"Like the sun peeking through the clouds, Rebecca DeWolf's groundbreaking book clears the fog that has long surrounded the Equal Rights Amendment. . . . Anyone who wants to understand why the ERA is not yet law would be well advised to read this book."

—JOHANNA NEUMAN, author of *Gilded Suffragists: The New York Socialites Who Fought for Women's Right to Vote*

"Rebecca DeWolf has given us a book we desperately need—perhaps now more than ever. In *Gendered Citizenship* DeWolf peels back the layers of conflict surrounding the Equal Rights Amendment . . . to the core question regarding the true scope of American citizenship that arose in the wake of the passage of the Nineteenth Amendment securing women's suffrage in 1920."

—ANGIE MAXWELL, author of *The Long Southern Strategy: How Chasing White Voters in the South Changed American Politics*

"DeWolf's thoughtful analysis of [the] forty-year struggle [between the ERA's advocates and its foes] reveals that their disagreements were primarily ideological, not political. . . . This is a deep dive into the enduring constitutional struggle over the meaning of citizenship, a story that DeWolf tells with deep understanding and critical insight."

—CANDICE SHY HOOPER, author of *Lincoln's Generals' Wives: Four Women Who Influenced the Civil War—For Better and For Worse*

Gendered Citizenship

Gendered Citizenship

The Original Conflict over the Equal Rights Amendment, 1920–1963

Rebecca DeWolf

University of Nebraska Press
LINCOLN

Previous versions of chapters 3 and 4 originally appeared as "The Equal Rights Amendment and the Rise of Emancipationism, 1932–1946," *Frontiers* 38, no. 2 (2017): 47–80.

Library of Congress Cataloging-in-Publication Data
Names: DeWolf, Rebecca, author.
Title: Gendered citizenship: the original conflict over the Equal Rights amendment, 1920–1963 / Rebecca DeWolf, University of Nebraska Press.
Description: Lincoln: University of Nebraska Press, [2021] | Based on author's thesis (doctoral—American University, 2014) issued under title: Amending nature: the equal rights amendment and gendered citizenship in America, 1920–1963. | Includes bibliographical references and index.
Identifiers: LCCN 2021007225
ISBN 9781496215567 (hardback)
ISBN 9781496227959 (paperback)
ISBN 9781496228284 (epub)
ISBN 9781496228291 (pdf)
Subjects: LCSH: Sex discrimination against women—Law and legislation—United States—History—20th century. | Women's rights—United States—History—20th century. | Equal rights amendments—United States—History—20th century.
Classification: LCC KF4758 .D49 2021 | DDC 342.7308/7809041—dc23
LC record available at https://lccn.loc.gov/2021007225

Set in New Baskerville ITC Pro by Mikala R. Kolander.

In loving memory of
John Edward DeWolf III

And to the bright lights of
Holland and Teddy MacGregor

CONTENTS

ACKNOWLEDGMENTS

In the time it has taken to complete this book I have relied upon the help, inspiration, and patience of many people. I would like to thank them now, though I fear that my words may not fully demonstrate the extent of my considerable gratitude. To start, I am thankful for the enriching advice and expertise of several scholars and mentors, including Linda Levy Peck, Marcy Norton, Andrew Zimmerman, Max Paul Friedman, Eric Lohr, Andrew Lewis, Kate Haulman, Peter Kuznick, Pamela Nadell, and Allan Lichtman. Through their teaching and research guidance, these scholars have challenged me to think more deeply about how we know and represent the past. They have also taught me the profound importance of unearthing all sides of a conflict, even when those battles may provoke firmly held beliefs and heartfelt reactions.

In particular, I wish to thank Allan Lichtman, Peter Kuznick, and Pamela Nadell, who were willing to assist me with this project from the beginning. They were not only a motivating force but also a dependable presence as I researched, drafted, and revised my work. I am especially indebted to Peter Kuznick for his thought-provoking perspectives on my research, as well as to Pamela Nadell for her reassurances and insights. I am eternally grateful for the careful and efficient help given to me by Allan Lichtman. Over several years he provided me with unyielding encouragement, sage advice, and enlightening criticism. I would not have been able to complete this book without his supreme professionalism and skillful mentoring.

My research and writing were supported in part by a Graduate Fellowship at American University, an American University Robyn Rafferty Mathias Research Award, a Dirksen Center Congressional Research Grant, an American University Doctoral Student Research Grant, an American University Merit Award, and an American University Clendenen Dissertation Fellowship. I gratefully acknowledge these grants and fellowships, as they significantly assisted in my ability to carry out the research for this project.

I extend my gratitude to the numerous librarians and archivists who worked with me at the institutions where I conducted research throughout this process. The staffs at the Library of Congress, Belmont-Paul Women's Equality National Monument, Schlesinger Library at Radcliffe Institute for Advanced Study, the Hayden Library at Arizona State University, and the Kansas State Historical Society, as well as the presidential libraries of Franklin D. Roosevelt, Harry S. Truman, and Dwight D. Eisenhower, were all exceptionally accommodating in their efforts to help me locate the various materials that contributed to my study.

In many ways this book emerged from my experience at the ERA in the 21st Century Conference, held at Rogers Williams University in the fall of 2013. At that conference I presented a paper that was later published as an article, "The Equal Rights Amendment and the Rise of Emancipationism, 1932–1946," *Frontiers* 38, no. 2 (2017): 47–80. I would like to thank the University of Nebraska Press for permission to use in revised form portions of that article in this book. I would also like to extend my sincere thanks to the organizers of that exciting and vibrant conference. In particular I want to thank Laura D'Amore, the main director of the conference, as she later provided me with productive feedback on my research, as well as vigorous support for my book manuscript.

I am excited to be publishing my first book with the University of Nebraska Press, and I am deeply thankful to Alicia Christensen, the editor who signed me to a precompletion contract. She saw the potential in my research and gave me the initial encouragement that I needed to transform my study. Emily Wendell, who later took over my project, showed immense patience with my endless questions and concerns. As well, I am thankful for the publishing guidance from Joeth Zucco, Ann Baker, Abigail Goodwin, Maureen Bemko, Rosemary Sekora, and Tayler Lord. I am infinitely grateful to all of the editors and staff with whom I worked at the University of Nebraska Press for their diligence and amiability in assisting me, regardless of the task, which made working with this press a genuine pleasure.

Several friends from the academic and scholarly world have supported me in the completion of this project in ways they might not fully realize or that I can adequately capture in the space here. Johanna Neuman not only inspired me to "write for the ear," but she also lifted me up whenever I needed a confidence boost. Christopher Hickman was always ready to offer fruitful research advice, and Shaadi Khoury shaped my thinking on several important scholarly trends. I am grateful to Jeneva Hinojosa for letting me talk about my research incessantly and for helping me to unfold numerous analytical entanglements. I am thankful for the unwavering support of Tracie Peterson and Karyn Strickler; your friendships have added a positive energy to my life, and I am incredibly appreciative of you both. I am also indebted to Laura Levillier Wang, Terumi Rafferty-Oaski, Jordan Grant, Eric Singer, Ryan Englekirk, John Little, Patrick Funiciello, Pete Veru, and Aaron Bell. In short, all these friends and colleagues have helped me wrestle with a number of challenging ideas, and they have been remarkable sources of comfort throughout this entire process.

I am blessed to have an amazing family. My marvelous mother, Susan DeWolf, sparked my obsession with books and my thirst for history. I still remember the joy of listening to her read to me at night when I was a child. My mother also made the careful effort to read through my manuscript line by line several times to cautiously point out any typos or inconsistencies. I am forever thankful for her unbounded encouragement as I have progressed through this journey. My brilliant siblings, Jennifer D. Farber, John E. DeWolf IV, and Melissa D. Kaufmann, have provided me with sources of ingenuity as well as much-needed respites from the stressors of completing a book. Additionally, I need to thank my wonderful MacGregor family, who housed me when I traveled to Boston to conduct research for this study.

Most of all, I must thank my life partner and co-parent, Michael MacGregor. He has been my everlasting rock since I first entered graduate school many years ago. More than anyone, he has been with me through the thrills and frustrations of writing a book. He has been a true co-parent to our two wildly crazy young children in every sense of the word. So much of what I have accomplished would simply not be possible without his partnership. Over our many years together he has added an unanticipated bliss to my life, and I am endlessly grateful for his steadfast belief in me. Since the time when I began work on this book, I have given birth to my two children, Holland and Teddy. They are both spirited dynamos in their own rights, and they have kept my life exciting, to say the least. The innocence that they bring to so many concepts has reinforced in me the great value in unraveling the origins of influential ideas; only through that process can we more fully understand why certain beliefs take hold in a community. For me, my young kids are beacons of hope; their bright lights reassure me that a more just and equitable future is possible. For that, I dedicate this book to them.

I also dedicate this book to the memory of my father, John Edward DeWolf III. My father had a larger-than-life presence and an awe-inspiring imagination. He instilled in me from an early age the self-assurance to chase my curiosity for historical knowledge. He taught me how to be brave and to believe in myself even when I was overcome with fear. To this day, when I feel my anxiety mounting, I reassure myself that I am my father's daughter; there is nothing that I cannot do. I will never forget the sheer delight in his smile and the amazement in his eyes when I told him about my precompletion book contract in July 2018. Although he passed away less than a month later, I know that he was proud of me and this work.

ABBREVIATIONS

AAUW	American Association of University Women
ACLU	American Civil Liberties Union
AFL	American Federation of Labor
AWSA	American Woman Suffrage Association
BPWC	Business and Professional Women's Clubs, National Federation of
CACSW	Citizens' Advisory Council on the Status of Women
CIO	Congress of Industrial Organizations
EEOC	Equal Employment Opportunity Commission
ERA	Equal Rights Amendment
FLSA	Fair Labor Standards Act
GFWC	General Federation of Women's Clubs
GWC	Government Workers' Council
ICSW	Interdepartmental Committee on the Status of Women
LWV	League of Women Voters
NACWC	National Association of Colored Women's Clubs
NAWL	National Association of Women Lawyers
NAWSA	National American Woman Suffrage Association
NCDURA	National Committee to Defeat the Un-Equal Rights Amendment
NCL	National Consumers' League
NCSW	National Committee on the Status of Women
NCW	National Council of Women
NIRA	National Industrial Recovery Act
NLRA	National Labor Relations Act
NOW	National Organization for Women

NRA	National Recovery Administration
NWP	National Woman's Party
NWPC	National Women's Political Caucus
NWSA	National Woman Suffrage Association
NWTUL	National Women's Trade Union League
OLC	Office of Legal Counsel, Justice Department
PCSW	President's Commission on the Status of Women
UAW	United Automobile Workers
UE	United Electrical Workers of America
VMI	Virginia Military Institute
WEAL	Women's Equity Action League
WJCC	Women's Joint Congressional Committee
WJLC	Women's Joint Legislative Committee
YWCA	Young Women's Christian Association

Gendered Citizenship

Introduction

The Equal Rights Amendment and American Citizenship

In the summer of 1923, a few months before Senator Charles Curtis
(R-KS) and Representative Daniel Read Anthony Jr. (R-KS) introduced the Equal Rights Amendment (ERA) into Congress, Felix
Frankfurter, the vibrant and eminent legal scholar who went on to
become an influential associate justice on the Supreme Court of
the United States, condemned the proposed amendment in a formidable letter to fellow ERA opponent and social reformer Ethel
Smith, of the National Women's Trade Union League (NWTUL).[1]
"Nature," Frankfurter declared in his letter, "made man and woman
different: the law must accommodate itself to the immutable differences of Nature." ERA supporters, Frankfurter concluded, "cannot
amend Nature."[2] In contrast, ERA proponents, like the wily Senator Curtis, who would later become vice president under Herbert
Hoover, maintained that the proposed amendment was "the logical conclusion to the suffrage struggle."[3] While ERA supporters saw
the amendment as the fulfillment of America's democratic aspirations, ERA critics insisted that such an amendment would not
only overturn the American legal tradition but also upset the natural sexual order. As we will see, the issues at play in this debate
punctuated the long-running struggle over the ERA from the 1920s
through the early 1960s.

The story of the ERA begins with the advent of federal woman
suffrage, because the Nineteenth Amendment profoundly altered

women's relationship to the state. Put briefly, the Nineteenth
Amendment disrupted the traditional understanding of American citizenship that had given men authority over women in law
and in custom. Yet, the Nineteenth Amendment failed to provide
a clear explanation of women's rights as citizens after sex had been
removed as a valid reason for withholding the right to vote. This
failure ignited a debate about the constitutional effects of federal
woman suffrage. Eventually, this debate evolved into a battle over
the nature of American citizenship. That battle—the original ERA
conflict—lasted more than forty years.

In the early 1920s disputes over the transformative possibilities
of the Nineteenth Amendment gave rise to two competing views of
American citizenship that I call emancipationism and protectionism. Emancipationists supported the ERA as a way to guarantee that
men and women could participate as citizens on the same terms.
Protectionists, on the other hand, opposed the ERA. They believed
that the presumably different societal functions of men and women
citizens required the law to be free to treat citizens differently on
account of sex. These two patterns of thought ultimately clashed
over the relationship between gender and citizenship, as emancipationists contended that American ideals affirmed the right of men
and women citizens to be held to the same legal standard while protectionists maintained that true sexual equity demanded two separate collections of rights for men and women citizens.

From the early 1920s to the early 1960s these two warring views
struggled over the very idea of rights. Protectionists eventually prevailed at the end of the original ERA conflict. In the process protectionists redefined the concept of American citizenship from a
single-gender (masculine) model to a dual-gender model. Despite
the generally well-meaning approach of many protectionists, their
victory in the original ERA conflict led to the advancement of a
gendered concept of citizenship that justifies a lack of equal treatment for women and the perpetuation of sex discrimination. The
original ERA conflict thus not only served as the vehicle through
which Americans forged new concepts of citizenship but it also
produced a lasting belief in the supposed justice of sex-specific
rights, a belief that still shapes American society.

In this study emancipationism signifies a particular form of thought that developed after the passage of the Nineteenth Amendment. It advocates for the complete equality of men and women citizens before the law. It also comprises the core ideas behind the pro-ERA position. As ERA supporter Donald Quigley Palmer of the American Newspaper Guild put it, "Adoption of the amendment is simple justice and the only means by which men and women will be given equal rights and equal responsibilities under the law."[4] The notion that a single standard of rights should apply to men and women citizens equally animated the emancipationist viewpoint. For ERA supporters the ERA was the logical and necessary outcome of the Nineteenth Amendment. From their viewpoint, the strength of the American political system relied upon the autonomy and equal rights of its voting citizens. A break from this model of equality, they cautioned, would undermine the country's guiding principles.[5]

The term "emancipationist" captures the pro-ERA position, because ERA supporters drew upon the notion of "emancipating" women from the thrust of legalized sex discrimination when they described the ERA's purpose. The ERA, according to Representative Louis Ludlow (D-IN), a major supporter of the amendment, was the "necessary corollary and supplement of equal suffrage. . . . [It is] the crowning act that will bring women to a status of the complete emancipation which they are entitled [to] by all the rules of right and justice."[6] During the original ERA conflict supporters of equal rights insisted that although the Nineteenth Amendment affirmed women's standing as citizens in their own right, sex-based laws and customs had continued to assign to women an inferior civic status. In amendment supporters' arguments for the ERA, they often pointed to how the remnants of the common law tradition of domestic relations, or the doctrine known as coverture, had sustained the constraints on women's civic autonomy. These restraints included limitations on women's rights to hold public office, serve on juries, have ownership of and control over their earnings, maintain an independent domicile status, have an independent nationality status, and work in certain occupations. For ERA supporters these persistent restrictions on newly legalized vot-

ers created not only fluctuating definitions of women's legal personhood but also constitutional inconsistencies with regard to the
rights of American citizens. In the mind-sets of ERA proponents,
complete constitutional sexual equality was the only way to fully
emancipate a class of electors from their legal subjugation.

As I use it in this study, the term "protectionism" represents a
specific way of reasoning that arose primarily after the advent of
federal woman suffrage. It does *not* refer exclusively to advocates
of special labor legislation for women. As I explain throughout
this study, the protectionist habit of thought existed among not
only liberal-minded persons who opposed the ERA and backed
special labor laws for women but also conservative individuals who
detested such labor laws. Put simply, protectionism espouses the
virtues of sex-specific rights. It encompasses the core ideas behind
the anti-ERA stance, since both conservative and liberal ERA opponents criticized the amendment as a threat to the sex-based legal
distinctions that upheld what they understood to be women's natural right to special protection. As one anti-ERA pamphlet alleged,
"Men and women are different in biological structure and social
function. State laws regulating working conditions for women, family support, guardianship of children, property, and inheritance,
marriage[,] and divorce recognize these differences."[7] From the
protectionist perspective the Nineteenth Amendment may have
acknowledged women's right to officially partake in the political
community, but it did not jettison the need for sex-based laws and
customs. To protectionists, sex-specific legal treatment recognized
men's and women's separate societal roles and responsibilities.

A shared desire to preserve the law's ability to treat men and
women citizens differently even after the passage of the Nineteenth
Amendment fueled the protectionist position. Alongside this desire,
protectionists believed that while the law should respect women as
rights-bearing citizens, it should not categorically group women's
rights with men's rights. At a 1938 Senate subcommittee hearing
on the ERA, for example, James O. Murdock, an ERA opponent
and prominent Washington DC lawyer, argued against the notion
of ensuring a commonality of rights for men and women citizens,
as reflected in the ERA, because such an idea, in his words, did

"not reflect the facts of life or represent a realistic consideration of the social structure of our society." He then surmised, "We all know that men and women are not in fact equal in many respects. It would be absurd to disregard the facts and by legislation, whether constitutional or otherwise, endeavor to create a theoretical equality."[8] In the protectionist social imagination, sex-specific laws and customs had created a legal framework that sustained both the American family and the American social order. As the chapters of this book detail, protectionists reasoned that actual fairness in the treatment of the sexes meant securing two distinct but equally valued sets of rights for men and women citizens.

Before the mid- to late 1960s the predominant gender norm assumed that women were biologically destined to be society's nurturers and caregivers.[9] Even the author of the ERA, Alice Paul, once commented, "Women are certainly made as the peace-loving half of the world and the homemaking half of the world, the temperate half of the world."[10] Still, Paul and other emancipationists thought that women should be free to choose how they would exercise their benevolent nature. Further still, emancipationists believed that natural differences between men and women did not preclude the law from holding men and women to the same civic principles. For emancipationists, sex did not represent a legitimate legal classification in and of itself. Protectionists, in contrast, insisted that biological differences between men and women necessitated differential legal treatment based on sex. ERA critic Elizabeth Dolan of the National Council of the Daughters of Isabella, for instance, contended at an ERA congressional hearing that "because of the fundamental differences between men and women in natural physical endowments and the circumstances which they meet during life, it is necessary that the law recognize these differences if the welfare of the women of the country is to be safeguarded."[11] In short, emancipationists and protectionists differed over the legal implications regarding the presumed inherent differences between men and women.

During the original ERA conflict, however, neither group separated gender, which broadly concerns the values and qualities a society attaches to men and women, from sex, which refers to the general anatomical attributes found within the spectrums of male and female persons. In general, the participants on both sides assumed that physical differences naturally resulted in disparities between men and women with regard to their personalities and behaviors.[12] Consequently, this study predominantly uses the term "sex" when explicating the arguments of both groups, as it is the term that best represents the contemporary views on the links and differences between men and women that dominated the ERA conflict from the 1920s to the early 1960s.

Until the early 1970s the long-running struggle between protectionists and emancipationists transcended conventional categories of political ideology. Throughout the original ERA conflict both the emancipationist and protectionist positions included pronounced liberal and conservative variations. Those who adhered to the emancipationist position, for instance, ranged from liberals such as Vice President Henry Wallace and feminist Emma Guffey Miller to conservatives such as Senator Edward Burke (D-NE) and Republican politician George Wharton Pepper. Likewise, those who followed the protectionist line of reasoning included liberals such as Secretary of Labor Frances Perkins and Senator Robert Wagner (D-NY), as well as influential conservatives such as Senator Robert Taft (R-OH) and Congress member James Wadsworth (R-NY). In addition, women's organizations that followed the maternalist reform tradition, such as the League of Women Voters (LWV), the National Consumers' League (NCL), and the NWTUL embraced protectionism during this period. Thus, in the original conflict both conservatives and liberals were attracted to the emancipationist and protectionist viewpoints.

Over the course of the early 1970s the ideological aspects of the ERA conflict did evolve to reflect what we now understand to be conventional political positions: more liberals came to adopt the campaign for gender equality, while more conservatives came to support the insistence on sex-specific legal standards. This alignment is due to an ideological shift that arose in the mid- to late 1960s. That shift transformed how people thought about the relationship between sex and gender, as intellectuals and activists moved away from the previous emphasis on biological determinism to begin deconstructing the cultural and social foundations of gender differences. This ideological leap allowed people to separate gender from sex to see how the stereotypical behavioral traits generally assigned to men and women were socially created concepts and not essential products of nature.

This new, more fluid understanding of gender theoretically expanded the societal position of women beyond what had been previously understood to be biologically inescapable roles in the domestic sphere. The theoretical expansion of women's roles encouraged more liberals to back the ERA as a way to ensure that social benefits applied equally to the male or female parent responsible for child care. As more liberals embraced emancipationism, the conservative wing of the protectionist position, which had been rebuilding its strength since the mid-1970s with its positive spin on pro-family values, grew to engulf the anti-ERA campaign effort.[13] Accordingly, by the late 1970s and early 1980s the new conceptualization of the relationship between sex and gender had heightened the liberal dimensions of emancipationism and the conservative components of protectionism.

But this book is more focused on retracing the scenes, details, and debates of the ERA struggle at an earlier time, when the conflict still surpassed the typical liberal and conservative disputes of twentieth-century America. By utilizing a wealth of primary source material, which includes a careful analysis of correspondence, public and private utterances, congressional testimony, and several court cases, my research shows that liberals and conservatives were not always opposed to one another when it came to the issue of absolute constitutional sexual equality. As the dynamics of the ERA conflict before the 1970s suggest, support for and opposition to the ERA are not positions that are fundamentally tied to either conservatism or liberalism. Ultimately, at its roots the ERA struggle reflects a battle between two different interpretations of American citizenship and not a typical political fight between liberals and conservatives.

On March 22, 1972, Congress passed the ERA and placed it before the states' legislatures with a seven-year deadline for acquiring the necessary ratifications of three-fourths of the states.[14] The vast preponderance of writing on the ERA is concerned with this later period in the ERA struggle. These works are preoccupied primarily with unraveling why the ERA failed to secure the necessary state approvals when its initial fate during the state ratification campaigns had looked promising. A number of these studies highlight the political difficulties that plagued the ERA, while others point to ERA supporters' strategic errors and misperceptions.[15] A considerable number of these studies also focus on Phyllis Schlafly's revitalization of grassroots conservatism and its devastating impact on the ERA ratification battle.[16] While this body of work has offered important insights, it places too high a premium on the significance of the later ratification struggle, which I identify as the second ERA conflict.[17] To fully understand the ERA's historical significance, we must return to the original conflict, because it provided the foundational arguments that concretized the notion of gendered citizenship in the United States.

The scholarship on the later ratification struggle has obscured the significance of the original ERA conflict because it often ignores the earlier conflict's dynamic history.[18] The congressional source materials that inform this study confirm that the amendment did not sit idly in Congress until 1970. On the contrary, Congress held a number of hearings on the ERA and issued several reports on it from the 1920s through the 1960s. Uncovering the longer history of the dueling civic ideologies embedded in the ERA conflict also sheds light on how the economic turmoil of the Great Depression and the political upheaval of World War II helped emancipationists generate a considerable societal drive toward the pro-ERA position. By the end of World War II, for example, the ranks of amendment backers had grown to include Democrats and Republicans, working-class and upper-class Americans, as well as white and Black Americans. Protectionists certainly regained the dominant position in the postwar era, but their victory was not a foregone conclusion to the original ERA conflict. Hence, the ERA was not a dormant issue until the 1970s; rather, it involved a spirited battle that was anything but static.

A group of scholars have looked at the ERA's earlier history to unearth its connection to the history of American feminism. These scholars primarily discuss the ERA struggle in the 1920s and early 1930s as a dispute among women, about women, and concerning only women.[19] In particular they frame the conflict as a fight between two feminist groups over the trajectory of the women's movement in the wake of the Nineteenth Amendment. According to their analyses, one group, typically labeled "social feminists," worked to expand women's involvement in social reform programs, while the other group of feminists, sometimes identified as "radical feminists" or "egalitarian feminists," single-mindedly focused on the effort to secure absolute sexual equality.[20] In all, this second body of ERA scholarship has primarily employed a female-centric narrative that underscores how the amendment influenced the history of the women's movement.[21]

Although these other scholarly explorations have provided invaluable research, my work contends that the original ERA conflict is best understood as a battle between competing civic ideologies and not mainly as a struggle between divergent feminist ideologies. To be clear, a crucial aspect of the original conflict did involve disputes among women activists over the priorities of the women's movement after the beginning of federal woman suffrage. The focus on these disputes, however, has concealed the larger story and significance of the ERA struggle. To begin with, the original ERA conflict was not active just in the 1920s and early 1930s; it lasted all the way up until the early 1960s. Furthermore, the original ERA conflict did not involve only women activists who had been associated with the suffrage movement. It actually included an array of men and women politicians, intellectuals, labor activists, social reformers, and government officials. Overall, the participants not only argued over women's constitutional status; they also contested the nature of American citizenship.

To be sure, both the emancipationist and protectionist ideologies contained feminist variations; however, feminism, as it pertains to the original conflict, did not completely encompass either ideology in its entirety. Those who adhered to the emancipationist position, for example, included explicitly feminist groups, such as the National Woman's Party (NWP). These emancipationists supported the ERA as a way to empower women, because they assumed that the amendment would expand women's opportunities in public life. But the emancipationist ideology also included followers who were not outright feminists, such as Edward Burke, a conservative senator from Nebraska. For those individuals, women's empowerment was not necessarily their top priority. Instead, they backed the amendment as a way to promote individual economic opportunity and to challenge government regulation of the economy.[22] Even with these differences, emancipationists as a whole supported the ERA as a way to ensure that a basic model of rights applied to men and women citizens equally.

Protectionism also contained policy makers and activists who identified themselves as feminists, such as Mary Anderson of the Women's Bureau. These persons opposed the ERA and proudly supported what they believed to be equitable sex-based laws. In their view, such laws improved women's status by attending to women's special needs.[23] Nonetheless, protectionism also included reform-minded individuals who avoided the feminist label, such as Dorothy Straus of the LWV.[24] Finally, protectionism incorporated conservative persons such as former antisuffrage leaders Elizabeth Putnam and Margaret Robinson, who denounced feminism.[25] Despite these distinctions, protectionists with both feminist and antifeminist stances still discussed their opposition to the ERA in terms of protecting what they understood to be the natural sexual order. Above all, protectionists believed that American society correctly acknowledged the presumably inherent differences between men and women by differentiation in law and custom. Although strands of feminism undoubtedly influenced the contours of the original ERA battle, the larger conflict encompassed a struggle over the fundamental principles of American citizenship.

Capturing the broader historical significance of the ERA requires an expansion of the interpretive focus on the amendment so that it reaches beyond the existing historiography's preoccupations with the question of failure and the amendment's impact on the women's movement. As such, this study seeks to contribute to recent scholarly trends that aim to disentangle the gendered ideas that are enfolded in the history of American citizenship. The relevant studies in this field of work primarily document how discriminations against women persisted after the ratification of the Nineteenth Amendment. An underlying contention of these works is that even after federal woman suffrage, political and legal authorities continued to deny women's full citizenship status by withholding their other rights as citizens. In order to explain the continuity of discrimination against women, a few historians have suggested that since the Nineteenth Amendment primarily dealt with the right to vote, it made women unequal participants in the public sphere.[26] Other scholars have looked at the development of "social citizenship" during the Great Depression to chronicle the persistence of sex discrimination; these scholars discuss how the social benefits that emerged from this concept largely benefited men as the primary breadwinners.[27] Finally, a number of legal scholars and historians have called attention to what they describe as a judicial commitment to exclude women from various obligations that men have had to perform as part of their citizenship. The exclusion from such obligations, these scholars argue, has provided the pretext for the restriction of women's other rights as citizens.[28] Even though this collection of works admirably underscores the continuity of discrimination against women, it fails to take into account how the original ERA conflict changed the actual notion of rights during the post–Nineteenth Amendment era.

This book offers a different perspective on the historical basis for the gap between men's and women's citizenship. For starters, the continuity of discrimination against women after the Nineteenth Amendment cannot be simply explained away as lawmakers and legal authorities being intent on denying women their rights as full citizens. Indeed, ERA opponents actually insisted that they were *protecting* the distinct rights of women as citizens. Through the course of the original ERA conflict, protectionists moved the argument against equal rights away from the pre–Nineteenth Amendment emphasis on the reasons to exclude women from certain rights of citizenship toward a post–Nineteenth Amendment emphasis on the need to protect a distinct citizenship for women that purportedly came with its own set of rights. For protectionists, women's special rights included being exempt from military service, shielded from the ravages of industrial capitalism, and kept safe in their domestic roles. In this sense protectionists modernized the justification for sex-specific treatment by forming a new notion of full American citizenship that included two separate standards of rights for men and women citizens.

A work on the multifaceted importance of the original ERA conflict needs to start with a full discussion of the radical potential embedded in the Nineteenth Amendment, because the beginning of federal woman suffrage provided the springboard for the original ERA conflict. The first section of this book thus retraces how the Nineteenth Amendment dislodged the traditional, masculine understanding of American citizenship that had given men control over women. As chapter 1 explains, a period of uncertainty regarding women's rights as citizens ensued after the passage of the Nineteenth Amendment. This period, moreover, prompted several individuals to consider drafting an additional constitutional amendment to clarify women's standing in the post–Nineteenth Amendment era. Chapter 2 looks at how the arduous, almost three-year effort to draft this amendment produced two very different interpretations of American citizenship: emancipationism and protectionism. Taken together, chapters 1 and 2 argue that the Nineteenth Amendment may have opened the door to complete constitutional sexual equality, but protectionists slammed that door shut.

The second section of this work, chapters 3 and 4, details how the changes to the original ERA conflict during the 1930s and 1940s underscore the dynamism of the struggle before the later ratification battle. In particular, these chapters reveal the ways in which the destabilizing nature of the Great Depression and World War II pumped life into the ERA campaign and revitalized the emancipationist position. In sum, chapters 3 and 4 show that when events disrupt the traditional sexual order, they produce a potential for the dominant cultural consensus to align with the ethos of emancipationism.

The final section of this study confronts the decline of emancipationism in the postwar era and the eventual triumph of protectionism at the end of the original ERA conflict. As chapters 5 and 6 document, protectionists subdued the emancipationist impulse by creating alternative comprehensive measures to address the changing position of women more directly while also sustaining their belief in the different rights of men and women citizens. By the end of the original ERA conflict in the early 1960s, protectionists had further perfected America's gendered citizenship by forming the concept of intermediate constitutional equality for men and women. This notion upholds the constitutional affirmation of both men and women as full citizens through the Fourteenth Amendment without completely dislocating the government's ability to treat citizens differently on account of sex.

Although a reenergized women's activism gave way to the rebirth of the ERA campaign in the 1970s, the spirit of protectionism eventually prevailed at the end of the second ERA conflict. The epilogue, then, explores how the legacy of protectionism affected the later ratification battle and how it helped to fashion the formation of the modern constitutional doctrine of gender jurisprudence. As the epilogue argues, even though developments in recent years have sparked a renewed interest in the ERA, protectionist beliefs still influence America's social practices, which have continued to keep women in a disadvantageous position.

In the end the original ERA conflict supplied the terrain that allowed Americans to reconceptualize the concept of citizenship so that it corresponded to the changes in women's status after the passage of the Nineteenth Amendment. By bringing to light the competing civic ideologies embedded in the ERA struggle, the chapters of this book show how the original conflict encapsulates the defining narrative for the changing nature of American citizenship in the post–Nineteenth Amendment era. In an effort to preserve the rationale for sex-based distinctions in law and in custom after the introduction of federal woman suffrage, protectionists modernized the justification for sex-specific treatment. In the process, they created separate and distinct standards of rights for men and women citizens. Overall, the protectionists' triumph over emancipationists at the end of the original ERA conflict produced a confidence in the legitimacy of sex-specific treatment that still informs the dominant cultural consensus to this day. However, this protectionist notion of limited sexual equality also sustains the restrictions on women's autonomy, because it excuses the discriminatory outlook that rights should be dependent upon one's sex.

1

The Radical Nineteenth Amendment

Masculine Citizenship and Women's Status

In 1931 Chief Justice Arthur Prentice Rugg of the Supreme Judicial Court of Massachusetts bemoaned in his *Commonwealth v. Genevieve Welosky* ruling that "the change in the legal status of women wrought by the Nineteenth Amendment was radical, drastic, and unprecedented." He concluded that while the amendment "is to be given full effect in its field, it is not to be extended by implication."[1] Justice Rugg had issued this glaring rebuke of the Nineteenth Amendment in an effort to dismiss claims that the amendment had not only acknowledged women's right to vote but that it had also made women eligible to serve on juries. More than a decade after its ratification, Justice Rugg, along with others, had continued to fear the potentially subversive nature of the Nineteenth Amendment. As this chapter discusses, the emergence of federal woman suffrage shook the earlier societal framework that had given men authority over women. From the early days of the republic, American political leaders had upheld a single standard for full American citizenship, which venerated masculine strength and followed the common law tradition of domestic relations—the doctrine known as coverture. The Nineteenth Amendment, however, upset this paradigm because it removed sex as a legitimate reason for denying the right to vote, which implicitly acknowledged women's ability to hold their own civic identities. The transformative possibilities of this development produced a period of constitutional

uncertainty in which American political leaders and legal scholars debated the Nineteenth Amendment's meaning and scope.
Most important, this period of uncertainty eventually gave way to
what would become the original conflict over the Equal Rights
Amendment (ERA).

Masculine Citizenship

The maleness of rights-bearing citizenship is an idea deeply embedded in Western political thought. Like their Enlightenment predecessors, America's founders imagined their new nation as a domain
ruled by equally independent male agents. In this gendered outlook
the idealized man, like the idealized citizen, exhibited freedom,
responsibility, and the ability to govern.[2] The civic republicanism
that infused the American Revolution also followed the contention that active political participation should be limited to citizens
who could demonstrate their civic virtue by bearing arms to protect the new republic. As scholar Carole Pateman puts it, "Republican citizens were thus men and soldiers."[3]

The commitment to this benchmark of citizenship implicitly
barred all women from full citizenship status, because early American political thinkers assumed that women were unfit for combat. At the time of the revolution most Americans connected men
to productivity, reason, and self-control, while linking women to
seduction, manipulation, and dependency. According to political scientist Mark Kann, America's founders sought to establish a
republic "based on male governance and female subordination."[4]
All in all, America's earliest political and legal authorities sought
to institutionalize exclusive opportunities for white men in order
to create a society that was regulated by, in the words of historian
Joan Hoff, a "masculine system of justice."[5]

To be clear, early political leaders counted women, albeit only
white women, as citizens of the country in the sense that they understood these women to be inhabitants of the new nation. Still, the
status of being a rights-bearing citizen excluded all women. The
legal basis for this exclusion derives from the English common law
doctrine of domestic relations known as coverture. This body of
status law presumed that a woman held no civic identity separate

from her husband's status. In essence it submerged a woman's civic identity into her husband's identity. Thus, a husband's civic status *covered* his wife's status. The early modern English jurist William Blackstone—revered by American jurists—described the philosophy behind this doctrine, writing that "by marriage the husband and wife are one person in law: that is, the very being or legal existence of the woman is suspended during the marriage, or at least is incorporated and consolidated into that of the husband: under whose wing, protection, and cover, she performs everything."[6]

A dominant belief in early American society was that the majority of women married; consequently, coverture correspondingly stood for the legal process by which unmarried women (*femmes soles*) became married women (*femmes coverts*). As the House Judiciary Committee explained as late as 1884, "The exceptional cases of unmarried females are too rare to change the general policy, while expectancy and hope, constantly being realized in marriage, are happily extinguishing the exceptions and bringing all within the rule which governs wife and matron."[7] The nineteenth-century theologian Horace Bushnell put it more bluntly, writing, "What we have to say is, that all women alike are made to be married, whether they are or not."[8] If a woman remained unmarried, the law assumed that she was dependent on male relatives for economic support and political representation, since the majority of political and cultural leaders believed in the inherently weak nature of all women. For a woman, then, marriage was the move from dependent daughter or relative to dependent wife.[9]

Coverture also denoted a system of sex-specific marital duties in which wives were thought to owe their husbands services such as childbearing and homemaking. In return, the legal tradition presumed that husbands provided their wives with shelter and financial support.[10] In treating women as "covered" by their husbands, coverture imposed several restrictions on married women; it was, for example, unlawful for married women to hold property, draft wills, control their earnings, sue and be sued, vote, hold public office, serve on juries, and enter into contracts. Hence, coverture privileged the man/husband as the sole rights-bearing person of the household.[11]

Because coverture favored the male head of the household, it placed harsh constraints on women's right to control their own bodies, as the old doctrine of domestic relations sprouted from the belief that upon marriage the husband gained a right to his wife's body. "The married woman's civil identity," historian Linder Kerber explains, "was 'covered' by her husband's. Since her husband had control over the body of his wife, he controlled her will."[12] The presumed right of the husband to the sexual services of his wife's body was central to coverture. Tapping Reeve, a prominent early nineteenth-century American legal scholar, illustrated this point when he contended in one of his legal treatises that "the right of the husband to the person of his wife . . . is a right guarded by the law with the utmost solicitude; if she could bind herself by contracts, she would be liable to be arrested, taken in execution, and confined in a prison; and then the husband would be deprived of the company of his wife, which the law will not suffer."[13] In other words, coverture centered on the principle that upon marriage a woman's body became her husband's possession. His right to the services of her body exceeded all other obligations she might have held. For these reasons the emphasis on the self-governing individual wrapped in the notion of rights-bearing citizenship excluded women, since the old law of domestic relations denied women self-possession of their own bodies.

Beginning in the mid-nineteenth century, statutes enacted in the United States sought to reform the common law doctrine of coverture by giving a number of married women the capacity to enter into legal transactions. In general, this reform started with the passage of the married women's property acts, which allowed wives to hold property in their own right. Sometimes these statutes also conferred on wives limited dispositional powers over their property. A second wave of reform legislation permitted wives to assert property rights in the labor they might perform outside of the household and granted wives various forms of legal agency respecting their separate property, including the capacity to contract and file suit.[14]

It might be tempting to attribute these apparent legislative achievements to the burgeoning woman's rights campaign of the mid-1800s.[15] But demands for gender equity were not the sole motivations for the nineteenth-century marital reform legislation. Rather, economic anxiety, as a number of historians have shown, was a primary instigator for the reforms. Looking at early versions of the married women's property acts, several historians have argued that matters of land law, debtor-creditor relations, and family welfare had pushed lawmakers to initiate the reforms. In several cases the acts allowed families to hold assets in a wife's name and thus enabled families to protect property from a husband's creditors. In short, the reform legislation afforded households a degree of security in the unpredictable antebellum economy. Overall, these reforms were a part of a complex shift in social, economic, and cultural values that coincided with the rising industrial market economy.[16]

Most important, though, the reforms did not fully liberate wives from the restraints of coverture. During the industrial period, socio-economic forces separated men's work from the household setting. These same forces, however, imprinted gender on the work that most women continued to do in the family sphere. As a result, women's domestic labor became separate and distinct from market labor. In the wake of the marital reform legislation, as legal scholar Reva Siegel persuasively argues, coverture evolved into an "integral part" of the industrial economy; it was not an ancient relic of a precapitalist society. While the reform statutes gave married women property rights in work they might perform outside of the household, many of the acts continued to protect the presumed right of husbands to their wives' services, especially in regard to women's domestic labor. In this sense the reforms actually helped to modernize the tradition of sex-specific marital duties embedded in the doctrine of coverture so that it was consistent with the mores of America's budding industrial capitalist economy.[17]

The limitations to the marital reform acts were also due to an antagonistic judiciary, which drew upon the gendered discourse of the industrial era to frame the family and market as separate and distinct spheres of work. In the late nineteenth and early twentieth centuries judges rejected the notion that the earning statutes, which were a part of the second wave of reform legislation, gave wives a right to the monetary value of their domestic labor. In 1889, for instance, the Iowa Supreme Court refused to enforce an interspousal contract for a wife's domestic services on the grounds that "the marital obligations of husband and wife in the interests of homes, both happy and useful, have a higher and stronger inducement than mere money consideration."[18] The Court of Appeals of Kentucky issued a similar ruling in 1910 when it decided that it was against public policy to permit either husband or wife "to make an enforceable contract with the other to perform such services as are ordinarily imposed upon them by the marital relation, and which should be the natural promoting of that love and affection which should always exist between husband and wife."[19] For family matters the predominant judicial interpretation presumed that love, selflessness, and duty motivated work. In the market, however, the courts positioned self-interest and the desire for material gain as the driving force for encouraging individuals to complete work outside of the home. Ultimately, the marital reform acts of the mid- to late nineteenth-century, as well as the judicial interpretation of those acts, preserved the tradition of sex-based marital duties rooted in the doctrine of coverture such that it would continue to regulate gender relations in the changing socioeconomic environment.[20]

After the conclusion of the Civil War, core elements of coverture remained vibrant parts of the American legal tradition. Although the Reconstruction Amendments represented a significant effort to move toward a constitutional recognition of the rights of persons who were not white men, American courts were still inclined to locate women's legal personhood in the common law tradition. It is true that the Fourteenth Amendment confirmed that all women were citizens in that they counted as members of the country, but the courts limited the implications of the Fourteenth Amendment as it pertained to women's rights as citizens. In 1873 the U.S. Supreme Court demonstrated this point with its ruling in *Bradwell v. Illinois*, which held that a married woman could be refused admission to the bar. The case concerned Myra Bradwell, who had passed the Illinois bar examination in 1869 but was denied admission to the state's bar because she was a married woman. Even though Republican senator Matthew Hale Carpenter of Wisconsin argued on behalf of Bradwell before the court that professional licensing was a privilege of citizenship protected under the Fourteenth Amendment, the court still upheld Bradwell's exclusion. "The civil law, as well as nature herself," Justice Joseph P. Bradley reasoned in his concurrent opinion for the case, "has always recognized a wide difference in the respective spheres and destinies of man and woman." Justice Bradley went on to claim that women's civic status did not confer upon them the privilege to engage in any and every profession, occupation, or employment in civil life. He concluded that women's proper societal role remained in the domestic sphere, since "the paramount destiny and mission of women [were] to fulfill the noble and benign offices of wife and mother."[21]

In another case, *Minor v. Happersett* (1875), the U.S. Supreme Court further limited women's autonomy under the law by rejecting a new legal strategy devised by Francis and Virginia Minor. This strategy, which the woman's movement called the "New Departure," had aimed to enhance women's civic status through the Fourteenth Amendment by arguing that, since the amendment had affirmed women's citizenship, it had subsequently recognized women's right to vote. The high court disagreed with this assessment. It maintained that even though the Fourteenth Amendment had conceded that women were citizens, it did not establish women's right to directly participate in the governance of the country.[22] With its decisions in *Bradwell* and *Minor*, the court continued to harness women's civic membership to the domestic realm of the country even with the constitutional reform of the Reconstruction era.

The exclusion of women from the Reconstruction Amendments was not a simple, incidental legal interpretive error. As the Republican Party designed the constitutional amendments and the legal provisions that would free enslaved persons and protect their rights as citizens, the party's leadership was mindful that this new body of law, if not carefully crafted, could undermine various components of the common law tradition of domestic relations.[23] The architects of Reconstruction feared upsetting the legal paradigm of marital-status law because it had traditionally empowered male heads of the household with the right to govern their wives and to represent them in the political realm.[24] During the congressional debates on Reconstruction, for example, Republican representative John Martin Broomall of Pennsylvania justified expanding the franchise to include former enslaved men, but not women, explaining that he thought indirect representation should prevail in the cases of "women, children, and all those under the legal control of others." He concluded, "Adult males are supposed to represent the family, and the government is not bound to look further than this common consent or submission."[25] To avoid taking away the control over women that the law of marriage had traditionally given men, the framers of the Fourteenth and Fifteenth Amendments constructed their amendments in ways that recognized the rights of newly freed men while preserving women's dependent status.[26]

In the early twentieth century central concepts of coverture continued to play a determining role in the confinement of women's civic identity. In 1907, for example, Congress passed the Expatriation Act, which caused an American woman to lose her nationality status if she married a foreigner.[27] The act reflected an enduring devotion not only to the maleness of rights-bearing citizenship but also to the legal principle that a wife must be loyal and obedient to her husband above all else, even her country.[28]

In 1915 the Supreme Court upheld the Expatriation Act with its ruling in *Mackenzie v. Hare*. The case concerned Ethel Mackenzie, an active supporter of woman suffrage who had been born in California and had married a British subject. After California affirmed women's right to vote in 1911, the Board of Election Commissioners denied Mackenzie her voter registration, holding that upon marriage to a British subject she had ceased to be a citizen of the United States.[29] Even though Mackenzie challenged the law, claiming that Congress had exceeded its authority, the U.S. Supreme Court ruled against her. In an opinion reminiscent of its decision in *Bradwell*, the high court proclaimed, "The identity of husband and wife is an ancient principle of our jurisprudence. It was neither accidental nor arbitrary, and worked in many instances for her protection . . . and this relation and unity may make it of public concern in many instances to merge their identity, and give dominance to the husband."[30] With this decision, the court signaled its commitment to the core principles embedded in coverture, and it showed that from the court's perspective those principles were still robust parts of America's constitutional culture.

Women's Activism and the Suffrage Movement

In the early twentieth century new understandings of what the state owed its citizens perpetuated the distinction between men's and women's civic standings. As industrialization pushed more women into the workforce, policy makers decided that the state was obligated to provide distinct legal measures to shield working women from the havoc of capitalism. As the historian Melvin Urofsky describes it, most lawmakers and state courts embraced special economic protections for women that followed "the best common law tradition, attempting to meet the new social and economic conditions of the country."[31] These special measures included laws that specifically regulated labor conditions for working women by barring them from working at night, establishing maximum work hours, and prohibiting women from employment in certain occupations. Judges in Massachusetts, for example, accepted a restriction on the working hours allowed for women and children in 1876 and again in 1895, as did judges in Pennsylvania, Nebraska, and Washington in 1902. By 1908 nineteen states had banned night work or established maximum hours for women. In 1912 Massachusetts adopted the nation's first minimum wage law for women; within eight years, fourteen other states had passed similar laws.[32] By 1914 twenty-seven states had enacted laws limiting the hours of female workers.[33]

Yet, the rise of special labor legislation did not transpire seamlessly. In *Ritchie v. People of Illinois* (1895) the Illinois Supreme Court declared unconstitutional a special labor law requiring an eight-hour day for women working in factories. The court ruled that the law had violated women's right to contract freely.[34] The dependent woman theory embedded in coverture helped social reformers such as Florence Kelley of the NCL succeed in preventing more *Ritchie*-like decisions. That theory justified the special treatment of women by operating from the deep-seated belief that women were physically weaker than men and biologically destined to be mothers and caretakers of the household. In particular, Kelley and her social reform allies argued that since women's activities were imbued with the public interest, their roles as mothers and homemakers invoked the police power of the state. Police power refers to the inherent power of a state to pass laws that protect the health, safety, and welfare of its citizens.[35] In this manner Kelley not only encouraged the cultural conservatism of American judges by drawing on the common law view that women were dependents; she also constructed a set of legal precedents that enlarged the police power of the state and secured what she described as "ethical gains."[36]

When the U.S. Supreme Court embraced the dependent woman theory with its ruling in *Muller v. Oregon* (1908), it essentially admitted sex-specific economic protection into federal practice. *Muller* dealt with the constitutionality of an Oregon law that had barred women from working in laundries for more than ten hours a day. In its decision the high court asserted that there was a public interest in regulating the employment relations of women on the basis that all women were mothers or potential mothers.[37] Writing for the majority, Justice David J. Brewer declared that surely women's bodies and their maternal obligations placed every member of the sex "at a disadvantage in the struggle for subsistence." He went on to claim that "the physical well-being of a woman becomes an object of public interest and care to preserve the strength in vigor of the race."[38] At a time when women in unprecedented numbers were entering the labor market and earning college degrees, the high court's opinion fortified the idea that women workers were weak, dependent, and incapable of enjoying the same economic freedom as men.[39]

For its ruling in *Muller* the court relied upon the Brandeis Brief, a pioneering legal document that detailed the supposed evidence of women's exceptional susceptibility to workplace hazards. Florence Kelley and labor reform advocate Josephine Goldmark prepared the document, while Louis Brandeis presented it to the court. The brief included testimonies from European and American scientists and physicians to argue that overwork inflicted especial damage on women. The brief described, for instance, how British scientists attributed nervous disorders in women to "over-action." It went on to cite the conclusion of the Massachusetts Labor Bureau's experts in 1875, which claimed that "the back . . . gives out. Girls cannot work more than eight hours, and keep it up." Another expert quoted in the brief described a woman's knee as a fragile "sexual organ" that could be damaged by standing. The experts urged lawmakers to fight against overwork for women, as it would "unfit" women to "the burden of motherhood which each of them should be able to assume."[40] In the end the brief persuaded the justices to rule that women's innate dependency demanded that the state give women special legislative protection.

In a peculiar way *Muller* represented a victory for both social reformers and laissez-faire advocates. By following the social reformers' argument that maternity and women's household activities were filled with a public interest, the courts justified their regulation of women's work without renouncing their attachment to a free market in masculine labor.[41] In the wake of *Muller* the NCL and other reform groups began what historian William Chafe has described as a "national crusade to place a floor under woman's wages as well as a ceiling over their hours."[42] In a 1916 NCL pamphlet that discussed the advantages of special labor legislation for women, Kelley explained her reasoning for sex-specific labor laws: "for married women wage earners it is especially necessary to have the working day short and work regular. For when they leave their workplace it is to cook, sew, and clean at home, sometimes even to care for the sick."[43] Kelley's success in advancing special labor legislation for women prompted legal scholar Felix Frankfurter to assert in 1953 that Kelley "had probably the single largest share in shaping the social history of the United States during the first thirty years of the century."[44]

From revolutionary-era republicanism to nineteenth-century democracy, the political realm officially excluded women. Yet, to portray women simply as victims is to deny their historical agency. As Kelley's social activism suggests, women constructed important roles for themselves that allowed them to contribute (albeit informally) to the public sphere. By first embracing what historian Linda

Kerber has identified as "republican motherhood" and, then, by drawing upon what scholar Barbara Welter has called the "cult of true womanhood," thousands of women in churches, clubs, and other voluntary associations maneuvered within the male-dominated polity.[45] This women's activism aimed at reforming factories, slums, prisons, asylums, and brothels. Overall, women provided important energy that fueled voluntary associations and reform movements, which then became the precursors of state-dispensed social welfare.[46]

Many women also fought for the expansion of their rights, especially in relation to the franchise. Public discussion of votes for women largely began in 1848 with the Woman's Rights Convention at Seneca Falls, New York. After constitutional reform during the Reconstruction era had failed to institutionalize principles of universal suffrage, the woman suffrage movement created its own organizational structure. Steadfast campaigning for woman suffrage started in 1869 with the founding of two competing organizations: the National Woman Suffrage Association (NWSA) and the American Woman Suffrage Association (AWSA). Elizabeth Cady Stanton and Susan B. Anthony assumed leadership of NWSA, while Lucy Stone, Henry Blackwell, and others led AWSA. Unlike Stanton and Anthony, the members of AWSA continued to support the Fifteenth Amendment and the policies of the Republican Party.[47]

Eventually, in 1890 these two groups joined forces to form the National American Woman Suffrage Association (NAWSA).[48] In general suffragists asserted that women were the equals of men in their natural entitlement to exercise the franchise. As such, their position challenged the traditional conception of the state as a collection of independent male agents.[49] In 1894, for instance, suffragist Mary Putnam Jacobi wrote in an essay supporting woman suffrage that the state should be based on "individual cells" and not households. She concluded that women ought to be "brought into direct relations with the state, independent of their 'mate' or brood."[50] A few years earlier Stanton had made a similar point in a speech she delivered upon her resignation as the first president of NAWSA. In the speech, titled "The Solitude of Self," Stanton eloquently outlined her argument for woman's rights. She contended,

"In discussing the sphere of man, we do not decide his rights as an individual, as a citizen, as a man [by] discussing his duties as a father, a husband, a brother, or a son. . . . Just so with woman. The education that will fit her to discharge the duties on the largest sphere of human usefulness will best fit her for whatever special work she may be compelled to do."[51] In their full-throated attack on the patriarchal establishment, early suffragists challenged the gender-hierarchical organization of the family and state to advocate for woman's rightful place to freely partake in public life.[52]

In 1892 the indomitable Susan B. Anthony became president of NAWSA; she remained in office until 1900. While Stanton continued to work on an array of causes, many of which were rather controversial, such as the denunciation of Christianity, most of NAWSA's leaders (including Anthony) insisted that the movement focus primarily on the vote. Because of this new approach, NAWSA's leadership decided that the organization should avoid association with more radical issues.[53] It was during this time that the language of the suffrage movement began to shift, as many suffragists increasingly came to argue that women needed the vote for purposes of social housekeeping. Later suffragists appealed to women's special status as caregivers to pull together their argument that if women were enfranchised, then they would be able to secure a range of reforms, which would purportedly improve the health and welfare of America's families.[54] Historian Aileen Kraditor notably described this development as a strategic move toward "expediency," or, in other words, the decision to use traditional ideas about the "woman's sphere" for constructive purposes.[55] Due to this trend, a considerable number of later suffragists argued that as women brought their interest with them into the public domain, they would also purify politics. Kelley, who was not only an influential social activist but also a prominent suffrage supporter, asserted, for example, that woman suffrage would reinforce the "moral power" that society "sorely need[ed] to counterbalance the excessive pressure of business interest."[56]

As the suffrage campaign became a more mainstream component of women's organized activities in the late nineteenth and early twentieth centuries, so too did many suffrage advocates come to voice the racial and ethnocentric prejudices of the white middle class.[57] NAWSA's membership, for instance, frequently employed racist claims in their arguments for woman suffrage. NAWSA's members often maintained that white women were more qualified to vote than immigrant and Black men. Many of its members also asserted that the adoption of woman suffrage would help the South restore white supremacy, as it would increase the numbers of white voters.[58] Thus, by the turn of the twentieth century a considerable number of woman suffrage backers had increasingly adopted the argument that the vote would help white middle-class women utilize their supposedly superior moral sensibilities. This assessment, though, does not mean that Black Americans were uninterested in the suffrage campaign. On the contrary, Black women activists significantly contributed to the suffrage movement. As historian Sara Evans explains, Black women looked to the vote as a defense against "sexual exploitation as well as a guarantor of their economic rights." However, the racially charged claims of the predominantly white middle-class national organizations created a hostile environment for Black women activists; consequently, they developed their own reform groups. For instance, by 1900 they had formed the National Association of Colored Women (NACW) and local suffrage groups in numerous cities.[59]

From the mid-nineteenth century to the early twentieth century, calls for woman suffrage grew from a small fractious campaign into a powerful movement.[60] In part, this development was due to suffragists' appeals to traditional images of womanliness as well as the racial prejudices of the white middle class. By the early twentieth century the movement had further expanded to become not only an influential part of women's organized activities but also a prominent force in the spectrum of American politics. The tactics of acclaimed suffragist Carrie Chapman Catt contributed to this outcome, as she was able to harness NAWSA's power base and political strength. In particular, Catt mastered what historian Robert Booth Fowler calls "practical politics."[61] Catt's "Winning Plan," for example, helped to advance the federal suffrage amendment because it called for suffragists in states where women already had the vote to exert pressure on their national representatives.[62]

The bold strategy of suffragist Alice Paul of the National Woman's Party also mobilized support for the movement. From 1913 to 1916, Paul created a separate suffrage organization after she had become dissatisfied with the leadership and direction of NAWSA.[63] Thanks to Paul's use of tactics such as protesting and open public demonstrations, the NWP brought to light the more militant side of the suffrage movement. The NWP, for instance, was the first group to picket the White House for a political cause. During these protests police officers arrested NWP demonstrators and imprisoned them on charges of obstructing traffic.[64] While confined, the NWP's members objected to their arrests with hunger strikes, which caused prison officials to forcibly feed the imprisoned suffragists. NWP member Doris Stevens famously recorded this ordeal in detail in her 1920 account, *Jailed for Freedom.*[65] Paul was a brilliant strategist for attracting the attention of the press (and the general public) to the movement. By way of illustration, Paul organized a large, theatrical suffrage parade during President Woodrow Wilson's inaugural celebration in March 1913. The parade successfully seized the nation's attention by featuring more than eight thousand suffragists.[66] Because of Paul's proclivity for public spectacle, she was able to force the cause of woman suffrage to the forefront of public debate. With Paul's guidance, the NWP drew national focus to what had appeared to be the duplicity of a nation that championed democracy in World War I while still denying its own female citizens the right to vote.[67]

When American legislators finally moved to support federal woman suffrage with the ratification of the Nineteenth Amendment in 1920, they did unsettle the masculine model of full citizenship status. By passing the Nineteenth Amendment, as legal scholar Reva Siegel describes it, American lawmakers "were breaking with understandings of the family that had organized public and private law and defined the position of the sexes since the founding of the republic."[68] In other words, the constitutional appreciation of women's right to vote was a big deal. To be clear, the Nineteenth Amendment did fall short in fully overthrowing the potency of legalized sex discrimination. The many limitations of the amendment will be discussed later in this chapter. Nonetheless, the Nineteenth Amendment is an impressive achievement to behold when one considers the obstacles that the suffragists had to overcome in order to push federal woman suffrage forward. Due to decades of relentless determination and persistence, women were able to ensure that sex would no longer be a commanding reason for denying the right to vote in a country that had been founded on a profound commitment to the maleness of rights-bearing citizenship.

The "Radical" Nineteenth Amendment

While it was a tremendous achievement, passage of the Nineteenth Amendment not only left many matters unresolved; it also opened the door to an array of other questions concerning women's rights as citizens. Even though the Nineteenth Amendment disrupted the earlier societal framework that had given men authority over women, it failed to provide a unified set of principles for determining women's rights as citizens after the amendment had removed sex as a barrier to voting. Because of the destabilizing nature of the Nineteenth Amendment, a period of constitutional uncertainty arose in which political leaders and legal scholars clashed over the constitutional implications of federal woman suffrage. In the end this period of uncertainty prompted several individuals to consider pursuing additional federal legislative measures to clarify women's legal personhood in the post–Nineteenth Amendment era. Eventually this work evolved into the original collaborative effort to draft the ERA.

In assessing the impact of the Nineteenth Amendment, a strand of previous scholarship has suggested that the start of federal woman suffrage not only failed to uplift the status of women but that it also (ironically) led to a decline in women's political activism. In general this scholarly narrative tends to suggest that while suffragists claimed that women would purify the political world, many women failed to vote, and those women who did vote did not do so as a bloc. As a result, the narrative maintains, politicians lost their new-found reverence for women voters and they relegated women to minor roles in party politics. This account argues that the women's movement lost the single issue that held it together—the vote.

Consequently, as the story goes, many former suffragists became politically apathetic and the few remaining activists fought among themselves over the trajectory of the women's movement. Scholars who have employed this assessment often look to the vote, particularly how many women voted and how they voted, to measure the historical significance of the Nineteenth Amendment. Yet, the focus on women's political behavior has created gaps in this scholarship regarding the general feeling of uncertainty among political and legal authorities over the constitutional ramifications of the Nineteenth Amendment.[69]

Although past scholars are right to pinpoint the ways in which sex discrimination persisted after the Nineteenth Amendment (and even up to this day), the traditional emphasis on failure tends to minimize and even devalue the historical significance of the Nineteenth Amendment.[70] Furthermore, the emphasis on failure neglects to recognize how contemporary Americans viewed the amendment's ratification as a transformative event. Indeed, Harry Burn, the legislator who, inspired by his mother's pleas, cast the deciding vote for ratification in Tennessee, described the amendment as an act that had "free[d] seventeen million women from political slavery."[71] For a number of his contemporaries the Nineteenth Amendment had implications beyond the vote. In their view the amendment had ushered in an era of change regarding how Americans understood state, gender, and political power.[72] Several observers even argued that it did not matter if women actually voted. For them, simply having the constitutional affirmation of women's right to vote was significant enough. On this point Judge Florence Allen, one of the first women to serve as a federal judge, asserted, "Whether or not the ballot is exercised at all, whether it is exercised foolishly, there is a potential power in the franchise which makes its holder more influential than the one who does not have the vote."[73] In a similar line of thought, Molly Lifshitz, a Russian immigrant and the secretary of the White Goods Workers Union, wrote in the women's journal *Woman Citizen* that "of course, it makes a difference to women to have the vote. It is a mark of recognition."[74]

In the years immediately following passage of the Nineteenth

Amendment, a climate of change coalesced around questions regarding women's legal personhood, which rattled how American lawmakers and legal authorities had previously understood women's status as citizens. During this time it seemed as though the amendment had helped to trigger more movement toward the recognition of women as sovereign individuals. Federal judges hearing the case *United States v. Hinson* (1925), for example, ruled that the federalization of suffrage had nullified old common law rules about husbands' responsibility for wives' criminality.[75] Into the 1930s, moreover, state courts generally agreed that age and literacy qualifications for suffrage had to be identical for both sexes.[76] The apparent spirit of change even affected the Deep South state of Georgia. In *Curtis v. Ashworth* (1928) Georgia's state Supreme Court ruled that husbands were no longer responsible for torts committed by their wives, since recent legal changes had "greatly modified the principle that the civil existence of the wife is merged in that of the husband. . . . The wife is now made, in all important affairs of life, the equal of the husband."[77] In significant ways, then, it seemed as though the Nineteenth Amendment had created an opening for women's rights activists to fully uproot the societal apparatus that had previously confined women to second-class citizenship.

The passage of the Married Women's Independent Citizenship Act of 1922 (the Cable Act) marks the most significant move toward recognition of women's civic autonomy since the passage of the Nineteenth Amendment. As Representative John Rogers (R-MA) declared during the congressional debate on the Cable Bill, "There was no particular force in the demand for this bill until the nineteenth amendment became part of the organic law of the land. . . . At that moment the doctrine of dependent or derived citizenship became as archaic as the doctrine of ordeal by fire."[78] Also speaking in the language of change driven by the passage of the Nineteenth Amendment, Representative Isaac Siegel (R-NY) contended during congressional debate on the bill that "as to the right of the woman to be an independent American citizen in her own right there can be no controversy, because the nineteenth amendment to the Constitution has settled that for all time."[79] As these Con-

gress members' comments suggest, the Nineteenth Amendment
had made the passage of the Cable Act possible.

Nicknamed the Cable Act for its congressional sponsor, Representative John Cable (R-OH), the measure essentially set out to
affirm a woman's right to an independent nationality status. The
act provided that the right of any woman to become a naturalized citizen of the United States would not be denied on account
of sex. The act also recognized that marriage to a non-American
national did not erase an American woman's national identity.
As such, the act repealed provisions in the Naturalization Act of
1855, which had established that an immigrant woman's citizenship derived from her husband's status, and the Expatriation Act
of 1907, which had caused an American woman to lose her American nationality status if she married a foreigner. Consequently,
the American legal system no longer considered women's nationality to be simply contingent and disposable.[80]

Despite these advancements, the Cable Act of 1922 had significant
limitations.[81] These weaknesses reflect the contemporary public hostility toward immigrants, especially those seen as racially unassimi-
lable, as Congress had passed the Cable Act in the early 1920s amid
an expanding anti-immigration movement. That movement had
been fueled by white Americans' fears that non-Protestant immigrants from the Mediterranean, Eastern Europe, Russia, and Asia
were overrunning American culture. As a result, the 1921 Quota
Act, and its culmination, the Immigration Act of 1924, largely constrained immigration by establishing maximum quotas for groups
by national origin. Due to the ever-growing anti-immigration atmosphere, the Cable Act did nothing for American women who had
married persons deemed ineligible for citizenship by naturalization (which primarily referred to Asians but also anarchists and
polygamists). Even with the act's passage, these women still lost
their nationality status. The act also kept in place other sharp distinctions between husbands and wives by specifying that an American woman still lost her nationality status if she lived two years in
her foreign-born husband's country or five years in any foreign
nation. Congress, then, did not permit an American woman who
had married a foreigner to retain her nationality status absolutely.[82]

The Cable Act did eradicate the American man's traditional authority to bestow his foreign-born wife with his nationality status merely by marrying her. In its place the law provided a simplified naturalization process for foreign-born wives, which required them to be a resident for only a year, rather than the standard five years. The law also allowed foreign-born wives to circumvent the typical stage of declaring intent.[83] Congress members defended these aspects of the act by arguing that such measures would encourage foreign-born wives to gain better knowledge about American society and become "equal partners" with their American husbands. Moreover, lawmakers reasoned that these changes would push foreign-born wives to become active recipients of American citizenship, which would make them better suited for raising American children. Congress, however, failed to even consider paving a clear route to naturalization for American women's foreign-born husbands.[84] Pressure from several women's groups, as chapter 3 discusses in detail, prompted Congress to amend the Cable Act in 1930, 1931, and 1934 in order to adhere more fully to the principle that women should have the right to an independent nationality status.[85]

Not everyone approved of the changes driven by the advent of federal woman suffrage. From the viewpoint of several individuals, the addition of the Nineteenth Amendment to the Constitution had severely violated states' rights. In Baltimore's newspaper, *The Sun*, one critic characterized the amendment by writing, "A State which does not control its own 'suffrage' is not a 'State' but a mere 'province.' Its citizens are not self-governing freemen, but helpless subjects of irresponsible outsiders."[86] Another steadfast enemy of federal woman suffrage, legal scholar George Stewart Brown, claimed that the Nineteenth Amendment attacked the very sovereignty of the people and that it exemplified "irresponsible government by constitutional amendment."[87] To stop the momentum of change, opponents of federal woman suffrage first challenged the actual legality of the Nineteenth Amendment. Immediately after federalization, opponents filed a number of lawsuits disputing the ratification of the amendment. Battles exploded in Tennessee, Vermont, Connecticut, West Virginia,

Missouri, Ohio, and Maryland. In general, critics alleged that several states, especially Tennessee and West Virginia, had improperly ratified the amendment.[88]

The most successful of these attempts came from William L. Marbury, a longtime foe of the Fifteenth Amendment. Marbury contested the Nineteenth Amendment on the grounds that it exceeded the legitimate scope of Article V of the Constitution. His argument went all the way to the U.S. Supreme Court in the case of *Leser v. Garnett* (1922).[89] Marbury reasoned that by changing the gender composition of the electorate, the Nineteenth Amendment had unlawfully transformed the fundamental identity of the state and in essence had created an entirely new state.[90] To bolster this claim, Marbury argued that "the amendment . . . remakes—reconstitutes—every State in the Union that has not already by voluntary internal act re-made itself, into a state governed equally by male and female votes. It abolishes a distinction in political power that has been since the world began."[91] For Marbury the Nineteenth Amendment reordered the constitutional compact so that women counted equally with men among the ranks of "We, the people." As a result, he claimed, the amendment had fundamentally changed the political nature of the country.[92]

Many individuals had hoped that the U.S. Supreme Court would provide a solid answer not only to the legality of the Nineteenth Amendment but also to Marbury's claims about the amendment's impact on the character of the American political community. As one observer put it, the high court's ruling in *Leser v. Garnett* should provide "a judicial interpretation of our exact status, and of what State and local political rights still survive under recent Constitutional legislation."[93] But the U.S. Supreme Court neither denied nor confirmed Marbury's depiction of the body politic; it only spoke to the validity of the *procedure* by which the body politic had been rearranged.[94] Justice Louis Brandeis delivered the opinion of the court. "This Amendment," he maintained, "is in character and phraseology precisely similar to the Fifteenth. For each the same method of adoption was pursued. One cannot be valid and the other invalid. That the Fifteenth is valid . . . has been recognized and acted on half a century."[95]

In an effort to justify the legality of the Nineteenth Amendment, the high court had drawn a parallel relationship between the Nineteenth and Fifteenth Amendments. However, the court's acknowledgment of this relationship raised even more concerns about the scope and meaning of the Nineteenth Amendment. In particular, the court's ruling in *Leser* begged two important questions. First, did the Nineteenth Amendment support political rights for women in the same manner that the Fifteenth Amendment had intended to support the political rights of Black men? Second, did the Nineteenth Amendment acknowledge women's position as a historically discriminated group in the same way that the Fifteenth Amendment had attempted to do so for Black men? If the answers to these two questions were yes, meaning that the Nineteenth Amendment had essentially the same constitutional effect as the Fifteenth Amendment, then there would be an implied link between the Nineteenth and Fourteenth Amendments for women, as there was between the Fourteenth and Fifteenth Amendments for Black American men. An implied connection between the Fourteenth and Nineteenth Amendments is important for understanding the constitutional ramifications of the Nineteenth Amendment, because such a connection would seem to suggest that lawmakers could subsequently hold men and women to the same legal standard.[96]

Even with the ambiguities raised in *Leser*, the high court's subsequent decision in *Adkins v. Children's Hospital* (1923) appeared to suggest that the court would uphold a broad interpretation of the Nineteenth Amendment's effect. Ruling against a minimum wage law for women, the court indicated that the Nineteenth Amendment had placed women in the same legal category as men. In his opinion on the case Justice George Sutherland reasoned, "In view of the great—not to say revolutionary—changes which have taken place . . . in the contractual, political, and civil status of women, culminating in the Nineteenth Amendment . . . woman is accorded emancipation from the old doctrine that she must be given special protection or be subjected to special restraint." The court, it seemed, was interpreting the Nineteenth Amendment as an act that had elevated women to an equivalent civic position with men.[97]

In *Radice v. New York* (1924), however, the court backtracked on the implications of its previous views by ruling in favor of a law that had banned night work for women. Also delivering the opinion in this case, Justice George Sutherland concluded, "The loss of restful night's sleep cannot be fully made up by sleep in the day time. The injurious consequences were thought by the legislature to bear more heavily against women than men, and, considering their more delicate organism, there would seem to be good reason for so thinking." Accordingly, the court had returned to the idea entrenched in the common law tradition, which presumed that since women were naturally weaker than men, they must require special legal protection. In contrast to *Adkins*, then, the court decided to restrict the reach of the Nineteenth Amendment in this subsequent ruling.[98]

Although the U.S. Supreme Court recognized that the Nineteenth Amendment had redefined citizenship for women in ways that disordered the traditional subservient place women had occupied in America's constitutional culture, the high court failed to provide a consistent answer on how these disturbances would affect women's legal personhood going forward. Did passage of the Nineteenth Amendment mean that women should be treated as citizens on the same terms as men? Or did the amendment imply that women could enjoy a new, but different type of citizenship from the one occupied by men?

As the inconsistent court rulings suggest, authorities differed on the answers to these questions. One reporter described the situation as the "suffrage war after the suffrage war."[99] Social science educator Augustus S. Beatman simply asked, "Just what was the Nineteenth Amendment?"[100] For years political leaders and legal experts would contest this question. For the most part the disputes centered on three specific concerns: women's right to serve on juries, women's right to hold public office, and women's right to an independent domicile. At issue in these debates was whether the Nineteenth Amendment afforded other rights beyond the vote.

After the ratification of the Nineteenth Amendment, a main area of contention concerned women's right to serve on juries. Jury service is a fundamental component of full citizenship status (or the status of being a primary citizen who has access to the full range of benefits and opportunities in a society). Jury service is a civil right in that it is a matter of individual protection against state authority. It is also a political right as it is a form of democratic participation in the exercise of law and justice. "The right of trial by a jury of one's peers," as suffragist Catharine Waugh McCulloch put it, "is more important than any other guarantee of liberty."[101]

Since the country's founding, the American legal system had largely excluded women from serving on juries.[102] The early modern English jurist William Blackstone, a main architect of coverture, offered insights into the reasoning behind this exclusion in his writings. For Blackstone, a jury should be a group "consisting of twelve free and lawful men" because, according to his description, "under the word *homo* also, though a name common to both sexes the female is however excluded, *propter defectum sexus.*" From Blackstone's perspective, the anatomical makeup of female persons burdened women with inherent flaws and frailties, which prevented women from exercising the independent judgment necessary for service on a jury.[103] Up until the early twentieth century, American courts and legislatures generally followed this belief, as they mostly denied women the right to serve on juries.[104]

After the constitutional removal of sex as a legal restraint on the right to vote, supporters of women's jury service insisted that such civic activity complemented women's newly elevated standing as direct participants in the body politic. For example, as discussed in an article in the *American Bar Association Journal*, Judge Robert Marx of Cincinnati, Ohio, believed that "since women vote[,] their service upon the jury is a broadening experience to them and increases their capacity for civic usefulness."[105] Helen Sherry of the Maryland State Federation of Republican Women offered a similar view in her testimony in support of female jury service before the state legislature when she argued, "Now that women have the vote, [they] are ready to assume the burdens as well as the benefits of citizenship."[106]

A number of state legislators and courts agreed that women should have the right to serve on juries. By the early 1940s twenty-eight states had moved to allow women to serve on juries. In a few cases state legislatures passed new laws that permitted female jury service. In the other cases the courts found that women became qualified for jury service when they became electors.[107] In *People v. Barltz* (1920), for instance, the Supreme Court of Michigan ruled, "The moment a woman became an elector under the constitutional amendment she was entitled to perform jury duty, if she was possessed of the same qualifications that men possessed for that duty. In other words, she was placed in that class of citizens and electors, from which class jurors were, under the statute, to be selected."[108] Additional state court decisions ruling that elector status provided voters with the right to serve on juries include the Supreme Court of Nevada's ruling in *Parus v. District Court* (1918), the Supreme Court of Iowa's ruling in *State v. Walker* (1921), and the Supreme Court of Indiana's ruling in *Palmer v. State* (1926).[109] These courts connected voting and jury service rights through *Neal v. Delaware* (1881), a case in which the U.S. Supreme Court ruled that Black American men were eligible for jury service due to their status as electors under the Fifteenth Amendment.[110] Thus, these courts' decisions interpreted the legal recognition of the right to vote as an act that furnished broader political rights in a manner similar to what the Fifteenth Amendment had set out to do for the rights of Black American men.[111]

Nevertheless, support for women's right to serve on juries was far from being a unanimously held position because a considerable number of people continued to cling to the earlier belief that women were innately unfit to deal with issues of law and justice. In the weekly publication *The Independent*, for instance, an opponent to female jury service asserted, "Juries deal with all manner of crimes, from innocuous offenses to the vilest and most revolting aberrations of the human beast. Their educations, their habits of mind, their points of view have not prepared women to deal with such cases. . . . The great majority of women hardly know that such things exist."[112] In a different publication another person claimed that women should be exempted from jury service because "women are not only embarrassed themselves by service on a jury, but they are sometimes very embarrassing to lawyers on both sides of a case who do not know the psychology of a woman's mind and are not sure which way she is going to jump."[113] Hence, gendered ideas about women's feeble nature had continued to breathe life into the arguments against women's ability to serve on juries even after the passage of the Nineteenth Amendment.

An array of state courts also proved to be resistant to the further expansion of women's rights in the area of jury service. These courts reasoned against female jury service from two angles. First, they maintained that the Nineteenth Amendment did not explicitly mandate jury service for women, and as a result it did not automatically make women eligible for such service. In particular the New Jersey Court of Appeals ruled in *State v. James* (1921) that suffrage did not make women qualified for jury service and that the common law restrictions on women's jury service still held.[114] A New York court also denied that women's newly acquired suffrage status made a difference, ruling that there was "no connection whatever between the right to vote and jury service," concluding that "women were not entitled as citizens to act as jurors."[115] In a second line of reasoning, courts opposed to female jury service had decided that when states used the word *person* in old jury statutes, they had in mind a man. Therefore, they insisted, the original intent of those statutes precluded women from serving. On this matter the Supreme Court of Illinois ruled in *People ex rel. Fyfe v. Barnett* (1925) that the legislative intent was for an assembly of persons that accorded with the old jury law, which contemplated only male jurors. If women wanted to partake in jury service, then they would have to push for new legislation.[116]

As mentioned in the introduction to this chapter, Chief Justice Arthur Prentice Rugg of the Supreme Judicial Court of Massachusetts wrote a wretched opinion that strongly condemned the notion that women had a right to serve on juries. In *Commonwealth v. Genevieve Welosky* (1931) Rugg pointed to understandings of the term "person" in his state's election law. Although the law specified that a "person" qualified to vote could sit on juries, Rugg ruled that the law implied male persons. Accordingly, he maintained, it excluded women from jury service.[117] In his ruling Rugg also described the passage of the Nineteenth Amendment as an extremely distressing event. He argued that as the amendment "conferred the suffrage on an entirely new class of human beings . . . it

added to qualified voters those who did not fall within the meaning of the word 'person' in the jury statutes." He surmised, "The
change in the legal status of women wrought by the Nineteenth
Amendment was radical, drastic, and unprecedented. While it is
to be given full effect in its field, it is not to be extended by implication." Echoing fellow woman suffrage opponent William Marbury's earlier argument against the Nineteenth Amendment in
Leser, Rugg maintained that women were an entirely new "class"
of voters and that the "drastic" Nineteenth Amendment had created a feminized electorate.[118] Although a few legal authorities had
seen the Nineteenth Amendment as an act that provided women
with rights outside of the realm of suffrage, others sought to contain the "radical" implications of the amendment by upholding
the legitimacy of sex-based legal limitations on women's right to
serve on juries.

Up until the early 1970s courts generally followed Justice Rugg's
reasoning against female jury service. The resistance to women's
jury service culminated with the U.S. Supreme Court's ruling in *Fay
v. New York* (1947) in which the court declared that women did not
have a constitutional right as citizens to serve on juries.[119] As late
as 1961 the Supreme Court continued to adhere to this position
when it decided in *Hoyt v. Florida* that Gwendolyn Rogers Hoyt, a
battered wife convicted of killing her husband, did not have a constitutional right to a trial by a mixed-sex jury.[120] Even though the
Civil Rights Act of 1957 had recognized women's right to serve on
federal juries, more than twenty states continued to refuse to place
women on juries well into the 1960s.[121] By 1973 women could insist
on the right to jury service in all fifty states, but nineteen states
still allowed voluntary exemption for reasons such as pregnancy,
a fear of public life, or maternal demands.[122] It was not until 1975
that the Supreme Court ruled against the systematic exclusion of
women from jury service by holding that such an exclusion violated the right of an accused person to a trial by a jury "drawn
from a fair cross section of the community."[123]

Women's right to hold public office was another area of debate
in which lawmakers and judicial authorities wrestled over the Nineteenth Amendment's implications. Throughout the early 1920s a

few state legislatures and courts had issued favorable opinions with regard to women's right to serve in public office. In Maine, for example, the state legislature reacted to the Nineteenth Amendment's ratification by passing a statute announcing that the right to hold state office could not be denied because of sex. The state's highest court also ruled that its governor could appoint a woman as justice of the peace, because "every political distinction based upon the consideration of sex was eliminated from the Constitution by the ratification of the amendment. Males and females were thenceforth, when citizens of the United States, privileged to take equal hand in the conduct of government."[124] Similarly, in *Preston v. Roberts* (1922) the Supreme Court of North Carolina held that a woman was qualified to serve as a notary public and deputy clerk to the state superior court because the Nineteenth Amendment had removed the ban on women from holding public office.[125] Hence, in the view of certain legislative and judicial authorities the Nineteenth Amendment had afforded women broader political rights on top of the vote.

In alignment with this thinking is the Supreme Court of Texas's decision in *Dickson v. Strickland* (1924). This case dealt with the candidacy of Miriam "Ma" Ferguson, who was the Democratic candidate for governor of Texas in 1924. Miriam Ferguson's opponent, Charles Dickson, challenged her candidacy with claims that she was simply a figurehead candidate standing in for her husband and campaign manager, James "Pa" Ferguson. (James Ferguson had been impeached while serving as governor of Texas a few years earlier, making him ineligible to run for that office again.) Dickson also contended that Miriam Ferguson was not qualified to hold public office because she was both a woman and a wife.

Nonetheless, the Supreme Court of Texas denied his claims, ruling that women were eligible to hold public office, and a few days later the people of Texas elected Miriam Ferguson as their governor. "It is to blind one's eyes to the truths of current history," Justice Thomas Benton Greenwood proclaimed in his ruling for the case, "not to recognize that the last vestige of reason to sustain a rule excluding women from office was removed when she was clothed with equal authority with men, in the government of the

state and nation, through the ballot. When the reason for the rule
of exclusions has failed, the rule should no longer be applied."[126]
In its richly complex decision to uphold Miriam Ferguson's right
to hold public office, the Texas court did deny a direct effect by
the Nineteenth Amendment on the state's rules regarding eligi-
bility for office holding. Even so, as legal scholar Gretchen Ritter
explains, the Texas court drew attention in its ruling to what it
understood to be the normative impact of the Nineteenth Amendment on the judicial views regarding women's rights.[127]

As with female jury service, however, support for women holding public office was not a consistently backed position. A number
of state-level officials across the country disagreed with the notion
that the Nineteenth Amendment had confirmed women's right to
hold public office. In 1921, for example, Maryland attorney general
Alexander Armstrong Jr. delivered an official statement in which
he decided that the masculine pronoun in the laws that create
public offices excluded women from taking such positions.[128] As
well, in 1927 the high court of New Hampshire declared that even
though the Nineteenth Amendment made women eligible for elective office the "framers of the Constitution understood that office
holding was limited to men by that document." The court went
on to argue that the connection between the Nineteenth Amendment and office holding pertained only to elective office and not
in the cases of appointive office, where the common law restrictions against women should remain.[129] Thus, even in the realm of
political rights, a number of legal authorities insisted upon main-
taining a narrow interpretation of the Nineteenth Amendment's
impact on women's status.

In a final field of contention, authorities clashed over the Nineteenth Amendment's bearing on women's right to an autonomous domicile.[130] Domicile, or the status of being a resident of a
particular jurisdiction, forms a crucial component of one's legal
existence.[131] As Albert Levitt, an up-and-coming legal scholar who
would go on to help the NWP draft the ERA, wrote, "The domicile is the legal home. It is the place where that law can act upon
the status of the individual no matter where the person may be
in corpore."[132] In legal terms a person's domicile affects his or her

taxation, political representation, and legal estate. But under the common law doctrine of domestic relations a husband's domicile determined his wife's domicile, no matter where she actually lived. Following the original impetus toward change in the years immediately following the passage of the Nineteenth Amendment, several state legislatures granted married women more control over their domicile. Several states, including Maine, Massachusetts, Michigan, New Jersey, Ohio, and Pennsylvania, attempted to resolve issues surrounding the location of married women's residency by allowing married women to choose their own domiciles for voting purposes. These states, however, left other restrictions on married women's domicile otherwise intact.[133]

The Supreme Court of Virginia's ruling in *Commonwealth v. Rutherford* (1933) sheds light on the basis for these post–Nineteenth Amendment limitations on women's rights. The case involved Helen Rutherford, resident of New York, and her husband, John Rutherford, who was a resident of Virginia. Helen Rutherford was a financially independent woman who had lived separately from her husband with his consent. The state of Virginia, however, had levied income taxes on Helen Rutherford by alleging that since her domicile was the same as her husband's, she was a resident of Virginia.[134] Ruling in favor of Helen Rutherford's claim that she was a legal resident of New York, the Virginia court concurred with the argument that to do otherwise "would deprive her of her property in derogation of the Fourteenth and Nineteenth Amendments of the Constitution of the United States."[135] In the ruling the Virginia court explicitly recognized a relationship between the Fourteenth and Nineteenth Amendments; such a recognition would seem to suggest a considerable expansion of women's rights as citizens. The court also went on to call into question one of the primary aspects of coverture: the doctrine of marital unity. In regard to this point the court condemned the doctrine as the "common-law fiction that the entity or being of the wife is merged into that of the husband . . . that they are one and that one is the husband."[136] In a significant way, then, the decision in *Rutherford* hinted at considerable progress toward the legal affirmation that women should be regarded as sovereign individuals.

However, as Ritter has noted, court decisions like the one in *Rutherford* also offered what appeared to be an escape route from the idea that the changes to woman's legal personhood necessitated that the law treat men and women citizens alike.[137] In *Rutherford*, for instance, the Supreme Court of Virginia refused to dismiss the notion of coverture in its entirety. "The authorities are not uniform," Justice George L. Browning stated in his opinion for the case; "they are diverse; but we think that the statutory invasion of the fiction, certainly in this state, has broken it down as far as the political, civil and property rights of the wife are involved; but as to purely domestic relations it is, at least in part, preserved and it ought so to be."[138] Accordingly, the Virginia court favored enriching women's domicile rights insofar as that expansion did not infringe upon the traditional domestic obligations between husband and wife.[139]

As explained at the beginning of this chapter, coverture not only submerged the civic identity of a woman into her husband's status. It also upheld a model for domestic relations in which the legal culture assumed that wives were obligated to provide their husbands with household services; in return, husbands were expected to provide wives with financial support and shelter. In the sphere of "domestic relations" various legislative and judicial leaders decided that the old rules of marital duties should continue even after the Nineteenth Amendment had expanded women's ability to autonomously participate in the public realm. As Reva Siegel has shown in her work on the history of coverture, the Nineteenth Amendment may have unsettled the doctrine of marital unity, but the second piece of the common law tradition, with its emphasis on what husbands and wives owed to each other within the household, continued to shape how legislative and judicial authorities thought about the outlines of women's civic presence well into the mid- to late twentieth century.[140]

Yet, as the court noted in *Rutherford*, the authorities were not uniform in their interpretation of women's status in the post–Nineteenth Amendment era. Because the Nineteenth Amendment had allowed for the separation of a woman's civic identity from her husband's identity, it undermined a central component of coverture—the doctrine of marital unity. Various groups inter-preted this change as lifting women up to the same legal standing as men. Others, however, insisted that women still required dif-ferential legal treatment. So, the question remained: what were women's constitutional rights now that the Nineteenth Amend-ment had removed sex as a legally acceptable reason to withhold the right to vote?

The Beginning of the Equal Rights Campaign

The concept of a constitutional amendment to ensure the equal rights of men and women citizens materialized during this period of constitutional uncertainty. But the idea did not immediately fol-low the passage of the Nineteenth Amendment; rather, it devel-oped from an effort to pass a limited federal bill that sought to remove a short list of legal discriminations against women. As the debate over the meaning and scope of the Nineteenth Amend-ment grew, the campaign for the limited federal bill evolved into a larger effort to draft an additional constitutional amendment to clarify women's rights in the post–Nineteenth Amendment era.

As discussed previously, the NWP, which would become the major organization behind the ERA, represented the more mili-tant side of the suffrage struggle. After the passage of the Nine-teenth Amendment, the organization did not immediately pursue an equal rights campaign, nor for that matter did it immediately seek the passage of an additional federal amendment. On the contrary, the organization's leader, Alice Paul, and its other offi-cers voiced their concern about the future direction of the party. A few officers insisted on dissolving the organization, while others suggested that the NWP needed to reorganize and develop a new campaign. Because of these concerns, Paul announced in Novem-ber 1920 that the NWP would hold a convention in February to dis-cuss the organization's future, and if the membership wished the party to continue, then they would create new guidelines of opera-tion.[141] Thus, the NWP's campaign for equal rights developed over time and in conjunction with the growing debate over the consti-tutional effects of the Nineteenth Amendment.

It was only after the convention in February 1921 that the NWP

announced its new goal, which in the words of the party's leadership was the removal of "the remaining forms of subjections
of women, beginning with the legal disabilities."[142] On the NWP's
new objectives, Paul declared, "Now that political freedom has
been won, we hope to wipe out sex discrimination in law, so that
the legal status of women will be self-respecting."[143] Another NWP
leader, Elsie Hill, who was the newly elected temporary chair of
the group's national council, made a similar pronouncement in
her correspondence during this time: "We are launched on the
open road towards greater power for women."[144] In short, by February 1921 the NWP had developed a new campaign to carry out
the removal of other sex discriminations from the law.

This campaign, however, still did not involve the pursuit of an
additional constitutional amendment. The NWP's original strategy was twofold, the first goal being to introduce a federal bill into
Congress. The bill would include the theory of equality between
men and women, as well as a short list of discriminations to be
eliminated. In a letter Paul wrote during this planning period, she
described the limited objectives of the bill, explaining that it sought
to make women's nationality status independent of the husband's
status, to eliminate discrimination against women in government
service, and to remove existing legal discriminations based on sex
in the code of the District of Columbia.[145] The NWP hired a lawyer,
Shippen Lewis, to help draft the federal bill. Shippen Lewis was
the son of Dora Lewis, a suffrage leader and founding member
of the NWP. He was also counsel to the Pennsylvania Consumers'
League.[146] The second component of the NWP's post–Nineteenth
Amendment strategy involved the introduction of state-level bills
that would be modeled on the federal measure.[147]

In early April 1921 the NWP continued its new campaign to elim-
inate additional sex discriminations in the law by meeting with
President Warren Harding at the White House. About sixty peo-
ple went to the meeting, including Elsie Hill, Anita Pollitzer, and
Izetta Jewel Brown. The group met with the president for almost
an hour, and Paul described the meeting as "very gratifying."[148]
Pollitzer also believed that the meeting had gone successfully. "He
[President Harding] began with the usual remarks about evolu-

tion, slow progress," Pollitzer explained. "Then he told that the Republicans meant to keep their platform pledges, that he greatly desired to see the fulfillment of the Nineteenth Amendment, and would see that our measure was brought to the attention of the proper authorities in Congress."[149]

When members of the delegation informed President Harding that they had enlisted the support of Republican senator Charles Curtis of Kansas, President Harding responded, "You have strong backing."[150] Senator Curtis had promised to introduce the equal rights model bill when Congress convened. Representative Simeon D. Fess of Ohio agreed to introduce the bill in the House of Representatives.[151] These politicians' support can be partly attributed to the desire of the Republican Party to secure what it presumed to be a woman's voting bloc. Indeed, in the period immediately following the passage of the Nineteenth Amendment both parties had rushed to appease women voters in the hopes of obtaining the so-called woman's vote.[152] In these favorable surroundings the NWP was able to take a few steps toward what President Harding had referred to as "the fulfillment of the Nineteenth Amendment."[153]

Even with what appeared to be positive movement on the federal bill, the NWP's leaders still wavered over its wording and the strategy as a whole. To start, the NWP's officers were concerned about their own lack of legal expertise. "The task of getting the bill in shape," Elsie Hill wrote to Shippen Lewis, "is of course, absolutely beyond us. We can only cling with determination to the idea, while a skillful sympathetic critic like yourself hammers it with technique."[154] In a similar fashion Pollitzer later wrote that the NWP had delayed publicizing drafts of the federal model bill because the NWP's leaders feared it might not be "in the right language, or amateurish."[155]

Leaders of the NWP were also apprehensive about upsetting supporters who might possibly see the NWP's new strategy as an effort to create uniform, national lawmaking. Paul, for example, understood that many of the NWP's backers were wary about giving the federal government too much power through far-reaching legislation. In one letter Paul advised journalist Florence Sanville, who had been drafting an article on the NWP's proposed bill, to use "legislation in place of words like 'a blanket law'" in her proposed piece. As Paul explained it, the lawyers with whom the NWP had consulted were "not certain whether it [would] be possible to combine in one law all the legislation, which we wish to have passed in each state."[156]

During the early spring of 1921, moreover, Paul feared that a considerable number of the NWP's members would readily reject the prospect of a model federal bill because those members might see the bill as an overreach by the federal government into local issues, especially those imbued with racism like state segregation laws. NWP supporter Ella Clapp Thompson, for instance, criticized the proposed federal bill early on. "In working for the federal [Nineteenth] amendment," she contended, "we asked to have sex discrimination removed—always saying that we were willing in each state to be subject to voting qualifications required of the men in that state. To go into a fight on the race question is distinctly against my taste, to say the least. To my mind, each state is the best judge of that problem." She finished her criticism by writing, "California knows the Jap, New York the alien, and the South the Negro. No outsider can understand. For my part, I am frank to say that I belong to a white woman's party or none."[157] One of the many shortcomings of the Nineteenth Amendment was that even though it had removed sex as a permissible barrier to voting, it left other specific requirements for voting in place. As a result, several state legislatures, mainly in the South, were still able to employ prejudiced measures, such as literacy tests, to withhold the right to vote from many Black American women. As the above quote suggests, a number of NWP members continued to support those racially discriminatory practices.[158]

Disillusioned with their original strategy, Elsie Hill and Alice Paul sought help from a talented young legal scholar: professor Albert Levitt of The George Washington University.[159] As noted earlier, Levitt had been working on the expansion of women's domicile rights, and he would go on to marry, and eventually divorce, Elsie Hill. With regard to the history of the ERA, Levitt not only helped to develop the concept of a constitutional amendment to ensure women's status as full citizens, but he also convinced Paul to move in that direction.[160] The historic meeting occurred on a Sunday afternoon in mid-May 1921 as Paul, Hill, and Levitt were discussing the federal bill. In Hill's description of the meeting, she wrote, "I have never seen more continuous mental effort than those two put into this."[161]

Halfway through the meeting Levitt proposed that they pursue an additional constitutional amendment. He argued that such an amendment would enshrine a "'Woman's Bill of Rights' into our national constitution."[162] While Paul is credited as the main creator of the ERA, Levitt not only pushed for the idea, but he also crafted the first, albeit tedious, draft of the amendment. The first section of the proposed amendment stated, "The legal rights, duties, powers, privileges, capacities and opportunities of a citizen of the United States shall not be abridged or denied by the United States or any State on account of sex." Eight more sections followed, all detailing the specific rights that the amendment intended to secure, which included women's rights to serve on juries, hold public office, and maintain their own domicile.[163] Overall, for Levitt, an additional constitutional amendment was the key to determining the rights of women as citizens in the wake of the Nineteenth Amendment.

During the meeting Levitt offered to show the draft of the proposed amendment to his old friend and advisor, Harvard law professor Roscoe Pound. As Hill later described it, "Finally, Levitt sprang up and said: 'What would it mean to you if you could have Dean Pound's opinion on this!' Whereupon we sent him to the telephone and in a few minutes, he had Dean Pound at Harvard on the wire. And an appointment made for Monday at four pm at Cambridge." Levitt dined with Paul and Hill until ten thirty that night, and then he took the midnight train to Boston to meet with Pound. The possibility of having Pound's assistance boosted the credibility of Levitt's idea, and as a result Hill and Paul signed onto it.[164] After their meeting with Levitt, Hill gleefully but mistakenly exclaimed to a friend, "It looks to me as though it [the amendment] will be ready for introduction in ten days."[165] But the amendment would not be ready for introduction that summer, or even that year, as an arduous, almost three-year drafting process ensued after Levitt, Paul, and other collaborators failed to reach a consensus on the contours of the amendment's intent.[166]

Conclusion

Before the start of federal woman suffrage, American political leaders and legal authorities had followed a single, masculine model for full citizenship status that venerated the doctrine of coverture. But the Nineteenth Amendment challenged this legal paradigm, because it implicitly recognized women's right to hold their own civic identities. Due to this development, a period of uncertainty resulted in which the country's leaders wrestled over the constitutional effects of federal woman suffrage. At issue was whether voter status commanded other civic rights. Eventually the ambiguities over the Nineteenth Amendment's meaning and scope prompted several individuals to consider drafting an additional amendment to clarify women's rights in the post–Nineteenth Amendment era. Yet, as the next chapter discusses, the once collaborative project eventually fell apart as the participants strongly disagreed over the implications of the proposed amendment.

2

"The Right to Differ"

The Power of Protectionism, 1920–1932

In December 1922 Florence Kelley, executive secretary of the National Consumers' League, skewered the proposed ERA in an article for *Survey*, a leading journal of social work and reform. In this piece she declared that the ERA would deprive American wage-earning women for all time of the right to differ and that it would "place upon them forever the yoke of uniformity with the legislative achievements of working men." Finally, she argued that the amendment would violate women's "eternal, fundamental" right to differ from men.[1] Kelley, who, as discussed in the previous chapter, was a prominent social reformer who had helped to fashion the legal basis for women's special labor legislation, believed that women's welfare and the stability of American society required that the law be free to treat men and women citizens differently. While Kelley had been initially curious about the ERA in its earliest forms, she now feared that it would infringe upon what she viewed to be an essential need for women to have their own set of rights.

The creation of the ERA, which had caused Kelley so much distress, was rooted in the constitutional uncertainty that ensued after the passage of the Nineteenth Amendment. In the late spring of 1921 a number of lawyers, politicians, and activists came together to write an additional constitutional amendment. Their intention was to quell the persistent arguments over women's legal personhood with a subsequent amendment that would solidify women's rights as citizens. But, as this chapter reveals, the toilsome, nearly three-year struggle to draft the additional amendment resulted in the creation of two very different interpretations of American citizenship.

Drafting the Equal Rights Amendment

The initial effort to draw up a constitutional amendment to enshrine women's rights as citizens lasted until the fall of 1921. For the most part it consisted of cooperation and teamwork among various legal minds and political activists. During this period the leaders of the National Woman's Party, along with other political activists and legal experts, worked together on the phrasing of the proposed amendment. Since a number of those involved in the drafting process supported special legislation for women, a primary concern in the early effort involved the inclusion of a "saving clause" to protect sex-specific labor legislation. However, the failure to construct a saving clause that satisfied all of the positions led to the collapse of the original collaborative effort.[2]

From the very beginning of the drafting process, the NWP's leaders and supporters called attention to the proposed amendment's intended impact on women's status in the post–Nineteenth Amendment era. Sociologist and NWP supporter Mary Burt Messer described the purpose of the amendment as "straightening out the status of woman at every point."[3] In the eyes of Lavinia Egan, an NWP official, the amendment would recognize the "duties and responsibilities of women in the light of their right of citizenship."[4] NWP leader Elsie Hill held a similar sentiment. As she put it, "we are attacking and revolutionizing ten centuries of English Common Law tradition. All the great lawyers we have consulted believe this should be done."[5] Hence, many of those involved in the drafting process not only insisted on the need for an additional constitutional amendment to determine women's rights as citizens in the wake of the Nineteenth Amendment, but they also hoped that the newly proposed amendment would eradicate the remaining elements of coverture, specifically the common law tradition of sex-specific marital duties.

As discussed in the previous chapter, in May 1921 Albert Levitt, an up-and-coming legal scholar, had persuaded Alice Paul toward the idea of writing an additional constitutional amendment. Soon after that fateful encounter Levitt traveled to Boston to meet with Roscoe Pound about the proposed amendment. Upon Levitt's return, he presented to Paul another draft of the amendment; Pound had significantly revised Levitt's original draft. First, he condensed the language of the amendment.[6] As Pound later explained to Levitt, "I think it is wise to have the amendment as short and concise as possible."[7] Most important, though, Pound inserted into the second section of the amendment a "saving clause" that exempted legislation based on the "physical constitution of women" from the provision of equality.[8] Both Pound and Levitt supported the preservation of special legislation for women.[9] As the prior chapter describes, special legislation, which had flourished in the beginning of the twentieth century, regulated the labor conditions of working women and was driven by the idea that women required extra legal protection as mothers or potential mothers.

At first Paul and other NWP leaders supported the inclusion of a saving clause. Even before Levitt had convinced Paul to pursue a constitutional amendment, she specified that the NWP did not want to threaten special legislation for women, clarifying in one letter, "We, of course, are stating definitively that our [federal model] bill does not in any way contemplate changing minimum wage laws or hours of labor for women, as, while society is as it is at present, we women need this protection."[10] Other NWP members also favored special legislation for women. Elsie Hill, for example, cautioned that the amendment "should be so drawn that it will not prevent us from passing constructive and social legislation after we secure equal rights before the law."[11] Thus, during the first stage of the drafting process many of the NWP's leaders openly supported special legislation for women, and they explicitly expressed their desire to include a saving clause in the amendment.

Almost immediately after deciding to proceed with a constitutional amendment, the NWP's officials began to solicit the support of Florence Kelley, leader of the NCL. Hill wrote that the prospect of Pound's support seemed so promising, because they assumed that "his opinion . . . [would have] added weight with Ms. Kelley."[12] As noted, Kelley had been one of the major architects of special legislation for women; moreover, she had helped to promote the dependent woman theory that justified such legislation. Although Kelley fiercely supported woman suffrage, she did not like grouping the interests of men and women into a single and, to her mind, masculine standard. Before the idea of a constitutional amendment had entered into the picture, Kelley warned Hill to think twice about the ramifications of theoretical equality, exclaiming, "To say Equality, Equality when there is no Equality, when Nature herself has created permanent physical inequality, can, however, be as stupid and as deadly as to cry, Peace, Peace, when there is no peace." Still, Kelley insisted that "sex disabilities" against women should be eliminated. For Kelley, these disabilities included women's exclusion from jury service as well as restrictions on women's right to hold public office. In Kelley's view, these rights justly belonged to women as citizens of the country.[13]

Despite her concerns, Kelley did provide feedback and suggestions to the NWP's leaders and their legal experts in the initial effort to craft legislation to prevent sex discrimination. Early in the spring of 1921 Kelley met with Maud Younger of the NWP to discuss the organization's equal rights campaign. Afterward Kelley wrote of the meeting, "Miss Younger seemed disposed to accept all my suggestions and I hope she may succeed in convincing her colleagues. . . . She understands the dangers to be feared from loosely drawn laws."[14] Early on in the drafting process of the ERA, Kelley also continued to communicate with Hill about the proposed amendment. In one letter Kelley concluded, "This draft looks less alarming than some of its predecessors."[15] While Kelley remained wary of the developing equal rights campaign, she was initially willing to at least entertain the NWP's ideas.

Throughout the summer of 1921 the NWP continued to solicit help from various legal minds, especially from notable persons who supported special legislation for women. At the start of June, Elsie Hill wrote to Felix Frankfurter, the future associate justice of the Supreme Court, and asked for his assistance in drafting the proposed amendment. When Frankfurter responded, however, he expressed significant concerns about the amendment. First,

Frankfurter contended that such an amendment could overturn
minimum wage laws for women, because judges might interpret
those laws as not falling under the exemptions in Pound's saving clause, which only protected legislation explicitly based on
the "physical constitution of women." Second, Frankfurter conveyed his fears over the general implications of equal rights. In
his response to Elsie Hill, Frankfurter reasoned, "If I may say so,
the form in which you have attained your end begets new difficulties. I do not like to be merely destructive but . . . this is a task
of considerable delicacy and requires not a little consideration. I
am positive, however, that the amendment in its present form is
fraught with mischief that I know you are anxious to avoid."[16] Hill
replied, "We are determined to avoid difficulties."[17]

At this point in the course of drafting the amendment, Alice
Paul and other leaders of the NWP were determined to convince
Felix Frankfurter, as well as others who supported special labor
legislation, that an amendment could be drawn up that would satisfy all positions. For this purpose Paul traveled to Boston in mid-
June 1921 to meet with Frankfurter in person. After the meeting
Paul wrote to a friend that she believed she had convinced Frankfurter to reconsider his stance. Furthermore, she thought that
she had persuaded Frankfurter to outline a more inclusive saving
clause with the help of Roscoe Pound.[18]

But Paul had misunderstood the outcome of her meeting with
Frankfurter. By the end of June, Frankfurter wrote to Paul that,
after further discussion with Pound, both had decided that the
prospect of a constitutional amendment to ensure the rights of
women as full citizens was "fraught with the greatest dangers." He
continued, "I confess I do not see how any intelligent amendment
can be drawn without prior knowledge of what is sought to be
changed—not generally but specifically. A Constitutional amendment such as you are contemplating is an extra-hazardous instrument and can only be fashioned upon full knowledge." Frankfurter
went on to assert that laws discriminating against women varied too
much from state to state, and a constitutional amendment could
not remedy the problem until an extensive investigation into the
variations in women's status had taken place.[19]

Even with Frankfurter's criticisms, Paul pressed on, and by the beginning of July 1921 she had begun to sketch out the amendment herself. Previously Levitt and Pound had modeled their versions on the language of the Fourteenth Amendment. Paul, in contrast, based her early drafts on the language of the Thirteenth Amendment. Her basis for avoiding the language of the Fourteenth Amendment, she suggested in her correspondence, was to circumvent the freedom of contract issues, which arguably posed threats to special legislation for women.[20] One of these earlier drafts stated in its first section, "Neither political nor common law disabilities on account of sex or marriage shall exist within the several states, the United States, or any place subject to the jurisdiction of the United States."[21] Paul quickly gathered opinions on her drafts from several lawyers, including not only Albert Levitt but also Shippen Lewis, who had helped with the federal model bill, as well as Dean Acheson, who was clerking for Justice Louis Brandeis and would later become an influential foreign policy advisor to several U.S. presidents, and Frank Walsh, former chair of the Commission on Industrial Relations and a former joint head of the War Labor Board.[22]

Paul also looked to the Thirteenth Amendment, because she considered that marriage under the common law tradition of domestic relations formed a type of involuntary servitude. Speaking to this claim, Paul wrote to Caroline Spencer, a lawyer serving as secretary of the Colorado State Committee of the NWP, that "marriage always abridges the rights, privileges, and immunities of citizens, that is[,] the rights, privileges and immunities of a married man or of a married woman are necessarily abridged by obligations which they take on through marriage."[23] Paul thought that Acheson agreed with her view of marriage; she even wrote to Levitt that Acheson had suggested to her "that perhaps it might be well for the amendment to declare that the whole system of coverture should cease to exist."[24] Levitt, however, did not like the direction Paul was taking the amendment. He cautioned against gathering advice from "too many cooks" and recommended that they should not try to "do away with the legal institutions of marriage and the family."[25] Even so, Paul's early attempts to prepare the amendment in such a way that it directly addressed coverture reflects the degree to which she and others had sought to reform the remaining influential components of the common law tradition of marital duties in the wake of the Nineteenth Amendment.[26]

In mid-July 1921 Paul sent Frankfurter a copy of her draft modeled on the Thirteenth Amendment; Paul was still determined to win Frankfurter over.[27] Yet, Paul's persistence only increased Frankfurter's annoyance with the whole concept. Demonstrating his frustration with the topic, Frankfurter grumbled in an ensuing letter to an NCL official, "I made it perfectly clear that I would not undertake its drafting and I do not approve of the amendment."[28] In response to Frankfurter's intransigence, Levitt traveled to Connecticut in mid-July to meet with Frankfurter at his summer home. The meeting did not go well. In a subsequent letter to Paul, Levitt underscored the futility of the meeting with Frankfurter, writing, "The net result of the interview is nothing." As Levitt put it, Frankfurter was "temperamentally against the Federal Amendment in any form and so will never see any good in any amendment you may draft. . . . He is in the state of mind where he will protect his own at all hazards, and beyond peradventure of a doubt."[29] Before the meeting had concluded, Frankfurter gave Levitt an extensive memorandum that listed what he saw as the many problems entrenched in the proposed amendment. In short, Frankfurter still thought that the amendment would endanger special legislation for women— the legislation he had worked diligently to achieve for most of his career. As Frankfurter explained in his memo, "I do not believe the amendment even in this form is free from the danger of the contention that women cannot by law be treated differently from men—a calamity which is to be most zealously guarded against."[30] In the end Frankfurter refused to support the amendment no matter how it was worded, because he fundamentally believed that the law should be able to hold men and women to different legal principles.

Paul eventually realized Frankfurter would not change his opinion, so she decided to move on and enlist help from others who supported special legislation for women but were also open to the idea of writing an additional amendment to establish women's rights as citizens.

During this time Paul gained the support of labor activist Frank Walsh.[31] As well, Paul sent her NWP colleague Maud Younger to visit Ethel Smith of the NWTUL. At that meeting Younger listened to Smith's concerns, especially those surrounding the amendment's potential impact on minimum wage legislation for women.[32] Around this time Paul met with Mary Anderson, director of the Women's Bureau. At this meeting Paul showed Anderson a potential saving clause to be included in the amendment: "This article does not undertake to deal with the field of industrial legislation."[33] Anderson would later become one of the strongest, most vocal opponents of the ERA, but, at least according to Paul, Anderson had offered a tentative approval of the saving clause and the proposed amendment during this earlier meeting.[34]

Anderson's apparent approval excited Paul, and she turned once again to collecting the advice of Levitt and Pound. Contrary to Frankfurter's claim, Pound was still willing to help draft the amendment, because, in Elsie Hill's words, he saw it as "saving time and being more effective at present than state action."[35] Still, Pound did not like Paul's latest draft, which led him to write yet another version of the amendment. The proposed amendment now stated that neither "political nor legal disabilities on account of sex or marriage" shall be permitted in the United States. The second section provided a saving clause that read, "This article shall not be interpreted by the courts . . . as prescribing legislation based upon the exercise of the police power of the several states, [and] the United States."[36] Both Pound and Levitt still believed that an additional constitutional amendment could resolve the confusion over the contours of women's rights in the post–Nineteenth Amendment era, but they insisted that such an amendment must include a saving clause to protect special legislation for women.[37]

Several individuals criticized Pound's latest version in its wording of the saving clause, especially its reference to the "police power" of the federal government in a constitutional amendment. As explained before, "police power" refers to the supposed inherent power of the state to pass legislation that protects the health and welfare of its citizens. A few of the NWP's legal advisors cau-

tioned against referencing such power in a constitutional amendment. As one lawyer commented to Caroline Spencer of the NWP,
"Section two is exceedingly dangerous. No lawyer can tell what
legislation might be enacted under it nor what legislation under
it might be upheld by the courts."[38] Paul also expressed unease
about Pound's saving clause, remarking, "I think this is as bad as
earlier ones about the physical constitution of women which we
have been trying to get away from[;] it seems to me that everything we want to avoid would be let in under the police power."[39]

Given the friction caused by ongoing concern about the inclusion of a possible saving clause, the original collaborative effort fell
apart in the fall of 1921. Previously, Paul had been determined to
win over persons who supported special legislation for women. In
the spring and summer months of 1921, for example, she eagerly
asked for their advice and brought them into the drafting process. But by the end of 1921 Paul had become annoyed with her
legal advisors' apparent inability to draw up a saving clause that
would please everyone. She also began to second-guess altogether
the merits of special legislation for working women. Throughout
the fall and winter of 1921 the initial cooperative effort collapsed
as Paul and her supporters began to reassess exactly what they
meant by equality.

In the fall of 1921 Paul and other NWP leaders started to entertain the notion of abandoning a clause safeguarding special legislation for women. This move was partly due to the advice of a
few of the NWP's legal advisors, including Frank Walsh, Shippen
Lewis, and George Gordon Battle. These lawyers maintained that
a saving clause was unnecessary, because the amendment would
not interfere with women's special legislation.[40] In fact Lewis even
presented to Paul his own report on Supreme Court rulings, which,
he argued, showed that the amendment without a saving clause
would not affect special legislation, because the amendment dealt
only with the political and legal restrictions on women's rights and
was not intended to touch the industrial field.[41] Others contended
that not only was a saving clause unnecessary but, in the words of
Judge Robert Kerr of Colorado, it put an "added weapon in the
hands of the enemies of section one." He asserted that it "is either

contradictory of section one or is superfluous or both and should be stricken out before the bill is introduced."[42]

By this time Paul had begun to work with Shippen Lewis to draft yet another version of the amendment. This version also reflected the Thirteenth Amendment, but it did not include a saving clause.[43] It stated, "Section One. Neither political nor civil disabilities or inequalities on account of sex or marriage shall exist within the United States or any place subject to their jurisdiction. Section Two. Congress shall have power to enforce this article by appropriate legislation." Paul planned to introduce this form of the amendment into Congress in the winter of 1921.[44]

In the fall of that year the NWP went public with the proposed amendment by releasing copies of the draft to the *New York Times* and the *Washington Post*.[45] Several prominent legal minds also publicly endorsed the amendment. Frank Walsh, for instance, told the *New York Times*, "The political civil and legal disabilities and inequalities leveled against woman, on the sole ground of sex, are so great in number . . . that I can see no way of approximating justice as affecting the sexes, except by the passage of such an amendment."[46] Lending another voice of support, Matthew Hale, former national chair of the Progressive Party, declared, "Now that women have been granted the franchise, it is a particularly opportune time for the introduction of a Constitutional amendment, removing all political, civil, and legal disabilities on account of sex."[47] As well, amendment supporters contended that an amendment guaranteeing the equality of men and women citizens needed to follow the Nineteenth Amendment to ensure women's status as rights-bearing citizens. As Harry Slattery, former counsel to the National Conservation Association, remarked in a statement provided to the NWP, the Nineteenth Amendment "did not give to women the status that the Fourteenth and Fifteenth amendments gave to the colored citizen. In fact, the suffrage amendment, is in a sense, a half-way house on the road to equal civil, legal, and political rights for women."[48] As these legal thinkers saw it, the Constitution required an additional amendment to remove any further undue legal disabilities against women and ensure the autonomy of America's voting citizens.

The wide publicity of an amendment draft, especially one without a saving clause, incited a fury of opposition from many activists and legal scholars who supported special legislation for women. Felix Frankfurter, for example, wrote of his "shock" that Paul would go ahead with her amendment in spite of his warnings that it would allow the courts to invalidate protective legislation for women. He went on to doubt the good intentions of the leaders of the party, who "seem either indifferent to or ignorant of the consequences they will bring upon millions of wage-earning women."[49] Florence Kelley too conveyed her distress over the publication of the draft. Writing to Frankfurter, she called the proposed amendment "terrifying." In her view it would only intensify the confusion over women's legal standing.[50] For her part, Ethel Smith of the NWTUL demanded that Maud Younger, now legislative chair of the NWP, make clear the party's stance on special legislation for women. In one letter Smith exclaimed to Younger that "until the Woman's Party declares itself on these points, it necessarily shows itself ruthless, to say the least, in its dealing with working women."[51]

In addition, Smith wrote a detailed letter about her concerns to the NWP's legal advisor, George Gordon Battle, who was a prominent attorney and Democratic Party politician. First, Smith wrote that she feared the proposed amendment would strengthen the argument against laws requiring a minimum wage for women workers; she specifically mentioned the challenge to the District of Columbia's minimum wage law taking place in the District of Columbia Court of Appeals. As discussed in the previous chapter, this case, *Adkins v. Children's Hospital,* would continue on to the U.S. Supreme Court in the spring of 1923, with the high court overturning the law, citing women's elevated status after the Nineteenth Amendment. Second, Smith pointed out that even though a few lawyers had contended that the planned amendment would not affect special laws for women, other lawyers, including Felix Frankfurter, Ernest Freund, and Roscoe Pound, disagreed with that assessment. Smith concluded, "When lawyers differ, what else can we expect of the courts?" In Smith's view the proposed amendment would hardly clarify women's other rights after suffrage because it would add more confusion to the already complicated situation.[52]

Albert Levitt too was upset about the course of events and how his advised amendment had turned out. "I am very disappointed," he confessed in a letter to Roscoe Pound, "at the result which they have reached. In the last month they have entirely revamped it until now it is in a form which I think entirely faulty. . . . They seem to have gotten started on a theory of equality which no amount of persuasion on my part seems to effect [*sic*]."[53] To Alice Paul he wrote that he realized she no longer cared for his opinions and that his advice was now "worthless" to her. But, he continued, "at the same time my interest in the problem you are trying to solve is so genuine and keen that I am moved once more to urge upon you that a construing clause in your proposed amendment will do no harm and will do considerable good."[54] When Paul eventually responded to Levitt, she wrote of her reluctance to return to the prospect of a saving clause. She explained that "no one seems to have been able up to the present to devise a clause satisfactory to the leaders of the movement for protective legislation for women." In her closing remarks she indicated her impatience with the whole saving clause situation, snapping, "I would suggest that you take up your suggestion with Mr. Frankfurter again, who seems to be a general legal adviser of the welfare workers."[55]

In a furious reply Levitt laid bare how deeply upset he was over the turn of events. In red ink he cried out that to him the opinions of Florence Kelley, Felix Frankfurter, and Ethel Smith did not matter. In all capital letters he bellowed, "THEIR APPROVAL OR DISAPPROVAL IS A MATTER OF VALUE ONLY IF YOU ARE PLAYING POLITICS!" He persisted, "I am not interested in persuading the legal adviser of The National Consumers League [Frankfurter] to phrase a construing clause. I am content with the approval of Dean Pound." In closing, Levitt wrote, "I do care that the National Woman's Party does not sacrifice welfare legislation for a possible *emancipation* of women. . . . I am urging you to do the thing which, I submit, will do the least harm and at the same time bring about the greatest amount of good." Levitt still believed in the possibility of creating a constitutional amendment that would establish women's rights as full citizens while also preserving special legislation for women. Paul, however, was fed up with the saving clause issue.

She ultimately refused to respond to Levitt's subsequent letters, and she effectively shut him out of the drafting process altogether.[56]

The collapse of the initial collaborative effort deepened when Kelley invited Paul to meet with her and other prominent women activists on December 4, 1921, the day before Congress was set to resume.[57] A flashpoint unfolded at this meeting as the NWP openly modified its position on special legislation for women. During the meeting Maud Wood Park of the LWV asked Paul to state the NWP's stance on women's right to special protection. Paul answered that "the Woman's Party had taken no stand on this question. . . . The Woman's Party wish[es] to deal only with those things upon which they [are] united, namely, political, civil, and legal disabilities, and not touch the industrial field." Later in the meeting Park declared that special labor "legislation is very precious to us, and I do not want to take the seats away from tired working women, as Miss Paul does." According to the NWP's report, "Miss Paul let this pass unnoticed."[58]

Unlike its previous supportive stance, the NWP now insisted that it held no official position on the issue of special protection for women. There are a few reasons for this development. As demonstrated in Paul's correspondence with Levitt, by this time she had become aggravated with the concept of a saving clause; she now considered it a waste of time. More important, though, Paul had started to reassess the advantages of special labor legislation for women. As she wrote to an NWP member in October of that year, such legislation "should be by trades and not along sex lines." She added that "even if by any chance our proposed legislation should result in throwing out protective legislation for women, it would not be a bad thing because it would hasten the enactment of this legislation for both men and women."[59] While Paul's organization now took no official stance on special legislation, she had begun to voice her own opposition to the issue in private.

Also, during the December 1921 meeting the representatives of the NCL, the NWTUL, and the LWV indicated that they would not support the amendment in any form.[60] In reality, Kelley, Smith, and Park had started to question the NWP's motives long before the December meeting. In particular, they had suspected that the

NWP's leaders no longer supported the idea that women required extra legal protection. Furthermore, they feared that the NWP might actually want to demolish the existing welfare laws for working women.[61] Paul's refusal to endorse special legislation at the meeting only reinforced their suspicions. As NWP officials noted in their report of the meeting, Kelley seemed "deeply distressed and concerned for the welfare legislation."[62]

The situation continued to deteriorate when Dean Acheson visited Paul a few days later. Acheson had hoped to resolve the dispute between Paul and the other activist women. At this encounter he presented Paul with his own draft of a saving clause, which would have exempted hours and minimum wage legislation from the provision of equality.[63] According to Acheson, Paul rejected his saving clause, fearing that "anything like this would look as though she approved of welfare legislation and lose her supporters." When Acheson strongly encouraged Paul to reconsider, he reported that "she accused me of insulting her and she had a glorious time telling me about myself."[64] Acheson recounted this story to Frankfurter, who passed it along to Kelley. For Kelley, Acheson's explosive meeting with Paul only fortified her fears about the NWP and its proposed amendment.[65]

Kelley was now fully convinced that the amendment posed a serious threat to sex-specific labor legislation, which in her view was justly based on the dependent nature of women. Consequently, she issued a direct appeal to Representative Simeon D. Fess of Ohio, the Republican who was set to introduce the amendment in the House of Representatives. In what would later become a widely distributed pamphlet, Kelley proposed "twenty questions" to Representative Fess. Kelley asked what would become of the Mann Act (which outlawed white slavery), a husband's obligation to support his wife, dower rights, penalties for rape, maternity legislation, and women's exemption from military service. In regard to labor laws for women Kelley prodded, "What safeguards will wage earning women have to compensate the disadvantages which they everywhere tend to suffer in competing with men?" To Kelley's mind, the amendment would not only topple labor legislation for working women but it would also threaten

what she understood to be women's inherent right to special protection under the law.[66]

Representative Fess had been a supporter of the suffrage movement and was an early backer of the NWP's equal rights campaign.[67]
Yet, Kelley's rhetorical triumph in her twenty questions swayed the
Congress member to pause and rethink his position. As Representative Fess wrote to Smith and others, he ardently believed that in
order to secure women's status as rights-bearing citizens, a constitutional amendment had to follow the Nineteenth Amendment.
At the same time, he explained, he supported working women's
welfare legislation, and he did not want to advance an amendment
that would jeopardize such legislation. As a result, he decided to
withdraw his support for the proposed amendment.[68]

That December Paul found herself in a challenging situation.
Not only did the volatile meetings with Kelley and Acheson alarm
her, but she had lost crucial congressional assistance from Representative Fess. At the end of the month Paul turned to William
Draper Lewis, dean of the University of Pennsylvania Law School,
for help. She pleaded, "We feel greatly perplexed and worried as
to what to do."[69] William Draper Lewis suggested that Paul revisit
the idea of a saving clause.[70] But Paul did not want to return to
the saving clause matter. Instead, she decided to further explore
the legal implications of complete constitutional sexual equality.[71]

The Emergence of Competing Civic Ideologies

After the disastrous events in December 1921, Paul chose to hold
off on the amendment's introduction into Congress. In the meantime she set out to gain a better understanding of the legal consequences of the proposed amendment. First, she returned to her
law school studies, which she had put on hold the previous summer.[72] Second, she decided to follow Frankfurter's suggestion from
months earlier. As noted earlier, Frankfurter had argued that the
legal status of women varied too much from state to state and that
an additional constitutional amendment would only worsen the
confusion over women's constitutional rights. To help dispense
with this confusion, Frankfurter suggested that Paul and her supporters conduct a study on women's status with the intention of

developing specific legislation for specific problems. Frankfurter thought that this proposed study would encourage the NWP to move away from its focus on a blanket approach. As it turned out, however, the study only bolstered the NWP's determination to fight for a constitutional amendment.[73]

Paul launched an extensive investigation into the status of women in the early winter months of 1922. As Paul explained to other officials of the NWP, she believed that this study would help them be sure of their "ground before proceeding."[74] The massive project was conducted by the Legal Research Department of the NWP under the guidance of Burnita Shelton Matthews. Matthews, a lawyer and legal scholar, felt that the project would assist the NWP in having "a definite working basis in place of vague ideas prevailing as to the legal disabilities of women in the United States." In all, the purpose of the research campaign was to acquire concrete information about the variations in women's legal standing in the post–Nineteenth Amendment era.[75] The project lasted for several years, and reports were issued throughout the 1920s and early 1930s. The NWP's investigation not only covered the debates around women's right to serve on juries, hold public office, and control their own domicile, but it also chronicled the numerous other legal discriminations that continued to restrict women's civic autonomy.[76]

The NWP's research focused in particular on dissecting the common law basis for legal prejudices against women. As discussed in the previous chapter, central to the common law tradition of domestic duties was the notion that the husband was the head of the family. As such, the legal tradition understood the husband to be the natural guardian of his wife and children. Most important, with the husband as the head of the family, his rights were favored over those of his dependents, particularly the rights of his wife. In unsparing detail the NWP documented how this disparity created several discriminations against women concerning guardianship laws, inheritance laws, and married women's economic rights.[77]

With regard to guardianship laws, the NWP revealed that in a number of states, including Georgia and Maryland, the father had a right to will away the custody of a child from its mother.[78] In

Michigan, New York, and Massachusetts the father alone was entitled to the services and earnings of a minor child.[79] In Iowa and
Minnesota the right to recover damages or losses from a child's
injury belonged primarily to the father.[80] Thus, according to the
NWP's research, even after the Nineteenth Amendment the legal
thinking in America still privileged husbands and fathers as the
primary rights-bearing individuals within the household.

The NWP also rooted out how the common law tradition of
domestic duties led to discriminations against women with regard
to inheritance laws. The NWP's reports noted that the laws of the
District of Columbia, Idaho, Maryland, and New York supported
the father over the mother in granting administration over a child's
estate. In Arkansas, West Virginia, and a number of other states,
only a father could inherit the estate of a child who died without
a will or descendants.[81]

In addition, the NWP's research brought into fuller view how the
common law tradition of domestic relations still affected married
women's economic rights. According to common law, the wife's
domestic services belonged to her husband, since he provided her
with protection. Following this notion, the American legal tradition
upheld the right of the husband to hold dominion over his wife's
economic value. As one NWP report stated, "In at least forty states
marriage is not a partnership between equals, where each partner owns his own labor. Nor is it a partnership where the partners
jointly own the property acquired by their mutual efforts."[82] In forty
states, for example, property acquired through the joint efforts of
husband and wife was still legally considered the sole property of
the husband. In a few of these states, such as Georgia and Vermont,
married women's earnings legally belonged to their husbands. In
Illinois, Colorado, Delaware, Nebraska, Michigan, Mississippi, Missouri, New York, and Tennessee a husband had the right to sue for
damages that resulted in the loss of his wife's services and labor.[83]
What is more, state laws in Michigan, Nebraska, West Virginia, Florida, and Texas continued to restrict married women's right to enter
into contracts without the consent of their husbands.[84]

In its reports the NWP also called attention to how the dependent
woman theory embedded in the common law tradition negatively

affected women. That theory appealed to conventional images of women's presumed physical and mental weaknesses to justify sex-specific legal treatment. According to the NWP's research, however, this legal footing produced harmful discriminations against working women because it discounted women's capabilities from the start. To bolster this point, the NWP argued that sex-specific labor legislation hampered women's chances to find and maintain gainful employment. The NWP claimed, for instance, that laws that prohibited night work for women unfairly shut women out of certain employment opportunities, such as dining service, where night work was often more profitable than day work. As one NWP account asserted, "Equal pay, equal opportunity for promotion, equal recognition of work are incompatible with special protective laws limiting the service with which women may offer their employers while not limiting the service which their male competitors may offer."[85] The NWP's reports suggested that minimum wage laws for women hindered women's ability to compete in the labor market, since those laws made women "expensive luxuries" for employers.[86] Overall, the NWP maintained that laws prohibiting women from night work, overtime, and certain manufactory procedures, as well as requiring minimum wages exclusively for women and children, forced working women out of good jobs and into poorly paid inferior positions.[87]

By the fall of 1922 the leaders of the NWP had armed themselves with documentation showing how sex-based legal distinctions continued to negatively affect women. Thanks to the exhaustive research effort, the organization's leaders now felt confident in insisting that absolute constitutional sexual equality was the only way to emancipate women from their legal subjugation to men. "It is obvious," one research assessment asserted, "that if women are to become first-class citizens, only a fundamental and country-wide means of doing away with inherited legal disabilities can be effective."[88] In sum, the NWP's research campaign fueled the organization's conviction that women needed to be emancipated and that such an emancipation could be secured only through the strength of a constitutional amendment.

In November 1922 the NWP held a meeting to discuss with its leading members the initial findings of the legal research campaign and the overall philosophy of the organization moving forward. It was during this meeting that the principal members of the NWP unanimously adopted its Declaration of Principles.[89] The declaration began by proclaiming "that women shall no longer be regarded and shall no longer regard themselves as inferior to men, but the equality of the sexes shall be recognized. That women shall no longer be the governed half of society, but shall participate equally with men in the direction of life." The declaration went on to list several goals that promoted economic, political, and social equality between the sexes. The declaration ended by concluding "that women shall no longer be in any form of subjection to men in law or in custom, but shall in every way be on equal plane in rights, as she has always been and will continue to be, in responsibilities and obligations." Overall, the declaration asserted for women the right to participate as citizens on the same terms as men.[90]

The NWP's declaration of principles also offers insight into the organization's newfound commitment to complete sexual equality in the industrial field. The declaration's economic goals included equal opportunities in education, employment, and job promotions, as well as equal pay for equal work. In addition, the NWP's freshly articulated economic goals affirmed the organization's denunciation of sex-specific labor legislation by declaring "that women shall no longer be barred from any occupation, but every occupation open to men shall be open to women, and restrictions upon the hours, conditions, and remuneration of labor shall apply alike to both sexes."[91] Thus, by the fall of 1922 the NWP's official party line involved formal opposition to special labor legislation for women.

In the last fourteen points of its declaration the NWP directly took on a remaining influential feature of coverture: the established tradition of sex-based marital duties. In an effort to focus on the rights of married women, the NWP insisted that married women should have rights to their earnings and property, as well as grounds for divorce, control over their children, and an independent nationality status. Moreover, the NWP challenged the notion that a husband should have authority over his wife. In its declaration the organization proclaimed "that the headship of the family shall no longer be in the husband alone, but shall be equally in the husband and wife. That the husband shall no longer own the wife's services, but these shall belong to her alone as in the case of any free person." With their Declaration of Principles, the members of the NWP had announced their intention to revolutionize the common law tradition of domestic duties.[92]

At the November 1922 meeting the attending members of the NWP passed a resolution to continue working on a constitutional amendment. Even though the NWP's leaders were still considering the exact phrasing of the intended amendment, they agreed that the party should aim to introduce the amendment at some point during the following year.[93] In the meantime the organization set out to embark on an educational campaign to inform the American public about women's numerous legal disadvantages. For this purpose the NWP launched its weekly publication, *Equal Rights*, to underscore the organization's recently adopted principles and advance its campaign for a constitutional amendment.[94]

Once the leaders of the NWP solidified their party's goals and overall philosophy, they began to espouse a certain form of thought, which I describe as emancipationism. At the core of this complex conglomeration of ideas is the belief that a solitary collection of rights must be applied to men and women citizens equally. For emancipationists, the highest ideals of American democracy could be fulfilled only by a comprehensive move toward constitutional sexual equality. As an *Equal Rights* editorial exclaimed, "It is liberty we seek, not repression. We wish to free women, not to restrain them. Our aim is to enable women to do what their own abilities and preferences and necessities urge them to do."[95] Mary Winsor, a prominent member of the NWP since the days of the suffrage campaign, also emphasized the need to free women from the harms of legalized sex discrimination in her arguments for a subsequent constitutional amendment. In an article for *Equal Rights* she declared, "Women in America should emancipate themselves fully at home so as to be ready to play a part in the emancipation of women throughout the world."[96] In all, emancipationists believed that women should be free to enjoy the range of opportunities and respect that came from full participation in the public life of a democratic society.

An intense desire to ensure the complete release of women from the restrictions embedded in the common law tradition of domestic duties enlivened the emancipationist outlook. Due to emancipationists' formidable belief that women needed to be freed from the legal paradigm of marital-status law, emancipationists often cited the limited gains that the Nineteenth Amendment had provided for women. Emma Wold, a lawyer and a leading member of the NWP, argued in an article for *Equal Rights* that after the passage of the Nineteenth Amendment "the great majority of the American mind" felt that women should be able to claim the "equal protection of the laws guaranteed to 'persons' by the Fourteenth Constitutional Amendment." But, as she maintained, women soon "learned that the ballot, while it might be an 'outward and visible sign of an inward and spiritual grace,' in the republic, was not a token of equality before the laws."[97] Put another way, emancipationists recognized that even though the Nineteenth Amendment had removed sex as a permissible reason for withholding the right to vote, it had failed to fully unseat the centuries-old legal foundation that had given men authority over women in law and in custom. The failure of the Nineteenth Amendment to place women on equal legal footing with men drove the emancipationist demand for an additional constitutional amendment to guarantee the full status of women as rights-bearing citizens.

In the early 1920s the majority of emancipationists were members of the NWP. Nonetheless, as the organization embarked on its equal rights campaign, it did enlist other supporters. In 1923, for instance, William Cabell Bruce, an American writer and future Democratic senator from Maryland, announced his support for the planned amendment, asserting, "I am fully in sympathy with the movement to free women from all clinical and legal discriminations that tend to deny to them the full equality of opportunity that men enjoy."[98] State senator George Condon of Michigan also confirmed his backing of the NWP's equal rights campaign in a statement to the organization. In it he proclaimed, "The placing of women on an equal plane with men as far as the law is concerned will someday be regarded as a natural and logical step in their emancipation as the granting of their political rights. The old common law disabilities . . . [are] inconsistent with the modern conception of both thinking men and women as a factor in the social programs and economic life of today."[99] Above all, from the emancipationist perspective the nation's legal practices could not be considered consistent with the country's avowed political ideals until the country adopted a cohesive, basic standard of rights for its men and women citizens to enjoy equally. For emancipationists, the integrity of the American political structure relied upon the equal rights of its electors. Deviations from this model, they warned, jeopardized the ideals of equality upon which the country had been founded.

Over the summer of 1923 Alice Paul, with help from a handful of legal advisors within the NWP, wrote a straightforward draft of the proposed amendment. It stated, "Men and women shall have equal rights throughout the United States and everyplace subject to its jurisdiction. Congress shall have the power to enforce this article by appropriate legislation."[100] To lawyer and NWP member Caroline Spencer, the draft seemed "beyond every other suggestion in clearness of meaning, perfection of form, consistency with our program as announced, and with the advantage of being a positive rather than a negative statement."[101] The statement's simple language went against the complications of the almost three-year drafting process. The straightforward amendment, moreover, embodied the emancipationist call for the equal treatment of men and women citizens before the law.

The NWP announced the final form of the proposed amendment at an outdoor pageant in Seneca Falls to commemorate the seventy-fifth anniversary of the first woman's rights convention. Paul had hoped that the publicity about the pageant would help launch a national effort for passage of what was now formally called the Lucretia Mott Amendment and commonly referred to as the Equal Rights Amendment (ERA).[102] Paul, who had been quite a media genius during the days of the suffrage campaign, was successful in gaining the national spotlight for the planned amendment, as the *New York Times, Baltimore Sun, Chicago Daily Tribune, Washington Post, Los Angeles Times*, and other major news outlets covered the pageant.[103] On the spectacle of the event, *The Nation* wrote that the NWP's "boldness and sense of dramatic values never fail it. . . . With a sure instinct, the NWP invariably challenges public attention and climbs to the top of the first page of newspapers."[104] The local press estimated that almost two thousand people participated in the affair.[105] In this fashion the NWP had successfully drawn the public's attention to its ERA by the summer of 1923.

But the publicity for the finalized draft had also unleashed a wave of intense opposition. For starters, Roscoe Pound, William Draper Lewis, Felix Frankfurter, Florence Kelley, and Dean Acheson all came out against the final version.[106] As opposition to the ERA mounted, amendment opponents began to craft their own way of thinking about the rights of men and women citizens, which I identify as protectionism. As the term is applied in this work, protectionism represents a form of thought that primarily developed after the passage of the Nineteenth Amendment as a way to continue justifying sex-based legal distinctions in American laws and customs. As a whole, protectionism celebrates the assumed equity of sex-specific rights.

The belief that nature and/or God had ordained different but equally important roles for men and women citizens forms a central tenet of the protectionist position. Giving voice to this notion, an NCL pamphlet that criticized blanket equality measures declared, "Sex is a biological fact. . . . Men do not bear children, and are free from the burdens of maternity."[107] In a 1922 letter to Florence Kelley, lawyer and legal expert Henry Bates articulated a similar argument against the proposed amendment. In the letter he contended that the difference between men's and women's social positions was based on "something more or less permanent in human nature and the development of human society. . . . It is the accumulation perhaps of the ages of human life."[108] For protectionists, the implicit constitutional inclusion of women in the political community as a result of the Nineteenth Amendment did not negate the necessity of sex-specific treatment. In their view, sex-specific treatment recognized that men and women fundamentally differed in their biological and social functions. Thus, unlike emancipationists, protectionists maintained that sex by itself constituted an appropriate legal classification.

A potent maternalist impulse shaped the intricacies of the protectionist position during the original ERA conflict. Maternalism flourished around the late nineteenth and early twentieth centuries. In general, it upheld the essential nature of women's domestic roles and strongly associated women with children's well-being. As historian Molly Ladd-Taylor explains it, women who followed the maternalist tradition believed that "there was a uniquely feminine value system based on care and nurturance." Maternalists, in other words, envisioned women as occupying a special role within society as its natural caregivers. In this outlook, motherhood was the vivid embodiment of womanhood.[109]

Maternalism consisted of conservative and liberal variations during the early twentieth century, since conservatives and liberals often differed over the particulars of women's maternal destiny. In the view of conservative maternalists, blatant activism and overt involvement in the public domain on the part of women reflected a corruption of motherhood. Therefore, before the Nineteenth Amendment, conservative maternalists had strongly opposed woman suffrage.[110] Even so, conservative maternalists adjusted their stance on women's participation in the public realm once American legislators had passed the Nineteenth Amendment. In the 1920s conservative women came to see the vote as a crucial way to defend the traditional social order.[111] Conservative maternalist Elizabeth Lowell Putnam of Boston, for example, had opposed federal woman suffrage, but after the Nineteenth Amendment's passage she subsequently described voting as a "new political duty" that she would do with all her "heart."[112] The election returns of 1924 reflect especially well the robust female conservative vote of the 1920s, as women surpassed men in voting for Republicans and conservatives. In the wake of the Nineteenth Amendment, then, conservative maternalists went on to justify their involvement in the political arena by claiming that their vote was necessary to preserve what they had understood to be essential American values.[113]

Central to these American values, according to conservative maternalists, was the belief that the vitality of American society depended on the preservation of traditional sex-based responsibilities in the home. In particular, conservative maternalists were suspicious of any reform effort that they saw as a replacement of such responsibilities with state paternalism. For this reason conservative maternalists steadfastly opposed the Sheppard-Towner Maternity and Infancy Act of 1921, which provided federal funding for maternity health services and child care. For conservative women such measures undermined the rightful household governing powers of fathers. From the perspective of conservative maternalists, social reform measures confused natural sex roles and endangered the stability of the American family. In sum, conservative maternalists viewed women as guardians of the home who had to sometimes partake in the public sphere to ultimately protect the home from what could be perceived as subversive influences, such as communism, socialism, and feminism.[114]

In contrast to their conservative counterparts, liberal maternalists supported the consistent and direct involvement of women in the shaping of public life. Because of this support, several liberal maternalist groups contributed to the suffrage movement in the early twentieth century. After the Nineteenth Amendment, liberal maternalist organizations such as the NCL, NWTUL, LWV, the Women's Joint Congressional Committee (WJCC), and the Women's Bureau vigorously campaigned for the Sheppard-Towner Act, the Cable Act of 1922, and the proposed Child Labor Amendment.[115] Liberal maternalists also supported state-level measures to secure women's right to serve on juries; in general, liberal maternalists backed female jury service as a way to enhance women's maternal role by extending its influence in the public arena.[116] Groups that followed the liberal maternalist reform tradition supported the removal of what they considered *unfair* restrictions on women's ability to fully participate in public life. But they also maintained that sex-based laws and practices could in theory be equitable because, they believed, men and women differed in their primary social roles.

Liberal maternalists defended women's public activism by adhering to the mainstream cultural ethos of female passivity, humility, and self-sacrifice. Observing these standards helped liberal maternalists establish professional careers. As scholar Jan Doolittle Wilson describes it, liberal maternalists' insistence on "women's differ-

ences from men and their emphasis on women's special mothering qualities and aptitude for child care tended to reinforce the
concept of immutable sexual difference. . . . Yet a gendered, maternalist politics also provided the basis and the rationale for separate female organizations through which women gained access to
the public sphere."[117] With appeals to conventional ideas about the
mother-child relationship, liberal maternalists successfully created
policy-making bodies that centered on social work, public health,
and home economics. For liberal maternalists, these social reform
programs naturally belonged to the female sphere of influence.[118]

Social reformers who had aligned with the liberal maternalist
influence formed a major source of support for sex-specific labor
legislation. From the liberal maternalist perspective, sex-based
labor laws protected women's roles in the home. For example,
Mary Van Kleeck, a prominent social scientist who had worked
alongside Eleanor Roosevelt at the Women's City Club of New
York, claimed in an anti-ERA article for *Congressional Digest* that
special labor laws worked to "protect children and to preserve the
right of mothers to be safeguarded in the family group."[119] Liberal
maternalists backed special labor legislation because they recognized that the hardships of the modern world often compelled a
number of married women to enter the labor force. Nevertheless,
liberal maternalists believed that work outside of the home should
not overburden married women who had young children. Overall, liberal maternalists maintained that the state had a moral obligation to regulate women's activity in the industrial field in order
to safeguard society's mothers and potential mothers against economic exploitation.[120]

Because conservative and liberal maternalists held opposing
views about the correct extent to which women should participate in public life, as well as disagreed about the overall legitimacy
of social reform programs, these two groups often found themselves at odds when it came to policy proposals and politics. But
the implicit resistance rooted in the emancipationist position to
the maternalist idea that motherhood encompassed all of wom-
en's primary social contributions caused both conservative and
liberal maternalists to denounce the ERA as an affront to the nat-

ural sexual order. Alice Hamilton, a leading academic in the field of public health and a follower of the liberal maternalist reform impulse, expressed this point in an article for *Forum* magazine. On the ERA she argued that the proposed amendment failed to recognize women's "special needs"; as a "working mother is handicapped by her own nature, she cannot take the sleep that she needs until the demands of her children are satisfied; the father can and does."[121] In a similar line of reasoning, conservative maternalist Margaret Robinson of the *Woman Patriot* insisted that the ERA "would drive women into unprotected 'survival-of-the-fittest' competition with men."[122] To stop the ERA and thereby defend women's distinct status as society's caregivers, liberal and conservative maternalists found themselves appealing to the same form of thought: protectionism.

Since protectionism incorporated the maternalist drive, it featured liberal and conservative branches during the original ERA conflict. So, those who followed the cluster of standards and beliefs that molded the protectionist habit of mind included conservative politicians like the formerly forthright woman suffrage opponent Congress member James Wadsworth (R-NY). In 1925 Wadsworth, then a senator, wrote of his opposition to the ERA in a letter to a New York clubwoman, explaining, "I think men are expected, and in some instances should be required to do the rough work of life and assume the responsibility for it. At that, their task will never be as difficult as the normal task assigned to women."[123] In all, conservative ERA foes believed that women required special protection, but they insisted that such protection should primarily come from the male head of the household.

Liberal amendment critics, in contrast, insisted that government reform initiatives, such as sex-specific labor laws, could also serve as effective instruments of protection for women. On the reasons why women needed more protection than men, liberal amendment critic Mary Anderson of the Women's Bureau justified sex-specific labor laws, writing, "The wear and tear on the mother is something to be thought of too. She cannot be a very good mother if she is so tired she is ready to drop."[124] Liberal and conservative protectionists also differed on what they counted as an unfair or

unreasonable discrimination against women. Conservative protectionists, for example, opposed women's right to serve on juries,
while liberal protectionists generally supported it.[125] Even so, both
liberal and conservative ERA adversaries opposed the amendment
to *protect* what they understood to be the separate roles of men
and women citizens. From their standpoint, a fundamental American value was the preservation of the traditionally ordered family—an arrangement that maintained men's position as providers
and women's position as caregivers.

In an effort to preserve the law's ability to treat citizens differently on account of sex, ERA opponents started to develop a new
way of understanding full American citizenship that accentuated
the separate but equally important rights of men and women citizens. ERA opponent John Commons of the University of Wisconsin, a progressive scholar and labor historian, gave voice to this
emerging concept when he argued in a statement presented to
the LWV that "women should have preferential rights instead of
equal rights. . . . These are needed in order to make them really
equal to men."[126] Linna Bresette of the National Council of Catholic Women, who was a teacher and social justice advocate, gave a
related justification for her opposition to the ERA during one of the
early ERA congressional hearings. The ERA, she proclaimed, was a
reckless pursuit because "the responsibilities of men and women
are not identical and for that reason it is necessary that some of
their rights be held different both in legislation and custom."[127]

There is a subtle but crucial distinction that marks the anti-
ERA stance and sets it apart from the previous arguments against
equal rights for men and women citizens. Before the passage of the
Nineteenth Amendment, arguments against equal legal treatment
tended to dwell on the reasons to exclude women from certain
rights of citizenship. Assumed in these claims was the suggestion
that since women were dependents who did not possess an autonomous relationship to the state, the law was therefore not required
to provide women with all the rights that came from having full
American citizenship. The Nineteenth Amendment altered the
political and legal landscapes, because it implicitly gave women
a direct connection to the state and constitutionally removed sex

as a legal reason for blocking a citizen's immediate involvement with the governance of the country. Due to these changes, those who opposed the prospect of complete constitutional sexual equality increasingly came to focus on the need to form and protect a distinct citizenship for women, which supposedly came with its own collection of rights. As a result, these protectionists began to create a second, coequal standard for full citizenship status that upheld motherhood and the stereotypical gendered attributes generally assigned to women, like inherent altruism. In the process of defending what protectionists had understood to be women's natural domestic roles, they started to develop a new notion of American citizenship that included separate sets of rights for men and women citizens.

Even as the opposition to the ERA grew over the fall of 1923, the NWP was still able to find two members of Congress who were eager to introduce the amendment into the Senate and the House in December of that year. They were Senator Charles Curtis, who had long supported the NWP's equal rights campaign and would be Herbert Hoover's running mate in 1928, and Representative Daniel Read Anthony Jr., nephew of Susan B. Anthony. Both men were Republicans.[128] Following the emancipationist insistence on complete constitutional sexual equality, Senator Curtis proclaimed that the ERA would write the principle of equality "forever into the highest law of our land." He concluded, "To my mind, it is the logical conclusion of the suffrage struggle." Likewise, Representative Anthony declared that he proudly supported the amendment because it "will establish what I have been brought up to feel a democracy should establish—equality for men and women in all fields."[129] At last the long, perplexing struggle to draft the amendment had ended and the fight over passage of the ERA in Congress had begun.

The Power of Protectionism

From 1923 to 1932 Congress held six hearings on the ERA.[130] The protectionists dominated these hearings. Throughout the hearings, protectionists successfully advanced a three-pronged argument: the amendment was too vague, it threatened states' rights, and it violated America's legal tradition. Because of these alleged flaws, protectionists insisted that the amendment posed a serious threat to American society. Emancipationists, in contrast, stumbled through their early congressional testimonies; apparently, they were overwhelmed by the protectionist attacks. Although emancipationists attempted to highlight instances of women's legal disadvantages, at this point they were unable to offer consistent and persuasive counterarguments to the protectionist line of reasoning.

Throughout the congressional hearings of the 1920s and early 1930s, protectionists argued against the ERA by boldly charging that it would create even more confusion over women's legal personhood and that it would threaten all the rights of American citizens by destroying the American legal system. At the 1929 Senate subcommittee hearing, for instance, Everett Fraser of the University of Minnesota Law School, who was a legal scholar and political enthusiast, warned in a statement presented to the committee, "The equal rights amendment would operate like a blind man with a shotgun. No lawyer can confidently state what it would hit."[131] The former Speaker of the Massachusetts state legislature's House of Representatives, the conservative Benjamin Loring Young, articulated a similar complaint at the same hearing when he claimed that the amendment would "destroy all our judicial machinery."[132]

During these hearings protectionists cautioned that passage of the ERA could allow the federal government to impose a condition of universal, nationwide equality onto the American people despite regional and local differences. Florence Kelley brought up this contention at the 1929 hearing when she asked, in a rhetorical manner, "Does it mean that a black woman will have the same rights as a white man[?] . . . Who is to be equal and what is the equality to be[?] . . . What kind of equality is to be and among whom?"[133] Mrs. William J. Carson of the LWV argued from a related line of thought at the 1932 House Judiciary Committee hearing on the ERA. "There is nothing in the amendment," she declared in her testimony, "to prevent a court decreeing that a woman in North Dakota shall have equal rights with a man in Georgia." She went on to contend, "Though we are one Nation our points of view and standard of social relations differ greatly in different sections of the Country. . . . The States should be free from dictation in such matters by the Federal Congress."[134] By raising the specter of states' rights, as these quotes demonstrate, protectionists were attempting to suggest that the ERA would recklessly pave the way toward complete racial equality.

In their congressional testimonies, protectionists conceded that the Nineteenth Amendment had tacitly recognized that women should be treated as rights-bearing citizens; however, they insisted that this development did not mean that women should have the exact same rights as men. As Edgar Bancroft, a lawyer and diplomat, put it at the 1925 House Judiciary Committee hearing on the ERA, the amendment "not only removes so-called disabilities; it destroys and prevents all special rights and privileges of women."[135] Thomas Cadwalader, a leading member of the Sentinels of the Republic states' rights group and an outspoken conservative foe of social reform legislation, offered a related objection to the ERA when he asserted at the 1929 Senate Judiciary subcommittee hearing that the amendment would take away women's right to be exempted from military service.[136] In the context of women's right to special treatment, a number of liberal protectionists brought up the issue of sex-specific labor laws during the early congressional hearings. "We seek protection for woman in industry because she needs it on the job," exclaimed Selma Borchardt, representing the American Federation of Labor (AFL), in her testimony at the 1932 House Judiciary Committee hearing on the ERA. She went on to argue that a working woman requires extra protection "because she needs it for the protection of her own health, and for that of her children."[137] The ERA, according to the views of conservative and liberal protectionists alike, would not provide women with more rights. On the contrary, protectionists maintained, the amendment would actually rob women of the distinct rights that they needed to carry out their duties as mothers and caretakers of the home. These rights included women being exempted from military service, shielded from the ravages of capitalism, and being kept safe in their domestic roles.

The belief that the ERA violated America's legal tradition also guided the protectionists' arguments against the amendment during the early ERA congressional testimonies. From the viewpoint of protectionists, the American legal tradition rightfully upheld the different societal functions of men and women citizens. In order to bolster the assertion that men and women citizens naturally had different societal roles, protectionists appealed to the common law tradition of sex-specific marital duties. Sentinels of the Republic official Thomas Cadwalader, for example, alleged in a statement given at the 1925 congressional hearing that the ERA "would destroy all rights both of the wife and the children to be supported by the husband and father." He concluded, "The family relations would be altered for the worse by a novel piece of legislation that practically could not be cured and henceforth must be endured."[138] At the same hearing Katharine Ludington, a member of the LWV executive committee, asked in her testimony, "What would be the effect of identical legal status upon a woman's right to support from her husband?"[139] According to protectionists, the ERA stood to subvert the old law of domestic relations, which had provided a legitimate structure for sustaining the biologically destined familial arrangement: wives took care of the household and, in return, husbands gave their wives financial support and protection.

While protectionists admitted that the common law tradition of marital duties may have produced some laws and customs that had become outmoded, they insisted that the underlying principle of the doctrine remained valid. At the 1929 Senate Judiciary subcommittee hearing Cadwalader likened the possibility of having such outdated practices to the existence of a "great many flies" that might come "in the summertime and annoy you and get all over the place." But, he cautioned, "you do not get a stick of dynamite to get rid of those flies."[140] As a remedy for outdated practices, protectionists recommended what they had named the "specific method." In the words of LWV official Ludington, this approach aimed at "amending, altering, or legislating law by law, State by State," particular limitations or disabilities that unfairly restricted women's autonomy.[141] A few ERA opponents also enlisted Felix Frankfurter's advice from the early days of the drafting saga by suggesting to Congress that state-level studies on women's legal status should be conducted so that activists and lawmakers could understand what legislation, if any, was needed.[142] At this time ERA critics insisted that if women's legal status demanded some sort of corrective action, then that action should primarily come at the state level, with specific legislation for specific problems.[143]

Finally, protectionists promoted what they described as "real" or "true" equality for women in their congressional testimonies in order to undermine emancipationists' calls for equal rights. "To demand identical rights for men and women is absolutely unsound," Agnes Regan, a social reformer and an official of the National Council of Catholic Women, argued during one congressional hearing. She went on to maintain that "the difference in function—the result of natural law—impl[ies] essential differences in rights and duties. There can be no question that woman should have in law definite, specific rights, in accordance with the definite specific duties, which nature has imposed upon her."[144] Put another way, "real equality," according to Katharine Ludington of the LWV, meant ensuring that women were able to perform for "the community, and for civilization, their characteristic function as women."[145] For protectionists, true sexual equity involved securing a distinct citizenship for women with its own assortment of rights.

Throughout the early ERA congressional hearings, committee members peppered the emancipationists with antagonistic questions and observations. At the 1925 House Judiciary Committee hearing, for instance, several members repeatedly interrupted Burnita Shelton Matthews's testimony to ask her for the NWP's membership numbers. Matthews attempted to deflect the questions, but to no avail. At one point Maud Younger of the NWP reportedly sighed, "Oh no." Matthews and Younger had good reason for trying to avoid questions about the NWP's membership; at this time the majority of emancipationists were NWP members, and that membership was dwindling. One congressional representative even suggested at the 1925 hearing that the NWP hardly seemed to represent the "women of the country."[146]

In each of the early ERA hearings emancipationists faltered in their attempts to provide sufficient counterarguments to the pro-

tectionist claims. At the 1932 House Judiciary Committee hearing, emancipationists tried to assert that the ERA was not vague,
because it conveyed one of the highest ideals of American democracy: establishing the common rights of all citizens.[147] Somewhat
paradoxically, however, emancipationists had insisted at the 1925
House Judiciary Committee hearing that they were not trying to
bring about a universal condition of equality. When asked about
states' rights, for example, Younger avowed that the amendment
would "not impair the power of the States to make laws or to adopt
such standards of equality as they may desire."[148] And, at the 1929
Senate subcommittee hearing Matthews maintained, "There are
various States which have provisions to the effect that men are to
have equal rights but they have not been interpreted to mean that
the laws for all men must be identical." In response, committee
member Charles Waterman (R-CO) told Matthews, "I think that
suggestion will give you something to think about."[149] In an effort
to sidestep the states' rights issue and avoid extended discussions
on racial equality, emancipationists claimed that their amendment
would allow states to determine their own "standard of equality."
In the process, though, emancipationists had undermined their
other assertion that the ERA would follow a basic principle of
American democracy: the equality of all citizens before the law.

When addressing the concerns of liberal protectionists about
special labor legislation for women, emancipationists once again
argued from two rather contradictory angles. First, emancipationists contended that the ERA would improve rather than harm welfare legislation. Annie Warburton Goodrich, an American nurse,
academic, and ERA supporter, expressed this logic in a statement
presented at the 1925 ERA Senate subcommittee hearing. "Once
the equality is established," she alleged, "legislation may then be
enacted which will insure the protection of the young, the weak,
and the handicapped and thereby safeguard the race."[150] Yet, at
the 1931 Senate subcommittee hearing NWP official Anita Pollitzer
appealed to the freedom of contract principle, which was the reasoning courts typically used to dismantle welfare legislation, in her
attempt to build support for the ERA. As Pollitzer envisioned it, passage of the ERA would allow women to "be free as men to decide

for themselves when they will work and how they will work."[151] In the end the protectionists' three-fronted attack, combined with the emancipationists' inconsistent defensive effort, doomed the ERA in its first congressional hearings. Although Congress held several hearings on the amendment from the 1920s to the early 1930s, none of them resulted in committee reports. Congress would continue to table the amendment until the mid- to late 1930s.

Congress was not alone in its dismissive attitude toward the ERA. During the 1920s and up until the early 1930s public opinion favored the protectionist position. "There are a great many people of both sexes," the *Youth's Companion* reported in 1923, "who still believe that the social and economic functions of men and women should be allowed to differ, who distrust the theory that the two sexes should of right be treated exactly alike, and who fear the results of society encouraging economic and political competition between them."[152] Other magazines and newspapers published criticisms of the ERA during this period. In 1925, for example, a *Chicago Tribune* editorial decried the "equal rights crusade" as a "hysterical" attempt to "ignore the facts of women's nature and obey a theory of equality which can never be realized." The author concluded that the amendment had no sympathy "from normal women who have too much respect for their sex to wish to be men, or to be considered men."[153] Two years earlier the *New York Times* had reported that a multitude of organizations remained resolute against the ERA, among them not only the LWV, the NCL, the NWTUL, the AFL, and the National Council of Catholic Women but also the Council of Jewish Women, the National Association for Labor Legislation, the Women's Christian Temperance Union, the American Association for Organizing Family Social Work, the National Federation of Federal Employees, the General Federation of Women's Clubs (GFWC), and the American Civil Liberties Union (ACLU).[154]

What accounts for the dominance of protectionism during this period? In the post–World War I era a gap emerged between Americans who were still committed to a national identity driven by late nineteenth-century Victorian cultural tenets and those Americans who became allied to the gradually pluralistic trends of the twen-

tieth century. Those who resisted the pluralist influences of the
postwar period eventually united with business leaders to create a
new conservative consensus that linked support for private enterprise to white Protestant cultural values. This new conservative
consensus shaped American politics throughout the 1920s. Thus,
by the time emancipationists had introduced the ERA into Congress, there was already a growing move throughout the country
toward what President Warren Harding had called a "return to
normalcy."[155] Of course, not all protectionists were conservatives at
this time. Nevertheless, the emphasis in the new conservative consensus on the traditionally ordered family directly corresponded
to the protectionist call for clear lines between the rights of men
and women citizens.

Certainly the 1920s marked an exciting change in American cultural forms, particularly in regard to gender and sexual standards.
The "new woman" of the 1920s, for example, directly challenged
the sexual mores of the Victorian era with her short hair, ciga-
rettes, and sexually experimental attitude. Moreover, the numbers
of working women, which grew during the early twentieth century,
had called into question traditional gender norms, especially the
perception of the workplace as a masculine domain. Even so, these
challenges did not eradicate traditional values, as women's entry
into the workforce eventually provoked a backlash among white,
middle-class American men. Because of this reactionary attitude,
many employers had relegated women to jobs that were deemed
to be within the conventional sphere of female work. As a whole,
then, the 1920s witnessed challenges to prescribed gender roles,
but those challenges were ultimately limited and eventually met
with social ostracism and public condemnation.[156]

Distaste for the ERA continued into the years immediately following the stock market crash of 1929, since many Americans blamed
the economic crisis on the increased presence of women in the
labor force. When Samuel Harden Church, president of the Car-
negie Institute, wrote of the economic meltdown in a letter to
the *New York Times*, he lamented that "the tragedy of this is that
the man has no work at all—the women have crowded him out of
his birthright."[157] In the early years of the Great Depression many

Americans questioned the right of women to hold jobs when vast numbers of men were unemployed. As a result, pressure on working women to leave their jobs mounted, which fortified the protectionist notion that women's primary roles should be in the home as caregivers and homemakers.[158] This trend, however, would not hold. As the next chapters discuss, ongoing economic troubles and intense worldwide political turmoil would soon rouse a backlash against protectionism.

Conclusion

In order to protect sex-based legal distinctions in the midst of the emerging ERA campaign, amendment opponents began to modernize the justification for the differential treatment of men and women. In the process these protectionists started to create a new way of understanding American citizenship that advocated for the different but equally important rights of men and women citizens. Up until the early 1930s most Americans sided with the protectionist view that the law should be free to treat citizens differently on account of sex. Societal attachment to women's traditional domestic duties and the political conservatism of the 1920s all contributed to the early dominance of protectionism. Nonetheless, the supremacy of the protectionist position would not last forever, as worsening economic conditions and the onset of another world war would push more Americans to adopt the emancipationist way of thinking.

3

"To Be Regarded as Persons"

Emancipationism on the Move, 1933–1937

At a 1937 House subcommittee hearing on the ERA, veteran NWP member Elsie Hill declared, "Females are persons and citizens of the United States; and we do not want to be discriminated against and we want to be regarded as 'persons' under the Constitution of the United States." She went on to observe, "There is a great sympathy with the subject. . . . People declare for equal opportunity."[1] Hill, the ever-steadfast supporter of the ERA who had backed the amendment from the very moment Alice Paul decided to pursue it, felt quite confident in the ERA's chances for congressional passage in the late 1930s. Where did Hill's buoyant optimism come from, especially given the strong current of aversion to the amendment during the previous decade? As this chapter explains, support for the ERA began to increase in the mid-1930s because the NWP's Depression-era economic campaign had helped the organization build an important network of alliances with other women's groups. The renewed drive for the ERA also stemmed from the failure of liberal protectionists to fully confront the attacks on women's right to work that had accompanied the early 1930s. As the Depression years moved forward, more groups came to back the ERA as a way to defend women's economic rights as citizens and affirm women's value as persons.[2]

American Citizenship and the Great Depression

The rise in support for the ERA corresponded to the profound changes in social policies created by the Great Depression. Those changes not only transformed the concept of American citizenship, but they also opened up a pathway for ERA supporters to better articulate their case for the amendment. To start, political theorist T. H. Marshall describes the 1930s as a period that saw the emergence of "social citizenship," or the notion that citizens possess the right to social well-being.[3] The Great Depression also gave way to the idea of "economic citizenship," which, as historian Alice Kessler-Harris explains, not only means the right to work but also denotes a status that holds the full play of authority that defines participation in the marketplace.[4] In short, the Depression brought about the recognition of the right of citizens to a broad guarantee of economic security. The social policies that came out of the Depression, moreover, affirmed the positive rather than the negative rights of workers. Negative rights, such as the right to "freedom of contract," guarded citizens from the risk of legislative intrusion. Positive rights, on the other hand, called for government action to protect the economic and social welfare of its citizens. In sum, the Depression discredited the idea that social progress rested on the unrestrained pursuit of wealth, as it recast the expectations of the government and advanced the idea that the nation-state must protect its citizens from economic turmoil.[5]

In truth, the very notion of social benefits had originated from the efforts of women reformers in the late nineteenth and early twentieth centuries. Still, until the 1930s recipients of social benefits remained more pitied than entitled, as historian Linda Gordon has observed.[6] The social and economic citizenship that came out of the New Deal programs differed from the goals of earlier reform movements in that they aimed to bolster the rights of the family provider to achieve economic and social well-being. Hence, the New Deal programs primarily benefited men, because government officials assumed that most families relied on a single male breadwinner.[7]

The programs rarely discounted women explicitly (except in the case of the Civilian Conservation Corps), but they hardly ever provided women with relief as individuals and potential wage earners. For instance, the Works Progress Administration job-creation agenda aided a significantly smaller number of women than what their proportion in the labor force should have commanded. In addition, several of the National Recovery Administration (NRA) codes allowed for lower minimum wages for women than for men. The National Labor Relations Act (NLRA) also barely affected women, since they seldom held union membership.[8] In addition, the gendered disparities of the Social Security Act effectively resulted in the creation of a two-tiered welfare state that had women receiving noncontributory, means-tested social assistance, while men gained non-means-tested contributory social insurance.[9]

In many ways the social policies that grew out of the Depression led to the fortification of the common law tradition of domestic duties by favoring husbands and fathers as the principal wages earners and encouraging the dependency of wives and mothers.[10] Yet, the typical scholarly emphasis on the ultimate exclusion of women from the rights of social and economic citizenship has overlooked how the Depression-era economic and social disadvantages against women did inspire many people to adopt the emancipationist cause and back the ERA. As the sections of this chapter detail, the emancipationists' gains in the mid-1930s suggest that the Depression was not simply a time of advancement for men's rights to the detriment of women.

Emancipationism during the Great Depression

The growth of emancipationism can be fully understood only with reference to the Depression-era economic campaign of the NWP. In the early 1930s members of the NWP still accounted for the majority of emancipationists. This gap, though, would narrow after the NWP shifted its policy objectives and embarked on a nationwide economic campaign. Certainly the ERA remained a priority for the NWP's members, but party leaders increasingly came to emphasize the need to defend women's economic rights in particular. Muna Lee, director of national activities for the NWP, explained

the reasons for the organization's shifting objectives in an article
for *Equal Rights*: "Now is an excellent time to cut through to the
hard fact underlying all sentimental generalizations about the difficulties of night work and long hours and force a comparison of
these with the difficulties of existing in hard times with no work
at all."[11] At a 1933 national council meeting, officials of the NWP
elaborated on the party's economic campaign. They announced
that the future work of the party would be aimed at defining and
developing an "intelligent concept of women's status as worker
and as a wage earner[,] affirming the right of any and all women
to engage in the occupation of their choice and reaffirm[ing] as
a cardinal principle equal pay for equal work, urging that all legislation [relating] to workers as such be regardless of sex difference."[12] In a 1934 newsletter party leaders further expounded on
their campaign by insisting that "the right of women to economic
freedom is at stake, and under constant fire, and women themselves must assemble to fight for their right to work on equal terms
with men."[13] By the early to mid-1930s, as these declarations make
clear, the NWP had placed the defense of women's economic rights
at the forefront of its policy objectives.

The NWP redirected its efforts due in large part to the condem-
nations of women's right to work that had marked the early years
of the Depression. When the Depression began, numerous public and private institutions responded to the economic calamity by
restricting women's work in the hopes that such restrictions would
open up more jobs for men. As a result, the initial years of the
Great Depression brought about an increase in the regulation of
working women; these policies emphasized limiting women's work
hours and controlling their wages. As the restrictions on women's
work grew, the economic discord of the Depression reenergized
another policy that private and public institutions had previously
used to reduce the number of women in the workforce: the firing of married women. As Depression-era social investigator Ruth
Shallcross showed in her reporting, throughout the early years of
the economic crisis public utilities, banks, and insurance compa-
nies, as well as state and municipal governments, formally and
informally limited the employment of married women.[14] In Janu-

ary 1931, for example, legislators in Massachusetts and New York introduced bills that called for the removal of married women whose husbands also held government jobs. Around this time the governor of Kansas too proposed a policy to bar married women from state employment, and the California State Assembly reviewed three bills that attempted to either discharge working wives or ban them from taking civil service examinations.[15]

During the early part of the Depression, critics of married women in the workforce advanced a twofold argument. First, they charged that working women who were married ignored their social responsibilities in the domestic sphere. Second, they claimed that married working women exacerbated the economic turmoil by taking jobs from men who needed employment to support their families. In 1932 C. W. Galloway, vice president of the Baltimore and Ohio Railroad, gave voice to these arguments when he justified his company's firing of several married women workers in Maryland, declaring that once a "girl" married, she essentially forfeited her job to "take her place in the home where she ought to be."[16] A few months earlier New York state legislator Arthur L. Swartz reiterated that same line of thought at a luncheon with NWP official Mildred Palmer. When asked about his stance on married women in public employment, he reasoned that "with the present unemployment there is no doubt in my mind that most married women could be, and should be, relieved of their public positions . . . their pride and patriotism should prompt them to resign during the depression."[17]

The hostility toward married working women that infused the opening years of the Depression developed from the idea that women who worked outside of the domestic sphere contributed to the demoralization of the home. Although this idea had existed long before the economic collapse, its intensity grew as the extent of the economic devastation became apparent in the early 1930s.[18] As noted in the previous chapter, the dominant cultural consensus of the early 1930s still aligned with the ethos of protectionism, which had dominated the 1920s. This mind-set assumed that a woman with children belonged at home. If she continued to work, the thought process went, then she was motivated by dire need or careless selfishness.[19] Even with the blatant disdain for married women's presence in the workforce, the expanding regulation of women's work outside of the home eventually backfired by the mid- to late 1930s, as it caused a wave of discontent among several women's groups and ultimately ruptured the power of protectionism.

The NWP cultivated this discontent with its nationwide economic campaign, which attacked with particular force the escalating discrimination against working women. The NWP's economic campaign consisted of publicizing the discrimination against women, filing formal protests, and organizing lobbying groups. When in 1930, for instance, the executive committee of the Cotton-Textile Institute recommended fewer hours and the abolition of night work for women, the NWP not only published editorials on the recommendation but also sent two of its leaders to New York to file an official protest with the president and chair of the institute's board of directors.[20]

There are countless other examples of the NWP's Depression- era efforts to curtail the restrictions on women's right to work. In 1931 NWP officials sent letters of protest to northern and midwest- ern governors when their state legislatures passed laws restricting women's employment. That same year party leaders held meetings with Governor Gifford Pinchot of Pennsylvania and Governor John Pollard of Virginia in the hopes of promoting industrial equality for the sexes. And in the early 1930s the NWP sent party member Josephine Casey to organize women workers in the textile indus- try in several states. She was especially successful in Rhode Island and Georgia. In the latter her lobbying efforts helped to defeat a bill that would have prohibited night work for women. While the NWP did have some successes, these activities did not end all of the discriminatory practices public and private institutions used in their attempts to reduce the number of women in the workforce. Nonetheless, the NWP continued to spearhead efforts to resist the Depression-era subjugation of women workers.[21]

One of the most important activities of the NWP's economic campaign was in leading the fight against Section 213 of the Econ- omy Act of 1932. This work would later help the NWP form valu- able connections with other women's groups. When Section 213 passed Congress, it signaled the federal government's entry into the assault on women's ability to work. "No single thing in recent years," according to an NWP pamphlet on the measure, "has done so much to retard the progress of women in industry."[22] Section 213 was problematic because it required personnel reductions to be made at the expense of persons whose spouses were employed by the government. In other words, it barred two people from the same family from simultaneously holding federal employment. Whereas the measure read "persons," the intent was clear, because legislators had originally worded the bill to read "married women." (The House committee in charge of the bill had changed its phrasing so that the bill would pass the House without protest.)[23] The federal government justified the clause as a way to spread around jobs on the rationale that it was wrong for one family to have two jobs while other families went without one. The measure, however, mostly resulted in wives leaving federal employment, because their husbands usually held the higher-paying job.[24]

Shortly after Congress passed the bill, the NWP began an extensive campaign for its repeal. At this time the organization formed the Government Workers' Council (GWC) as the main unit directing the repeal efforts. Edwina Austin Avery served as the director of the campaign. As part of its work the GWC organized meetings with members of Congress and directed a large letter-writing campaign.[25] A considerable amount of the GWC's efforts focused on documenting the ill effects of Section 213. At one GWC meeting, for instance, the group's leaders reported, "The lowest paid women workers are bearing the brunt of this misguided attempt to spread employment. . . . Most of the married women discharged under the law have been obliged because of financial obligations to seek employment in the lower grade and more crowded occupations. Those who remain at home displace domestic helpers."[26] In all, the GWC contended that the exclusionary policy represented by Section 213 not only violated women's ability to find and maintain work, but it also hampered the economic recovery by exacerbating the unemployment problem.

A number of members of Congress took note of the GWC's work, especially Republican senator Hiram Bingham of Connecticut. In

January 1933 Senator Bingham attached a rider amendment onto
an appropriations bill that called for the repeal of Section 213. Senator Bingham, who was the chair of the Senate Economy Committee, called a subsequent hearing on the measure and invited GWC
members to testify in support of his rider. During Edwina Austin
Avery's testimony for the GWC, as well as the NWP as a whole, she
argued that Section 213 undermined women's right to work and
that it lowered the standard of employment. "It makes the criterion of employment," Avery insisted, "the fact of whether or not
the employee is married to another employee, rather than whether
he or she is efficient or qualified for the position and the work to
be done."[27] Even though the committee voted to reject the rider,
the NWP continued to fight Section 213. Over the coming years, as
discussed later in this chapter, the NWP would recruit several other
women's organizations to join its struggle against the measure.[28]

Alongside the NWP's fight against Section 213 and throughout its
economic campaign as a whole, party leaders stressed the unconditional right of women to work outside of the home. As party member Alma Lutz declared in a pamphlet for the NWP, women were
not "casual and temporary workers or extras."[29] When in 1930 the
Iowa Federation of Labor called for the replacement of married
working women with jobless men, a member of the NWP, Elizabeth Seldon Rogers, decried in an article for *Equal Rights*, "Married men are not to be asked to give their jobs to the needy, they
are to be left undisturbed with their salaries and wages. . . . But
is a married woman who wishes to earn money to raise the standard of living for herself to be penalized for that ambition? Must
her brains and powers be suppressed in order to give some man
a chance to use his? No!"[30] Although individuals in favor of limiting women's work argued that unbounded female employment
created economic chaos, the leaders of the NWP maintained that
women's economic rights mattered just as much as men's economic
rights. Further still, party leaders asserted that a citizen's right to
work outside of the home should not be based on a person's sex.

As the leaders of the NWP stressed the unconditional right of
women to work, so too did they use the increasing regulation of
working women to sharpen their arguments against sex-specific

labor legislation. For starters, party officials contended that such legislation handicapped women's ability to compete in the labor market, particularly during times of economic turmoil. To back up this claim, NWP official Burnita Shelton Matthews contended in a 1934 speech before the GFWC that it was dangerous to continue the promotion of sex-specific labor laws, because that trend "in times of economic stress when jobs are scarce, encourages campaigns to pass 'restrictive' legislation intended to make women ineffective as competitors."[31] According to NWP party leaders, the impulse to pass special labor laws for women often swelled during times of economic unrest, because those laws were intended for the protection of men, not women. Matthews went on in her speech to note how New York waitresses had petitioned to be exempted from a law barring women from night work. But, as Matthews described it, a representative of the State Federation of Labor had objected to the petition on the basis that such an exemption would throw thousands of men out of work. To Matthews, the situation proved that night work laws were not "for the protection of women but for the protection of the men who wanted their jobs."[32] In their arguments for women's economic rights, members of the NWP asserted that the Depression-era expansion of sex-specific labor laws showed that the main purpose of those laws was to preserve men's place as the primary economic actors. As party member Vee Terrys Perlman later put it in an NWP pamphlet, "regulations which arbitrarily restrict one section of a group of workers instead of protecting, victimizes that section."[33]

Even though the NWP condemned special labor laws for women, the organization did not oppose government involvement in the economy altogether. On the contrary, party members insisted that government regulations should apply equally to both sexes. Anna Kelton Wiley, head of the NWP in the early 1930s, spoke to this point when she explained in a letter to the president of the National Federation of Business and Professional Women's Clubs (BPWC) that "a shorter working day is of course the trend of the times and should be welcomed by all workers in industry, but a limited statutory working day for *women only* will work a hardship to women and make it harder for them to secure employment. . . . Such a law should be for *persons, all persons in industry*, and not for women only."[34] For leaders of the NWP it stood to reason that since men and women worked for the same purposes, they should be held to the same labor standards.

For the most part the NWP actively supported economic legislation that embraced sex-neutral policies. In 1933, for example, the NWP backed the Black-Connery Bill calling for a thirty-hour work week, because the labor regulation in the bill was originally intended to apply equally to men and women.[35] In the spring of that year Maud Younger of the NWP explained her organization's support for the bill in her testimony before the House Committee on Labor. "All regulations," she maintained, "should be based upon the nature of the work, and not upon the sex of the worker." Younger concluded that passing policies that encouraged the replacement of women workers with jobless men would only lead to a larger unemployment problem.[36] As Younger's testimony illustrates, the NWP not only advocated for women's right to compete with men in the marketplace but it also supported regulatory measures that promoted economic stability and the welfare of all workers.

The NWP even backed a number of the New Deal economic recovery measures. Indeed, the NWP endorsed the National Industrial Recovery Act (NIRA), which established the NRA. Vee Terrys Perlman called the act "revolutionary," because it made a "legal minimum wage for *both men and women* compulsory."[37] In Maud Younger's view, the NRA's inclusion of men in the government's oversight of employment practices had changed "the psychology of the nation towards protective laws, placing men and women on the same basis."[38] For the leaders of the NWP the inclusion of men in government economic regulatory practices with acts such as the NIRA had ushered in a positive change in how political authorities envisioned the rights of men and women citizens. From the NWP's standpoint, policy makers were now appearing to be applying the same economic principles to both men and women.

Even after several of the NRA's codes permitted rampant sex-based differentials in wages, the NWP continued to highlight the positive aspects of the NRA.[39] In one article for *Equal Rights* party leader Jane Norman Smith commented, "Though wage scales for women are lower than those for men under the codes, by including men in hours and wage regulations, the principle of equality of opportunity, for which the Woman's Party . . . has labored for years, seems to have been established."[40] Of course the NWP opposed the codes that allowed for sex-based differentials in wages, but party officials advocated for the reform of such codes and not the disbanding of the NRA entirely. Ultimately, party officials continued to support the act, because they believed that it advanced the equality of the sexes, at least in principle.[41]

The right of all citizens to economic self-fulfillment undergirds a central component of the emancipationist ideology. Yet, this emphasis on economic rights has led many scholars to conclude that members of the NWP fundamentally supported uncontrolled competition in the marketplace. Historian Sandra VanBurkleo for example, describes the objectives of the NWP as fitting "comfortably into the laissez-faire paradigm that a good many legal and social reformers were struggling to dismantle."[42] Likewise, historian Nancy Cott contends that at its heart the NWP maintained a philosophy that understood society to be composed of "atomistic individuals" who were only joined "by competition and contract."[43] In most cases scholars are correct to surmise that in the 1920s members of the NWP upheld the unrestricted right of women to compete with men in the marketplace. But, the civic ideology that members of the NWP and emancipationists in general espoused did not *necessarily* align with conservative economic policies.

At the core of emancipationism is the notion that a single standard of rights should apply to men and women citizens equally. In the 1920s the discourse of emancipationism reflected the ideas underlying the freedom of contract principle, because that was the doctrine that legal and political authorities predominantly appealed to when discussing the conventional rights of citizenship. In the 1930s the discourse of emancipationism shifted as the concept of American citizenship changed. Similar to the emerging concept of social citizenship, emancipationists began to embrace the rights of all citizens to economic and social well-being. In a display of this trend, one Depression-era *Equal Rights* editorial called to mind President Franklin Roosevelt's famous "forgotten man speech" when it pleaded with policy makers to stop neglecting the "forgotten woman" in their New Deal recovery plans.[44] All the more, NWP leader Muna Lee remarked that her party was not opposed to improving economic and social conditions through union action, labor legislation, or "the reorganization of society on a non-capitalistic basis," but, she maintained, "whatever the method adopted it should be carried out without distinctions based on sex."[45]

To be sure, emancipationism would continue to uphold a woman's right to choose how she would contribute to society. Emancipationists consistently supported this type of individualism, because another fundamental tenet of their ideology was the rightful emancipation of women from the common law tradition of domestic duties. And certainly a number of emancipationists would continue to favor fiscally conservative policies.[46] Even so, support for conservative economic policies was not an essential component of the emancipationist ideology. As the economic campaign of the NWP reveals, many emancipationists had begun to better articulate the need for a middle ground between economic freedom and government oversight, as they increasingly asserted that men and women citizens should enjoy the same degree of economic opportunity and security.

Emancipationism on the Move

As the NWP moved its attention toward combating the mounting discriminations against working women, it was able to form alliances with other women's groups. The development of these connections, moreover, pumped life back into the emancipationist movement. Over the Depression years various women's groups had grown more open to coordinating their work with the NWP because of the deepening economic crisis and the resulting increase in the regulation of working women. These factors had forced those groups to recognize the potential disadvantages embedded in sex-specific labor laws. In 1932 twenty-two groups went on record opposing special labor legislation for women. These groups included the National Association of Women Lawyers (NAWL), the Business and Professional Women's Legislative Council of New York, the League of Advertising Women, and the American Alliance of Civil Service Women.[47] In 1934 several groups joined the NWP in its opposition to liberal protectionists' attempts to pass minimum wage laws that applied to women and children only. These groups included the NAWL, the New York League of Business and Professional Women, the American Alliance of Civil Service Women, the Zonta Clubs of Albany and New York, the Brooklyn-Manhattan Women's Railroad League, Typographical Union No. 6, the Women's Equal Opportunity League, and the Equal Rights Association. As NWP member Vee Terrys Perlman noted in an NWP pamphlet on the matter, these were organizations not only for business and professional women but also for working-class women. For example, the Typographical Union, the Women's Equal Opportunity League, and the Equal Rights Association largely consisted of working-class women.[48]

Beginning in the mid-1930s the NWP strengthened its standing with other women's groups by presenting itself as a leading defender of women's economic welfare. Party leader Muna Lee asserted in an article for *Equal Rights* that during "strenuous" times it was the NWP that took the initiative to "defend and improve the status of women throughout the country."[49] An array of individuals and groups also took notice of the NWP's actions and applauded the organization's efforts. As one NWP official put it at a 1933 national council meeting, "members of various powerful organizations are taking an interest in the work of the party and realizing the importance of it."[50] Before the growth of the NWP's economic campaign, it was common to view the organization as a group of radical activists who were determined to impose abstract and destructive principles of equality on helpless women. But, in the mid-1930s the NWP was able to counteract that view by shifting its efforts toward tackling the concrete economic ramifications of sex-specific treatment. As a result, the organization started to appear as a principal guardian of women's economic interests.

In the mid-1930s prominent women's organizations joined the NWP in its opposition to Section 213 of the Economy Act of 1932, the federal measure that had prohibited two spouses from working for the federal government at the same time. As discussed, the measure had predominantly forced married women to leave their federal jobs, because their husbands usually held the higher-paying position. In the summer of 1932 the leaders of Zonta, a service organization of women executives, proclaimed at their annual meeting that Section 213 encouraged other institutions to "make it an open season on married women, and vent their suppressed prejudices against giving them employment."[51] As a sign of unity, members of the BPWC, NAWL, the American Association of University Women (AAUW), and the Women's International League for Peace accompanied NWP officials Florence Bayard Hilles and Elsie Hill to a meeting with federal budget director Lewis W. Douglas to protest Section 213 in April 1933.[52]

In January 1935 the movement against Section 213 intensified after Representative Emanuel Celler of New York introduced a bill that called for the measure's repeal. The NWP, through its subsidiary organization (the GWC), immediately initiated work on building support for Celler's bill. Edwina Austin Avery and Bessie I. Koehl led these efforts. In addition to conducting meetings with members of Congress and reaching out to other women's groups, the GWC requested and eventually received a hearing on the bill. That hearing was held in April 1935 before the House Civil Service Committee.[53] Representatives from fourteen other organizations attended the hearing with members of the NWP and testified in support of Celler's bill. These organizations included the American Federation of Teachers, the NAWL, the BPWC, the League of American Civil Service, and the National Education Association. Protectionist groups such as the LWV and the NWTUL joined the other organizations in their support for Celler's bill. Thus, opposition to Section 213 actually produced a brief alignment among emancipationists, soon-to-be-emancipationists, and a number of liberal protectionist groups.[54]

Even so, there are significant differences in how protectionist and emancipationist groups attacked Section 213. All of the organizations maintained that the measure produced harmful discriminations against working women. But emancipationists, and soon-to-be-emancipationists, predominantly accentuated women's right to work in their criticisms while liberal protectionists stressed the economic factors that compelled many women to enter the workforce. The emancipationist position on Section 213 is exemplified by Dorothy Dunn's congressional testimony at the 1935 hearing. Dunn, representing the BPWC, an organization that would endorse the ERA in 1937, posited that the measure symbolized the general "hysteria" aimed at women workers. She concluded that the measure was a "blow to all women who worked. . . . It established a precedent by Federal Government [that] can be cited by private employers as a justification for refusing to employ married women."[55] In equally intense testimony at the same hearing, Anita Pollitzer of the NWP argued that "Section 213 of the Economy Act by its very nature, discriminates against women. . . . [It] violates a fundamental principle of our government." For emancipationists, and soon-to-be-emancipationists, measures like Section 213 blighted women's unconditional right to work.[56]

In contrast to the emancipationist emphasis on framing women's employment in terms of a citizen's right to economic opportunity, protectionist critics of Section 213, mostly liberal-leaning protectionists, blasted the measure as a terrible bias against women who were forced to work out of economic necessity. As Mrs. Harris Baldwin, vice president of the LWV, argued in her testimony at the 1935 congressional hearing, Section 213 did not take into account "the economic status of the family, the total family income, the number of dependents, and other conditions" that compelled some women to work. She went on to explain that in certain circumstances the salaries of both wife and husband were needed "to support dependent children . . . to support a mother or father or younger brothers or sisters." The measure, she concluded, "work[ed] a great hardship in the family."[57] Protectionists like Baldwin visualized women's employment around the family, because such employment was often vital to the family's survival. Because the protectionists who opposed Section 213 had tied their justification for women's employment to the family, they primarily criticized the measure as an assault on families whose economic circumstances demanded two sources of income.[58]

The success of the NWP's economic campaign in rehabilitating its relationships with other women's groups helped to reenergize the movement for the ERA by the mid-1930s. One of the earliest signs of the growing influence of emancipationism is the 1933 ERA congressional hearing. For the first time individuals outside of the NWP testified in support of the amendment during the hearing. Republican senator John Townsend of Delaware opened the hearing in favor of the ERA, and several women's groups sent members to testify in support of the ERA. These groups included the Bindery Women's Union Local, Quota International, the Married Women's Teachers' Association of Philadelphia, and the Business Women's Legislative Council of California.[59] The expanding support for the ERA prompted NWP leader Rebekah Greathouse to declare in her testimony that the opposition was now "growing fainter."[60] Over the next few years the majority of groups that had supported the NWP's economic campaign eventually moved to endorse the ERA. By 1937, for example, the list of official backers of the amendment had expanded to include the NAWL, the BPWC, the American Association of Medical Women, the National Women's Democratic Club, Quota International clubs, Zonta International, the American Federation of Soroptimist Clubs, the American Alliance of Civil Service Women, the National Women's Real Estate Association, the Association of American Women Dentists, and the Women's Osteopathic Association. In addition, by 1935 the GFWC and the National Council of Women (NCW) had both retracted their original opposition to the amendment and initiated an overall review of the measure.[61]

In addition to gaining momentum from the NWP's economic campaign, emancipationism's increasing influence also benefited from the progress in women's nationality rights during the mid-1930s.[62] As noted previously, liberal-minded protectionists had also fought for improvements to the Cable Act of 1922; the 1930 and 1931 Cable Act revisions in particular are mostly the result of the lobbying achievements of the WJCC, a protectionist group.[63] Nonetheless, the final reform of the Cable Act—the Equal Nationality Rights Act of 1934—came about largely due to the work of emancipationists. Even after the 1930 and 1931 Cable Act revisions, U.S. immigration and naturalization laws still disadvantaged women in two significant ways. First, American women could not transfer their nationality to their children. Consequently, the nationality of the father still determined the status of the child. Second, American women with foreign spouses could not automatically receive the quota breaks enjoyed by immigrating women married to citizens or resident aliens. An international campaign led by two veteran leaders of the NWP, Alice Paul and Doris Stevens, encouraged Congress to pass the final Cable Act reform to address those remaining restrictions.[64]

From the late 1920s to the mid-1930s Paul and Stevens focused much of their energy on the Inter-American Commission on Women. The Pan-American Union had established the Inter-American Commission on Women in 1928 with the purpose of collecting data on the civil and political status of women in the Americas. While conducting work on the commission, Paul and Stevens turned their attention to creating and directing an international nationality rights campaign. Their campaign consisted of two goals: congressional passage of an equal nationality rights bill, which would amend the Cable Act, and ratification of an equal-nationality treaty.[65]

Both measures sought unconditional equality between men and women with regard to their nationality rights. Paul and Stevens pursued a two-front campaign for women's nationality rights partly because they recognized that the global patchwork of nationality laws still left many women stateless upon marriage even if the United States moved to amend the Cable Act. In essence, they had realized that improvements to women's nationality rights necessitated national as well as international work.[66] Eventually their efforts paid off when in 1930 Paul and Stevens successfully persuaded the Inter-American Commission on Women to unanimously adopt their treaty proposal, which read, "The contracting States agree that . . . there shall be no distinction based on sex in their law and practices relating to nationality."[67]

From December 3 to December 26, 1933, the Pan-American Union held its convention in Montevideo with the Inter-American Commission's equality-nationality treaty on its schedule. Before the conference began, most of the attending countries had expressed their intention to sign the treaty. The United States, however, was not one of those countries, because the Roosevelt administration did not want to settle the question of women's nationality rights through an international agreement that appeared to adhere to the notion of blanket sexual equality.[68] As I explain later in this chapter, the Roosevelt administration epitomized the liberal protectionist stance. While it supported enhancing women's position in society, it did not approve of introducing absolute equality among the sexes. At the time of the convention newspapers reported that it was Eleanor Roosevelt, a firm critic of the ERA, who had been primarily responsible for her husband's reluctance to endorse the treaty.[69] In fact, the First Lady had previously called the ERA, as well as the overall concept of blanket sexual equality, "a foolish thing." Although she later denied any direct involvement in her husband's handling of the treaty, she criticized the measure as an act that would cause "confusion in our nationality laws."[70]

Leaders of the LWV shared Eleanor Roosevelt's concerns. The *New York Times* reported in December 1933 that according to LWV official Dorothy Straus, her organization favored practical methods for improving women's nationality rights and "opposed all blanket legislation in any form." Straus, a lawyer who was a legal advisor to the LWV, went on to explain why: "We of the league are very much for the rights of women, but we are also for the proper working out of problems by modes of orderly procedure. We are not feminists primarily; we are citizens."[71] Straus had gone even further in her criticisms, insisting in an LWV memo on a related matter that such treaties represented a "fundamental change in our legal philosophy" because it challenged "the method of the common law."[72] As Straus's comments suggest, the LWV's leaders still conceptualized women's citizenship around a model that they had anchored to the common law tradition. The liberal protectionists who opposed the treaty also feared that, if passed, it might open the door to the abolition of all laws based on sex. For them, passage of the measure could encourage more people to join the emancipationist cause.[73]

Nonetheless, opponents of the international agreement had misjudged the level of support for it among many women's organizations. When the administration's dislike of the treaty became evident in early December 1933, a delegation from the NAWL swiftly gathered at the White House to voice its objections. (The NAWL would go on to become an ERA backer in 1935.)[74] As the Pan-American Union's conference in Montevideo reached its second week, the *Washington Post* reported that "feminine pressure" for the White House to support the treaty had reached "unexpected proportions." According to the same report, treaty supporters had been "shower[ing]" Secretary of State Cordell Hull, who headed the U.S. delegation to the Pan-American Union convention, with cables urging him to back the treaty.[75] On December 20, as Florence Bayard Hilles of the NWP was gathering a delegation to protest at the State Department, Secretary Hull announced that he would follow new instructions from the president and back the treaty.[76] The president had apparently surrendered to public pressure. When the international conference ended on December 26, the Equal-Nationality Treaty carried the signatures of delegates from several countries, including the United States.[77]

A couple of months after the conference had adjourned, Congress held a hearing on the NWP's equal nationality rights bill in March 1934. The bill would amend the Cable Act, as it called for complete sexual equality in the nation's immigration and naturalization laws. Since 1932 members of the NWP had been lobbying Congress to pass this bill. While the NWP continued to focus on its economic work, the organization had reallocated some of its resources to assist Alice Paul and Doris Stevens in their international nationality rights campaign.[78] Through the NWP's lobbying efforts, the organization enlisted two important congressional sponsors: Democratic representative Samuel Dickstein and Democratic senator Royal Copeland, both of New York. The lawmakers introduced the bill in 1932 and 1933.[79] As Representative Dickstein saw it, the purpose of the bill was "to complete the provisions of the Cable Act of 1922 so as to establish complete equality between American men and women in the matter of citizenship for themselves and for their children."[80] The bill was commonly referred to as the "equalization bill," because, according to Representative Dickstein's explanation, the bill sought "to equalize the citizenship rights of male and female citizens."[81] By the 1934 hearing, the bill had gained the backing of important women's groups, including the GFWC, BPWC, NAWL, National Women's Medical Association, and the Zonta Clubs.[82]

The NWP's bill, however, faced considerable opposition from the State Department and the White House. On the day the House began its March 1934 hearing on the NWP's bill, Secretary of State Hull sent a letter to Democratic representative William Bankhead of Alabama, who chaired the House Rules Committee. Hull informed Bankhead that the State Department harbored "serious objections" to the bill. Because of these concerns, Hull requested that action on the bill be delayed until further investigation into the extent of the discriminations against women's nationality rights had been completed.[83] In an earlier letter to Representative Dickstein, Hull had explained that to avoid judicial confusion he thought it better to dismiss blanket bills in favor of piecemeal legislation.[84] Evidently, Hull was still intent on avoiding blanket equality measures of any type despite the controversy over the nationality treaty.

A larger political and cultural context lay behind the State Department's aversion to the NWP's international nationality rights campaign. More than a year before the 1934 hearing, State Department officials had expressed their unease with the NWP's equal nationality rights bill, because the bill provided citizenship status to children of women living abroad. In the early 1930s many Americans had accepted the notion that a strong country relied upon its citizens' undivided allegiance. Due to this mind-set, some Americans questioned the loyalty of children born to American women residing in other countries. In a February 1933 letter to Representative Dickstein, Assistant Secretary of State Wilbur Carr explained that he thought the NWP's bill would create a class of absentee "alien" Americans. He warned, "It is hardly necessary to say that, when a woman having an American nationality married a man having the nationality of a foreign country and establishes her home with him in his country, the national character of that country is likely to be stamped upon the children so that from the standpoint of the United States they are essentially alien in character."[85] From Carr's perspective, the NWP's bill meant granting American citizenship to a group of persons who were non-Americans in practically every respect.

In addition to the fears from State Department officials that the NWP's bill would impose irresponsible, blanket sexual equality onto the country's nationality laws, Secretary of Labor Frances Perkins, a staunch challenger of the ERA, expressed concerns about the NWP's international nationality rights campaign. Before President Roosevelt had nominated Perkins in 1933 to be the first woman secretary of labor, she had been a prominent social worker in the world of New York politics. She was an ardent champion of special labor laws for women and a follower of the reform impulse that had shaped the liberal protectionist stance. Around the time of the March 1934 hearing on the NWP's equal nationality rights bill, Perkins informed Representative Bankhead that she too supported delaying action on the bill until the president's Interdepartmental Commission on Nationality had completed its report. Roosevelt had set up that executive committee in April 1933 to review the nationality laws of the United States and to make recommendations for removing certain discriminations. It seems as though officials in the White House, the State Department, and the Department of Labor understood that passage of the NWP's equalization bill would hasten the Senate's ratification of the equal-nationality treaty. Consequently, they held out hope that the House committee would follow Hull's and Perkins's suggestions and delay action on the bill indeterminately.[86]

Despite the opposition's best efforts, action on the NWP's bill progressed in the spring of 1934, as the Roosevelt administration had underestimated the pragmatic tenacity of the NWP. When NWP leaders realized that the administration was intent on dragging its feet on the bill and the treaty, they sent a deputation to the White House on March 26 to meet with presidential secretary Marvin McIntyre. In the words of one NWP party member, the deputation was a "very splendid and large group of prominent Democratic women."[87] During the meeting the deputation announced its intention to publicly accuse the executive branch of backtracking on an international agreement and obstructing the legislative process.[88]

The group's threat apparently disturbed Hull, Perkins, and possibly even the president.[89] Given the NWP's threat, both secretaries sent letters to Congress disavowing any attempt on their part in delaying the federal government from acting on the advancement of women's nationality rights.[90] In the end their retreat cleared the way for the bill's passage.[91] The president signed the Equal National- ity Rights Bill into law on May 24, 1934—the same day that the Sen- ate approved a resolution for ratification of the Equal-Nationality Treaty. In the earlier words of Representative Dickstein, the bill's passage was intended to "complete" the Cable Act, as men and women Americans were subsequently able to enjoy the same nat- uralization benefits for their foreign-born spouses, while moth- ers gained the same rights as fathers to transmit their citizenship to their children.[92]

In principle, the Equal Nationality Rights Act of 1934 set out to instill sexual equality into the processes of naturalization, expa- triation, repatriation, and immigration for men and women. In the coming years, however, the passage of subsequent immigra- tion and nationality laws would muddle the original promise of sexual equality embedded in the 1934 act by permitting different requirements for the transmission of U.S. citizenship to children born abroad and out of wedlock based on whether the child had an American citizen mother or an American citizen father.[93] Nev- ertheless, the 1934 act was an impressive achievement for the NWP and its allies. As historian Candice Lewis Bredbenner describes it, the passage of the 1934 act showed that the NWP had "orchestrated a successful end to a splendid crusade," as women of the United States had finally gained an independent nationality status.[94]

The mid-1930s progress in women's nationality rights together with the growing support for the NWP's economic campaign pro- duced significant congressional movement on the ERA. The height- ened support for the NWP prompted Democratic representative Louis Ludlow of Indiana to write a letter to Anita Pollitzer in Decem- ber 1934 in which he exclaimed, "I believe this is the psycholog- ical time to press the amendment." He then urged Pollitzer to push the primary work of the NWP back to the ERA and "make the best drive possible" for the amendment's congressional passage.[95] Ludlow, who had previously been a prominent newspaper corre- spondent before entering Congress in 1928, would later emerge as a national leader of the war referendum movement.[96] Regarding the ERA, Ludlow became a vocal and consistent proponent of the amendment starting in the mid-1930s. As Ludlow wrote in a subsequent letter to Pollitzer, he strongly supported the amendment, because he was dedicated "to the struggle to emancipate women from unwarranted discriminations imposed on account of their sex."[97] Like all emancipationists, Ludlow believed that an additional constitutional amendment needed to follow the Nineteenth Amendment, because in his view the cohesion of American democracy necessitated a single standard of rights for its voters to ensure the fair application of justice. Two months after Ludlow's correspondence with Pollitzer, he wrote to NWP leader Anna Kelton Wiley to announce that he had "been canvassing members of Congress." He continued, "Members are more deeply aroused than ever over discriminations that are now practices against women and there is a growing realization of the utter nonsense of trying to wipe out these discriminations by pop gun acts of state legislatures."[98] In Ludlow's opinion, the mood of the country was changing, and that change was in the ERA's favor.

By December 1934 the leadership of the NWP had wholeheartedly agreed with Ludlow's optimistic assessment of the ERA's fate. What is more, leaders of the organization had expressed similar views even before Ludlow's correspondence. At the organization's national council meeting in the summer of 1934, Maud Younger reasoned that with regard to the amendment it was "unquestionably the time . . . to get Congress converted[;] . . . so much of the hostility of a few years ago has vanished."[99] Likewise, in the fall of that year NWP member Anna Milburn had observed, "The friendly attitude of the members of Congress toward the Equal Nationality legislation passed during the past session, and the growing realization of the justice of all Equality legislation, makes us feel that during the coming session of Congress the Equal Rights Amendment will pass."[100]

As NWP officials recognized the advantageous situation, party leaders developed a new plan to maximize congressional backing of the amendment, which they initiated in January 1935. Under the management of Anita Pollitzer and Betty Gram Swing, the NWP's congressional committee carried out the party's new congressional strategy.[101] As a whole, the new congressional committee favored a behind-the-scenes approach for building congressional support. For this purpose, it directed a large letter-writing campaign and held several private meetings with members of the House and Senate Judiciary Committees. The success of the group's campaign was largely due to its private meetings with principal members of those congressional committees. These meetings, NWP organizers explained in a report on the new strategy, showed that they were not in fact facing strong opposition from many congressional leaders, because, in the words of the report, "when our position [is] actually understood . . . when we get to talking it over, [members of Congress] find that the thing that we want is the same as what they want."[102] Through the NWP's private meetings with Congress members, the organization was able to advance its position without distracting interjections from ERA opponents. As Pollitzer put it in an article for *Equal Rights*, the NWP was conducting "an offensive rather than defensive campaign" with its new congressional strategy.[103]

Whereas in the 1920s the NWP favored congressional hearings as a way to build public support, by 1935 it wanted to avoid the publicity that came along with those hearings. At this time the NWP's strategists preferred private methods to public spectacles, because they did not want to provoke the "formidable opposition" within the Roosevelt administration. The organization's leaders recognized that the White House had only signed the Equal Nationality Rights Bill into law under political duress and that it still strongly opposed blanket equality measures. As Swing explained, "we wish to avoid hearings at all costs, to work quietly with individual members so as to avoid letting our opponents know just what we are doing."[104] Thus, the party's strategists had decided by this time that it was best to develop support quietly to avoid provoking ERA opponents and providing them with the opportunity to prepare a strong counterattack.

Over the course of the next year and a half the new congressional strategy proved effective, as several members of Congress either fully endorsed the amendment or privately pledged to reconsider the measure. As early as April 1935, for instance, Pollitzer had reported to the NWP's national council that the results of the strategy "had been most gratifying."[105] The following month Representative Matthew Dunn of Pennsylvania, described by NWP leaders as "a strong labor man," announced his support for the amendment in an article for *Equal Rights*. "We cannot truthfully say that our Government is a government of the people, by the people and for the people," he proclaimed, "unless we give to the women the same rights and privileges the men now enjoy."[106] The NWP's congressional campaign had particular success with members of the House Judiciary Committee; by the fall of 1935 seven committee members had expressed their support for the ERA.[107] These congressional gains prompted Betty Gram Swing to declare, "We have the best chance of winning Equal Rights now that we have ever had since the Amendment was first introduced."[108]

Swing's assessment of the ERA's standing in the House turned out to be quite accurate. On May 30, 1936, a House subcommittee reported the ERA favorably to the House Judiciary Committee. This was the first positive congressional action on the ERA since its introduction into Congress in 1923. The chair of the subcommittee, Representative Francis E. Walter, a Democrat from Pennsylvania, made the recommendation with the concurrence of a fellow Democrat, Representative J. L. Adair of Illinois, and Republicans U. S. Guyer of Kansas and W. H. Wilson of Pennsylvania.[109] The encouraging congressional activity prompted Representative Ludlow to hail the action as "an epochal event in the advancement of the cause of women in America."[110] The achievement particularly thrilled Swing, who cheered in an article for *Equal Rights*, "We may well rejoice. . . . *This is the first real action ever to be taken by Congress on the Amendment.* It is the first step, which is always the hardest."[111] For ERA proponents the positive congressional action had marked a significant victory for the amendment and the emancipationist movement.

Congressional action on the ERA continued throughout the next year. In May 1937 a subcommittee of the House Judiciary Committee held an informal hearing on the ERA with only ERA supporters in attendance. The small number of attendees included

Representative Ludlow along with NWP members Emma Wold and Elsie Hill, as well as Rebekah Greathouse, who now represented the NAWL. Representative Zebulon Weaver of North Carolina, a Democrat and supporter of the Nineteenth Amendment, chaired the subcommittee. The subcommittee also included Republican representative U. S. Guyer of Kansas and Democratic representative Walter Chandler of Tennessee. The hearing was intended as an informal meeting to provide ERA supporters with an opportunity to address some of the committee members' concerns.[112] The emancipationists, however, took it as an opportunity to electrify a refined argument in support of complete constitutional sexual equality.

In this refreshed line of reasoning, the emancipationists who testified at the hearing argued that the ERA would provide women with a permanent guarantee of their rights as full citizens while preserving the doctrine of states' rights. According to Elsie Hill's testimony, the ERA would simply "make equality permanent."[113] Still, Emma Wold, a lawyer and teacher, cautioned that the ERA would not make the states enforce the same standard of equality. "We are not asking for equal rights between the inhabitants of the various states," she remarked, "but it is equal rights between men and women wherever they may be living."[114] In other words, emancipationists were now trying to convey as clearly as possible that the ERA was not intended to impose a national, uniform legal standard for all the states to follow. Rather, emancipationists maintained, the purpose of the ERA was to create a federal mandate for the states to "harmonize" their own laws so that women and men could have the same legal standing within a particular jurisdiction.[115]

In emancipationists' arguments about states' rights during the 1937 hearing, they also revealed how they had adjusted their approach to discussing the ERA's relationship to the Fourteenth Amendment. For instance, Rebekah Greathouse argued in her testimony that the essential purpose of the ERA was to guarantee that the equal protection clause of the Fourteenth Amendment also applied to women. "I don't think," she surmised, "it would affect the states in their relations to each other any more than a phrase already in the Constitution affects them." Nonetheless, she contin-

ued, the ERA would establish a "definite principle for the body of
the Supreme Court and other judicial bodies for interpreting laws
in regard to women." In her mind the ERA would "erase the common law precedent that women are to be treated differently than
men."[116] In the 1920s emancipationists tended to avoid referencing
the Fourteenth Amendment in their congressional testimonies,
because they did not want to open themselves up to protectionists' claims that the ERA would harm working women's welfare by
subjecting them to the freedom of contract principle. As discussed
in more detail in the next chapter, the economic calamity of the
Great Depression brought about seismic changes in how legal and
political authorities located the rights of citizenship. By 1937 these
authorities had started to move away from the freedom of contract
principle by interpreting the Fourteenth Amendment in terms of
positive rather than negative rights. As a result, emancipationists
felt freer to appeal to the Fourteenth Amendment in their explanations of the ERA's purpose. Similar to the Fourteenth Amendment, they reasoned, the ERA would ensure the equal treatment
of men and women citizens before the law.

Throughout the 1937 congressional hearing, emancipationists argued that only with the addition of the ERA would the U.S.
Constitution be able to uphold women's value as persons, since
the ERA would provide the Constitution with a concrete recognition of women's status as full citizens in their own right. As mentioned early in this chapter, Elsie Hill skillfully summarized this
point during her testimony when she declared that women wanted
to simply "be regarded as 'persons' under the Constitution of the
United States." For Hill and other emancipationists, only a constitutional declaration of men's and women's equal rights would
remove outworn sex discriminations from America's laws and customs and fully emancipate women from the enslavement of common law.[117] The House subcommittee members at the 1937 hearing
had apparently empathized with the emancipationist position,
because in June 1937, almost a month after the informal hearing,
the subcommittee reported the ERA favorably to the House Judiciary Committee. That same month a subcommittee of the Senate
reported the ERA favorably to its Judiciary Committee.[118]

Thanks to the increased support for the NWP and its renewed arguments for the ERA, a number of conservative-minded politicians voiced their backing of the amendment in 1937. In February of that year Senator Edward Burke (D-NE), a critic of the New Deal, announced his endorsement of the amendment, declaring, "It is a disservice to our women workers to throw about them protective legislation which can have only one ultimate effect, and that is to take their jobs away from them."[119] That month conservative Democratic senator Royal Copeland of New York, who had been a primary backer of the NWP's equal nationality rights bill, endorsed the ERA. "As the adoption of the Suffrage Amendment was necessary to give political rights to women, so I am of the opinion that the adoption of the Equal Rights Amendment . . . is vital to the establishment of equal legal rights" was how Copeland explained his support for the ERA in an article for *Equal Rights*.[120] Like other emancipationists, Copeland believed that the ERA would ensure that American democracy did not exclude a class of electors from all the rights of citizenship.

Throughout the coming years, the ERA would continue to attract the approval of more conservative-leaning politicians who were critical of the Roosevelt administration, among them Senators Warren Austin (R-VT), John Townsend (R-DE), and Frederick Van Nuys (D-IN). As explained before, not all emancipationists followed conservative economic principles; moreover, many emancipationists supported New Deal policies. Even so, the failure of the Roosevelt administration's court-packing plan in 1937 had emboldened a handful of New Deal critics to advocate for the ERA. Due to the amendment's inherent challenge to special labor legislation for women, these pro-business conservatives found in the emancipationist position arguments that aligned with their support for private enterprise. For these conservative-minded ERA proponents, the amendment provided a vibrant tool for attacking government regulation of the economy and undermining the authority of the Roosevelt administration.[121]

By the end of 1937 emancipationists had an assortment of reasons to feel optimistic about their amendment's future. At this time several women's groups had become official backers of the ERA and Congress had issued its first favorable actions on the amendment. The amendment had also started to pull in support from a number of influential politicians. While these gains were substantial, a few more developments were needed for emancipationism to become a formidable force in the spectrum of American politics. Until then, ERA proponents would have to continue to endure the considerable threat of liberal protectionism.

Protectionism and the Great Depression

The stock market crash of 1929 had plunged America into the longest and deepest depression in its history. The resulting economic turmoil had also moved the center of American politics away from the conservatism of the 1920s toward the New Deal liberalism of the 1930s. Indeed, the economic hard times had largely reduced women's conservative activism. By 1932, for instance, the conservative publication *Woman Patriot* had shut down and the predominantly conservative Daughters of the American Revolution (DAR) had moved away from politics.[122]

Most significantly, the dynamics of the ERA conflict had changed as the political strength of conservatism diminished. In the 1920s conservatives and liberals alike had participated in the ERA opposition work. By the early to mid-1930s, however, the rising power of the Roosevelt administration and its New Deal liberalism had propelled liberal protectionists to the forefront of the Depression-era ERA opposition effort. As a result, conservative ERA opponents retreated from active participation in the conflict; prominent conservative opponents would not return to the controversy until the later part of the next decade. Liberal protectionism thrived during the changing political landscape of the early 1930s, yet by 1936 the growing influence of emancipationism had started to crack the liberal protectionist hold on the ERA conflict.

To understand the liberal protectionist opposition to the ERA, it is important to first discuss the women who had contributed to the New Deal. The "network of New Deal women," a description borrowed from historians Susan Ware and Linda Gordon, included First Lady Eleanor Roosevelt; Mary (Molly) Dewson of the Democratic National Committee; Mary Anderson, head of the Women's

Bureau; Secretary of Labor Frances Perkins; Frieda Miller, head
of the women's division of New York State Department of Labor
and later head of the Women's Bureau; and Rose Schneiderman,
formerly of the NRA (until the Supreme Court overruled it). A
generation of common experiences, such as the woman suffrage
campaign, Progressive-era reform movements, and the social welfare activities of the 1920s, engendered the formation of this New
Deal women's policy network. In sum, the New Deal women created a network of friendship and cooperation that shaped the planning and administration of social legislation until the late 1930s.[123]

This network of New Deal women included social types who
were ready to make larger claims for women in the public sphere,
but they also opposed the ERA. While these women had sought
to improve other women's lives, they favored economic policies
that aimed to restore the male-breadwinner model of the family.
In truth, as historian Nancy Cott observes, many of these women
were "themselves career-oriented and mostly self-supporting. Of an
identifiable group of influential women policy-makers and reformers, two thirds had never been married, and even fewer had children. . . . But they did not take themselves as the norm."[124] These
women did not recognize any contradictions in the gendered ideas
that they were promoting. Even though they held notable positions in the public arena, they believed that domesticity was the
desirable arrangement for most women. Eleanor Roosevelt articulated this position in a radio speech she gave in 1935 in which she
insisted that "the normal woman feels that her home must come
first and that if she falls in love and has children, this is the life
which probably will bring her the greatest lasting happiness."[125]
In general, the New Deal women claimed that for the most part
a wife and mother (especially one with small children) could not
sustain a full-time career successfully. Further still, they assumed
that most women wanted husbands and children and would seek
only part-time or ill-paid employment out of economic necessity.

To be sure, the New Deal women had recognized the difficulties that working women faced during the Great Depression.[126] For
instance, Mary Anderson, leader of the Women's Bureau, asserted
that women workers suffered the most during the economic crisis,

because they were the last to be hired, received the worst jobs, and were underpaid.[127] The New Deal women had certainly wanted to better the conditions of working-class women, but their ideological framework confined their actions. A prime example is how these women and other liberal protectionists opposed Section 213 of the Economy Act.[128] As noted previously, the liberal protectionist defense of women in the workforce largely centered on the need to work, rather than the right to employment.[129] A speech Eleanor Roosevelt made in 1933 illuminates this point. On measures like Section 213, she contended, "in the present depression it may be necessary for a married woman who is working, to voluntarily give up her job in order that some other family may have her salary but . . . this should not be done as a matter of law because legislation cannot take into account individual situations."[130] Eleanor Roosevelt opposed a legal mandate that had effectively pushed married women out of the workforce; however, she did not oppose the underlying principle that women held only conditional rights to work. Following the liberal maternalist reform tradition, the New Deal women had wanted to help destitute women whose economic circumstances forced them to work. Even so, they preferred to restore the husband-father's role as wage earner. Overall, liberal protectionists like the New Deal women supported the traditional view of the family in which the husbands remained principal earners while their wives were homemakers.

As a whole, liberal protectionists, not just the New Deal women, supported increases in special labor legislation during the Depression to alleviate the problems encountered by working women. In particular, liberal protectionists had campaigned for minimum wage laws for women as well as legislation that limited women's work hours. Liberal protectionists found success with these campaigns when in 1934 they convinced seven eastern state legislatures to approve uniform labor legislation for women and children. These interstate compacts regulated women's and children's hours, established a mandatory wage for certain industries, and prohibited night work in manufacturing, mercantile, and mechanical operations establishments.[131] While emancipationists, and soon-to-be emancipationists, criticized such laws as unfair restrictions on women's right to work, liberal protectionists maintained that minimum wage laws for women and children boosted purchasing power and enhanced economic stability.[132] Besides, liberal protectionists asserted, their sex-specific labor laws safeguarded women from economic exploitation.[133] In support of this claim, Democratic senator Robert F. Wagner of New York, a liberal protectionist and staunch supporter of the New Deal and the labor movement, declared in a speech, "To the legion of women who toil in mill and factory, store and laundry, this legislation has provided essential aid in overcoming the many handicaps that beset them.... These women ... have been peculiarly subject to ruthless exploitation, as everyone familiar with our industrial history will know."[134] In all, liberal protectionists viewed the appearance of women in the workforce as an unavoidable evil of the modern world, especially one that was enduring an economic crisis.

By and large, liberal protectionists had wanted to ensure that the women who needed work were able to find and maintain reasonable employment. Consequently, liberal protectionists opposed workplace practices that they considered unfair, such as the temptation to take advantage of women's cheap labor. But there were variations within liberal protectionism on what constituted fair and unfair labor practices. Liberal protectionists who had followed the maternalist tradition, particularly women who belonged to social reform organizations, criticized practices that they believed *unfairly* privileged men workers, such as sex-based wage differentials and laws that forced married women out of the workforce. Yet, the male-dominated organized labor faction of liberal protectionism was less inclined to condemn these policies, particularly the replacement of married women workers with men workers. A few unions had even promoted discriminatory policies against married women workers. Early in the Depression, for example, the Brotherhood of Railway and Steamship Clerks had declared that no married woman whose husband could provide for her was entitled to a job.[135] With these differences aside, liberal protectionists as a whole supported special labor legislation as a necessary government intervention to ensure the health and well-being of society's mothers, potential mothers, and children.

Liberal protectionists also failed to see any connection between their special labor laws and what they considered unfair practices. They maintained that unlike imbalanced labor practices, their policies attended to the special circumstances of women workers, which, in turn, promoted fairness. To back up this claim, Mary C. Wing, legislative secretary of the NCL, asserted in a letter to Democratic senator Pat McCarran that special labor laws created "an actual equality" between men and women workers.[136] Along a related line of thought, Senator Wagner proclaimed in an address to the New York Institute of Women's Professional Relations that there was "no inconsistency in holding on the one hand that women should receive equal treatment with men for the same kind of work, and on the other hand that women should receive special consideration based upon their special circumstances."[137]

From the liberal protectionist viewpoint, there was a double demand on a working woman's energy, as she was not only a wage earner but also a wife and mother. Therefore, they argued, she was subject to a double day: work at the factory and work at home. "Many women," as Mary Anderson of the Women's Bureau put it, "must attend to home responsibilities before and after their day at a paid job. They thus make a double economic contribution to the family. . . . In looking after the food, clothing, shelter, and health of the family, in caring for children and any sick members she is involved in an endless round of tasks."[138] In an effort to ease the harsh conditions of working women's lives, liberal protectionists sought out labor policies that they had assumed would make it easier for working women to fulfill their primary roles as mothers and homemakers. In the minds of liberal protectionists, unfair labor practices exacerbated the economic hardship of working women, while special labor laws affirmed the central importance of women's domestic roles to sustaining American family life. Be that as it may, the idea that women's work outside of the domestic realm was secondary and conditional reinforced the inferior status of women when they did pursue activities that extended beyond the conventional boundaries of the home.[139]

The growing support for the ERA in the mid- to late 1930s did not escape the attention of liberal protectionists. In particular, the

1936 congressional action on the ERA persuaded several liberal protectionist women to form a new opposition group. As Mary Anderson later recalled, "In 1936 when the agitation for the equal rights
amendment was very intense, several of us felt that we should have
a conference."[140] In response to the mounting support for the ERA,
a cohort of liberal protectionist women met in the fall of that year
to devise a new resistance strategy. Attendees included Mary van
Kleeck of the Russell Sage Foundation, Frieda Miller of the New
York State Department of Labor, Lucy Mason of the NCL, and Elisabeth Christman of the NWTUL.[141]

During the meeting these women decided to create a loosely
connected organization, which they called the Women's Charter
Group. As Anderson explained, the organization's objective was to
draft and advance "a general statement of the social and economic
objectives of women . . . insofar as these can be embodied in legislation and government action."[142] This statement, or the Women's
Charter, as Mary van Kleeck described it in a letter to Felix Frankfurter, would "fulfill all the constructive purposes of the equal
rights amendment, while safeguarding special labor legislation for
women."[143] Van Kleeck also wrote in another letter that the Wom-
en's Charter should include "a statement of principles and a formation of a program for common action."[144] In general, the Women's
Charter was intended as a declaration of principles for women's
organizations to adopt as well as a set of guidelines for institutions
to follow when they enacted policies that affected women.[145]

The somewhat lengthy charter began by declaring full civil and
political rights for women. It then went on to outline women's right
to special consideration. Most notably, it professed that women "shall
be assured security of livelihood, including the safeguarding of motherhood." As a Women's Charter Group memorandum summarized
it, the measure would promise women protections "against harmful
working conditions and other forms of exploitation; for the right to
leisure, for the safeguarding of motherhood; and for security of livelihood for themselves and for their families."[146] While the charter
championed full civil and political rights for women citizens, it qualified that principle of equality by proclaiming that women, as mothers
and potential mothers, had a natural right to special treatment.

In its calls for equality and special consideration, the Women's Charter represents the first protectionist attempt to develop an alternative comprehensive measure to compete with the ERA. As van Kleeck contended, "We seek to go far beyond the demand for 'equal rights.'"[147] In a similar vein, Elinore Morehouse Herrick, director of the Regional Labor Board and a Women's Charter Group member, announced that, unlike the ERA, the charter would "really face facts." Furthermore, she continued, "if women really want 'equal rights' here is their opportunity."[148] Likewise, Blanch Freedman, a New York lawyer long active in the NWTUL and also a Women's Charter Group member, suggested that the charter would create "genuine equality," because in contrast to the ERA it would recognize "woman's function of motherhood in conjunction with her role as a worker, and society's responsibility for the special problems involved."[149] From the perspective of the Women's Charter Group members, their measure promised a sensible equality between men and women citizens that would acknowledge the need for women to have special rights in light of their roles as mothers and caregivers.

Despite about a year of concerted work on the measure, the charter movement ultimately failed. As Anderson described it, "nothing worked out the way we had wanted it to. The movement was a complete flop."[150] For starters, the group's members fought over the publicity strategy. A few members had wanted to publicize the idea of the Women's Charter as soon as possible, while others had advised taking a more cautious approach toward announcing the measure in order to avoid giving the NWP an opportunity to publicly condemn it.[151] Women's Charter Group members also expressed concerns about how to explain the purpose of the charter and its relation to special labor legislation. In a letter to Ruth Hanna of the Young Women's Christian Association (YWCA), Lucy Mason of the NCL, a Women's Charter Group leader, wrote that when explaining the charter to other women's organizations, she felt it necessary to "avoid the use of the phrase 'protective legislation for women' and to say instead 'legislation which affects women only.'" In her view "the word 'protective' acts as a red rag to the bull."[152] But Anderson dismissed these concerns. She insisted that the charter should include a strong and explicit endorsement of special labor legislation for women. "I think it is too bad," she complained in one letter, "that some of our good organizations quibble over words when after all, all that they need to do is to endorse the principles that they have always stood for."[153]

A deeper methodological problem had plagued the charter movement as well. In the mid- to late 1930s many liberal protectionists still favored the "specific method" as the best strategy for defeating the ERA. As explained in the previous chapter, the specific method was the predominant protectionist alternative to the ERA in the 1920s and early 1930s. This position held that if women's societal standing needed improvement, then action should come primarily at the state level, with specific legislation for specific problems. For a considerable number of liberal protectionists the specific method still provided the best counterargument to the emancipationist call for complete constitutional sexual equality. Even Lucy Mason, one of the founders of the Women's Charter Group, expressed reservations about the movement's objectives: "If it is a question of attempting to go farther in an endeavor to meet the Woman's Party point of view[,] . . . I want to put myself on record as saying I think it is impossible for those of us interested in the charter ever to meet the Woman's Party point of view. The more we concede to them the more danger there is that they will misinterpret what we have said."[154] While the charter upheld the protectionist doctrine of separate standards of rights for men and women citizens, at this time too many liberal protectionists feared that an alternative comprehensive declaration of equality would fuel rather than break the ERA's momentum.

Although liberal protectionists had failed to rally around the Women's Charter in the mid-1930s, the rising support for the ERA continued to strike a chord with several liberal protectionists. In the spring of 1937 Ruth Hanna of the YWCA wrote to Lucy Mason that she was "rather disturbed" at the "increasing support of the Woman's Party view."[155] A few days after New Year's Day in 1938, Dorothy Straus of the LWV also expressed her concerns to Molly Dewson, head of the Women's Division of the Democratic National Committee, about the amendment. "It is amazing," Straus commented in her letter to Dewson, "how the measure [ERA] seems to have recovered from the various doses of anaesthetic that it has from time to time been given." She went on to claim that ERA opponents needed to issue a direct attack on the measure, complaining, "I think it is about time that we got annoyed. . . . There is no reason why we should not express ourselves with rather more force than we have in the past." She also grumbled, "What I should like to do is to kill it once and for all."[156] As the next chapters convey, it would take many years for protectionists to curtail the rise of emancipationism. Most of all, they would have to return to the strategy underlying the charter initiative; they would have to develop their own comprehensive approaches for advancing their belief in the distinct rights of men and women citizens.

Conclusion

The Depression years had marked a turning point in the ERA conflict, as support for the amendment steadily increased from the mid- to late 1930s. Similar to the destabilizing nature of the Nineteenth Amendment, the economic turmoil of the Depression had undermined the traditional sexual order. Most notably, the economic instability had highlighted the concrete ramifications of sex-specific treatment, which eventually caused more women's organizations to oppose sex-based labor legislation. The Depression had also thrust liberal protectionists to the forefront of American politics; however, inherent ideological limitations narrowed their ability to adequately respond to the mounting discriminations against women in the workforce. In contrast, the NWP directly attacked the Depression-era restrictions on women's right to work. Moreover, the NWP's economic campaign encouraged more women's groups to embrace emancipationism and back the ERA. As support for the ERA grew among women's groups, Congress became receptive to the idea of constitutional sexual equality and it issued its first favorable actions on the amendment. Although a few more developments were needed for emancipationism to become a pronounced influence in American politics, the changing political and socioeconomic conditions of the Great Depression had cleared the path for the rise of emancipationism.

4

"We Women Want to Be Persons Now"

The Rise of Emancipationism, 1938–1945

At a 1945 Senate subcommittee hearing on the ERA, Emma Guffey Miller, who was a prominent Democratic Party member and an emerging authority within the NWP, declared, "We women want to be persons now because we are still not persons in the Constitution of the United States."[1] Miller was one of the most influential Democratic women in the state of Pennsylvania. In 1932 she had been elected a member of the Democratic National Committee from her home state; it was a post she would hold until her death in 1970. For several years Miller had also been serving as the official hostess for her brother, Democratic senator Joseph F. Guffey. That such a leading force within the Democratic Party had joined the ranks of prominent ERA supporters demonstrates the extent to which the emancipationist movement had grown by the end of World War II.[2] At the close of the war a range of cultural and political luminaries had endorsed the ERA, which invigorated the emancipationist momentum.[3] Both political parties had also backed the amendment in their party platforms by this time, and the rising support for the ERA had spurred significant congressional action on the amendment during the 1940s. As this chapter discusses, the Fair Labor Standards Act (FLSA) and World War II strengthened the growing energy behind the ERA, because these developments had further dislocated conventional sex boundaries. Protectionism would return to its leading position in the postwar era, but the rising support for the ERA from the late 1930s through the mid-1940s shows that the protectionist victory was not a foregone conclusion to the original ERA conflict.

Advancement in the Senate

In the early winter weeks of 1938 members of several liberal protectionist organizations, including the NCL, the NWTUL, and the LWV, flooded the office of Democratic senator Henry Ashurst of Arizona, who chaired the Senate Judiciary Committee, with letters urging him to call a hearing on the ERA. These leaders had hoped that such a hearing would provide them with the opportunity to publicly condemn the ERA and ultimately kill the amendment's momentum.[4] Due to their letter-writing campaign, Democratic senator Edward Burke of Nebraska, who chaired the Senate Judiciary subcommittee on the ERA, called a public hearing on the amendment. The subsequent hearing began on February 7 and lasted four days; it was the longest and most extensive congressional hearing on the amendment since its introduction into Congress in 1923.[5]

Dorothy Straus, a legal advisor to the LWV, orchestrated the protectionist strategy for the 1938 congressional hearing. As noted in the previous chapter, Straus was an ardent foe of the emancipationist position, and in the beginning of 1938 she had found the increased support for the ERA quite alarming.[6] As an urban professional woman who had backed socially active government policies, Straus was a member of the liberal protectionist cohort that fiercely despised the ERA. While she believed that women should have an expanded public role, she felt that women required a distinct set of rights. With regard to the hearing, Straus enlisted a variety of figures, including legal scholars, religious authorities, political leaders, and social reformers, to testify and submit statements on behalf of the protectionist cause. Most of these figures were liberal protectionists, as the liberal wing of the protectionist position was still dominating the opposition effort. Even so, a handful of conservative protectionists did testify at the hearing.[7]

Before the hearing Straus explained to Democratic Party organizer Molly Dewson that she was "very keen" to make sure that ERA opponents moved beyond their tendency to focus on the "labor aspect" of their arguments against the amendment. Straus believed that the growing antipathy toward sex-specific labor policies had made that aspect "somewhat less important."[8] To be clear, a number of protectionists who had testified at the 1938 hearing did touch upon women's need for special protection in the industrial realm.[9] But to a large extent this diverse group of individuals chose to emphasize another criticism of the ERA, or what Straus had identified as the most "dangerous aspect" of the amendment: its threat to American society.[10]

At the hearing the protectionists argued that the ERA would imperil the American legal tradition and subvert the American social order. To make this argument, they claimed that the legal framework of American society affirmed the importance of men's and women's natural roles. On this point, Straus testified, "distinctions in the law recognized what we consider established biological factors." She went on to declare that those who supported the amendment erroneously wanted to "legislate" and "recreate" woman in the "image of man."[11] Thus, as with the congressional hearings of the 1920s and early 1930s, protectionists once again argued that the American legal system correctly acknowledged biological differences between men and women and rightly held them to separate standards.

In their defense of the American legal tradition, protectionists continued to appeal to the dependent woman theory embedded in the common law tradition of domestic duties in an effort to justify sex-based rights. At the 1938 hearing, for example, a well-known Chicago lawyer, Edgar Bronson Tolman, claimed that the amendment "would take from women protection now given by law. . . . It might deprive them of present exemptions and immunities; such as compulsory military service, poll tax, and labor on the roads." In a similar line of argument, William J. Millard, a justice of the Washington state Supreme Court, advised in a statement presented to the Senate subcommittee, "The effect of the amendment, I fear, would be to deprive women of rights they now have, and to which they are entitled, because they are women."[12] In short, protectionists still maintained that the ERA would endanger women's distinct status and their distinct set of rights.

It is important to remember here that for protectionists the natural family arrangement followed a precedent that was set by the
common law tradition of domestic relations: wives supplied their
husbands with children and household services, and in return
husbands provided their wives with financial support and protection. In the protectionist mind-set, however, the ERA subverted this
old law of domestic relations and destabilized the conventional
responsibilities of husband and wife. Justice Millard put this view
into words in his statement by simply asking the Senate subcommittee, "Does this equality mean that the law requiring a man to
support his wife will apply equally to women?"[13] Dean Acheson,
an ever-resolute critic of the ERA, further explained what he saw
as the amendment's legal implications during his testimony. He
argued that "in all the States and Territories except 14, the husband
has the legal obligation to support his wife, and the wife does not
have the legal obligation to support her husband. What would be
the effect of the amendment upon that? Would it mean the wife
would be subject to the duty of supporting her husband . . . that
runs through all the relations of husband and wife." Protectionists
believed that the old law of domestic relations provided a structure
that sustained the American family and ensured social stability. In
the end, protectionists asserted, the ERA would undermine the
traditional family structure by destroying women's special status.[14]

Similar to the congressional hearings of the 1920s and early
1930s, protectionists maintained that they were not against the idea
of equality altogether; rather, they avowed, they favored practical
measures that promoted "real equality" between the sexes. Even
the conservative Mrs. Rufus M. Gibbs, who had begun her testimony by proudly proclaiming that she had "always been against
feminism, socialism, and communism," commented that she was
not necessarily against "justice and fair play for the sexes." But, she
claimed, the ERA "was not the way." In her view the amendment
went against "the condition of human nature" and constituted "a
very serious handicap to our civilization."[15] Longtime social activist
Ethel Smith of the NWTUL further expounded on the protectionist notion of equality. She stated that she and other amendment
opponents backed measures that brought "women up to the sta-

tus of men and at the same time secure[d] . . . women's separate, independent needs."[16] Above all, for protectionists practical equality meant affirming sex differences and preserving sex boundaries.

Protectionists also continued to acknowledge that the old tradition of domestic relations had produced a number of outdated laws. But they insisted that the doctrine should be reformed and not completely set aside. As Mrs. John Hader of the NCL exclaimed in her testimony, "We do not believe in throwing the baby out with the bath water."[17] For handling women's legal disadvantages, protectionists once again advocated for the "specific method." According to Dorothy Straus, only the specific method would achieve "real equality" because it would attend to the particular needs of women and therefore "bring women up to a state of equality."[18] As before, protectionists contended that the specific method would allow lawmakers to carefully address certain legal disabilities while leaving the otherwise equitable legal distinctions intact.

Although protectionists provided an extensive analysis of what they had perceived to be the amendment's inherent threat to American society, the 1938 hearing actually turned out to be another considerable victory for emancipationists. For starters, more than fifteen organizations in addition to the NWP sent representatives to testify in support of the amendment. Additionally, numerous national as well as state and local organizations had gone on record in support of the ERA, and a handful of prominent individuals, including activist Helen Keller, artist Georgia O'Keeffe, and playwright Rachel Crothers sent statements endorsing the ERA to the Senate subcommittee.[19]

Despite protectionists' hopes, the hearing had actually given emancipationists a public platform on which to display their amendment's growing support. In addition, the Senate subcommittee members acted quite receptive to the amendment during the 1938 hearing. Toward the beginning of the hearing, for instance, Republican senator Warren Austin of Vermont suggested that he believed there was potential for the ERA to act in accordance with "what was contemplated by the founders of our American system."[20] This positive interest in the amendment was rather different from the open hostility that other members of Congress had displayed during the ERA congressional hearings of the 1920s and early 1930s. The sympathetic attitude of the subcommittee was partly due to the work of its chairperson, Senator Edward Burke.[21] As explained in the previous chapter, Senator Burke had been one of several New Deal critics who had become active ERA supporters in the mid- to late 1930s.

Besides Senator Burke's support, there were other factors accounting for the success of emancipationism at the 1938 hearing. From its outset, emancipationists effectively connected their position to the more pressing concerns that were preoccupying the attention of the nation's leaders. To capture the senators' attention during the hearing, for example, emancipationists linked the ERA to issues that dealt with the ongoing socioeconomic changes of the Great Depression, as well as the destructive influence of rising totalitarian governments and the subsequent worldwide political upheaval. In particular, emancipationists argued that the ERA would assist the economic recovery and fulfill America's democratic promise. Moreover, they contended that the ERA would strengthen the country as a whole, as it would reinforce American political and economic ideals, which would help the country to withstand the rising tide of fascism. With regard to the period's economic turmoil, emancipationists contended that in a world plagued by irregular work and persistent unemployment, most families had grown to rely on the financial contributions of men and women alike. At the 1938 hearing Dorothy Ashby Moncure of the NAWL asserted in her testimony that "economic conditions have forced women to assume the same burdens formerly assumed by man." She ended her testimony by stating, "If the conditions of today had existed at the time the Bill of Rights was adopted, the equal rights amendment would have been included therein."[22]

Emancipationists were actually on the right path in their assessment of women's Depression-era employment experiences. As detailed in the previous chapter, the Depression did witness a rise in discriminations against working women. By almost every measure, however, women's participation in labor conducted outside of the home actually *increased* during the 1930s. During the Depression women's share of the labor force grew from 22 to 25 percent,

while the percentage of all adult women who were in the workforce grew from 24.3 to 25.4 percent. Additionally, the proportion
of married women who were employed grew from 12 to 15 percent.
As will be discussed later, the socioeconomic demands of World
War II accelerated this trend; by 1945, for example, women's share
of the civilian labor force had risen to 36 percent.[23]

Thus, despite the numerous attacks on women's right to work,
the number of women who worked outside of the home had continued to grow. This increase can be partly attributed to the fact that
women generally worked for lower wages.[24] The Depression also
dealt a sharper shock in sections of the economy with higher numbers of male workers, such as mining and heavy industry; areas in
which female workers dominated, such as service and clerical fields,
had suffered less of a hit. The sexual stratification of the workforce,
then, persisted during the Depression. This persistence forced the
increasing number of women entering the labor force into lower-
paid positions.[25] So, in the face of the attacks on women's right to
work, the number of working women grew, but that increase was
generally in low-level, low-skilled, low-paid, dead-end jobs.

Even with these limitations, emancipationists believed that
the Depression era had ushered in a new social reality that could
broaden the scope of women's social functions and open the door
for women to gain economic independence. From the emancipationist perspective, the growth in women's work outside of the
home was a considerable step toward the release of women from
their enslavement under the common law tradition of domestic
duties. Nonetheless, according to the emancipationist viewpoint,
sex-specific labor legislation hampered the economic recovery
and therefore distorted the potential of this new social reality.
"While it might be very attractive to have all women leading a life
of ease and leisure at home," Emma Guffey Miller asserted at the
1938 hearing, "we must face the facts and acknowledge that such
a time[,] if it ever existed out of Eden, has gone forever." Miller
finished by stressing that if the country's leaders wanted to raise
millions of "low-lived people to a higher standard, the only way to
do it . . . will be to have more than one breadwinner in the family."[26] At the hearing emancipationists claimed that equal economic

opportunities for men and women were essential for advancing the economic recovery. They reasoned that both men and women needed access to adequate incomes in order to raise their families' standard of living. In all, emancipationists argued that the ERA would encourage an economic upturn by removing the barriers that unfairly prevented women from earning a sufficient living.

Furthermore, during the hearing, emancipationists claimed that the rising international threat to democracy demanded that America pass the ERA to show that it stood firm in its democratic beliefs. Sarah Gibbs Pell, who had been a noted supporter of the suffrage movement and was a member of the NWP, articulated this position in her testimony. She declared, "This is a critical time in the world's affairs. . . . Democracy is no longer safe. . . . The issue is crystal clear. Shall the women citizens of this Nation be given, in constitutional form, the final and fullest expression of the liberties they deserve?"[27] For emancipationists the situation was urgent. To withstand the increasing threats to American political ideals, they argued, the country needed to fulfill its democratic promise and pass the ERA.

In the view of several influential protectionists the hearing had been a disappointment. In their opinion, too many subcommittee members had simply dismissed the merits of their claims. On the apparent failure Dean Acheson wrote to Elisabeth Christman of the NWTUL that while he was "very glad" to have testified at the hearing, he believed that the majority of committee members were "in favor" of the amendment.[28] Mary Dublin, general secretary of the NCL, expressed similar concern to a colleague, noting that she found it "appalling" that amendment proponents had been able to "marshal so much influence" with the senators.[29] In the weeks immediately following the hearing a *New York Times* article reported that Dorothy Straus was in the process of creating an organization dedicated to stopping the ERA and that she planned to call it "The Campaign Committee of 500 against the Equal Rights Amendment." As the article explained, amendment opponents needed to create a unified organization, because a "crisis ha[d] arisen in our fight against the Equal Rights Amendment." It went on to observe that there was "a serious danger that the amendment may be reported out of the Judiciary Committee for vote on the Senate floor."[30] Due to the events that transpired after the hearing, this anti-ERA campaign committee failed to take off. Nonetheless, amendment opponents would resurrect this idea in the next decade, when the ERA made progress through Congress once more.

In March 1938 the full Senate Judiciary Committee voted to report the ERA to the Senate floor. The committee, however, reported the amendment without recommendation. While this was a limited victory, it was the first time the measure had reached the floor of either legislative chamber.[31] On the relative victory, Emma Guffey Miller wrote in an article for *Equal Rights* that the recent development reflected a "growing sentiment throughout the country for a New Deal for women."[32] But the imperfect achievement was short-lived. When the Senate reached the amendment on May 5, a steadfast critic of the ERA, Republican senator William E. Borah of Idaho, moved to have the measure recommitted to the Senate Judiciary Committee.[33]

Although the ERA failed to make substantial progress immediately after the 1938 hearing, the hearing itself had pushed emancipationists to develop a more appealing line of reasoning for the ERA, which further connected the amendment to the economic recovery and the unfolding turmoil wreaking havoc on the sphere of international politics. Emancipationists would continue to turn to these arguments over the next several years to build even more support for the ERA. At the close of the 1930s, for example, emancipationists would argue that the ERA could improve New Deal initiatives such as the FLSA, and, when the United States' entered World War II in 1941, emancipationists would insist that the passage of the ERA could uphold American political ideals to help the country withstand the escalating international threat to democracy. By situating the foundational arguments for the ERA against a backdrop of many pressing contemporary concerns, emancipationists were able to emphasize how they saw the ERA as an act that would enhance American principles and not transform them. As a result, their efforts advanced the trend toward emancipationism that was already under way.

The Fair Labor Standards Act and the Equal Rights Amendment

During the beginning of Franklin Roosevelt's presidency, the U.S. Supreme Court had strongly resisted the administration's effort to move to a new constitutional understanding that would allow the federal government to act aggressively in tackling the economic depression. As late as 1936 the Supreme Court had insisted in two decisions, *Carter v. Carter* and *Morehead v. New York ex rel. Tipaldo*, that the Constitution prohibited both Congress and state legislatures from regulating the conditions of labor.[34] Therefore, it seemed as though the high court was determined to sustain a strict interpretation of the Commerce Clause and uphold the freedom of contract principle. The Supreme Court's reluctance to move toward a new constitutional understanding dates back to the so-called *Lochner* era of the early twentieth century. During that time the high court had held that under the Due Process Clauses of the Fifth and Fourteenth Amendments, citizens were entitled to make free contracts without government intrusion. Consequently, courts had found that the majority of government efforts to regulate the terms of work (wage hours and working conditions) were unconstitutional. Yet, the Supreme Court had for the most part excluded women from that freedom of contract principle. This exclusion began with the court's ruling in *Muller v. Oregon* (1908). As discussed in chapter 1, the high court had reasoned that women required special protection on the assumption that women were inherently weaker persons. As well, the court had maintained that special protection for women safeguarded the overall health and safety of the public, because women were presumed to be society's caregivers.

Months after President Roosevelt had won a landslide re-election victory in the 1936 election, the Supreme Court surprised almost everyone by handing down a series of decisions that ushered in what a number of scholars have described as "the first constitutional revolution."[35] This revolution included decisions that upheld many of the Roosevelt administration's Second New Deal social policies. In the process the high court moved away from the freedom of contract doctrine and its traditionally narrow interpretation of the Commerce Clause. More broadly speaking, the court's decisions provided a constitutional validation for the new under-standing of liberty that was developing alongside the emerging con-cepts of economic and social citizenship. Thus, it appeared that the Supreme Court was henceforth in agreement with the notion that civic liberty meant protection against economic exploitation as well as the right to act collectively. This notion of liberty, more-over, espoused a positive view of the state and its ability to act in the interest of the larger public.[36]

The New Deal constitutional revolution began with the high court's ruling in *West Coast Hotel Co. v. Parrish* (1937). In this deci-sion the court upheld a law establishing a minimum wage for working women. To reach this conclusion, the court denied the freedom of contract principle. "The Constitution," Chief Justice Charles Evans Hughes wrote in the majority opinion, "does not speak of freedom of contract. . . . The liberty safeguarded is lib-erty in a social organization which requires the protection of the law against the evils which menace the health, safety, morals, and welfare of the people." In other words the court was now envision-ing rights as being historically positioned and related to the wel-fare of the public.[37] In *West Coast Hotel* the court advised that the state could intervene in the economy on behalf of men workers as well women workers. On this groundbreaking suggestion the court declared, "The argument that the legislation in question consti-tutes an arbitrary discrimination, because it does not extend to men, is unavailing. . . . The legislature is 'free to recognize degrees of harm and it may confine its restrictions to those classes of cases when the need is deemed the clearest."[38] In *Muller* the court had justified state intervention for women by setting women workers apart as a distinct group. In *West Coast Hotel*, however, the court suggested that the state had a right to intervene in the economy to protect both men and women workers. For the court the dif-ference was just a matter of degree between the levels of protec-tion.[39] Four years later the court would draw upon this logic when it upheld the FLSA in *United States v. Darby Lumber Co.* (1941).[40]

Two weeks after the Supreme Court's ruling in *West Coast Hotel,* it upheld the National Labor Relations Act in *National Labor Rela-tions Board v. Jones and Laughlin Steel Corporation* (1937). This decision affirmed a revised interpretation of the Commerce Clause that enlarged the scope of the federal government's regulatory power.[41] With these two decisions, the Supreme Court had undermined the strict interpretation of the Commerce Clause and the sanctity of the freedom of contract doctrine. Since the judicial hurdles to a national labor standard had been removed, President Roosevelt sent to Congress a comprehensive bill on wages and work hours in late May 1937.[42]

Due to the bill's turbulent journey through Congress, it would take a little more than a year before President Roosevelt was able to sign a limited version of his bill into law. Nonetheless, once that bill was enacted the FLSA established the unprecedented principle that the federal government had the right to control the wages and hours of both men and women engaged in occupations related to interstate commerce. The statute instituted a forty-four-hour work week, which would be reduced in three years to forty hours and require overtime pay for those working more than forty hours. It created a minimum wage of twenty-five cents per hour; this level would slowly increase until it reached forty cents in seven years. Unlike the codes of the previous National Recovery Administration, the FLSA did not permit classifications by sex for minimum wage purposes. Hence, it was intended for the minimum wage clause to apply equally to men and women workers. Until the FLSA was amended with the Equal Pay Act of 1963, sex-based wage differentials above the minimum wage level were still legal.[43] Even so, the FLSA had established for the first time in the United States a national labor standard that covered male and female workers alike.[44]

For most liberal protectionists, the act symbolized the victory of a principle: the establishment of the government's right to intervene on behalf of men and women workers. In general, they believed that increased hours and minimum wage legislation would help end the Depression. More specifically, New Deal protectionists thought that the FLSA would remedy certain societal ills, or what Secretary of Labor Frances Perkins called the "evils of child labor, sweatshops, and low wages." New Deal protectionists also claimed that the FLSA would do away with the problem of "wage cutter" businesses that sold their products at a lower cost than the competition because they paid penny-pinching wages.[45] Altogether, New Deal protectionists believed that the FLSA would protect employees, grant more security to businesses through the minimum wage, create more purchasing power for citizens, and eventually trigger economic growth.

But, the FLSA had significant flaws. It barred from coverage so many groups of workers that its provisions applied to only 20 percent of the labor force.[46] The law disproportionately excluded women workers, including those who worked in the low-paid jobs of retail, restaurant and hotel service, domestic labor, and clerical vocations.[47] While the measure covered 39 percent of adult working men, its provisions extended to only 14 percent of working women. The bill also excluded many Black women workers, as more than a third of them worked as domestic servants. Male industrial workers benefited the most from the act. This was largely due to the overtime provisions, which mandated time-and-a-half wage rates for hours worked beyond forty a week. Special labor laws prevented most industrial female workers from taking advantage of the extra-pay clause, because such laws restricted the hours of working women.[48]

These flaws are partly due to the compromises that occurred during the FLSA's tumultuous congressional journey. But the act's limitations too stemmed from the gendered principles of the administrative officials who drafted the original bill. As historian Suzanne Mettler persuasively argues, "it was in the quiet drafting of the bill by administration officials that the majority of low-paid women workers and non-white men, those who could have benefited most from national labor standards, were exempted from coverage."[49] The intentions behind the group that drafted the initial labor bill are important for understanding the original ERA conflict because that group included prominent amendment opponents such as future Supreme Court justice Felix Frankfurter and Roosevelt's secretary of labor, Frances Perkins.[50] New Deal protectionists and liberal protectionists in general had wanted a national labor standard to place a floor under workers' wages as well as a ceiling over their hours. Yet, their intention was not to have the FLSA displace

the rationale for sex-based labor policies. The liberal protectionists who contributed to the drafting of the labor bill had intentionally designed the measure so that it left the state-level special
labor laws for women workers intact.[51] Perkins assured Congress
of this point during an FLSA congressional hearing when she testified that the bill was only intended to "supplement" the state-
level special labor laws that were already in place.[52]

The architects of the FLSA had hoped that a national labor
standard with narrow coverage would enhance state-level laws for
women and encourage the development of extra state-level initiatives. From their viewpoint, state measures were more effective for dealing with the special needs of women workers.[53] In a
later congressional hearing on the ERA, for instance, Perkins contended that unlike the FLSA, state-level labor laws were specifically
"designed to safeguard women" by providing women "with days
of rest and rest periods" and by "prohibiting dangerous work or
work at night or in places deemed unwholesome to the morals
and health of women." She concluded that these state-level special labor laws were based on "the unique biological function of
women and their responsibilities as homemakers and mothers of
future citizens."[54]

The framers of the FLSA had crafted the measure in such a way
that it not only left special labor laws in place but also ensured that
the states remained free to regulate women's work in rather different ways from how it dealt with men's work.[55] They had excluded
a large proportion of the female labor force from the measure
because they assumed that the typical experience of working women
was essentially dissimilar from that of working men. To start, they
thought that most women's occupations belonged to an entirely
separate realm than those industries in which men had usually
constituted most of the workforce. When, for example, journalists brought up southerners' concerns that the FLSA might mandate that housewives "pay your negro girl eleven dollars a week,"
President Roosevelt insisted, "No law ever suggested/intended a
minimum wages and hours bill to apply to domestic help."[56] The
persistent belief that women's true place was in the home—and
that when they did leave the home they were best suited to doing

work that replicated their natural domestic duties—consequently reduced women's work to being seen as unskilled and amateurish. This protectionist mind-set resulted in a marketplace segregated by sex, which consistently valued men's work over women's work.[57]

Although emancipationists had challenged this view for years, protectionists believed that men had dependents and women typically did not. In the view of liberal protectionists, men needed a family wage to ensure that married women did not have to work. At the FLSA congressional hearing, for instance, labor leader John Lewis of the Congress of Industrial Organizations (CIO) proclaimed that "a husband and father should be able to earn enough to support his family." He went on to assert that he was not against "the employment of women, or even of wives," when it was a result of their "own free choice." But, he concluded, "I am violently opposed to a system which by degrading the earning of adult males, makes it economically necessary for wives and children to become supplementary wage earners, and then says, 'See the nice income of this family.'"[58] Lewis clearly voiced his belief that if a woman had chosen to work, then she was entitled to a fair wage; however, his main concern was with the struggle of working men. In his mind, normal families relied on the financial income of a single male breadwinner. In a similar line of reasoning, Perkins contended at an ERA congressional hearing that, unlike men, women workers were "not the primary family breadwinners . . . they are frequently casual workers."[59] In short, New Deal protectionists excluded most women workers from the provisions of the FLSA because they believed that the average woman worker was incapable of the labor patterns and activities performed by men. In all, liberal protectionists saw in the FLSA the establishment of a dual system of labor standards: a national standard that promised sufficient wages and reasonable work hours for a mostly white, male workforce and the continuance of a state-level standard that promoted sex-specific, regional initiatives to help working women fulfill their primary duties in the domestic realm.[60]

The Supreme Court upheld the FLSA in its 1941 landmark decision in *United States v. Darby Lumber Co.* The newly elevated chief justice, Harlan F. Stone, had written the majority opinion. In the

decision Justice Stone stated that civic liberty did not require a
total absence of government regulation or support in the work
realm. Most important, he ruled that the "statute is not objec-
tionable because [it] applied alike to both men and women."[61]
Emancipationist Helen Elizabeth Brown, president of the Wom-
en's Bar Association of Baltimore, admired that such a statement
had been "made at all." In her view, the ruling suggested that men
and women were moving closer toward the attainment of "equal
working rights."[62]

While liberal protectionists maintained that the FLSA merely
supplemented women's special labor legislation, emancipationists
insisted that the FLSA, along with the *Darby* ruling, had effectively
dislodged the rationale for such legislation. As Dr. Lena Madesin
Phillips of the BPWC announced, "Whatever the situation may
have been in the past, the Fair Labor Standards Act has now set
the standard."[63] From the emancipationist viewpoint, the FLSA and
Darby had begun to alter the legal sexual order by extending the
government's protective umbrella to include men citizens. What is
more, emancipationists contended that these acts validated their
assertion that economic regulation could be based on the nature
of the work and not on the sex of the worker.[64]

For emancipationists, the FLSA and the ruling in *Darby* had
made claims for sex equality more attractive because equality no
longer meant access to negative freedoms, such as the freedom
of contract doctrine. As Caroline Lexow Babcock of the NWP put
it, "the chief objection to the Equal Rights Amendment has been
eliminated by the *Darby* decision. . . . The Equal Rights Amendment would unquestionably hasten the universal application of
this principle in industry as elsewhere."[65] As this comment suggests, emancipationists argued that the FLSA and *Darby* had neu-
tralized the labor aspect of amendment opponents' arguments,
since it appeared that labor safeguards could legally apply to men
and women alike.[66]

Even though emancipationists saw the FLSA as a step toward
constitutional equality for men and women citizens, they recognized that the measure had significant flaws. As explained, the
FLSA applied to "persons" engaged in interstate commerce. The

measure, however, left in place state-level labor laws that specifically regulated women's work. As a result, women workers engaged in interstate commerce did not benefit from all the provisions of the FLSA, such as the overtime clause, because special labor laws prevented women from working extra hours. Consequently, the NWP argued in *Congressional Digest* that "equal pay for equal work is impossible of attainment when men and women do not work under the same regulations."[67]

For emancipationists, the continuation of sex-specific labor laws had rendered largely symbolic the equality principle embedded in the minimum-wage provision of the FLSA. Emancipationist Nora Stanton Barney, granddaughter of Elizabeth Cady Stanton, elaborated on this viewpoint in a pamphlet titled *Women as Human Beings.* In it she maintained that while the FLSA had extended labor protections to include men, it left in place laws that encouraged occupational segregation of the sexes. She explained that with sex-specific labor laws, a married woman could not teach, which resulted in hundreds of women being forced out of work. She also noted that several labor laws had prohibited women from carrying objects over a certain weight, which then forced women out of waitressing jobs. Laws that had banned women from working at night gave rise to the exclusion of women from obtaining jobs as printers, proofreaders, musicians, singers, and factory workers. Finally, she noted that laws that had required women's work to be consecutive hours of the day and not in split shifts subsequently disqualified women from jobs such as streetcar conductor and bus driver. For Barney and other emancipationists, sex-specific labor laws had continued to deny women their personhood because such laws unfairly restricted women's economic rights. Since those laws remained intact, emancipationists maintained that there was still a battle to be won to ensure that women enjoyed all the benefits of the FLSA as persons under the law.[68]

In their critiques of the FLSA, emancipationists had returned to one of their main arguments from the 1938 hearing, which was that the passage of the ERA would improve America's economic recovery. To support this claim, they contended that the ERA would enhance the FLSA and lead to better labor conditions for all workers. "The Equal Rights Amendment," members of the NWP claimed in an article for *Congressional Digest*, "will actually place labor legislation on a sounder basis by making it necessary to regulate the hours, wages, and conditions of work of all adult workers on an equal basis."[69] As this comment suggests, emancipationists believed that the ERA would not only ensure that sensible labor regulations applied equally to men and women but also that it would remove the inequitable regulations that had marked women as being less capable and more dependent in the economic domain.

The FLSA and *Darby* eventually encouraged more people to adopt the emancipationist position and publicly endorse the ERA. In *Congressional Digest*, for example, Arthur Meier Schlesinger Sr., an acclaimed scholar of American history, pointed to the changes in American labor standards to explain his support for the amendment. "In recent years," he reasoned, "legislation has extended to men wage-earners most of the advantages earlier granted exclusively to women. . . . No substantial objection of a practical character remains for treating the two groups of workers differently, whereas the principles of democracy require that they should be treated alike."[70] Anna Kelton Wiley and Lucy Dickinson, by this time associated with the GFWC, an organization that would endorse the ERA a little more than two years after the *Darby* ruling, also looked to the changes in labor standards to promote the amendment. In a letter to their congressional representatives, they declared, "We believe that labor laws should be based on the nature of the work. . . . The Supreme Court in the Darby Lumber case in 1941 held that maximum hour and minimum wage legislation may be applied to both men and women." As a result, they argued, "'equality of rights' under the law for women is a principle which should be incorporated in our Constitution because it is a basic human right."[71]

Two years after President Roosevelt had signed the FLSA into law, the Republican Party endorsed the ERA in its party platform in June 1940. With the help of platform committee chair George Wharton Pepper, a new supporter of the emancipationist cause, members of the NWP successfully lobbied for the ERA at the Republican National Convention in Philadelphia.[72] To understand this development, it is important to return to a trend discussed in the previous chapter. Starting in the mid- to late 1930s, the ERA began to draw the support of a number of pro-business, conservative-minded politicians who were not firmly committed to the notion that sex constituted a legitimate legal classification in and of itself. Conservative ERA proponents, moreover, argued that the amendment would help remove unnecessary government regulations that unfairly restricted women's ability to freely compete in the marketplace.[73] Pepper, a conservative-leaning public figure and a New Deal critic, moved to support the ERA as a way to back private enterprise and challenge the power of the Roosevelt administration. In the end Pepper, along with a handful of the NWP's members, successfully convinced the Republican Party to endorse the ERA in its platform as a symbol of the party's commitment to individual economic self-fulfillment.[74]

The passage of the FLSA and the Republican platform endorsement prompted a number of emancipationists to declare that the country's two major political parties had practically agreed on the issue of sexual equality. In a 1941 radio broadcast Democratic senator Guy Gillette of Iowa, who would go on to become an influential supporter of the ERA, asserted, "It might be said that there are no party lines in regard to the equal-rights amendment. The Republicans have declared for it in their national platform. The Democrats have passed legislation which the courts have interpreted as wiping out the only objection to it." He ended by stating that "both parties are united on this measure which is so important to complete our democracy and bring our Constitution up to date." Overall, the FLSA inspired more support for the ERA because it had undermined much of the logic behind special labor legislation for women, and with the Republican Party's subsequent endorsement of the ERA the emancipationists were now able to assert that it appeared that both political parties generally favored equal treatment under the law for men and women citizens.[75]

Emancipationism Progresses in Wartime America

The Japanese attack on Pearl Harbor in December 1941 threw the United States into a global war that affected American society in its entirety. World War II made extraordinary economic demands on women, and it disordered conventional societal arrangements on a broad scale. Most important for the ERA conflict was that the social ramifications of wartime America accelerated the trend toward emancipationism that had begun with the economic chaos of the Great Depression. There are three reasons for the emancipationist advancement during World War II. First, women's employment experiences in the war boosted the emancipationist viewpoint on women's natural capabilities by challenging the protectionist contention that women were biologically dependent persons who required special legal treatment. Second, emancipationists actively drew upon the wartime social and political developments, especially the avowed war aims of the United States, to bolster support for the ERA. Third, World War II created a patriotic atmosphere imbued with a zest for America's democratic principles and a general feeling of gratitude toward women. This environment nourished the emancipationist assertion that the ERA would fulfill America's political aspirations. These factors ultimately encouraged an array of public figures to voice their support for the ERA, which prompted emancipationists to believe that the amendment's passage could be imminent.

The rise in emancipationism was partly due to Americans' experiences during World War II, because those experiences belied several beliefs about women's conventional societal roles. In particular, the war pulled greater numbers of women into the labor force and put them to work in unprecedented ways.[76] As the war production demands grew, for example, traditionally male-dominated industries such as shipbuilding began to hire significant numbers of women workers. Women's war work further called into question the need for special labor laws, since many of the laws designed to protect women workers were suspended or relaxed during the war, with minimal harmful effects. As well, the federal government and private employers purposely encouraged women to enter the labor force through wartime initiatives. Government officials, for instance, allocated federal funds to help communities look after working women's children, and the National War Labor Board promised women would receive the same wage rates that men did.

Private employers also subsidized or created day-care centers at many work sites.[77] In this manner, the war was undercutting traditional assumptions about women's inherent potential, as highly skilled and highly paid women workers were producing the materials needed to win the war.[78]

A distinctive feature of the war period was the large public relations campaign that celebrated the virtues of "Rosie the Riveter." In particular, the scale of that campaign helped to enhance working women's public persona. In the 1940s popular magazines began to depict married women workers in a favorable light by illustrating them as able to handle their jobs competently while fulfilling their family duties.[79] Before the war, the dominant cultural consensus had generally viewed women's work outside of the home with censure and suspicion. But as the war further dislocated the conventional sexual order, public and private institutions started to celebrate women's economic contributions beyond the confines of the domestic sphere. To be clear, there were limitations to the wartime refashioning of sex roles, as many of the initiatives were based on the notion that women were only temporarily stepping outside of their customary role in the domestic realm. Nevertheless, the propaganda's depiction of the war as a struggle for freedom and democracy sharpened the disparity between American ideals and the reality of sex discrimination.[80]

Due to the new employment opportunities, the female labor force increased from thirteen million in 1940 to more than nineteen million in 1944. By March 1944 roughly one-third of all women over the age of fourteen were in the labor force. In addition, the number of women in industry grew about 500 percent, to one woman out of every three workers. The wartime economic opportunities also allowed scores of women to leave low-paid domestic service jobs; for example, between 1940 and 1944 the percentage of working women who held domestic jobs fell from 17.7 percent to 9.5 percent.[81]

Emancipationists successfully capitalized on these wartime societal developments to inspire more support for the ERA. In their arguments for the ERA, emancipationists pointed out that even though war production needs had pushed most state governments to suspend laws regulating women's employment, that suspension had not caused harm to women workers. "Nearly all the states," Rebekah Greathouse contended in an article for the *American Economic Review,* "have suspended their protective laws for the war emergency. And the women are getting along extremely well. They are holding hundreds of jobs that were formerly supposed to be unsuitable for them. They are belonging to unions. They are drawing excellent pay. And they are liking it."[82] Other emancipationists maintained in their public statements that as the war had widened women's participation in the labor force, it revealed women's endurance and their ability to handle strenuous conditions. In a 1943 article on the ERA, *Congressional Digest* reported Senator Gillette's declaration in favor of the amendment. In his statement he argued, "We are witnessing the mobilization of women in all enterprises, military and civilian, in the ranks, at the lathes, at the drills, at the assembly lines." In the same article Representative Louis Ludlow, a longtime ERA supporter, asserted that if women were "good enough" to "render splendid service working in the defense plants of our country [then] they are good enough to be entitled to enjoy equal rights with men under the laws of the land." In the end, he proclaimed, to refuse women their just rights would be "a stain on our flag."[83] For emancipationists, women's wartime service not only confirmed the extensive range of women's capabilities; it illuminated women's value as citizens.

Emancipationists also called upon the avowed war aims of the United States in their wartime campaign for the ERA. As the turmoil of the war progressed, emancipationists reasoned that if the nation was fighting for freedom and democracy around the world, then surely it must extend such promises to its own women citizens. As Emma Guffey Miller put it, how "dare we declare for real democracy and at the same time deny equality before the law to the women of the United States."[84] In a similar vein Alice Paul, the unceasingly dedicated originator of the movement for the ERA, urged in an article for *Congressional Digest* that "at this moment when the United States is engaged in a war with the avowed purpose of establishing freedom and equality for the whole world, the United States should hasten to set its own house in order. For the sake of a new and better world, as well as in justice to women themselves, we ask the immediate adoption of the Equal Rights Amendment."[85]

World War II produced a more fertile environment for emancipationism in general and the ERA in particular. The unique challenges of the war had spawned an atmosphere filled with a patriotic zeal for democratic ideas and a broad appreciation of women's wartime contributions. Moreover, during the war publications such as the *New York Herald Tribune* and the *Christian Science Monitor* began to publish articles in support of the ERA. In one editorial, for instance, the *New York Herald Tribune* stated, "When countless thousands of women have entered industry and the armed services to help save their nation, it is idle to attempt to withhold from them the equality to which they are entitled. . . . It [the ERA] would grant nothing which women do not deserve."[86] The war formed a social setting well suited for the flourishing of emancipationism, because the war had disrupted conventional sex boundaries on a large scale. Above all, women's wartime service showed that women were not inherently weak creatures incapable of handling the same rights as their male counterparts.[87]

Thanks to the wartime esteem for women and the overall patriotic mood of the nation, the ERA received more positive congressional action in the 1940s. In May 1942, for instance, the full Senate Judiciary Committee under the direction of Democratic chair James Hughes of Delaware reported the amendment favorably on a 9-to-3 vote.[88] Additionally, in January 1943 Democratic representative Louis Ludlow introduced the ERA in the House as the first resolution; forty-two members cosponsored it. That same month Democratic senator Guy Gillette introduced the amendment in the Senate with twenty-three cosponsors.[89] Plus, in February and March 1943 the subcommittees of the Senate and House Judiciary Committees reported the amendment favorably by unanimous votes.[90]

Although the ERA had garnered more support in Congress, several lawmakers still expressed concern about the amendment's constitutional impact. Indeed, as early as 1941 a few senators had asserted that while they supported constitutional sexual equality in theory, they objected to the amendment in its present form. They were worried that the Supreme Court would interpret the amendment in a way that would force all of the states to write identical legislation regardless of regional differences. Due in large part to these concerns, Democratic senator Joseph C. O'Mahoney of Wyoming suggested to Alice Paul in the spring of 1941 that a proper rephrasing of the amendment could ease apprehensions over its impact on the doctrine of states' rights but maintain the measure's original intent.[91]

To improve the amendment's chances of passage in Congress, Paul eventually heeded Senator O'Mahoney's advice, and in 1942 she returned to the drafting process. Unlike the previous drafting period, however, Paul now mainly solicited help from two main sources: George Gordon Battle, a legal scholar and prominent Democratic Party member who was a longtime supporter of constitutional sexual equality, and George Wharton Pepper, a political leader and key figure behind the Republican Party's platform endorsement of the ERA in 1940.[92] By January 1943 Paul had settled on an alternative version of the amendment that she and her advisors had based directly on the wording of the Nineteenth Amendment. It read, "Equality of rights before the law shall not be denied or abridged by the United States or any State on account of sex."[93]

The Senate Judiciary Committee began to review the revised amendment on May 16, 1943.[94] A little more than a week later, on May 24, it issued a favorable report on the modified amendment by a 12-to-5 vote with a request for early and favorable action.[95] Notably, the committee had added two more clauses to Paul's draft. First, it inserted a broadly worded enforcement statement: "Congress and the several states shall have power, within their respective jurisdiction, to enforce this article by appropriate legislation." By including the "several states" in the enforcement power, committee members had intended to neutralize the states' rights objection to the amendment.[96] Legal researcher Peter Seitz even advised steadfast ERA opponent Mary Anderson of the Women's Bureau that this clause had "eliminated" the charge that the amendment would threaten the doctrine of states' rights.[97] Second, the committee added a time-frame clause that called for the

amendment to take effect five years after ratification. Committee
members once again hoped that such a clause would ease fears
about the amendment's impact on the states, since it would purportedly give the states adequate time to update their laws.[98] On
June 22, 1943, a House Judiciary subcommittee followed the Senate committee's lead and reported the revised amendment favorably with a unanimous vote.[99]

The newly worded amendment's apparent removal of the states'
rights objection combined with the wartime appreciation of wom-
en's contributions gave way to several new endorsements for the
ERA. By 1944 twenty-four national organizations had endorsed the
ERA, including the American Economic Association, the American Political Science Association, the Society for Public Administration, and the National Education Association. This group of
new endorsers also included several prominent women's organizations, such as the GFWC and the NCW. Most notably, the amendment had also gained the backing of the National Association of
Colored Women's Clubs (NACWC), the first Black American wom-
en's organization to endorse the amendment.[100]

Emancipationists created the Women's Joint Legislative Committee (WJLC) in the spring of 1943 to organize the surge of groups
that were now backing the amendment. Headed by dedicated
ERA supporter Katherine Norris of the NWP, the group served as
a coordinating committee for the national, state, and local wom-
en's organizations that supported the ERA. Member organizations
included the NAWL, the BPWC, the NACWC, and the GFWC, as
well as the American Federation of Soroptimist Clubs, American
Medical Women's Association, and the Association of American
Women Dentists. The combined membership of the WJLC totaled
an impressive constituency of between five million and six million
members. The organization primarily focused its efforts on lobbying lawmakers to push the ERA through Congress.[101]

As the number of women's organizations supporting the ERA
multiplied, so too did the interest in the ERA among noted public figures. By the end of the war, for instance, the list of new ERA
supporters included a variety of cultural icons, such as actresses
Katharine Hepburn and Helen Hayes, opera singer Gladys Swarth-

out, radio broadcasters Rupert Hughes and Dorothy Thompson, prominent Catholic politician James Farley, and Cardinal Dennis Dougherty, as well as authors Pearl Buck, Carl Sandburg, Margaret Culkin Banning, Irving Fisher, Victor Hugo Duras, Struthers Burt, James Truslow Adams, Albert Field Gilmore, and Channing Pollock.[102]

Together with the cultural luminaries who endorsed the ERA toward the end of the war, a number of politicians expressed their approval of the amendment. In 1944, for example, former president Herbert Hoover spoke out in favor of the amendment.[103] That same year seventeen Republican and eight Democratic governors voiced their support for the amendment.[104] The war encouraged even more members of Congress to become vocal proponents of the ERA. In particular, the war produced the first woman congressional sponsor of the ERA: Democratic senator Hattie W. Caraway of Arkansas. In 1943 she explained her support for the amendment, writing, "I want [women] free to assume greater responsibilities as our Nation works its way out of this crisis. . . . I want them free to work equally with men to build a better world." That year Republican representatives Margaret Chase Smith of Maine and Winifred Stanley of New York followed Senator Caraway by becoming the first woman members of the House to endorse the amendment.[105]

During the war the number of Republican congressional proponents of the amendment expanded to include Senators W. Warren Barbour of New Jersey, Joseph H. Ball of Minnesota, William Langer of North Dakota, Homer Ferguson of Michigan, and Kenneth S. Wherry of Nebraska. Likewise, prominent Democratic congressional supporters now included Senators Dennis Chavez and Carl Hatch of New Mexico, George Radcliffe of Maryland, Claude Pepper of Florida, Harley Kilgore of West Virginia, Ernest W. McFarland of Arizona, Joseph Guffey of Pennsylvania, Sheridan Downey of California, and James Tunnell of Delaware, as well as former senator Robert L. Owen of Oklahoma and Representative William Fadjo Cravens of Arkansas.[106] As the dramatic expansion of the list of congressional ERA supporters indicates, the war encouraged more people to embrace emancipationism because the economic pressures of the war had lent a new legitimacy to the woman worker, which, in turn, assigned to women greater public responsibilities and enhanced their importance as citizens.

In 1944 the amendment gained the support of two important Democratic political figures: Vice President Henry Wallace and Senator Harry Truman, the future vice president and president. In January 1944 Vice President Wallace professed his support for the ERA when he declared, "Having long advocated EQUALITY in DEMOCRACY it seems to me that it naturally follows that there should be no inequalities under the law because of sex. Every man and woman should have an equal right to earn a living. . . . The surest method to eradicate the many discriminations and unjust practices against women is to pass the Equal Rights Amendment." Wallace was the first member of the Roosevelt administration to publicly issue an unqualified, straightforward endorsement of the ERA.[107] The next significant endorsement came in the spring of 1944, when Senator Truman wrote to Emma Guffey Miller. In the letter he avowed, "I am in sympathy with [the] fight for the Equal Rights Amendment because I think it will improve the standard of living. . . . I have no fear of the effect on the home life of the American people." As the *New York Times* would report in September 1945, the recently elevated President Truman moved to reaffirm his approval of the ERA at a White House conference with several amendment supporters.[108]

President Truman's subsequent endorsement is particularly significant because it would be the first time a sitting president had gone on record in support of the amendment. With the exception of Vice President Wallace, the Franklin Roosevelt administration had epitomized the liberal protectionist stance, as it was generally critical of blanket equality measures. As discussed in the previous chapter, the Roosevelt administration had supported enhancing women's societal position, but it did not approve of establishing absolute legal equality for men and women citizens.[109] In later years Alice Paul went so far as to claim that the death of President Roosevelt had eliminated the "greatest opposition" to the ERA.[110]

Almost a year before President Roosevelt's death in April 1945, emancipationists continued to ride the wartime wave of popularity for their amendment, as both political parties endorsed the ERA

in their party platforms in the summer months of 1944. A group
of Republican women laid the foundation for the 1944 platform
endorsement. Under the leadership of Jane Todd, vice-chair of
the New York State Republican Committee, and Mrs. Lulu Powell, a member of the Maryland State Republican Committee, the
group worked consistently to build support for the ERA among
Republican National Committee members in the months preceding the Republican convention. In June NWP leaders Alice
Paul and Helen Hunt West carried on the ERA lobbying efforts at
the Republican National Convention. Members of the NAWL, the
BPWC, and the GFWC helped Paul and Hunt with their ERA pro-
motional work. Due to all of these efforts, the Republican Party
once again included a plank supporting the ERA in its party platform, as it had previously done in 1940.[111]

Emancipationists prepared for a more intense fight at the Democratic National Convention in July. Longtime Democratic Party
member Emma Guffey Miller led the emancipationists' lobbying
efforts as she worked tirelessly to secure support for the ERA during
the platform committee hearings. The lobbying group for the ERA
included representatives from the NAWL, the BPWC, the American
Medical Women's Association, and the National Education Association. Legal scholar George Gordon Battle too presented a report to
the platform committee members that outlined the arguments in
favor of the amendment.[112] Even though various liberal protectionists, including Frances Perkins, Mary Anderson, and William Green
of the AFL, had offered meaningful objections to the ERA during
the committee hearings, the Democratic Party included an endorsement of the amendment in its party platform on July 20, 1944.[113]

There are two immediate reasons for the Democratic Party's
platform endorsement: the growing support for the amendment
within Congress and the general disorganization of the opposition
work. As NWP member Anita Pollitzer reported, the ERA's victory
was partly due to the rising support for the amendment among
Democratic senators. While the lobbying efforts of the pro-ERA
women's groups certainly contributed to the endorsement, several key senators on the drafting committee had convinced their
fellow Democrats to back the amendment. This group included

committed ERA supporters: Senators Carl Hatch of New Mexico, Joseph O'Mahoney of Wyoming, and James Tunnell of Delaware.[114] Another reason for the platform endorsement was the general disorganization among liberal protectionists and their inability to provide a clear answer as to whether or not the First Lady, Eleanor Roosevelt, continued to oppose the ERA. Although liberal protectionists had presented at the platform hearings a statement from the First Lady indicating that she still objected to the amendment, ERA proponents countered with their own statement purportedly from the First Lady (written to Emma Guffey Miller) in which she expressed her reluctance to speak against the amendment, citing the turmoil of the war.[115]

Despite the statement from the emancipationists, Eleanor Roosevelt remained opposed to the ERA. In fact she would continue to oppose the amendment until the early 1950s.[116] So what accounts for her conflicting statements during the fight over the Democratic Party's platform endorsement in 1944? The most likely answer is that the authenticity of the declaration from Eleanor Roosevelt written to Emma Guffey Miller is suspect. As historian Cynthia Harrison has shown, Miller was not opposed to altering documents from prominent Democrats to reflect opinions that were more favorable to the ERA. Nonetheless, liberal protectionists failed to deliver an additional statement from the First Lady before the drafting committee convened to finalize the proposed platform.[117] Because of this failure, liberal protectionists were unable to discredit the emancipationist claim that support for the amendment had grown to such an extent that even the First Lady was reconsidering the measure.[118]

As the platform endorsements suggest, the war had cultivated a surge within the emancipationist position so that it grew to include a more pronounced spectrum with regard to its conservative and liberal branches. By the mid-1940s the ranks of amendment proponents had expanded to include influential conservative individuals such as Republican political leader George Wharton Pepper and Representative Howard. W. Smith (D-VA). For conservative emancipationists the ERA's inherent threat to special labor legislation fell in line with their support for private enterprise and their criticisms of the government's involvement in the economy. The ERA had also gained the support of liberal public figures such as Vice President Henry Wallace as well as Senators Claude Pepper (D-FL), Hattie W. Caraway (D-AR), and Joseph Guffey (D-PA). In contrast to their conservative counterparts, liberal-minded amendment proponents maintained that the ERA would help policy makers expand government initiatives to benefit men and women alike.[119] Even with these differences, both conservative and liberal emancipationists backed the ERA as a way to ensure that men and women citizens could enjoy the same standard of rights.

Support for the ERA continued to build in the final months of World War II. In February 1945, for instance, Representative Louis Ludlow announced that seventy-four other representatives had pledged their support for the ERA.[120] On March 24 of that year the New York State Assembly and Senate adopted a resolution by unanimous votes that called on Congress to pass the ERA as soon as possible.[121] Additionally, in July the full House Judiciary Committee reported the amendment favorably for the first time since the amendment's introduction.[122] In its report the House Judiciary Committee cited the political parties' platform endorsements of the ERA as well as women's wartime service as its reasons for backing the amendment. The report concluded, "The laws of many states and of the United States, under the guise of protecting the safety and welfare of the female sex, have in fact discriminated against such sex."[123] The ERA was now out of the House Judiciary Committee, and emancipationists were jubilant. In an article for *Equal Rights* Amelia Himes Walker, lobbying chair for the NWP, hailed the victory as "another step forward."[124]

Several weeks after the Japanese surrendered in August 1945, a subcommittee of the Senate Judiciary called a hearing on the ERA. While the 1938 Senate subcommittee hearing had been more extensive, both sides still provided detailed presentations of their position at the 1945 hearing. At this hearing the emancipationists remained dedicated to their contention that the ERA followed an entrenched tenet of the American political community: equal access for all citizens to the complete range of power and influence that came from full participation in public life. Emma Guffey

Miller, for instance, asserted that the amendment was "nothing more nor less than an addition to the Bill of Rights."[125] Emancipationists also highlighted women's wartime service to support their argument that women were fully able to handle the same degree of civic responsibility that their male counterparts already enjoyed. "What has transpired during the war," declared Democratic senator George Radcliffe of Maryland, who had recently become an active ERA supporter, "has given the most convincing demonstration that women have done their full share and therefore they are entitled to their full opportunity."[126]

In ERA proponents' testimonies during the 1945 hearing, they put even greater emphasis on their assertion that the ERA was more practical and strategically advisable than the "specific method" advocated by protectionists. To support their claim, emancipationists presented an extensive series of charts that outlined the numerous sex-based legal distinctions that continued to restrict women's civic autonomy. The charts showed that Mississippi, Oklahoma, and Wisconsin still denied women the right to hold certain public offices. Many states continued to prohibit women from serving on juries; those states included Montana, Nebraska, New Hampshire, Arizona, Alabama, Delaware, Connecticut, Maryland, Missouri, and Arkansas, along with several others. In addition, the charts showed that numerous states persisted in keeping different laws for men and women with regard to the right to manage property, the right to contract, the right to control one's domicile, and the right to sue and be sued, along with many other examples. In general, these laws favored the man's or husband's rights over the woman's or wife's rights. In an effort to seize upon the inadequacies of the specific method, emancipationists asserted that the ERA was the quickest and surest way to eliminate the multitude of legal discriminations that had perpetuated women's disadvantaged position.[127]

A final concern animating the emancipationists' testimonies at the 1945 Senate subcommittee hearing was the claim that the ERA would recognize women's rights as citizens and affirm their value as persons. As mentioned in the introduction to this chapter, Emma Guffey Miller skillfully surmised this core concept of the emancipationist position when she exclaimed in her testimony, "We women want to be persons now because we are still not persons in the Constitution of the United States."[128] Hence, on one level, emancipationists envisioned the ERA as the long-overdue extension of the Fourteenth Amendment's equal protection clause. As Miller's quote suggests, emancipationists believed that the ERA would nullify the old common law tradition of domestic relations to ensure that the Fourteenth Amendment fully applied to women as persons under the law. More broadly speaking, emancipationists viewed the ERA in symbolic terms. For them, the amendment signified women's autonomy, and it would provide women with the respect they deserved as self-governing adults. Furthermore, emancipationists contended that passage of the ERA would acknowledge what the war had already established: that women were fully capable of participating in the public sphere in ways that extended far beyond the domestic domain. In short, for emancipationists the adoption of the ERA would signal the full constitutional incorporation of women into the sovereign power of the people.

At the 1945 hearing protectionists returned to the main contention underlying their criticisms of the ERA, which was that the amendment would upend the conventional sexual order and overturn the American legal tradition. The amendment, according to the testimony of Frank Donner of the CIO, would "strike down legislation which recognizes such differences in physical structure and [the] social functions of the sexes."[129] Notwithstanding that women's wartime experiences had defied the dependent woman theory embedded in the protectionist ideology, ERA opponents still clung to the notion that the American social order depended on sex-based distinctions in law and in custom.

As the anti-ERA testimonies at the 1945 hearing demonstrate, the protectionist position persisted in its belief that women's distinct physical nature and their roles as wives and mothers necessitated differential legal treatment for men and women citizens. In the words of Marvin Harrison, an ERA opponent and legal representative of the NCL, "I am old-fashioned enough to think that the basic sociological unit . . . is still the family. . . . Whether we like it or not . . . the function of the man is to go out into this world and bring home the money with which to support his wife." He later concluded in his testimony, "[The amendment] will, in short, be an attempt to repeal the laws of nature itself."[130] Even after the wartime challenges to traditional sex roles, protectionists thought that women's primary duties were to give birth to children and raise them. In sum, protectionists contended that men and women naturally performed different societal functions, which required sex-based differentiations in law.

For the moment, though, the energy remained with emancipationism. On January 21, 1946, the full Senate Judiciary Committee reported the ERA favorably with an 11-to-4 vote.[131] The committee's written report followed the classic emancipationist line of reasoning, concluding that the "well-known proposal . . . would prohibit inequalities under the law on account of sex and thereby complete the movement for equality for women begun by the equal-suffrage amendment."[132] An editorial in *Equal Rights* proclaimed the victory to be "a splendid climax."[133] And, surely, it was a significant culmination of triumphs for the emancipationists, as it appeared to them that the ERA now stood ready for a vote in both houses of Congress.

Conclusion

By the end of World War II the ERA had advanced through Congress, having gained supporters from across the political and cultural divides. Even before the war, as the 1938 congressional hearing demonstrates, emancipationists had polished and honed their arguments for the ERA in ways that emphasized how the amendment would enrich American ideals, not uproot them. Since the FLSA had displaced the rationale for sex-based labor legislation, emancipationists were able to claim with confidence that the ERA would not threaten the health and safety of women workers. Finally, World War II ignited even more support for the ERA because it further destabilized the traditional sexual order and assigned to women greater public responsibilities. Together these changes accelerated the drive toward emancipationism that had begun with the Great Depression. But, as the next chapters explain, the emancipationist momentum would fail to endure the return of protectionism in the postwar era.

5

"Motherhood Cannot Be Amended"

The Return of Protectionism in the Postwar Era

After the ERA had failed to gain the overwhelming level of support it needed to pass the Senate in the summer of 1946, a *New York Times* editorial proclaimed, "Motherhood cannot be amended, and we are glad the Senate didn't try."[1] As this quote suggests, the strength of the emancipationist momentum steadily declined in the postwar era. This decline was largely due to the work of protectionists who reorganized their opposition efforts into a unified group, which revitalized the anti-ERA campaign. When the war ended, social stability replaced military victory as the nation's top priority. In the wake of the war, then, many Americans had come to believe that the nation needed women to return to their conventional roles as wives and mothers. This emphasis on the traditionally ordered family produced a ripe environment for protectionists to reassert themselves. The legacy of World War II, however, did carry paradoxical elements that helped to sustain a lingering emancipationist impulse in the late 1940s. Even so, the renewed anti-ERA campaign combined with the postwar demobilization anxiety had begun to twist the national mind-set back toward the protectionist position.

The Revival of the Anti-ERA Campaign Effort

After the rise in support for the ERA during the war, Senate majority leader Alben Barkley (D-KY), an ERA supporter, pushed to have the amendment brought to the Senate floor for debate on

July 17, 1946.[2] Senator Barkley would go on to become President
Truman's vice president after the 1948 presidential election. On
his decision to move the ERA to the Senate floor, Senator Barkley
declared that since the amendment had been "before the country for a long time" he thought it was entitled to receive a vote.[3]
Besides, he insisted, bringing the amendment to the floor involved
an "element of good faith" since senators from both political parties had been elected on platforms that "pledged to submit this
amendment to the people." In conclusion, he urged, "If we who
were elected on that platform, which includes myself, are to say
that platforms are made to get in on and not to stand on after
getting in, I am not willing to adopt such a policy."[4] The ensuing
debate lasted three days; it was the first formal Senate floor debate
on the amendment since its introduction into Congress in 1923.[5]

Senators Claude Pepper (D-FL), Joseph Guffey, (D-PA), and
Arthur Capper (R-KS) joined Senator Barkley in representing the
emancipationist position during the Senate debate.[6] All four senators were notable New Deal proponents. Elected in 1936, Senator Pepper was a committed spokesperson for liberal policies.
Later on he would consider running in the presidential race of
1948 with his close friend and fellow ERA supporter Henry Wallace, the former vice president.[7] Senator Guffey, brother to leading
NWP member Emma Guffey Miller, had been serving in the Senate since 1935 and he had been a fervent supporter of President
Roosevelt's economic and social policies.[8] Senator Capper, on the
other hand, had been in the Senate much longer than most of his
colleagues; he had been serving since 1919. Senator Capper was
also a Republican, but he had nevertheless been a prominent supporter of President Roosevelt's relief policies when the economic
disaster progressed in the early 1930s.[9] As these senators' support
for the ERA indicates, the impact of the wartime enthusiasm for
the amendment may have dimmed, but it was nonetheless visible almost a year after the war ended because the emancipationist position now included a collection of well-known former allies
of the recently deceased President Roosevelt.

During the 1946 floor debate, Senate ERA supporters followed
the standard emancipationist line of reasoning, as they contended

that passage of the ERA would adhere to a fundamental American political principle, which was guaranteeing a single standard of rights for all citizens regardless of sex. "Is there anything extraordinary or revolutionary in that concept?" Senator Pepper exclaimed during the debate. He went on to question his Senate peers: "Is there any one who would contend that sex alone should deprive women of an equality of constitutional rights with men?"[10] In a similar manner Senator Capper maintained that "the women of this country are entitled to equality before the law, just as they are entitled to make the law."[11] Like other emancipationists, Senate ERA proponents held that the adoption of the amendment would complete the nation's democratic promise.

Pro-ERA senators also drew upon the nation's democratic aims in World War II to galvanize support for the ERA. Senator Guffey, for instance, likened the fight for the ERA to the struggle against Nazi Europe. On this claim he asked, "What kept the men and women of the countries of Europe, enslaved and devastated by the Nazis, from surrendering to their oppressors? It was that eternal hope of freedom born in the heart of mankind." He finished by observing, "It is this same hope of justice for which our women will continue to fight until the equal rights amendment is part of the Constitution."[12] In short, the senators who backed the ERA during the 1946 debate vowed that the amendment would ensure that America remained true to the democratic ideals it had recently gone to war to protect.

Senators Robert Wagner (D-NY), John Overton (D-LA), and William Revercomb (R-WV) spoke for the protectionist side at the 1946 debate.[13] During the Senate debate the emancipationist position was represented by New Deal liberals while conservatives and liberals alike argued for the protectionist viewpoint. As discussed in previous chapters, Senator Wagner, a dedicated ERA critic since the late 1920s, had also been a pioneer of New Deal legislation, a backer of the labor movement, and a close supporter of President Roosevelt.[14] In contrast, Senators Overton and Revercomb were more conservative in their politics. Elected to the Senate in 1932, Senator Overton had generally voted with the conservative coalition of Republicans and Southern Democrats.[15] Over the coming years, Senator Revercomb, who had been elected in 1942, would frequently oppose the domestic and foreign policies of President Truman.[16] Although these senators were diverse in their political leanings, they still followed the typical protectionist viewpoints. During the debate, for example, they alleged that passage of the amendment would threaten the American legal tradition and ultimately subvert the conventional sexual order. To Senator Wagner the ERA represented "a scatter-gun approach." He ended his comments by simply asking, "If a universal leveler is to be employed would we not also deprive married women of traditional protection in such matters as alimony and support?"[17]

Given the Senate protectionists' reliance on the claim that the ERA, if passed, would topple the American legal tradition, Senate protectionists were essentially alluding to the dependent woman theory embedded in the common law tradition of sex-specific marital duties in their attacks on the amendment. In spite of the fact that the war had challenged the dependent woman theory, protectionists continued to contend that the health and safety of the American family required the special treatment of all women citizens. Women, Senator Overton alleged during the 1946 debate, "are not as physically able to take care of world affairs as men are . . . their most appropriate sphere is motherhood and attention to domestic duties."[18] In an analogous contention, Senator Revercomb maintained in his remarks that women's place as mothers had entitled them to "special rights," and, he argued, the adoption of the ERA would "deprive women of the protection which they have enjoyed under the law, both the law of labor and the law of property rights."[19] Once again, protectionists insisted that passage of the ERA would imperil the distinct rights of women as citizens.

On July 19, 1946, the Senate voted on the ERA for the first time in the amendment's history. While the majority of senators had voted in favor of the ERA (38–35), the amendment fell eleven votes short of the two-thirds majority required for passage of a constitutional amendment.[20] On the disappointing outcome, ERA supporter Sally Butler of the BPWC decried in the *Chicago Daily Tribune* that "the Senate has let the women of America down. It has given women the run-around on a proposition that would have given us the rights of citizens under the law."[21]

Other emancipationists attempted to take a more optimistic stance on the development. The amendment, they asserted, had failed to receive the necessary two-thirds majority vote only because several of the Senate amendment proponents had been absent during the procedure.[22] As one *Equal Rights* editorial claimed, "Eighteen friends of the Amendment were away. . . . Had all of these 18 friendly Senators been present and voted yes, the total favorable vote would have been at least 56—possibly more."[23] Alice Paul too maintained that while the ERA had not received the commanding level of approval it needed to pass the Senate, the amendment had nevertheless collected a majority of favorable votes. Therefore, she surmised, the Senate vote simply showed that the amendment was still "gaining strength."[24]

For protectionists, however, the vote signaled a triumphant break in the emancipationist momentum. As noted in the introduction to this chapter, an anti-ERA editorial in the *New York Times* announced at the time of the Senate's vote that while the "so-called Equal Rights Amendment" had garnered an "imposing" amount of support, too many senators had come to realize that sex-specific legislation did not "presume inequality." Such legislation, the article stressed, merely recognized "the fact that women have babies and men do not." In the end, the editorial concluded, "Motherhood cannot be amended, and we are glad the Senate didn't try."[25] The *New York Times* editorial was not completely wrong in its assessment of the situation. As the Senate vote suggests, the drive behind the emancipationist movement had started to wane by the summer of 1946. Ultimately, the dynamics of the ERA conflict were changing, and that change was in the protectionists' favor.

The revival of the anti-ERA campaign almost two years earlier is one of the primary reasons the ERA failed to receive the two-thirds majority of votes it needed in the Senate after the 1946 debate. In September 1944 Mary Anderson, the former head of the Women's Bureau, organized a meeting of prominent liberal protectionists.[26] Reminiscent of the Women's Charter Group meeting in 1936, a collection of liberal-minded amendment opponents came together to create a new plan for defeating the amendment. The group included not only Mary Anderson but also Dorothy McAllister, former director of the Women's Division of the Democratic National Committee; Margaret Stone, a prominent member of the NWTUL; Frieda Miller, the new head of the Women's Bureau; and Frances Perkins, the secretary of labor.[27] Lewis Hines, a leading member of the AFL, also attended the meeting. By the end of the meeting the group had decided to set up a national organization to form a "formalized and coordinated program" for defeating the amendment. They named the organization the National Committee to Defeat the Un-Equal Rights Amendment (NCDURA).[28]

The primary purpose of the NCDURA echoed Dorothy Straus's fleeting "Campaign Committee of 500 against the Equal Rights Amendment," which had failed to take off after the 1938 Senate subcommittee hearing. Protectionists formed the NCDURA because the wartime advancement of the ERA, especially the political parties' platform endorsements of the amendment, had renewed their fears about the amendment's potential to pass Congress. As Dorothy McAllister described the situation, "it has become essential for organizations and individuals opposed to the so-called Equal Rights Amendment to unite their efforts, if they are to be effective in their fight against the Amendment."[29] In a similar vein Mary Anderson asserted in a letter to a prominent ERA opponent after the September meeting that "danger lies ahead. . . . There has therefore been organized a National Committee to implement the work of the other organizations by devoting its full time . . . to defeat this 'un-equal' amendment."[30] In sum, the founders of the NCDURA hoped to break the emancipationist energy by centralizing the opposition forces and launching a coordinated counterattack.

The NCDURA consisted of both state and national initiatives. On the national level the leaders of the organization established a directing committee to organize lobbying efforts, manage publicity strategies, and oversee a nationwide education campaign.[31] The leading officials of this group were "chairman" Dorothy McAllister; Margaret Stone, secretary; and Mary Anderson, treasurer.

Other influential members included Rose Schneiderman of the NWTUL, Eleanor Nelson of the CIO, Rose Glick of the YWCA, and Elizabeth Magee of the NCL.[32] On the state level the NCDURA set up local branches to develop community support for the protectionist position. The organization's leaders particularly hoped that such efforts would help persuade congressional members to join their cause and oppose the ERA. Dorothy McAllister, for instance, wrote that while members of the national office were meeting with Congress members, it was "exceedingly important" that "influence be brought to bear by the people at home."[33] The national directing committee also suggested that the state branches should investigate local, sex-specific laws and record any possible legal distinctions that might disadvantage women. Since the national committee members could not settle upon what exactly counted as an actual, harmful discrimination, they left that decision up to the state branches, as well as what action, if any, should be taken.[34]

After the NCDURA's inception in the fall of 1944, its leaders initially struggled to build a formidable opposition organization. For example, the NCDURA leaders struggled to raise the funds needed to create a substantial support base. Indeed, in an early letter to the head of the Massachusetts state branch, Mary Anderson exclaimed, "The Committee to Defeat the Un-Equal Right Amendment has no money!"[35] Nevertheless, the initial lack of interest in the NCDURA's work did not last long, as the events of the spring and summer months of 1945 would aid protectionists in their efforts to build more support for their anti-ERA campaign.

In April 1945 a clerk of the House Judiciary Committee notified the leaders of the NCDURA that the full Judiciary Committee intended to report the ERA favorably. This development alarmed the national directing committee, and it called an emergency meeting. During that meeting the NCDURA leadership resolved to intensify its opposition work. The organization's leaders developed a twofold strategy for stopping the ERA: convince influential Congress members to oppose the amendment and drive public opinion back toward the protectionist position.[36] Overall, the ERA's wartime progress through Congress had lent a new sense of urgency to the protectionist position, which then assisted the NCDURA's effort to restore the anti-ERA campaign effort.

After the emergency meeting in April, the NCDURA first looked to the House Rules Committee as a key to halting the amendment's advance. The NCDURA launched a large letter-writing campaign to influence the committee. In the view of Margaret Stone, letters from the constituents of the Rules Committee members needed to be sent "immediately."[37] As well, the NCDURA held private meetings with leading members of the Rules Committee. During this time the NCDURA met with Representative Adolph Sabath (D-IL), who chaired the House Rules Committee, and Representative Sam Rayburn (D-TX), the Speaker of the House, to encourage them to oppose the amendment.[38]

In addition, the NCDURA worked to gain the backing of a powerful Rules Committee member, the conservative Clarence J. Brown (R-OH). Ironically, the decision to pursue Representative Brown's support had come from a suggestion made by labor leader John Owens of the CIO. As Rose Glick of the YWCA reported, "Mr. Owens went on to say that Representative Clarence J. Brown is very powerful on the Rules Committee. Mr. Owens felt that he, Brown, could be seen and talked to, but the best groups to go to him were not labor groups."[39] According to Glick, "the all-powerful Clarence J. Brown" could certainly stop the amendment's progress in the House, even if it had obtained a favorable report from the House Judiciary Committee.[40] Glick's prediction was not far off the mark. After the full House Judiciary Committee reported the ERA favorably in July 1945, the leadership of the NCDURA used its budding connections with the Rules Committee to convince its membership to delay action on the amendment. Although the Rules Committee had placed the ERA on the House calendar, it did so in such a way that the House could not deal with the amendment until it attended to the various time-consuming international problems. As a result, the amendment failed to reach the House floor.[41]

Aside from the NCDURA's work to shape and direct the views of key congressional members, the organization set out to guide public opinion by expanding its publicity and education campaigns in the spring and summer months of 1945. During this time the NCDURA distributed anti-ERA pamphlets to underscore the amendment's alleged threat to American society. One pamphlet, titled *Warning! Look Out for the So-Called Equal Rights Amendment*, asserted that the ERA "won't create, it will destroy." It continued, "In the name of a spurious 'equality,' it would either deprive the wife of the right to support from her husband or give the husband an equal right to be supported by his wife."[42] Similarly, the leaflet *Don't Buy a Gold Brick* declared that the ERA "attacks the foundations of family life." It went on to ask, "Shall the law deprive 30 million homemaking women of their husbands' support or, in the name of equality, require them to support their husbands?"[43]

As part of its expanding publicity strategy, the NCDURA held public meetings and encouraged major newspapers to publish articles condemning the amendment. The summer before the Senate floor debate on the ERA, NCDURA members Frieda Miller of the Women's Bureau and Anna Lord Strauss of the LWV applauded a *Washington Post* opinion piece that condemned the ERA. The original piece, "Illusory Women's Rights," argued that the effect of the amendment would be "to refuse to make allowance for the different social positions of men and women as members of family groups."[44] In their follow-up letters, which were also printed in the *Washington Post*, Miller and Strauss claimed that the piece made an "excellent summary of the points" and that it demonstrated a "most constructive appreciation of the problems."[45] As Lewis Hines of the AFL put it at an earlier NCDURA meeting, the organization was setting out to "make plenty of noise to counteract the propaganda" of its opponents.[46]

In the summer of 1945 the NCDURA sent the bureaus of various newspapers a press release announcing that several leading women public figures had signed its statement of protest against the amendment. The statement read, "The Equal Rights Amendment would endanger present laws designed to protect women as mothers and potential mothers, thereby threatening the fundamental structure of the family. . . . The Equal Rights Amendment would deprive women of the substantial social protection without assuring them any real benefit." The statement carried the signatures of legal scholar Dorothy Kenyon; Carrie Chapman Catt, an acclaimed suffragist; Edith Abbott, former dean of the University of Chicago School of Social Service; and Maud Wood Park, veteran leader of the LWV.[47]

With its increased congressional lobbying efforts and its larger publicity plan, the NCDURA had created a sound base of support for its ERA opposition work. By June 1945 the organization had established fifteen state committees. It had also gained the official sponsorship of several influential national organizations, including the CIO, AFL, LWV, NWTUL, NCL, ACLU, National Council of Catholic Women, National Young Women's Christian Association, and Union for Democratic Action.[48]

Even though the NCDURA had reawakened the anti-ERA campaign effort by 1945, significant energy remained with the emancipationist movement. As discussed in the previous chapter, the full Senate Judiciary Committee reported the amendment favorably in January 1946. After this development, the NCDURA called another emergency meeting.[49] At the gathering the organization's leadership resolved to redouble its efforts to stop the ERA's advance. As Dorothy McAllister maintained, "it is especially important that the opponents of the Amendment be mobilized for action."[50] To stop the amendment's progress in the Senate, the NCDURA launched another letter-writing campaign.[51] In particular, the NCDURA reached out to a leading conservative senator, Robert Taft of Ohio. Senator Taft responded that he would assist the NCDURA's anti-ERA campaign because he believed that the ERA would cause "a good deal of harm." His view was that it would nullify "various state laws" that protected women's welfare.[52]

After the Senate Judiciary Committee's favorable report, the NCDURA's leaders turned their attention to President Truman and urged him to reconsider his support for the amendment.[53] In February 1946 Dorothy McAllister, who was not only a leading member of the NCDURA but also a force within the Democratic National Committee, wrote an extensive letter to the president detailing the NCDURA's case against the amendment. She contended that the amendment posed "serious threats to family support and other types of legislation affecting women as individuals and as citizens." She concluded that the ERA would be "destructive to the fundamental structure of American life." In her mes-sage McAllister asserted that her organization had the support of forty-three national associations and "millions of women" and that "every labor organization" opposed the amendment.[54]

In essence, McAllister's letter to President Truman had under-scored the emerging strength of the anti-ERA campaign, which alarmed the Truman administration. As presidential aide William Hassett expressed in a note attached to McAllister's letter, the ERA was turning into one "tough baby."[55] Political advisor David Niles concurred with Hassett's assessment. In another attached note he wrote, "This Equal Rights thing is dynamite which ever way you place it."[56] In mid-February the Truman administration gave in to the NCDURA's pressure. At this time presidential appointments secretary Matthew J. Connelly informed McAllister that because of her "careful analysis" President Truman had decided to "give some more thought to the Equal Rights Amendment." Evidently, the NCDURA had convinced the Truman administration that con-tinual support for the ERA would mean losing the backing of sev-eral influential national organizations.[57] Thanks to the NCDURA's criticism, President Truman did not speak publicly of the amend-ment during the rest of his years in office.[58]

In the early summer months of 1946, word reached the NCDU-RA's leaders that the ERA might be brought to the Senate floor for a vote. To secure the amendment's defeat in the Senate, the group's leadership returned to its twofold strategy from the previous year: build significant congressional support for the protectionist position and push public opinion away from the emancipation-ist cause.[59] On the congressional front the NCDURA increased its lobbying efforts to strengthen the protectionist presence in the Senate. Throughout June and the early days of July 1946 the orga-nization's members personally delivered to each senator another NCDURA pamphlet, *The Freund Statement.* This pamphlet consisted of an extensive essay by eminent legal scholar and longtime ERA opponent Paul Freund, which detailed the amendment's alleged threat to the American legal tradition. The pamphlet also listed the signatures of twenty-one law school deans as well as other renowned legal scholars who opposed the amendment.[60]

In an attempt to sway both Congress and public opinion, the NCDURA's leaders called attention to the various prominent women who remained opposed the amendment.[61] In the weeks preceding the Senate debate the leadership of the NCDURA had its allies in the Senate introduce a syndicated column recently written by Eleanor Roosevelt into the Congressional Record.[62] In the piece titled "On the Status of Women," the former First Lady presented the classic protectionist argument against the amendment. She avowed, "I am still opposed to the equal-rights amendment. . . . We cannot change the fact that women are different from men. . . . The best results are always obtained when men and women work together, with the recognition that their abilities and contributions may differ, but that in every field they supplement each other."[63]

At the time of the Senate debate the NCDURA issued two press releases: a joint statement of protest headed by Eleanor Roosevelt and a declaration against the amendment signed by three women from the House of Representatives. "Equal Rights," the joint statement proclaimed, "is a deceptive slogan. The proposed Amendment would not accomplish the purposes for which it is intended." It went on to contend that the amendment would endanger various state laws that protected women as workers, wives, and mothers. It included the signatures of Frances Perkins, now former secretary of labor; Mary McLeod Bethune, leader of the National Council of Negro Women; and Virginia Gildersleeve, former dean of Barnard College. Similar to the joint statement, the declaration argued that the amendment, if passed, would "cause chaos in 48 states in the status of all laws relating to women." The declaration carried the signatures of Representatives Helen Gahagan Douglas (D-CA), Chase Going Woodhouse (D-CT), and Emily Taft Douglas (D-IL).[64]

In the end the ERA failed to gain enough votes for the two-thirds majority necessary for passage in the Senate because the NCDURA had already started to weaken the emancipationist momentum when the ERA made it to the Senate floor in mid-July 1946. Although the wartime rise in support for the ERA was still visible, protectionists had been working for almost two years to assemble an organization strong enough to slow the amendment's advance. By the summer of 1945, for example, the NCDURA had created a sound base of support; a year later the organization used that base to launch an extensive attack on the ERA to undermine its progress in the Senate. With its relentless congressional lobbying efforts and its effective publicity strategy, the NCDURA had begun to rebuild the protectionist stronghold over the ERA conflict.

The Postwar Readjustment Anxiety

The anxiety of the postwar readjustment period created an apt atmosphere for protectionists and their reinvigorated anti-ERA campaign. As the previous chapters convey, the United States had experienced fifteen years of economic and political turmoil, shifting from a decade of depression to almost half a decade of war. This period of instability produced considerable changes regarding women's social status, as it extended women's public responsibilities and enhanced their value as citizens. When peace returned, however, it brought about a pervasive feeling of distress regarding the future of conventional societal arrangements, especially those that concerned women's traditional roles as wives and mothers. In the mid- to late 1940s this social angst developed into a ubiquitous desire to reestablish traditional sex roles, since many Americans felt that social stability would come only after women had returned to their traditional duties in the domestic realm.[65]

The anxiety surrounding the demobilization period can be partly traced back to the haunting memory of the Great Depression, as many Americans had not forgotten the substantial unemployment problem that had preceded the war. As historian William Chafe explains, "If the war had eliminated breadlines and relief rolls, peace threatened to re-establish them. In the eyes of many leaders, a cutback in women's employment offered one guarantee against the possibility of a new economic downturn."[66] In other words, various Americans feared that the dismantling of the war industries could force the country to return to an economy with limited job opportunities and a low standard of living.[67]

What is more, numerous policy makers and political figures had dreaded the very real possibility that women workers might not willingly relinquish their jobs to the returning veterans. In their view this predicament could create an unemployment problem and produce social unrest. On America's postwar domestic goals, Eleanor Roosevelt declared that "the first obligation of the government and of business is to see that every man who is employable has a job. . . . A woman does not need a job if she has a home and a family requiring her care and a member of the family earns an adequate amount of money to keep up a decent standard of living."[68] Even the new head of the Women's Bureau, Frieda Miller, a member of the NCDURA, publicly suggested that women in industry should leave their jobs and look for employment in the lower-paying service sector to free up jobs for the returning veterans.[69]

Policy makers encouraged the departure of women from the labor force with several initiatives. The federal government, for instance, ended day-care funding and gave veterans the right to replace wartime workers. As well, Congress removed married women from public payrolls to make room for unemployed men, even when women employees had been better suited for the jobs.[70] The federal government also passed the GI Bill of Rights, which overwhelmingly benefited men. Through this initiative millions of men received advantages that were available to only a few women, especially in areas of civil-service job preference, reemployment rights, and education.[71] In sum, government planners had placed the readjustment of sixteen million veterans at the heart of their postwar domestic priorities because they believed that the postwar readjustment would come more easily if women returned to their duties in the domestic sphere.[72]

In addition to its presence in the economic arena, the postwar anxiety manifested itself in cultural and legal realms. In the cultural domain it generated a considerable body of prescriptive literature on women's domestic responsibilities. This body of "demobilization literature" consisted of books, articles, novels, and short stories that were typically addressed to the wives of servicemen.[73] In general, such works instructed wives to promote domestic harmony by subordinating their interests and needs to those of their husbands. These instructions included the advice that women should cultivate feminine characteristics, such as dependency and submissiveness. In all, this body of work called upon women to restore the male ego by eschewing the assertiveness and competency that they had acquired from their experiences during the war.[74]

According to the works of several postwar psychological and child development theorists, women's roles should remain confined to the domestic sphere.[75] One of the most famous texts from this genre is Ferdinand Lundberg and Marynia Farnham's *Modern Woman: The Lost Sex* (1947).[76] Lundberg and Farnham argued that the independent woman was a contradiction in terms, as women were biologically and psychologically dependent on men. They asserted that when women turned away from their natural passivity, they disconnected themselves from their true calling to bear and raise children. This unnatural disconnect, they contended, resulted in psychological debilitation, which plagued society in its entirety. From the perspectives of Lundberg and Farnham, the demands of nature required women to embrace lives that were filled with mothering and domesticity.[77]

The Supreme Court's decision in *Goesaert v. Cleary* (1948) is the most striking example of the postwar anxiety's manifestation in the legal realm. This case concerned a Michigan law that prohibited women from working as bartenders unless they were married to or the daughter of a male owner of a licensed saloon. The Michigan law coincided with a national postwar effort by the International Union of Hotel and Restaurant Employees and Bartenders to exclude women from the union and from bartending.[78] The four main plaintiffs in the case were Margaret and Valentine Goesaert, a mother who owned a bar and her daughter who helped her, as well as bar owner Caroline McMahon and bartender Gertrude Nadroski. Their attorney, Ann R. Davidow, also filed a number of affidavits from other women bar owners and bartenders. These affidavits described the economic hardships that the law had caused to befall women, and they showed that women had fixed drinks without it being a detriment to themselves or their customers. In sum, the plaintiffs maintained, the Michigan law had violated their rights as persons under the equal protection clause of the Fourteenth Amendment.[79]

Despite these claims, the Supreme Court upheld the law in a 6–3 opinion, ruling that female bartenders might "give rise to social and moral problems." Staunch ERA opponent Felix Frankfurter, now a Supreme Court justice, wrote the opinion for the court, declaring, "The Fourteenth Amendment did not tear history up by the roots. . . . Michigan could, beyond question, forbid all women from working behind a bar." He concluded that even though many women "now indulge in the vices that men have long practiced," the law could still draw a "sharp line between the sexes" to defend against "social and moral problems."[80] Once more the Supreme Court restricted women's civic standing under the Fourteenth Amendment on the rationale that women required special protection under the law. Although women had previously demonstrated their competence during the war, the high court maintained that sex-based legal standards safeguarded women and protected society as a whole.[81]

The readjustment anxiety in the period following World War II had begun to drive the national outlook back toward the protectionist mind-set. As the above examples suggest, the postwar emphasis on the traditionally ordered family had corresponded to protectionists' calls for clear divisions between the rights of men and women citizens. Even so, there were divergent elements embedded in the legacy of World War II, which helped to sustain a small, but nonetheless significant emancipationist impulse at the end of the 1940s.

The Paradoxical Legacy of World War II

In the aftermath of World War II, it seemed as though the anxiety of the postwar era had reversed many of the war-induced changes in women's lives. Women did leave the workforce in the time immediately following the end of the war. By 1946, for instance, the female labor force had dropped from its wartime peak of 19,170,000 to 16,896,000.[82] In addition, the marriage rate, which was 84.5 per thousand women in 1945, jumped to 120.7 in 1946.[83] In a 1946 poll 53 percent of the participants answered that they believed it would be "a long time" before women would be "allowed an equal chance with men for any job in business and industry."[84] On the surface, then, it appeared as though after fifteen years of depression and war, most Americans had readily sought solace in the restoration of conventional sex boundaries.

Yet, it would be wrong to ignore the salient socioeconomic changes that were taking place below the surface. Although there was a dip in the number of employed women in the immediate postwar period, that figure had continued to rise over the long term. Even at their lowest point, the postwar figures reflecting women's numbers in the labor force were higher than those for 1940. By 1947 these numbers had begun to increase again as the long-term trend in women's employment reemerged.[85] A change also took place in the age distribution of women workers. By the close of the 1940s a large proportion of new workers were in their early forties, and women in their fifties were moving into the labor force at the same numbers as those in their twenties.[86] At the end of the decade the number of employed women was slightly higher than the wartime peak: close to 29 percent of all women were in the labor force, and they constituted 30 percent of all workers.[87]

The greatest postwar gains in women's employment occurred among married women. When the 1940s concluded, one in every four married women (with husbands present) was in the labor force, where they constituted 52 percent of all women workers.[88] Additionally, the number of couples in which both husband and wife worked jumped from 3 million, or 11 percent, in 1940, to almost 7 million, or 20 percent, in 1948. In 1948, moreover, approximately 4.5 million mothers with children under the age of eighteen were employed; they made up nearly 25 percent of the total female labor force. By 1952 approximately 10.4 million wives held jobs, which was 2 million more than the highest number of women employed during World War II and almost three times the number employed in 1940.[89]

There are several reasons for the rising number of women participating in the labor force during the postwar era. For starters, the war helped to validate women's work outside of the home, because it defined employment as a patriotic necessity. Furthermore, it eased employers' resistance to married and older women, and it allowed these women to prove their capabilities. The postwar era also triggered a boom in the demand for white-collar occupations such as clerical and sales positions, which were conventionally viewed as women's jobs. During the 1940s the proportion of women workers occupying these positions climbed from 31 to 37 percent; by 1950 more than half of all women workers were employed in white-collar jobs.[90]

By the beginning of the 1950s, work for married women had become an essential element in the lives of many American families, as it was a crucial means for attaining middle-class status. In the years before the 1940s, married women had primarily worked because their husbands received an income that placed the family below the poverty level. By 1950, however, most married women no longer worked because of dreadful economic circumstances. On the contrary, they worked to help their families purchase new homes, household appliances, and automobiles and to finance their children's education.[91] As one woman explained to a reporter for the *New York Times Magazine* in 1951, "the children get more things by my working; it's easier to buy them clothes and pay for school. We get more out of life."[92] Put another way, the postwar expansion of the American consumer society had altered the notion of economic need. In the Depression years economic need had meant what was essential for mere survival. In the late 1940s, however, it started to denote the quest for a better life. As the concept of economic need changed, more families came to rely on the incomes of both spouses to enable them to participate in the postwar consumer society. Therefore, the changing notion of economic need had encouraged the expansion of women's roles in the family. With the postwar growth of the American consumer society, women's employment became a more acceptable means for a family to seek upward social mobility.[93]

Still, the rising number of women in the labor force during the postwar period did have a significant limitation, as the breakdown of the sex-segregated labor force created by World War II did not survive. By the 1950s women had clearly become a permanent part of the working world; nevertheless, employers restricted women's postwar employment to jobs that had been traditionally designated for women. These restrictions were also due to the dismantling of the war industries, which pushed women back into conventional female occupations such as clerical work, sales, and domestic service. When women workers moved to these positions, they often lost the protection of labor unions. As historian Cynthia Harrison describes it, "Rosie the Riveter had become a file clerk."[94] As all these figures indicate, however, the loss of appealing job opportunities did not stop the overall increase in women's employment during the postwar years. Although women had lost their well-paid wartime jobs, they fought to stay in the labor market, even if it meant lower-paid employment.[95]

In the late 1940s the impact of the war years on women's economic lives remained clear: the war had softened the resistance to women's work outside of the home, and it had made women's employment a more acceptable part of American life. In the words of historian William Chafe, "At the turn of the century, the young, the single, and the poor had dominated the female labor force. Fifty years later, the majority of women workers were married and middle aged, and a substantial minority came from the middle class. In the story of that dramatic change, World War II represented a watershed event."[96] While the postwar readjustment anxiety had helped to push the dominant cultural consensus back to the protectionist mind-set, it had not erased the impression of the war on women's societal position.

The wartime appreciation for women's contributions outside of the home also remained imprinted in the postwar cultural outlook. In an October 1945 public statement, for example, President Truman underscored the enduring feeling of gratitude toward women: "To the women of America, I say—your untiring efforts to speed the winning of war . . . your effective work in advancing the great cause, need no tribute from me to make them shine as one of the glorious pages in our history."[97] Undoubtedly, traditional ideas about women's place had started to reassert themselves amid the postwar anxiety, but public appreciation for the value of women's extrafamilial roles did not instantaneously vanish when the war had ended.

For the ERA conflict, the remaining gratitude toward women combined with the deeper socioeconomic trends nourished a lingering emancipationist impulse in the late 1940s. In January 1947 the new leading congressional sponsor of the ERA in the House, Republican representative John Robsion of Kentucky, declared that the amendment's passage by Congress was "at hand." When Representative Robsion introduced the ERA that year, he had 102 cosponsors. That same year the NWP claimed it had pledges of support for the amendment from 64 senators.[98] Even though the emancipationist momentum began to decelerate after the war had ended, the ERA remained relatively popular in the late 1940s.

This enduring support led to a few notable victories for the ERA in the final years of the decade. In 1948, for instance, both major political parties once again endorsed the ERA in their party platforms.[99] As well, favorable congressional action on the amendment continued throughout the late 1940s. In 1948 subcommittees of the House and Senate Judiciary Committees voted to report the amendment favorably.[100] And, in the spring of 1949, the full Senate Judiciary Committee issued another favorable report on the amendment.[101] Emancipationism, then, did not immediately disappear amid the postwar readjustment anxiety and the resurrection of the anti-ERA campaign. These developments had undoubtedly weakened the emancipationist movement, but they did not destroy it. Over the coming years protectionists would realize that in order to fully suppress the remaining emancipationist influence, they would need to amend their current opposition strategy.

Conclusion

The emancipationist momentum steadily declined in the postwar years as ERA opponents began to rebuild the power of protectionism. The amendment's wartime advance had pushed several influential protectionists to form a unified opposition organization, which helped to bend Congress and the public back toward the protectionist position. The anxiety that had pervaded the postwar readjustment period also created a fitting environment for the revival of the anti-ERA campaign, since that period's emphasis on the reinstitution of traditional sex boundaries aligned with protectionists' calls for marked divisions between the rights of men and women citizens. These developments, however, did not extinguish emancipationism altogether. Deeper socioeconomic changes, as well as a lasting appreciation for women's wartime contributions, helped to sustain a small but noticeable emancipationist impulse in the late 1940s. Nevertheless, as the next chapter explains, protectionists subdued the remaining emancipationist influence in the late 1950s and early 1960s after they had developed their own comprehensive measures for addressing women's changing social and economic positions.

6

"Socially Desirable Concepts"

The Triumph of Protectionism, 1947–1963

In January 1947 Frieda Miller, head of the Women's Bureau and a member of the NCDURA, announced during a Labor Advisory Committee meeting that the creation of a new affirmative program would help ERA opponents remove the harmful discriminations against women while fighting to "retain the distinctions that are justified."[1] Miller, a dedicated labor activist who had long been committed to the anti-ERA campaign, believed that sex could be a legitimate legal classification when the law used that category to attend to women's special needs as mothers and potential mothers.[2] During the Labor Advisory Committee meeting that January, Miller concluded, "We do want continued what we have today if the distinction is based on socially desirable concepts."[3] In an effort to snuff out the remaining emancipationist influence, protectionists expanded their opposition strategy over the coming years to include new initiatives that would seek to enhance women's status while leaving the presumably reasonable sex-based legal distinctions intact. In the process ERA opponents developed a series of measures that obstructed the ERA campaign while helping amendment opponents refine their stance on the differences between men's and women's citizenship.

The Protectionist Resurgence

In the final weeks of December 1946 and the early days of January 1947 the leadership of the NCDURA held a series of meetings to devise a new opposition strategy for defeating the ERA. While the emancipationist energy had faded amid the postwar readjustment anxiety, ERA backers were still pressing congressional members for support in the winter months of 1946 and 1947. In the words of NCDURA member Louise Young, amendment proponents had "girded their bruised and mutilated loins for another round."[4] During the meetings the NCDURA's leadership developed a new strategy that consisted of two main goals: expanding the organization's support base by continuing to build relationships with prominent Republicans and enhancing the organization's image by creating a positive program that would provide alternative measures for improving women's opportunities.[5]

In January 1947, Dorothy McAllister, the devoted ERA opponent and Democratic Party leader who had persuaded President Truman to reconsider his support for the amendment, met with Marion Martin of the Republican National Committee in order to strengthen the NCDURA's political ties. Martin had served as both the founding head of the National Federation of Women's Republican Clubs as well as the Republican National Committee assistant chairperson in charge of women's activities. In McAllister's later recounting of this meeting to Frieda Miller, she relayed that Martin had promised to "write a number of key Republican women in the states asking them to use their influence with their Congressmen and Senators against the amendment." Martin also assured McAllister that she would write to Alf Landon, who had been the Republican presidential candidate in 1936, and encourage him to oppose the amendment. In all, McAllister reported that Martin was very "glad to help . . . in every way possible" because she had "always been opposed to the amendment."[6]

The NCDURA next developed a constructive program that aimed to defeat the ERA by advancing other comprehensive measures. Partly due to the advice of Eleanor Roosevelt, the group first decided to propose a joint resolution designed to eliminate the harmful discriminations against women while reaffirming the presumably equitable sex-based distinctions.[7] In the early weeks of January 1947, Mary Anderson, the always ardent ERA critic and former head of the Women's Bureau, and Peter Seitz, a legal advisor to the NCDURA, began crafting the proposed piece of legislation. Former secretary of labor Frances Perkins and Frieda Miller also contributed to the drafting process.[8]

For the most part the proponents of the joint resolution had designed the measure to confront the continuing threat of the ERA. The group explained in a memorandum that they had felt it was "important" to have the resolution ready for introduction into Congress "at the earliest possible time . . . in order to give members an opportunity to support the Joint Resolution rather than the 'Equal Rights Amendment.'"[9] But, the drafters maintained that the bill would "not be framed to win the support of individuals who would seem to be satisfied with nothing less than a declaration, in fundamental law, that women, however different from men in their physical structure, biological or social function must be accorded, by governments, identical treatment with men." The drafters, then, were not attempting to offer a compromise bill to broker a peace agreement with their emancipationist foes. On the contrary, they were determined to create competing legislation in the hopes of attracting individuals and groups who had wanted to enhance women's status but who were also not firmly committed to the ERA.[10]

The leaders of the NCDURA decided to propose a joint resolution rather than an alternative constitutional amendment for two reasons. First, they felt that since a resolution required only a simple majority in each house of Congress, it would be easier to pass than a constitutional amendment, as an amendment required a two-thirds majority in Congress and then approval by three-quarters of the state legislatures. Second, they believed that any constitutional amendment that attempted to tackle the complications embedded in women's legal status would stand a chance of endangering the supposedly equitable sex-based laws that protected the traditional sexual order. As one memo from the drafters put it, "an amendment (with or without safeguarding language) may expose family and labor laws to legislative and judicial attack." The memo went on to contend that, unlike an amendment, a carefully constructed joint resolution could advance "selective legislative action to eliminate unreasonable discriminations."[11]

The decision to pursue a joint resolution demonstrated a significant change in the protectionists' campaign against the ERA. Before this change, protectionists had typically argued that if women's status needed improvement, then legislative action should come primarily from the state level, with specific legislation for specific problems. With the proposed joint resolution, however, protectionists began to view the federal government as an essential vehicle for prompting legislative work on specific problems.

In early January 1947 Frieda Miller called a meeting of the Women's Bureau Labor Advisory Committee to discuss the NCDURA's new affirmative program, especially the proposed joint resolution. Prominent liberal protectionists attended the meeting, among them Katherine Ellickson and Esther Peterson of the CIO, along with Pauline Newman of the International Garment Workers and Elisabeth Christman of the NWTUL. Peter Seitz, one of the main drafters of the bill, also attended the meeting. It was during this meeting that Miller explained her intentions for the new positive campaign. In her words, it would "wipe out discriminations where they exist." But, as mentioned in the introduction to this chapter, Miller cautioned that the bill's backers "would fight to retain the distinctions that are justified." According to the meeting minutes, the committee overwhelmingly voted to support the "the shift in approach" to foster "a positive policy to get the wheels moving" for eliminating the harmful discriminations against women.[12]

The NCDURA changed its name to the National Committee on the Status of Women (NCSW) in the early spring months of 1947 to reinforce its new affirmative program. The newly elected head of the NCSW, Mary Anderson, described the change as "the beginning of a new phase in the controversy over the best method of attaining an improved legal status for the women of this country. Negative opposition has been transformed into a program of positive action."[13] Following the name change, the organization's leaders selected Louise Young as executive vice chairperson and

Ruth Craven as secretary. Additionally, they appointed Dorothy McAllister and Marion Martin to the national advisory council.[14]

In early February 1947 the NCSW's leaders and their affiliates finalized the draft of the proposed legislation. By this time the bill had gained the strong backing of two influential conservative Republican members of Congress: Senator Robert Taft of Ohio and Representative James Wadsworth of New York.[15] The people of Ohio had elected Robert Taft to the Senate in 1938, and he became a leader of the conservative coalition that had opposed the expansion of the New Deal.[16] Senator Taft later became involved with the ERA conflict in 1946, when the NCDURA had recruited him to help stall the amendment's progress in the Senate. He happily agreed to the NCDURA's requests, because in his view the ERA posed a threat to the various laws that protected women's welfare.[17]

Whereas Senator Taft joined the ERA opposition effort in the 1940s, Representative Wadsworth had been a vocal critic of the ERA since the early 1920s. Earlier still, Wadsworth, who had served as a U.S. senator before becoming a member of the House of Representatives in 1933, had been a prominent opponent of the woman suffrage movement. In a 1947 letter to ERA supporter and Republican Party member Jane Todd, Representative Wadsworth explained that he opposed the ERA because it would "prevent a continuation of certain preferential treatments to women (as contrasted to the treatment of men) which have been adopted down through the years by both the federal and state governments in recognition of the biological and social functions performed by women." In contrast to the ERA, Representative Wadsworth argued, the newly proposed joint resolution would allow for an "orderly repeal" of laws that actually disadvantaged women. "I doubt," he noted, "if there are any federal statutes discriminating against women, but it may very well be that there are certain rules and regulations which have that result." He went on to insist that the Women's Status Bill could "wipe out" the harmful federal regulations. He maintained, though, that the greatest numbers of legal discriminations against women were in state laws and that only a commission, as proposed by the bill, would allow for an "orderly" investigation into those laws to guarantee that the unjust practices be repealed. As he put it, "We would rather rely upon the people to ensure these things in their own communities than to depend upon the exercise of a nation wide federal power."[18] Wadsworth supported the bill because while it enlisted the authority of the federal government in its attempt to address the issue of sex discrimination, the bill put the greatest level of trust in the states to develop their own solutions for the various legal issues.

Senator Taft and Representative Wadsworth introduced the Women's Status Bill into Congress on February 17, 1947. The measure, which was commonly referred to as the Taft-Wadsworth Bill in the late 1940s, obtained a decent level of support in Congress. In the House of Representatives backers included Democratic members Helen Gahagan Douglas of California, Emanuel Celler of New York, Estes Kefauver of Tennessee, and Mary Norton of New Jersey, as well as Republican members Carl Lewis of Ohio and Edith Nourse Rodgers of Massachusetts. Prominent Senate supporters included Democrats Robert Wagner of New York and Howard McGrath of Rhode Island. On the notable degree of approval, NCSW leader Mary Anderson proclaimed that the bill had "attracted broad-bipartisan support."[19]

The somewhat lengthy Women's Status Bill contained two main parts. The first section established the basis for the bill. It asserted that women's current societal status required legislative action because "the economic, civil, social, and political progress of women has been burdened and impeded by discriminations arising in part from assumptions embedded in common law."[20] As Peter Seitz, legal advisor to the NCSW, had reasoned in an earlier memo, the bill included this statement because "many of the statutory sex discriminations of our times are attributed to common-law concepts of the status of married women." Seitz went on to claim that no "responsible" evaluation of such statutes had been attempted. "Presumably," he supposed, "many of them have a rational basis and it would be in the interest of women and society to retain them; others undoubtedly represent outmoded conceptions of the capacities and character of women."[21]

The second section of the bill detailed the measure's primary objectives, which were to declare a general national policy regard-

ing sex discrimination and to establish a commission on the status
of women. Regarding the national policy, the bill stated, "In law
and its administration no distinctions on the basis of sex shall be
made except such as are reasonably based on differences in physical structure, biological, or social function."[22] The drafters of the
bill proudly noted that the statement protected the "reasonable"
sex-based legal distinctions, including legislation that placed the
"duty of combat service on men exclusively," as well as legislation
that granted "maternity benefits to women but not men." Proponents observed that this statement required immediate action only
against harmful sex discriminations by federal government agencies; it did not entail immediate, compulsory action by the states.[23]
Thus, similar to the Women's Charter of the late 1930s, the policy outlined by the Women's Status Bill articulated a declaration
of limited equality that sought to empower women while preserving their right to special protection.

Most important, the bill's policy proposals called for the establishment of a presidential commission on the status of women.
The recommended commission would comprise nine members
appointed by the president and be tasked with making "a full and
complete study, investigation, and review of the economic, civil,
social, and political status of women, and the nature and extent of
discriminations based on sex throughout the United States, its Territories, and possessions."[24] Liberal protectionist and labor activist
Esther Peterson of the CIO reasoned that the commission would
provide a record of the "distinctions that should be kept, those
that should not be, and those in the middle group."[25] For the bill's
backers the purpose of the commission was to review the present
status of women, evaluate the various sex-based distinctions, and
make recommendations at the appropriate level of government,
whether federal, state, or local.[26]

The idea for the commission grew from two main sources. For
starters, it echoed Felix Frankfurter's original call for a study of
the variations in state laws affecting women's status in the years
following the ratification of the Nineteenth Amendment. As discussed previously, Frankfurter had suggested the idea to Alice Paul
when she had initially proposed the ERA in the early 1920s. From

Frankfurter's viewpoint, women's legal standing could be resolved only after an extensive evaluation of the various sex-based legal distinctions had taken place. Such a study, he maintained, would help lawmakers develop specific legislation for specific problems.[27]

The drafters of the Women's Status Bill also gained inspiration from the President's Committee on Civil Rights, established by President Truman's executive order in December 1946. The committee's report, *To Secure These Rights*, appeared in 1947. Although many of its recommendations were not enacted until the 1960s, the report had signified an important step toward national recognition of the problems caused by deep-seated racism and the need for government intervention.[28] In turn, many of the women behind the Women's Status Bill had hoped that a commission on women would result in a similar report and spur a national debate on women's status.[29]

On the whole the proponents of the Women's Status Bill saw the measure as an affirmative step that would address the changing societal position of women while defending women's traditional right to special legal treatment. Political party committee leaders Marion Martin and Dorothy McAllister articulated this point in a joint statement that they had prepared for the NCSW. "We see in the bill," they proclaimed, "a positive, constructive approach to the problems of how to eliminate unfair legal discriminations against women and at the same time retain those laws needed by women as mothers and workers."[30] In a letter to a potential backer of the bill, Representative Wadsworth gave a similar assessment. He wrote that in the end "the purpose of our bill is to accomplish the abandonment of the unjust discriminations . . . and yet at the same time maintain those protective measures which women should enjoy."[31]

Unlike the tepid response to the Women's Charter Group in the 1930s, ERA opponents largely approved of the Women's Status Bill in the late 1940s. Eleanor Roosevelt, for example, proclaimed that she solidly supported the bill. "It is perfectly clear," she explained in a press release for the NCSW, "that for biological reasons, women are different from men. . . . These things should be recognized but not used as a reason for making life harder for the woman who must earn her own living."[32] The bill also received backing from Carrie Chapman Catt, Dorothy Kenyon, and Frances Perkins.[33] Additionally, a *Washington Post* editorial declared that the bill represented an "intelligent method of procedure."[34] The list of organizations that officially supported the bill included the ACLU, the National Council of Jewish Women, the AFL, the CIO, the National Council of Negro Women, the American Federation of Teachers, the NCL, the NWTUL, and the National Council of Catholic Women.[35]

One of the most important groups to back the Women's Status Bill was the LWV, because it had been hesitant toward the Women's Charter initiative in the late 1930s.[36] Thanks to the changes to women's status wrought by the Great Depression and World War II, the LWV became more open to accepting alternative comprehensive measures for addressing women's legal personhood in order to compete with the campaign for the ERA.[37] In April 1947 the LWV announced its support for the Women's Status Bill in a widely distributed pamphlet, *Brief for Action: The Status of Women.*[38] In the pamphlet the leadership of the LWV asserted that although the Nineteenth Amendment had established that women were "intelligent" enough to be full citizens, it had not eliminated the need for women to have distinct, sex-specific rights. On this point the pamphlet stated that "laws favoring women as members of a family have always been held justified by society as a whole. . . . In physical structure, in biological and social functions, women differ from men. Society has always considered these differences in the making of laws and [their] application, and must continue to do so." The pamphlet further indicated that, unlike the ERA, the proposed Women's Status Bill offered "clear, positive, and quick action" for improving women's opportunities.[39]

As to be expected, dedicated emancipationists vehemently opposed the bill. Alma Lutz, an earnest ERA supporter and member of the NWP, insisted that "by legalizing so-called 'reasonably justified' sex distinctions, this bill would set women in a class apart as not quite human beings."[40] Likewise, Republican Party member Jane Todd announced in a letter to Representative Wadsworth that the Federation of Women's Republican Clubs of New York had passed a resolution denouncing the Women's Status Bill. The resolution stated that the proposed bill could serve "no useful purpose, save only to delay women in their achieving that equal status under law."[41] An editorial in *Equal Rights* too criticized the bill's proposed commission on the status of women as a superfluous endeavor, given that the NWP had already been investigating and collecting data on the variations in sex-specific laws for the past three decades.[42]

Despite these objections, the NCSW had versions of the Women's Status Bill introduced into Congress every year until 1954.[43] While the measure failed to pass Congress, it did succeed in undermining the emancipationist movement. As William Roach, a legal advisor to the NCSW, put it in an earlier letter to the organization, the measure served "as a good peg for those legislators who might . . . be regretting their support for the Equal Rights Amendment." He went on to reason that former amendment supporters could "gracefully ease over to the Bill without being inconsistent, on the face of things."[44] Roach's assessment of the situation proved to be fairly accurate, as a few of the congressional members who had previously endorsed the ERA subsequently changed their position in the postwar period and backed the Women's Status Bill as the best method for doing away with practices and laws that negatively affected women. These congressional members included Representative Mary Norton (D-NJ) and Edith Nourse Rodgers (R-MA).[45]

The Women's Status Bill diverted energy away from the emancipationist cause, since for a number of people the bill had represented a reasonable substitute for advancing women's position. In particular, the *New York Herald Tribune*, which had been a strong supporter of the ERA during the war, published an editorial in 1947 advising others to back the Women's Status Bill. The article urged women's organizations to "join forces" in support of the measure in order to resolve the decades-old problem of determining women's legal status in the wake of suffrage, as it had been a considerable length of time since the Nineteenth Amendment had removed sex as a permissible basis for withholding the right to vote.[46] Over the coming years a handful of former ERA supporters would move away from the amendment and back the Women's Status Bill as an attempt at conciliation. For these groups and individuals, the goal was always to increase women's influence, and they now hoped that they might be able to achieve this goal without the ERA.[47]

The Women's Status Bill represented the first protectionist endeavor to provide a viable, alternative comprehensive measure to compete with the ERA. To be sure, the proposed Women's Charter of the late 1930s had also been a protectionist effort to present a far-reaching policy that would espouse the idea of different but equally important rights for men and women citizens. However, the charter's advocates intended for the measure to be only a general strategy statement. With the Women's Status Bill, protectionists explicitly enlisted the power of the federal government to help establish a degree of equality for men and women citizens while preserving what they had assumed to be sensible sex-based laws and customs.

The Undercutting of Emancipationism

Even though the emancipationist momentum had diminished since the war's end, it was able to marshal a degree of influence over Congress during the final months of 1949 and the early days of 1950. In January 1950 the ERA made it once again to the Senate floor for a debate and vote.[48] In a situation similar to the 1946 Senate floor debate, ERA opponents and proponents followed the typical arguments made for and against the amendment. Senator Estes Kefauver (D-TN), an ERA opponent and backer of the Women's Status Bill, argued that the ERA would "eliminate rape as a crime." He also claimed that the amendment would lead to joint bathroom facilities. Like other protectionists, Senator Kefauver maintained that the strength of American society demanded sex-specific laws and customs.[49] Conversely, emancipationist senator Claude Pepper (D-FL) asserted that "the amendment proposes that at long last women shall be emancipated and placed before the law equal with the masculine portion of the population."[50] As with all emancipationists, Pepper claimed that the ERA would bolster American ideals and free American women from outworn discriminations.

Near the close of the debate Senator Carl Hayden (D-AZ) proposed a rider to the amendment. It read, "The provisions of this article shall not be construed to impair any rights, benefits or exemptions conferred by law upon persons of the female sex." Senator Hayden went on to argue that God had made men and women different and that his own mother had borne and breast-fed him, while his father had provided them food and shelter on the "wild Apache-infested frontier." He concluded that the law should recognize differences between men and women "by grant-ing rights and benefits and exemptions to women which are not necessarily granted to men."[51]

This rider was primarily Senator Hayden's idea, as he had been considering the idea of a saving clause since the ERA's advance during the war. After Hayden had served eight terms in the House of Representatives, the people of Arizona elected him to the Sen-ate in 1926. He would serve seven terms as a senator, setting a record as the longest-serving member of Congress. Throughout his time in office, Senator Hayden was a fervent ERA critic.[52] In his view, if the ERA were to pass, it would be "dire to our social structure."[53] While Hayden had preferred the specific method as the best strategy for enhancing women's status, he believed that at the very least his rider could offer a type of fail-safe mechanism in case Congress and the states were to pass the amendment. As he later claimed to a fellow senator, he felt that his rider would help protect the "special consideration" entitled to women due to their "social, economic, and physiological" nature.[54]

Apparently Hayden's colleagues were more than happy to take advantage of the opportunity that his rider had provided for them. On January 25, 1950, the Senate voted 51–31 for the Hayden rider and 63–19 for the ERA, easily over the two-thirds vote required for a constitutional amendment. The ERA then went to the House with the newly added Hayden rider. Similar to the Women's Sta-tus Bill, the Hayden rider offered politicians the chance to go on record in support of a different approach for enriching women's status—a way that embraced both equality and special protection for women citizens.[55]

Even with this support, several protectionist groups initially found the Hayden rider troublesome. These reservations came from the organizations largely associated with the NCSW, as they feared that

the rider would not adequately protect all the sex-based legal distinctions that they had assumed to be actual benefits for women.[56]
Katherine Ellickson of the CIO, for example, argued in a letter to
her congressional representative that the rider would increase the
"confusion" and would not "lesson the danger."[57]

Emancipationists of course openly criticized the Hayden rider.
As with their criticisms of the proposed saving clauses during the
ERA drafting process of the early 1920s, amendment proponents
argued that the addition of the rider would essentially nullify the
concept of complete constitutional sexual equality. Senator Pepper, for instance, declared on the Senate floor that the rider would
"emasculate the effect of the proposed constitutional amendment."[58]
Additionally, Alice Paul maintained to the *New York Times* that it
would be "impossible to imagine the Constitution containing two
such paragraphs."[59]

Ultimately, though, these criticisms did not matter, because
the Hayden rider proved to be an effective tool for halting the
ERA's progress. In 1950 the rider forced Katharine St. George, a
pro-ERA member of the House, to stop her attempts to have the
amendment released from the House Judiciary Committee. At
this time Representative St. George had gathered enough signatures to discharge the amendment from its committee; however,
fear of the Hayden rider eventually prompted St. George to withdraw her petition. Because emancipationists could conceive of no
other option, they chose to stall the amendment rather than have
it pass with the Hayden rider attached.[60]

As Representative St. George's failed effort to push the ERA out
of the House Judiciary Committee indicates, the amendment faced
another considerable hurdle in Congress: the intense animosity
of Emanuel Celler (D-NY), who chaired the House Judiciary Committee. Representative Celler, who had been serving in the House
of Representatives since 1923 and would end up serving in office
for almost fifty years, had been a proponent of civil rights legislation for Black Americans.[61] As noted in chapter 3, Representative
Celler first became involved with women's rights activism when he
assisted women's organizations in their fight against Section 213 of
the Economy Act in the early 1930s. Like most other liberal protec-

tionists, Celler opposed measures that he considered unfair labor practices against women, but he also supported the notion of equitable sex-based legal distinctions. In Celler's opinion the ERA was a "mischief-breeding piece of legislation," because he believed it threatened women's natural and essential right to protection. If the ERA ever became part of the Constitution, he argued, "then we shall realize how, with cats' paws, it worked itself quietly into our midst and then, once, in a whirlwind of activity, shattered, discarded and disrupted almost every phase of human relationships." Celler felt that ERA proponents had chosen to ignore what he saw as the "fundamental differences of physical capacity between men and women, the differences in social responsibility, [and] the pattern of our culture."[62]

Since Mary Anderson of the NCSW was aware of Representative Celler's deep antipathy for the ERA, she decided to meet with him in the days following the Senate's 1950 passage of the ERA, which had the Hayden rider attached. During the meeting Celler assured Anderson that he too held reservations about the rider. As Anderson later reported to fellow NCSW member Margaret Stone, Celler felt that "the best strategy in the House [was] to continue to keep it in Committee."[63] Celler remained true to his promise, as he refused to call a hearing on the ERA during the majority of his decades-long tenure as chair of the House Judiciary Committee. Consequently, the amendment remained bottled up in the House committee until 1970.[64]

Because emancipationists detested the Hayden rider, the protectionist groups that had originally been critical of it eventually came to realize that the measure did provide them with another valuable instrument for thwarting the ERA's advance. As such, in the early 1950s groups affiliated with the NCSW began to urge Senator Hayden to propose his rider whenever the amendment appeared to be progressing in the Senate.[65] Senator Hayden happily complied with these requests. He introduced his rider in 1951 and 1953, which effectively blocked the amendment from moving through Congress, as ERA proponents still refused to support the measure in its altered form.[66] On the success of the Hayden rider, the leadership of the CIO concluded at its convention in

1953 that "the strongest original proponents of equal rights have now lost interest in the amended constitutional amendment. It is not likely that much progress will be made in pushing the constitutional amendment further now that the Hayden amendment is incorporated within it."[67]

While the Hayden rider and Representative Celler's enmity had posed considerable obstacles to the ERA's progress in Congress, emancipationists did have a few reasons to hold out hope for their amendment in the early 1950s. In 1951 Eleanor Roosevelt put forward a cautious endorsement of the amendment. "For a long time," the former First Lady wrote, "I felt that the amendment was completely foolish. Men and women can be equal but they cannot be identical. They will always have different functions. . . . Nevertheless, I can see that perhaps it adds a little to the position of women to be declared equal before the law."[68] This hesitant endorsement was a result of the former First Lady's work at the United Nations, which had made her more sensitive to the international implications of constitutional equality for men and women citizens.[69] Even with this support, Eleanor Roosevelt continued to actively back what she understood to be more flexible approaches for addressing women's status, such as the Women's Status Bill, federal equal pay legislation, and a presidential commission on the status of women. For the former First Lady, these measures afforded better strategies for expanding women's place in society, because they did not completely set aside the basis for sex-specific legal distinctions.[70]

The result of the 1952 presidential election too gave emancipationists a glimmer of hope, because newly elected president Dwight D. Eisenhower initially appeared to favor the emancipationist position. When President Eisenhower entered office, he replaced the head of the Women's Bureau, Frieda Miller, the avid ERA opponent who had helped to establish the NCSW, with Alice Leopold, a Republican politician and former businesswoman. Although Leopold did not explicitly endorse the ERA, she did remove the bureau's formal opposition to the amendment during her time in office.[71] In October 1956, moreover, President Eisenhower offered a provisional endorsement of the ERA during an address delivered at Madison Square Garden. "We shall seek, as we promised in our Platform," President Eisenhower vowed during his speech, "to assure women everywhere in our land equality of rights."[72]

Nevertheless, there were significant drawbacks to President Eisenhower's apparent support for the ERA. First, the president did not fully understand the purpose of the amendment. In the notes of an April 1954 legislative meeting L. Arthur Minnich, the assistant staff secretary, recorded that when the amendment came up the president expressed his confusion over the issue as he "thought women had equal rights!"[73] Making matters worse for the ERA, the president's secretary of labor, James Mitchell, utterly opposed the amendment. He believed that women required special protection, especially in the industrial realm.[74] In the minutes of a February 1957 policy meeting Secretary Mitchell observed that, with regard to the ERA, President Eisenhower suggested that he was "for [it], but not quite." Consequently, Mitchell's notes indicate, the president advised the secretary to "fudge" on the issue.[75] President Eisenhower's support for the ERA was unenthusiastic at best. Although his public endorsement of the ERA at Madison Square Garden had excited emancipationists, his lackluster private support failed to help emancipationists propel the amendment forward in the hostile environment that protectionists had created in Congress.

In sum, the combination of the Hayden rider and Representative Celler's interference had successfully stymied the ERA's move through Congress. In 1957 Representative Celler alluded to the amendment's dismal prospects in Congress when he proclaimed in a *Los Angeles Times* article that the ERA was no longer a serious issue and that it was simply an "old hat." The article reported how "modern women" were more interested in "marriage, children, and security" and not the "kind of equality that their mothers and grandmothers [had] fought for."[76] As these comments suggest, the protectionist resurgence had effectively suppressed the allure of emancipationism by the late 1950s.

The Triumph of Protectionism

By the close of the decade protectionists had regained the dominant position in the original ERA conflict. Of course there were still ardent ERA supporters, but the campaign effort had largely evaporated over the course of the mid- to late 1950s. The NWP's journal, *Equal Rights*, had stopped publication in 1954, and throughout the 1950s the NWP had suffered from contentious internal disputes, which led to a significant decline in its membership.[77] As the ranks of ERA supporters diminished, the amendment languished in Congress. After the serious congressional movement on the ERA in the late 1940s and early 1950s, the amendment failed to receive meaningful congressional consideration again until 1970. This failure stemmed from the continual threat of the Hayden rider and Representative Celler's refusal to call a hearing on the amendment.[78] With the ERA's prospects in Congress dwindling, both political parties became less interested in the issue, and they eventually removed explicit support for the ERA from their party platforms in the early 1960s.[79]

As the threat of the ERA declined, so too did the participation of conservative protectionists in the opposition effort. To be clear, many conservatives still opposed the amendment, but by this time conservative amendment opponents had largely dismissed the ERA as a frivolous issue. In 1956, for instance, author Ida Mercedes Darden, a staunch conservative, asserted that ERA proponents represented just a few "aggressive supporters of Susan B. Anthony."[80] Likewise, lawyer V. L. Hash, another conservative-minded critic of the ERA, conveyed to an assistant of Senator Carl Hayden that he was no longer concerned with the amendment, because it simply did not represent the "universal desire of women." He further explained that he was more alarmed by "the socialistic legislation now being proposed before Congress . . . so-called Civil Rights."[81]

At this point conservatives were turning toward what they had understood to be a more pervasive menace: the supposed international communist threat. As historian Allan Lichtman explains, "By 1953, the right was swinging full circle from disengaged nationalism to a nationalism engaged with battling the global 'communist conspiracy.'"[82] For conservatives, especially those from the South, the movement toward civil rights for Black Americans had represented a significant component of the communist danger. Southern segregationists viewed federally mandated racial integration as endangering private property, religion, public safety, and states' rights. Put another way, they associated racial integration with communist subversion and the loss of what they believed to be essential American values. As the ERA campaign effort weakened over the course of the 1950s, conservative ERA opponents redirected their attention to what they had viewed to be a more pressing concern: the racial subversion embedded in the looming communist threat.[83]

While conservative ERA opponents had turned their attention to other issues, liberal protectionists came to see the ERA as more of an annoyance than an immediate hazard. Steadfast ERA critic and workers' advocate Esther Peterson became particularly annoyed with the ERA during the 1960 presidential election. Peterson, who had been a lobbyist for the CIO and a strong proponent of the Women's Status Bill, joined Senator John F. Kennedy's campaign once he had announced his intention to run for the presidency.[84] Peterson would later become the head of the Women's Bureau during President Kennedy's administration. She would also go on to serve as the primary director of the President's Commission on the Status of Women (PCSW). In the early 1960s Peterson explained to the *Washington Post* that she opposed the ERA because "it just happens that there are two sexes; they are biologically different and women need special consideration in certain areas as well as equality."[85] From Peterson's perspective, the ERA detracted from her and her allies' legitimate efforts to strengthen women's position. During the 1960 presidential election Peterson made her frustration with the few remaining ERA proponents clear by frequently calling the amendment a "nuisance" and describing ERA supporters as nothing more than a "pile of peanuts."[86]

Peterson's annoyance with the ERA came to a head in the fall of 1960, when Senator Kennedy replied to a letter from Emma Guffey Miller, the always fervent emancipationist. In the letter Kennedy expressed his support for women's equality, but he did not explicitly endorse the ERA. Peterson approved of this version of the letter before the Kennedy campaign sent it to Miller. According to historian Cynthia Harrison, Miller, unsatisfied with the vague response from Kennedy, took the matter into her own hands. She first changed the letter so that it included a specific endorsement of the ERA. She then had a colleague deliver it to the DNC, where a publicity committee assistant typed the letter on official Kennedy campaign letterhead. The assistant had the revised letter signed, by machine, without approval from Kennedy's campaign staff or Peterson. Thereupon, the updated letter now included explicit support for the ERA from Kennedy.[87] As one would expect, Miller's deceptive actions infuriated Peterson. Despite Peterson's anger, liberal protectionists within the Kennedy campaign understood that the ERA's chances were weak given that the Hayden rider and Representative Celler's blocking of the amendment in the House Judiciary Committee had continued to limit the amendment's prospects in Congress. As a result, the campaign decided to leave the matter alone so as to avoid calling attention to any discord within the organization.[88]

But Peterson did not set aside her frustration with Miller and the remaining ERA supporters.[89] Because of her annoyance with the ERA, Peterson set out to eliminate the amendment as an issue in its entirety. In her eyes the best way to get rid of the ERA was to simply make it unnecessary.[90] The outcome of the 1960 presidential election provided Peterson with the resources she needed to achieve this goal. Upon his election, President Kennedy appointed Peterson to two positions: director of the Women's Bureau and assistant secretary of labor. Peterson's assertiveness in these dual roles allowed her to wield considerable authority, especially over programs that dealt with women's societal position. Most important, this influence gave Peterson the opportunity to pursue a protectionist proposal that she had supported for more than a decade: the creation of a presidential commission on the status of women.[91]

Peterson was not alone in her consistent support for the proposed commission. Other unwavering advocates included Eleanor Roosevelt, Mary Anderson, Frances Perkins, and Frieda Miller. Liberal protectionists had consistently supported this proposal ever since ERA opponents had articulated the idea in the Women's Status Bill during the late 1940s. Liberal protectionists clung to the notion of a presidential commission well after the enthusiasm for the Women's Status Bill had faded among conservative protectionists in the mid-1950s.[92] While both liberal and conservative protectionists maintained that in theory sex-based distinctions in law and custom could be equitable, liberal protectionists were always more consistent in acknowledging that there were outdated discriminations that negatively affected women's opportunities. In short, liberal protectionists persisted in their belief that a presidential commission on the status of women could initiate a rational process for the removal of the harmful discriminations against women while leaving the otherwise equitable distinctions in place.

Upon President Kennedy's election, Peterson quickly revived the idea of creating a commission on the status of women. Approximately two months after Kennedy's inaugural speech in January 1961, Peterson met with trade union women and fellow liberal protectionists to discuss the idea. This small group of labor activists included Helen Berthelot of the Communications Workers of America (CWA), Dorothy Lowther Robinson of the Amalgamated Clothing Workers of America (ACWA), and Katherine Ellickson of the AFL-CIO.[93] Ellickson was the most prominent member of this group besides Peterson, since they would both exercise considerable influence over the commission once it was established.[94] Ellickson, who had been a fierce advocate for working mothers' welfare during the postwar years, had also been a notable member of the NCSW.[95] After this first meeting the group began to draft its proposal for a presidential commission on the status of women.[96]

In the spring and early summer of 1961 Peterson and the Women's Bureau staff, along with Ellickson, refined their arguments for the commission to win the support of Secretary of Labor Arthur Goldberg, who was a former labor counsel to the United Steelworkers and the CIO and an old friend of Peterson.[97] In June, Peterson secured Secretary Goldberg's support after she had sent him a persuasive overview of the proposed commission. She started the summary by arguing that the commission "would substitute constructive recommendations for the present troublesome and futile agitation about the 'equal rights' amendment."[98] Indeed, the specter of the ERA was very much on the minds of the commission's architects. For Peterson and her colleagues the commission could eliminate the ERA as an issue because it could deal with the changes in women's societal position and render the amendment pointless.[99] At one of the early trade union meetings where Peterson had reinvigorated the idea of creating a commission, Katherine Ellickson surmised that "women are in a better position to advance their cause if they don't key to the feminist view."[100] As well, in a draft of the overview that Peterson eventually sent to Secretary Goldberg, Peterson suggested that unlike the ERA, the proposed commission would be aimed "to effect more equitable treatment of women without jeopardizing the other necessary and desirable legislation."[101] From the viewpoint of the commission's organizers, their measure provided a more balanced approach for improving women's status. In yet another draft of her overview to Secretary Goldberg, Peterson maintained that there was surely a need for a commission because, as she put it, "questions continue to be raised about the status of women under our laws. . . . We need to examine our laws. . . . We must assure women their fundamental rights as citizens." But she again cautioned that the commission should be careful so as to not threaten the "necessary and desirable legislation" that afforded women special protection.[102]

In a subsequent memo on the proposed commission, Peterson and her collaborators expressed a similar view on the need to distinguish between reasonable and unreasonable sex-based policies. The memo explained that "some differences in economic, civil, and political rights of men and women arise from basic differences in social function—the fact that women are mothers and homemakers. However, certain other differences have no ready explanation, but appear to be based on prejudice, custom, or tradition."[103] Doing away with the underlying need for the ERA was not the only intention for the commission. More precisely, Peterson and her allies saw the measure as a way to promote a different program for enriching women's status—a program that would not threaten sex-based policies in their entirety.[104]

After gaining Secretary Goldberg's support in June, Peterson persuaded Katherine Ellickson to take leave from her position at the AFL-CIO and commit herself to work full-time on the creation of the commission. In the following months Ellickson, in coordination with Peterson, Goldberg, trade union women, and the Women's Bureau personnel, created a background report that outlined the reasons for establishing a commission.[105] In a draft of the paper, Ellickson stressed that the commission would recognize that "women's difficulties are intensified because . . . motherhood involves special needs and responsibilities and women's roles outside of the home are relatively new."[106] Thus, the commission's architects acknowledged that the increased participation of women in the labor force had enhanced women's public position. They assumed, however, that at society's core women's roles fundamentally differed from men's roles and that those differences necessitated sex-specific treatment. For them, a presidential commission could advance women's status without causing harm to women's supposedly natural roles in the domestic sphere. As they concluded in a draft of their proposal, their commission would be aimed "to strengthen home life by directing attention to critical problems confronting women as wives, mothers, homemakers, and workers."[107] In sum, they sought to enlarge women's social roles within the framework of the traditionally ordered family.[108]

In December 1961 President Kennedy agreed to the proposal and created the PCSW with Executive Order 10980. The order declared that the commission was needed, as "prejudices and outmoded customs act as barriers to the full realization of women's basic rights which should be respected and fostered." The order continued by asserting that the commission would promote measures that "contribute to family security, strengthen home life, and advance the general welfare." Overall, the order stated that the commission would review and make recommendations in the areas of private and federal practices, women's legal status, and family services.[109]

Peterson, as she had earlier told the *Washington Post*, intended to make the commission a representation of "the best brains in the country."[110] The membership of the PCSW included fifteen women and eleven men. The twenty-eight individuals who made up the commission were government officials, legal experts, social reformers, academics, labor organizers, and politicians. Notable members on the commission included Dorothy Height, president of the National Council for Negro Women; AFL-CIO secretary-treasurer William Schnitzler; Representative Edith Green (D-OR); Radcliffe College president Mary Bunting; Attorney General Robert Kennedy; Labor Secretary Goldberg; historian Caroline R. Ware; Henry David, president of the New School for Social Research; and Margaret Hickey, who was an editor for *Ladies' Home Journal.*[111] Peterson divided the commission into the following seven committees: Civil and Political Rights; Education; Federal Employment; Home and Community; Private Employment; Protective Labor Legislation; and Social Insurance and Taxes. Each committee was able to invite twelve to fourteen well-informed persons to participate in the research work and to make recommendations to the full PCSW.[112] In addition, Peterson selected Eleanor Roosevelt to serve as the "chairman" of the PCSW and Richard Lester, a Princeton University economics professor, to serve as the commission's vice-chair.[113] As will be discussed in more detail later, the PCSW included only one official, active ERA supporter: Marguerite Rawalt, a lawyer.[114]

While the membership of the PCSW and its subsidiary bodies included several persons, Peterson, Ellickson, and the Women's Bureau personnel dominated the commission's proceedings and operations. To begin with, Peterson held a key place on the commission as its executive vice-chair, and Ellickson worked as the commission's executive secretary. Since the commission met only eight times in the two years of its existence, and as the death of Eleanor Roosevelt in 1962 deprived the commission of its official chair, Peterson and her affiliates were able to exert considerable control over the commission's work.[115]

The PCSW released its findings and recommendations in its final report, published in October 1963 and titled *American Women.*[116] In general, the report endorsed the enlargement of women's access to education, the enhancement of women's employment opportunities, and the strengthening of women's participation in government. The report also captured the persistent legal discriminations that had continued to restrict women's ability to fully participate in the public realm. For instance, the report showed that three states still prohibited women from serving on juries, while twenty-six states maintained different standards for exempting men and women from jury service. The report advocated for the enactment of legislation "to achieve equal jury service in the states" to remedy these issues.[117] Additionally, the report called attention to the various state laws that had continued to limit married women's ability to enter into contracts, own property, engage in business, and maintain their own domicile. The report recommended further investigation into such laws to initiate a process for modernizing them.[118]

The PCSW's work resulted in several concrete actions aimed to benefit women. First, the commission successfully requested a review of a conventional practice within the federal government that had allowed agency heads to designate whether they preferred a man or woman for a given position. After the review, President Kennedy instructed all federal agencies to make selections based on a person's merit and without regard to sex, "except in unusual circumstances."[119] Upon the PCSW's recommendation, President Kennedy established two organizations: the Interdepartmental Committee on the Status of Women (ICSW) and the Citizens' Advisory Council on the Status of Women (CACSW). President Kennedy formed these two groups to encourage further action on the commission's research. The ICSW and the CACSW were essentially continuations of the president's commission. The former group, for example, included all the Cabinet members who had been on the president's commission, adding the secretaries of state and defense. As well, Kennedy named to the CACSW all members of the presidential commission who were not government employees. The PCSW's report, moreover, resulted in the formation of fifty state-level commissions that were set up to examine local sex-based laws and practices.[120]

Besides these accomplishments, the PCSW's work helped to further federal equal pay legislation. In truth, liberal protectionists who were associated with the NCDURA and the NCSW had been advocating for federal equal pay legislation since the mid-1940s. As explained in previous chapters, liberal protectionists who had aligned with the maternalist reform tradition opposed labor practices that they believed unfairly privileged men workers, such as sex-based wage differentials. In an effort to combat what they understood to be unfair practices, liberal protectionists such as Frieda Miller, Mary Anderson, and Dorothy McAllister had first called for state-level equal pay legislation. During the late 1930s, however, the initial state-level campaigns made little progress, as the male-dominated organized labor faction of liberal protectionism was less inclined to oppose labor practices that primarily benefited men. This obstacle largely disappeared after World War II, as more women entered labor unions and began to have an impact on the policies of organized labor. Thanks to the growing influence of women in labor unions, both the AFL and the CIO endorsed the principle of equal pay at the end of the war. At the same time, the United Electrical Workers of America (UE) and the United Automobile Workers (UAW) endorsed the concept of federal equal pay legislation.[121]

In the late 1940s the equal pay campaign had evolved to encompass a solid drive for federal equal pay legislation.[122] That effort eventually succeeded after years of advocacy work when the PCSW made its early calls for equal pay legislation known, which then advanced the political effort that became the Equal Pay Act of 1963.[123] As an amendment to the FLSA, the measure made sex-based wage differentials above the minimal wage level impermissible for men and women engaged in occupations related to interstate commerce. In other words, the act stipulated that employers involved in interstate commerce had to pay equal wages for equal work.[124] But there were significant limitations to the Equal Pay Act of 1963. Since the measure was only an amendment to the FLSA, all of the exceptions of the FLSA remained intact. Thus, in the early 1960s the act continued to exclude persons who worked in agriculture, hotels, motels, restaurants, and laundries. Furthermore, as an extension to the FLSA, the measure had left state-level special labor laws for women workers in place. As well, the act did not include any specific guidance for administrative enforcement. Women had to depend on the federal courts to enforce the provisions of the bill. Unfortunately, such litigation typically required employees to utilize their own resources; in many cases such resources were meager unless a local or national union backed the would-be plaintiff.[125]

The issues with the Equal Pay Act grew out of the deeper socioeconomic problem of the sex-segregated labor force and the traditions that acutely delineated the work that men and women were allowed to perform. On a practical level, equal pay for equal work meant little to the vast majority of women who were working in sex-

ually segregated occupations.[126] The act's limitations also sprang
from its turbulent congressional journey. The House and Senate
had voted on two different equal pay bills in 1962, but the conference committee that convened to work on those bills failed to
develop a compromise. The next year the Kennedy administration, under the guidance of Esther Peterson, endorsed a specific
(more limited) equal pay proposal, which led to the Equal Pay
Act of 1963. While Peterson and her liberal protectionist associ-
ates desired a comprehensive bill, they had come to realize that a
compromise bill was better than nothing.[127]

Notwithstanding the Equal Pay Act's substantial limitations,
liberal protectionists who had backed the legislation hailed it as
a positive move for eradicating the unfair practices that negatively affected women in the workforce. In the *Washington Post*,
Mary Anderson declared to a reporter that the measure marked
"a definite step forward in the recognition of women."[128] In sum,
the Equal Pay Act signified a broader victory for liberal protectionists. As they saw it, the measure had showed that it was possible to achieve concrete, legislative action to help women even in
the absence of complete constitutional sexual equality.[129]

Although the work of the PCSW produced considerable legislative and executive measures intended to benefit women, the ethos
of protectionism constrained the potential of the commission's
work. By way of illustration, the PCSW's Committee on Home and
Community insisted in its report that "over and above whatever
role modern women play in community . . . the care of the home
and the children remains their unique responsibility. No matter
how much everyday tasks are shared or how equal marriage partnership may be, the care of the children is primarily the province of the mother. This is not debatable as a philosophy. It will
remain a fact of life."[130] The PCSW's Committee on Education also
reflected the commission's insistence on enhancing women's status within the confines of the traditional sexual order. "The expec-
tation," the Committee on Education asserted in its report, "that
a woman will become a wife and mother differentiates the educational requirements of girl and boy from the very beginning."[131]
Last, but even more significantly, the full PCSW concluded in its

final report that "widening the choices for women beyond their doorstep does not imply neglect of their education for responsibilities in the home."[132] While the PCSW had worked to strengthen women's influence and eliminate the unfair disadvantages against women, it remained dedicated to the protectionist contention that women possessed a unique duty in the domestic realm to bear and raise children. Above all, the commission followed the protectionist view that sex roles could not fundamentally change.[133]

Alongside these pronouncements, the protectionist mind-set that infused the PCSW shaped and directed its handling of special labor legislation as well as the overall concept of sex discrimination. The commission, for instance, recommended that special labor legislation that regulated women's work hours should be "maintained and strengthened."[134] In addition, the commission ruled against expanding Executive Order 10925, which had barred discrimination by federal contractors on the basis of race, creed, color, or national origin. "We are aware," the PCSW remarked in an explanation of its decision, "that this order could be expanded to forbid discriminations based on sex. But discriminations based on sex . . . involve problems sufficiently different from discriminations based on the other factors. . . . Experience is needed in determining what constitutes unjustified discrimination in the treatment of women workers."[135] From the perspective of the PCSW, distinctions in law and practice based on sex were not always hostile acts. In the understanding of the PCSW, sex discrimination could be benevolent, since men and women differed in their biological and social functions. As historian Alice Kessler-Harris describes the PCSW's outlook, it was molded by popular conceptions of "fairness and justice rooted in the home."[136] As a whole, the PCSW sought to enlarge women's participation in public life while reinforcing the importance of conventional family roles.

When it came to the divisive issue of the ERA, the PCSW offered a different constitutional method for resolving the issues surrounding women's legal status. In actuality, there was very little chance, if any, that the PCSW would have endorsed the ERA. For starters, Peterson and the colleagues who had helped her to organize the commission were dedicated protectionists. Moreover, the membership of the PCSW overwhelmingly consisted of ERA critics, and not a single leading official of the NWP had been invited to join the commission.[137] Even though Peterson had envisioned the commission to be (in part) a tool for eliminating the ERA, she understood that the commission would not succeed in advancing policies to improve women's position if the controversy over the ERA sidetracked its efforts. In an attempt to prevent a backlash among ERA supporters, Peterson decided that when the commission formally started its work, it would avoid committing to a definitive stance against the amendment.[138]

In another move to mitigate potential criticism of the PCSW from ERA proponents, Peterson made sure that the commission included at least one known ERA backer: Marguerite Rawalt. In the years leading up to the commission Rawalt had been a prominent attorney and an influential advocate for women. In 1943 the Federal Bar Association elected Rawalt to be its president. She was the first woman to hold that position. Throughout her career Rawalt was also active with the BPWC.[139] Regarding the PCSW, Peterson asked Rawalt to serve on the commission because she had recognized that a commission without any ERA supporters would appear to lack sincerity in its proposed objectivity. In Peterson's view, Rawalt was a sensible advocate of the ERA. She was respectful of Peterson's beliefs, and in the past she had even commended Peterson for her commitment to bolstering women's status. For the PCSW, Peterson requested that Rawalt help direct the Committee on Civil and Political Rights. Peterson had hoped that her decision to include Rawalt on the commission would help garner support for the PCSW among the growing number of ERA proponents who were no longer vehemently attached to the idea of complete constitutional sexual equality.[140]

At Rawalt's urging, the Committee on Civil and Political Rights tackled the issue of women's constitutional status.[141] In its report the committee admitted that there were numerous ambiguities surrounding women's constitutional rights. The committee asserted that while the "legal status of women has improved greatly," it cautioned that outdated practices continued to restrict women's ability to fully participate in public life.[142] The final report of the PCSW concluded that "judicial clarification is imperative in order that remaining ambiguities with respect to the constitutional protection of women's rights be eliminated."[143] Although the PCSW had recognized that women's rights necessitated an official clarification, it did not endorse the principle of absolute constitutional equality as the best method for securing women's status as full citizens. Instead, the commission approved of a different, more flexible constitutional strategy for resolving the issues surrounding women's civic stature.

Pauli Murray, a prominent Black attorney connected to the civil rights movement, developed the new constitutional approach. Murray, who was a member of the PCSW's Committee on Civil and Political Rights, proposed in a lengthy paper that the commission recommend a concentrated effort to pursue litigation of a case involving a discriminatory state law. The goal of this tactic, Murray argued, would be to have the Supreme Court decide that arbitrary discriminations against women violated their rights as citizens under the Fourteenth Amendment.[144] Murray maintained that this judicial path would allow the high court to draw clearer lines between laws that unfairly discriminated against women and those that genuinely protected women's welfare. Murray's contention rested on her belief that the Supreme Court's decision in *Brown v. Board of Education* (1954) had indicated that the court would be more willing to issue a favorable ruling on women's standing under the Fourteenth Amendment. In Murray's assessment a favorable ruling in this regard could heighten the level of judicial scrutiny for sex discrimination cases without invalidating the basis for sex-specific treatment entirely.[145]

At the time of the PCSW's work, Murray was wary of the total equality advocated by ERA supporters. As Cynthia Harrison explains, Murray felt that sex-specific legal classifications could be appropriate when they protected women's family and maternal functions or when they dealt with women's traditionally disadvantaged position.[146] During this period Murray had backed legislation that applied to all women of childbearing age for the purposes of protecting potential mothers. Murray also supported special labor laws for working women.[147] Murray's position on the ERA would evolve in subsequent years, as Murray, like so many others, began to see the amendment as an alluring nexus for women's rights activism by the beginning of the following decade.[148] But at this earlier moment Murray clung to the notion that a judicial route based on an appeal to the Fourteenth Amendment could allow women to secure the constitutional recognition and personal dignity of being full citizens without risking their claim to sex-specific legal treatment in certain instances.[149]

In its final report the PCSW followed Murray's suggestion. It asserted that the Constitution already had equality provisions, in the Fifth Amendment and more notably in the Fourteenth Amendment, which affirmed women's civic stature as full citizens. Accordingly, it reasoned, an additional constitutional amendment "need not now be sought." The report went on to recommend that interested parties should actively pursue a "judicial clarification" of women's rights under the Fifth and Fourteenth Amendments to help distinguish between "justifiable" sex-based distinctions and "archaic standards."[150]

After the conclusion of the PCSW's work, Esther Peterson proudly wrote to Senator Hayden, "The commission is convinced that the U.S. Constitution now embodies equality of rights for men and women." She went on to describe how the PCSW recommended that concerned groups should bring forward judicial cases "involving laws and practices which discriminate against women" in order to test their validity under the Fourteenth Amendment. She cautioned, though, that this newly proposed plan to use the Fourteenth Amendment would be "directed solely against unreasonable and unjust legal discriminations."[151] In a statement on the PCSW's report, Senator Hayden hailed the new method as "refreshingly sensible." He suggested that the Supreme Court had a long history of interpreting the Constitution as permitting sex-specific legal treatment so long as such laws upheld reasonable sex-based distinctions. Consequently, he concluded that the PCSW's recommendation had provided a constructive way for making determinations as "to whether a given instance of differential treatment is reasonable and justifiable or whether it constitutes an arbitrary discrimination."[152] According to Peterson and Hayden, their alternative constitutional strategy offered a positive and practical method for dealing with the ambiguities surrounding women's legal standing. In their analyses this judicial approach could secure an intermediate but nonetheless appropriate level of sexual equality that would preserve what they understood to be equitable distinctions between the rights of men and women citizens.

As the sole active ERA supporter on the PCSW, Rawalt urged the commission to include in its final report the phrase "not now" in its assessment of the ERA. The PCSW's inclusion of this qualifying phrase encouraged a considerable number of remaining amendment supporters to back the PCSW's recommendation, since it was not an outright denunciation of the amendment. With the exception of the NWP, groups that had previously aligned with the emancipationist position, such as the BPWC, subsequently endorsed the judicial route as a limited but nevertheless suitable alternative. In the view of these previous ERA devotees, the newly advocated judicial strategy represented a more viable way for obtaining a constitutional recognition of women's rights, as the ERA was continuing to languish in Congress.[153]

In the end the PCSW had further refined the protectionist position. On the one hand, protectionists could now argue that an additional amendment was unnecessary, since the Constitution already included a provision—the Fourteenth Amendment—that could be used to confirm women's rights as citizens. As well, protectionists could contend that while the Fourteenth Amendment affirmed both men and women as full citizens, it did not preclude the law from treating citizens differently on account of sex. In sum, the protectionists' new constitutional approach aimed to heighten the level of judicial scrutiny for sex discrimination cases without setting aside sex-specific legal classifications completely. With this strategy, the PCSW had started to craft the concept of intermediate constitutional equality for men and women citizens. As the epilogue discusses, this intermediate notion of equality still helps to guide the modern constitutional doctrine of gender jurisprudence in the United States.

Conclusion

Starting in the late 1940s, protectionists changed their ERA opposition strategy to subdue the lingering emancipationist impulse. In
building their new affirmative program, protectionists had created a
series of alternative comprehensive measures not only to address the
problems embedded in women's societal status but also to defend
their belief in the different rights of men and women citizens. With
the Women's Status Bill, the Hayden rider, the Equal Pay Act, and
the PCSW, protectionists successfully promoted a campaign that
called for both equality and special protection for women. These
initiatives, moreover, boosted protectionists' claims that absolute
constitutional sexual equality was not essential for bettering wom-
en's status. By the close of the original ERA conflict, protectionists
had strengthened America's gendered citizenship. Most important,
they had developed a new strategy for obtaining the constitutional
affirmation of women's status as full citizens, which eschewed pronouncements of total equality and preserved the rationale for sex-
specific legal treatment. Although by the end of the original ERA
conflict protectionists had succeeded in restraining emancipationism, political and cultural developments in the mid- to late 1960s
did produce an ideological break that would change the dynamics of American society. As the epilogue explains, these changes
would eventually give birth to the second ERA conflict. Yet, despite
the momentous developments of the late 1960s and early 1970s,
the ethos of protectionism ultimately prevailed, as amendment
opponents defeated the ERA once more by returning to the contention that complete constitutional sexual equality would endanger the American family and imperil American society.

Epilogue
The Legacy of Protectionism

The original conflict over the ERA created America's gendered citizenship. Although the Nineteenth Amendment had changed women's relationship to the state, disparities in men's and women's positions persisted because protectionists modernized the justification for sex-specific treatment during the original ERA conflict. In particular, protectionists developed a new way of understanding American citizenship that upheld dual standards with sex-specific rights for men and women citizens. By the original conflict's end, protectionists had created the concept of intermediate constitutional equality for men and women citizens; this concept calls for the constitutional recognition of both men and women as rights-bearing citizens through the Fourteenth Amendment without fully setting aside the government's ability to treat citizens differently on account of sex.

In the mid- to late 1960s a reenergized women's activism led to a reawakening of the ERA campaign, which took off in the 1970s. During the second ERA conflict, amendment proponents and opponents both continued to draw from the core arguments of the original conflict. But societal developments had enhanced the liberal aspects of emancipationism and the conservative elements of protectionism. As a result, the second ERA conflict came to fall more in line with what we now understand to be conventional political positions: liberals demanded gender equality while conserva-

tives supported sex-specific standards that adhered to traditional
views of gender differences. Ultimately, ERA opponents defeated
the amendment for a second time by advancing a central protectionist notion, which was that true sexual equity requires the law
to be free to treat men and women citizens differently. Today the
protectionist concept of intermediate sexual equality still shapes
the modern constitutional doctrine of gender jurisprudence. Furthermore, the protectionist emphasis on limited constitutional
equality for men and women citizens continues to sustain wom-
en's disadvantaged position because it has failed to fully bridge
the gap between men's and women's citizenship.

The Renewal of Women's Social and Political Activism

The addition of the word "sex" to a section of a major bill aimed at
eradicating race discrimination set off a chain of events that eventually led to the revitalization of women's activism and the rebirth
of the ERA campaign. In February 1964 Representative Howard
W. Smith (D-VA) introduced an amendment to the proposed civil
rights bill that included sex in the list of prohibited discriminations in employment practices. Representative Smith's antagonism
toward civil rights was well known; consequently, Smith's proposal
appeared to many observers as a conservative attempt to prevent
the bill's passage. But Smith was a longtime supporter of the ERA.
At this time conservative-leaning amendment supporters such as
Smith backed the ERA partly as a way to ensure that Black Americans did not have an advantage over white women. Thus, it is quite
possible that Smith genuinely believed in formal legal equality for
white men and women. Smith had furthermore proposed adding
the sex provision to the civil rights bill at the request of the NWP.[1]
Whatever his motivation for the proposal, the Civil Rights Act of
1964 passed Congress with the inclusion of the sex provision.

At first the liberal protectionists who were largely associated with
the Women's Bureau and the PCSW had opposed the provision.
As historian Cynthia Harrison puts it, "the President's Commission on the Status of Women had not predicted or advocated so
sweeping a legal measure as Title VII of the 1964 Civil Rights Act,
and at the beginning its heirs preferred to ignore it and concen-

trate on their more moderate agenda."[2] The inclusion of sex in the list of prohibited discriminations in the workforce had problematic implications for liberal protectionists, since they were clinging to the notion that sex-specific treatment could be beneficial in a number of circumstances, especially in regard to women's special labor laws.

Due in part to the Women's Bureau's initial aversion to the sex provision, the federal agency charged with implementing the act, the Equal Employment Opportunity Commission (EEOC), had originally refused to enforce the stipulation, and it had approved of certain sexually discriminatory policies. In August 1965, for instance, the EEOC issued a ruling that permitted employers to advertise in sex-segregated want ads. This audacious and shortsighted action from the EEOC outraged many politically and socially active women and prompted them to question what exactly counted as an equitable sex-based division in treatment.[3]

These events eventually came to a head in 1966 when the attendees of the Third National Conference of Commissions on the Status of Women met in Washington DC. This conference was a part of a series of annual conferences that began in 1964, when the ICSW and CACSW began inviting representatives of the state commissions on the status of women to Washington DC to present their research and provide updates on their progress.[4] After the Third National Conference failed to pass a resolution that called on the EEOC to take a more active stance in preventing sex discrimination in the workforce, influential feminist leaders, including writer and activist Betty Friedan, legal scholars Pauli Murray and Mary Eastwood, and union organizer and civil rights activist Aileen Hernandez, decided to form a new organization. The founders of this new group, the National Organization for Women (NOW), believed that the EEOC would look at sex discrimination more critically if women had an outside civil rights organization to lobby as strongly for women as the National Association for the Advancement of Colored People did for Black Americans.[5]

In addition to the EEOC's troublesome attitude toward sex discrimination in the workforce, other developments had readied the political and social environments that fostered the resurgence of women's activism. Most prominently, the civil rights movement had inspired more women to fight back against their own disadvantaged position, and it had provided a model through its ideals and methods for how social advocacy groups could push for more effective government responses. As well, the changing pattern of women's labor, due to their growing presence in the workforce, had created a disconnect between the reality of many women's lives and a social backdrop that neglected to recognize and support women's work outside of the home. The PCSW, formed in part as a response to this disconnect, resulted in the establishment of a national network of information sharing with the set purpose of investigating these issues and bringing to light the limitations on women's opportunities. This network not only heightened social awareness of the various problems that affected women; it also raised expectations among women that these problems could be solved.[6]

But by the late 1960s the PCSW's alternative constitutional approach for ensuring that women could secure their place as full citizens had failed thus far to yield any substantive results with regard to the Supreme Court. As scholars Donald Mathews and Jane Sherron De Hart describe, until the early 1970s the Supreme Court continued to support the legitimacy of sex-specific treatment for the "flimsiest" of reasons.[7] Even before the PCSW gave its recommendation, the high court had upheld in *Hoyt v. Florida* (1961) a Florida law that exempted women from jury service on the basis that women were "still regarded as the center of home and family life."[8] The court's reluctance to move toward a substantial judicial reinterpretation of the Fourteenth Amendment would eventually encourage more groups of women to start questioning the legitimacy of legal distinctions based on sex altogether.[9]

In this politically and socially charged atmosphere, women activists banded together to form NOW. The goals of this new organization were to achieve effective and coherent solutions to the societal disadvantages that had continued to restrict women's autonomy. In its initial years NOW undertook efforts that resembled the PCSW's work in that it too focused on seeking government action to ease women's problems. Many of the people who had funded NOW in its early years were colleagues of members of the PCSW or members themselves. NOW also tended to emphasize employment and education issues. This emphasis made NOW more appealing to middle- and upper-middle-class women with professional training who had become interested in addressing discrimination against women after learning about such issues in the reports of the national and state commissions linked to the PCSW.[10]

Even so, NOW differed from the PCSW in crucial ways. First, as an independent organization, NOW was not attached to a government body. Hence, it was unrestricted by government power dynamics and was not indebted to one political party or presidential administration. NOW, then, maintained an autonomy of action that had few boundaries. In other words, it could take risks that the PCSW could not. Second, and most significant, NOW broke with the PCSW's position that sex roles were immovable and inflexible. In the view of NOW's leaders, men and women both had a duty to provide for their families and raise their children. This view stands in sharp contrast to the protectionist belief that had infused the PCSW. That formidable protectionist belief had insisted that while women might work outside of the home, they were still responsible primarily to their families and to their roles as homemakers. Because NOW did not accept that view, it could contend that men and women should be treated equally in the workplace, because fathers, like mothers, had a responsibility to take care of the home and look after the children.[11]

NOW's renunciation of the notion that sex boundaries were incontrovertible corresponds to the works of contemporary anthropologists and other intellectuals. Those works had been prompting increasing numbers of women activists to reconceptualize the relationship between sex (anatomical features found among the spectrums of male and female persons) and gender (the behavioral traits and qualities a society attaches to men and women). Around the mid- to late 1960s intellectuals and activists began to separate gender from sex to understand how gender differences were culturally and historically constructed and not biologically determined.[12] As early as 1963, for example, Betty Friedan, a founding member of NOW, had begun to question the naturalness of women's domestic roles in her massively influential text, *The Fem-*

inine Mystique. "Each suburban wife," Friedan wrote, "struggled with it alone. . . . She was afraid to ask even of herself the silent question—'Is this all?'" Overall, for Friedan the traditional family model had prevented women from developing their independence and individuality.[13]

NOW's embrace of and advocacy for the new conceptualization of sex and gender represents an ideological leap of tremendous importance. For the most part it allowed women activists to argue that assumptions unsubstantiated by anatomy had harmed both men and women but most especially women, since such assumptions had historically placed women under the aegis of their husbands and fathers.[14] The notion, moreover, that men's and women's roles were constructed by culture and society, rather than biologically ordained, released women from sole responsibility for child care (at least in theory). By arguing that women as well as men had dual responsibilities as workers and parents, NOW's leaders could cogently call for equality of treatment for men and women while requesting that special consideration be given to the male or female parent primarily responsible for child care.[15]

This flexibility toward women's responsibilities does call to mind the early insistence from emancipationists in the original ERA conflict that women should be given access to a range of opportunities in order to acknowledge and appreciate women's personhood. Yet, the ideological break of the mid- to late 1960s, which would change how people conceptualized the relationship between gender and sex, took the earlier emancipationist outlook even further because it broke away from the biological determinism that had so pervaded the first ERA conflict. During the original ERA conflict, as explained previously, even emancipationists had believed that women were biologically destined to be society's nurturers. But early emancipationists felt that women should be free to choose how they would apply their benevolent nature, whether it be through motherhood or some other compassionate cause. The subsequent separation of gender and sex freed women from the assumptions, stereotypes, and burdens that had come from being society's anointed caregivers, which then bolstered NOW's demand that women should be allowed to function as individuals.[16]

As NOW's work intensified over the years, other women's rights organizations began to form. For instance, in 1968 women activists who were unhappy with NOW's support for abortion rights left the organization to form the Women's Equity Action League (WEAL), which focused on educational and employment issues. The combined efforts of NOW and WEAL resulted in the launching of a major attack on sex discrimination in employment and education practices, while a third organization, the National Women's Political Caucus (NWPC), established in 1971, fought sex discrimination in the political arena.[17]

The surge of women's activism that had emerged by the late 1960s contained a pronounced feminist agenda. The participants predominantly identified themselves as feminists, and they largely expressed their goals in terms of women's empowerment and the desire to remove all the barriers that had restricted women's ability to fully participate in public life.[18] This resurgence of women's activism included two major strands or branches. The first branch aligned most clearly with the emancipationist position in that it too aimed to ensure that women had the same rights as men. This strand primarily consisted of the newly formed national women's rights organizations, including NOW, WEAL, and the NWPC. These organizations used established legal, political, and media institutions to secure measures that sought to combat sex discrimination and expand women's place in society.[19]

By the close of the 1960s a second branch of women's activism had appeared at the local, community level. This second thread, or what a number of scholars have described as the women's liberation movement, endeavored to expose the personal and political nature of oppression through "consciousness raising."[20] This strand had grown out of the antiwar struggle, the civil rights movement, and the New Left. In the fall of 1967 radical women began to form local liberation groups after becoming disenchanted with the biases and discriminations that they had faced in the other social-action movements. The women who formed these groups were committed to raising public consciousness about women's disadvantaged position by holding open and honest discussions about women's personal lives. The structure of the second branch was more fluid than organized because its participants had originally prided themselves on their lack of conventional modes of organization. The thousands of groups that shaped this radical branch of feminist activism were practically independent of one another, as their primary connection was through journals and newsletters. These locally focused groups would eventually go on to form community day-care centers, women's health collectives, as well as rape crisis centers.[21]

By the mid-1970s women who were associated with the second branch of feminist activism had started to create coalitions with the bigger, national organizations such as NOW in order to garner more help in obtaining state and federal support for local programs. In turn, the work of the smaller community groups had inspired NOW to focus on creating more local chapters. Around this time the two strands of women's activism began to fuse together, which helped to fashion an even more formidable movement for empowering women.[22]

The renewed women's activism of the late 1960s and early to mid-1970s led to several gains that have helped women to undermine sexually discriminatory institutions and practices. For starters, the work of women activists contributed to the passage of Title IX of the Education Amendments of 1972, which banned sex discrimination in any educational institution that received federal funds. As well, the rebirth of women's activism gave way to significant reforms in the common law tradition of domestic relations. By the late 1970s, for instance, most states had enacted changes that set out to neutralize the sex-specific aspects of laws and practices relating to alimony, head of household status, and domicile, as well as property and earnings rights.[23] Pressure from women's rights groups also helped to bring about the Supreme Court's ruling in *Roe v. Wade* (1973). That decision enlarged women's access to reproductive care by legalizing most abortions on the grounds that states outlawing abortions had infringed upon women's right to privacy.[24] Despite these advances, women activists sought a stronger, more concrete action to ensure women's civic autonomy. It was in this setting of feminist activism that the ERA became a galvanizing force.

The Rebirth of the ERA Campaign

In the late 1960s women's rights activists who were associated with NOW came to view the ERA as an essential tool for guaranteeing that women and men held the same access to political, economic, and social power. At this time the Supreme Court still appeared to be hesitant to offer a significant judicial reinterpretation of the Fourteenth Amendment, and the prospect of Richard Nixon's election to the presidency had raised fears that his election would lead to the appointment of conservative judges who would not be inclined to broaden women's civic status under the Constitution as it currently stood. Because of these factors, and after considerable internal debate, the ERA received a primary position in NOW's Bill of Rights for Women toward the end of 1967.[25]

Although women's rights activists had been facing judicial intransigence from the Supreme Court with regard to women's status under the Fourteenth Amendment, they were not willing to give up on the Fourteenth Amendment completely. By 1968 NOW had embraced a dual approach for enlarging women's constitutional standing. In an attempt to secure a major constitutional breakthrough, feminist strategists recommended that women activists pursue two paths to legal equality: ERA advocacy and litigation under the Fourteenth Amendment. Previously, with the PCSW's recommendation in the early 1960s, the Fourteenth Amendment strategy had been used as a diversion tactic to sway activists away from the complete constitutional equality reflected in the ERA. However, in this new climate of feminist mobilization activists started to believe that promoting both the reinterpretation of the Fourteenth Amendment and the ratification of the ERA could be complementary endeavors. Women activists, such as legal expert Mary Eastwood, reasoned that continuing to work for constitutional change through the Fourteenth Amendment could offer the potential for immediate relief with regard to ongoing litigation efforts, while passage of the ERA would provide a fuller, stronger, and more lasting declaration of men's and women's equal rights. In this sense women activists came to see the Fourteenth Amendment approach as a useful stepping-stone that could help chip away at sexually discriminatory practices, whereas their advocacy of the ERA would secure the permanence of complete constitutional sexual equality.[26]

In the early 1970s the ranks of ERA supporters grew to include groups that had historically opposed the amendment, among them the LWV, the ACLU, and the AFL-CIO. This widening of support for the ERA was partly due to a decisive move from the EEOC. In 1969, after facing years of significant pressure from NOW, the EEOC decided to interpret Title VII of the 1964 Civil Rights Act as a measure that prohibited special labor laws for women only. This substantial action prompted other groups and individuals to back the ERA.[27] Additionally, NOW's advocacy of a dual approach for constitutional change helped to persuade activists still attached to the Fourteenth Amendment strategy to support the ERA as a corresponding goal to their current efforts. Consequently, prominent liberals who had previously aligned with the protectionist position, including Pauli Murray and Dorothy Kenyon, began to express support for the ERA.[28] Esther Peterson's conversion to the pro-ERA position took more time than others; she eventually endorsed the amendment in the early 1970s. As legal scholar Serena Mayeri explains it, by this point Peterson had concluded that the Supreme Court was taking too long to issue a meaningful reinterpretation of the Fourteenth Amendment. That delay pressed Peterson to decide with "graciousness" that the ERA might be necessary after all.[29]

The new conceptualization of the relationship between sex and gender that had emerged in the late 1960s and early 1970s also fed the growing hunger for the ERA. The budding understanding that sex roles could be fluid had (theoretically) expanded the societal function of women beyond predetermined roles such as caregiver and homemaker. Because of this new conception, groups and individuals that had formerly adhered to the liberal protectionist position abandoned that ideology and turned to the ERA as the best way to secure social benefits for the male or female parent principally in charge of taking care of the children and the home.[30]

While cultural and societal factors had increased the number of liberal ERA supporters, and even though there were differences in the variations of arguments between earlier and later ERA supporters, new amendment proponents still appealed to the core, underlying emancipationist arguments from the original conflict. Well-known feminist activist Gloria Steinem echoed a central emancipationist claim in her testimony at the 1970 Senate subcommittee hearing on the ERA when she contended that women suffered a "second class treatment from the moment we are born." She further argued that "the law makes much more sense when it treats individuals, and not groups bundled together by some condition of birth."[31] Like before, ERA proponents maintained that the amendment, if passed, would erode women's second-class status by providing an explicit constitutional declaration of men's and women's equal rights and by eliminating sex as a legitimate legal classification in and of itself.

When the ERA came before Congress in 1970–72, Representative Martha Griffiths (D-MI), Senator Birch Bayh (D-IN), and Senator Marlow Cook (R-KY) submitted a new version of the amendment that kept the basic language of the first clause but changed the empowering clauses that detailed how the ERA would be put into effect and enforced. To deal with the criticisms of ERA congressional opponents, pro-ERA Congress members had added a seven-year limit to the time the states had to ratify the amendment, postponed its enforcement until two years after ratification, and took out the phrase "several states" from the second section. As scholar Jo Freeman notes, legislators had first used a seven-year deadline for ratifications of a constitutional amendment for the Eighteenth Amendment, and that practice later became commonplace in proposed constitutional amendments after World War II.[32]

At first the reawakening of the ERA campaign had panicked lawmakers. In response to the increased support for the amendment, politicians rushed to satisfy a constituency that potentially represented more than half of the voting public. Consequently, both political parties endorsed the amendment in their platforms in 1972. The amendment also gained the support of Presidents Richard Nixon, Gerald Ford, and Jimmy Carter. Support for the ERA reached a peak on March 22, 1972, when the Ninety-Second Congress passed the Equal Rights Amendment and sent it to the states for ratification.[33]

Even though the ERA failed during the ratification battle of the 1970s and early 1980s, its ratification had initially looked promising. By the end of 1973 thirty states had ratified the ERA. But its momentum rapidly declined after 1974. That year only three states ratified the ERA, and in 1975 only one state approved the amendment. The ERA did not receive a state ratification in 1976. It gained its final, pre-deadline state ratification in 1977. When the ERA reached its deadline on June 30, 1982, it remained three states short of the required three-fourths necessary for a constitutional amendment.[34]

Over the years scholars have spilled copious amounts of ink on trying to ascertain the reasons why the ERA failed to secure enough state approvals.[35] The rising controversy over abortion and accusations that the ERA would force women into combat on the same basis as men are just a few of the explanations that scholars have enlisted to explain the ERA's failure.[36] While there were numerous causes for the amendment's decline, the surfacing of a reinvigorated anti-ERA campaign did play a pivotal role in shaping the outcome of the second ERA conflict.

In the summer and fall of 1972 prominent right-wing author and grassroots organizer Phyllis Schlafly oversaw the emergence of the national "Stop ERA" campaign in which she wove together a network of Republican Women's Clubs, fundamentalist churches, and readers of her newsletters. Moreover, she brought an astute political expertise to the anti-ERA campaign effort by nourishing the fears of suburban and rural Americans and their disenchantment with the liberal order instituted by the New Deal.[37] As historian Allan Lichtman describes, "In concert with local opposition groups, Schlafly helped revive grassroots conservatism and won right-wing acclaim as the unmovable object that stopped the seemingly irresistible momentum of the ERA three states short of ratification." Under Schlafly's guidance, conservative ERA opponents seized a moral high ground by claiming that while ERA backers wanted to topple traditional values, they—the amendment opponents—were the true supporters of the American family. The strength of American society, they asserted, depended on the gendered distinctions that they were trying to protect. As they saw it, those distinctions were rooted in the traditional family arrangement, which would be upended by the passage of the ERA. With the revitalization of the anti-ERA campaign, Schlafly and her followers were able to help breathe new life into the conservative movement in the late 1970s and early 1980s to make it a dominating force in the spectrum of American politics once again.[38]

Amid Schlafly's ERA opposition work, the conservative wing of the protectionist ideology grew to take over the anti-ERA position. Like so many other changes during the second ERA conflict, this development was due to the new conceptualization of the relationship between sex and gender. The newer, more flexible understanding of sex and gender had left the protectionist stance largely in the hands of conservative ERA opponents, since that understanding of sex roles had pushed most liberals to back the ERA. Thus, during the second ERA conflict protectionism grew more conservative while emancipationism turned more liberal. As the conservative elements of the protectionist ideology intensified, ERA critics started to oppose any measure that might affect women's societal status as an assault on the traditional social order. Further still, conservatives came to view the renewed women's activism of the late 1960s and early 1970s as a symptom of the larger dangers embedded in the period's social movements. In the assessment of conservative ERA opponents, the amendment would decriminalize rape, legitimize homosexuality, integrate public bathrooms, and guarantee abortion rights.[39] For conservative opponents, the ERA increasingly appeared to be an immediate threat to their basic way of life.[40]

While a more pronounced conservatism impacted the anti-ERA campaign in the second conflict, amendment opponents still referred to the central protectionist convictions that had pervaded the original struggle. Most notably, opponents continued to express their opposition to the ERA in terms of protecting the American family and what they had assumed to be women's natural right to special treatment. For example, Phyllis Schlafly insisted in one of her writings that opposing sex-based roles and supporting the ERA was like "opposing Mother Nature herself." In Schlafly's view, immutable differences between men and women had "to be recognized as part of the plan of the Divine Architect for the survival of the human race through the centuries."[41] Akin to the protectionist arguments of the original conflict, Schlafly's claim was that the ERA would endanger the supposedly different societal functions of men and women citizens.

As seen with the original ERA conflict, a central component of the opposition's argument sprang from the idea that the ERA would destroy the principle of sex-specific treatment embedded in the American legal tradition. In a *Phyllis Schlafly Report* article titled "How ERA Would Change Federal Laws," Schlafly argued that the amendment would abolish laws that upheld "the traditional family concept of husband as breadwinner and wife as homemaker." Schlafly further maintained that under the ERA mothers would "no longer be entitled to any special benefits or protections for motherhood responsibilities."[42] In another article Schlafly asked, "Why should we lower ourselves to 'equal rights' when we already have the status of special privilege?" She went on to contend that the ERA would abolish the rights of women to be supported by their husbands and create "mandatory wife-support and child-support laws so that a wife would have an 'equal' obligation to take a job."[43] Similar to the original conflict, later ERA critics asserted that they wanted to protect a distinct citizenship for women. Again this distinct citizenship supposedly came with its own set of rights and privileges. In both conflicts ERA opponents successfully pushed forward the claim that the law needed to be free to treat citizens differently on account of sex.

Another prominent factor contributing to the ERA's ratification failure was the pitfalls rooted in the dual constitutional strategy. In 1971 the Supreme Court for the first time in its long history invoked the Fourteenth Amendment's equal protection guarantee to unanimously strike down a law discriminating against women. As discussed below, this case would be followed by several others in the 1970s that effectively produced a new understanding of the Fourteenth Amendment. With this judicial breakthrough, the high court raised sex to a quasi-suspect legal status, but the court would eventually stop short of declaring that sex required the strictest level of judicial scrutiny invoked by other categories such as race.

Despite the initial progress in the judicial arena, the simulta-
neous pursuit of Fourteenth Amendment litigation and a new
amendment created theoretical and tactical obstacles that wom-
en's rights advocates would fail to overcome. On one level the
Supreme Court's broadening of the Fourteenth Amendment's equal
protection clause diluted the sense of urgency behind the ERA's
momentum. The advance within the judicial arena also begged
an important question: if the principle of sex equality could be
found in the Fourteenth Amendment (as women's rights advocates maintained), why was an additional amendment necessary?
Ultimately, women's rights advocates found themselves struggling
to articulate the need for the ERA while insisting that the Fourteenth Amendment too protected women's rights. Though the
cause of the ERA might have been best served by sharply criticiz-
ing women's status under the Constitution as it currently stood,
women activists did not want to threaten the ongoing litigation
efforts that were already appealing to the Fourteenth Amendment.[44] In the end the ERA succumbed to a combination of the
shortfalls entrenched in the dual constitutional approach and in
the resurgent popularity of the protectionism embedded in the
anti-ERA campaign effort.

The Modern Constitutional Doctrine of Gender Jurisprudence

One month after the House passed the ERA in October 1971, the
Supreme Court used the Fourteenth Amendment to strike down
a sexually discriminatory law. The historic case, *Reed v. Reed*, dealt
with an Idaho law that gave preference to men in the appointment of administrators of estates. Feminist legal activists pulled
the state court case out of obscurity in the hope that it would push
the Supreme Court to issue a strict standard of review for sexually
discriminatory laws. With this case the attorneys of petitioner Sally
Reed introduced the argument that sex-and-race-based discriminations were analogous and that sex-based classifications should
be treated as "suspect." ACLU legal director Melvin Wulf recruited
Ruth Bader Ginsburg, then a law professor, to help craft the appel-
lant's brief to the Supreme Court. In the now-famous *Reed* brief,
Ginsburg developed the previous work of Pauli Murray to argue

that arbitrary discriminations against women violated their rights under the Fourteenth Amendment.[45]

Ginsburg saw *Reed* as an excellent opportunity to demonstrate to the high court the intrinsic injustice of sex-based classifications. With cases like *Reed*, Ginsburg and her colleagues sought to attack the assumptions that women were solely responsible for house-hold tasks and caretaking duties and that men should exclusively bear the burden of familial financial support. They argued that laws based on these assumptions unfairly distributed benefits and bolstered sex-based dependencies.[46]

While this argument made an impact on the high court, its over-arching judicial effects remained unclear. In a unanimous but cryp-tic opinion, authored by Chief Justice Warren E. Burger, the court declared in *Reed* that Idaho's preference for male estate adminis-trators was the "very kind of arbitrary legislative choice forbidden by the Equal Protection Clause of the Fourteenth Amendment." The court, however, explained that it was only invalidating the Idaho law because administrative convenience was not a rational or reasonable basis for upholding a sexually discriminatory law.[47] Even though *Reed* marked the first time the court invoked the Four-teenth Amendment to overturn a sex-specific law, the ruling was not a straightforward victory for women's rights advocates. In the ruling the court had applied the lowest level of judicial scrutiny: the rational standard of review. This standard assesses if a reason-able argument can be made for a discriminatory law or practice. Ultimately, *Reed* did not fully displace the old reasonableness cri-terion that the courts had traditionally used to permit sex-specific classifications as being logical extensions of different sex roles and supposedly fixed physical differences.[48]

In January 1973 Ginsburg argued a second major women's rights case, *Frontiero v. Richardson*, before the Supreme Court. As head of the newly created ACLU Women's Rights Project (WRP), Gins-burg hoped that with *Frontiero* the high court would provide a stronger standard of review for sex-discriminatory laws under the Fourteenth Amendment. The case dealt with U.S. Air Force lieu-tenant Sharron Frontiero's challenge to an armed services policy that allowed men to claim their wives as dependents regardless of whether they were actually financially reliant on their husbands but prohibited women in the armed services from claiming their husbands as dependents without proof that they had paid one-half of their husband's living costs.[49]

The high court's ruling in *Frontiero* signified another partial victory for women's rights activists. In May 1973 eight members of the court found the military's benefit policy unconstitutional, but the justices split on their reasoning for the ruling. While four justices applied the strictest level of judicial review, three found the statute unconstitutional on the authority of *Reed*, which was that administrative convenience failed to meet the rational basis for sex-based differential treatment.[50] Justice William Brennan Jr., who wrote the plurality opinion endorsing strict scrutiny for sex-based classifications, maintained that a departure from the rational basis of review was justified because "statutory distinctions between the sexes often have the effect of invidiously relegating the entire class of females to inferior legal status without regard to the actual capabilities of its individual members."[51] The ruling in *Frontiero* had come up just one justice short of establishing strict scrutiny as the standard of review for sex-discriminatory classifications. Though the victory was incomplete, it showed that change was taking place in the judicial realm with regard to women's standing under the Fourteenth Amendment.

Women's rights advocates had wanted the Supreme Court to use the strictest level of judicial review for sex discrimination cases, but the high court formed a different approach for evaluating sex-specific practices in subsequent rulings during the mid-1970s. This "Goldilocks solution," as legal scholar Serena Mayeri describes it, became known as the intermediate level of review.[52] Under intermediate scrutiny, a sex-based law must be substantially related to an important state interest to be upheld as constitutional. In other words, it requires the state or federal government to provide convincing evidence that a challenged sex-based classification is connected to a legitimate cause. This middle level places sex above the rational basis of review, which tests whether the discriminatory action bears a logical relationship to a reasonable public agenda. But it also places sex discrimination cases below the strictest level

of scrutiny, which only permits discriminatory classifications, such
as race, if there is no other way to achieve an essential state objective. Thus, the intermediate level of review does permit sex-based
differential treatment if such treatment can be substantially tied
to a presumably worthy, governmental cause.[53]

In general the court has relied on two criteria for permitting
sex-differentiating laws and practices. The first is whether the policy appears to benefit women. The court first expressed this line
of reasoning in *Kahn v. Shevin* (1974), in which it upheld a Florida statute that awarded widows, but not widowers, a five-hundred-
dollar property tax exemption. The court concluded that the state
law was properly designed to ease the "financial impact of spou-
sal loss upon the sex for which that loss imposes a disproportionately heavy burden."[54] The decision did not examine whether there
might be a more suitable factor than sex for assessing the extent
of a person's financial hardships.[55]

The second criterion looks at whether the sex-based practice
recognizes that men and women are not, in the words of the court,
"similarly situated." The court introduced this justification with
its ruling in *Schlesinger v. Ballard* (1975). This case dealt with a
federal statute that granted more time for female than for male
naval officers to achieve promotion before a required discharge.
The court concluded that the policy was consistent with the goal
of giving women fair career advancement opportunities. In particular, the majority ruling contended that in this case the different treatment of men and women "reflect[ed], not archaic and
overbroad generalizations, but, instead, the demonstrable fact
that [they] . . . are *not* similarly situated with respect to opportunities for professional service."[56] In 1981 the court appealed to the
not "similarly situated" argument to uphold a California statute
that had made statutory rape a crime that only men could commit against women.[57]

In 1976 the Supreme Court enshrined the intermediate level
of review as its standard for evaluating sex discrimination cases
with its ruling in *Craig v. Boren*. On the surface this rather lackluster case dealt with an Oklahoma law that prohibited the selling of
a certain type of beer to men under twenty-one while permitting

its sale to women over eighteen. The court found the law unconstitutional, ruling that a sex classification must "serve important
governmental objectives and be substantially related to achievement of those objectives." The court went on to conclude that in
this case sex did not "represent a legitimate, accurate proxy for
the regulation of drinking and driving."[58]

Craig marked a definite step away from the old rational basis
that had made it easy to uphold the feeblest of sex-specific laws
as supposedly being natural consequences of immovable gender
roles and unbending physical differences. But the ruling showed
that the court was unwilling to hold sex to a strict scrutiny standard, as it only overruled the sex-based law because the state had
failed to show that the law was substantially related to an important legislative interest. As Serena Mayeri explains, those who find
fault with Pauli Murray and Ruth Bader Ginsburg's race-sex analogy
have often rationalized the intermediate level of review. According to this outlook on America's judicial review hierarchy, racially
discriminatory laws are almost never justifiable because racial differences are mutable and fluid, but sex-based laws are permissible in certain instances because gender differences are somehow
more concrete and biologically inescapable.[59]

In later cases, the high court demonstrated the inherent mer-
curial disposition of the intermediate standard. In *United States v.
Virginia* (1996), for instance, the court moved to fortify intermediate scrutiny when it invalidated the Virginia Military Institute
(VMI) policy of excluding female students. In the ruling for that
case, now-Justice Ginsburg emphasized that there needed to be
an "exceedingly persuasive justification" for any sex-based legal
classification to be ruled constitutional.[60]

A subsequent case, however, highlighted the continuing limitations of intermediate scrutiny and the susceptibility of the robust
ruling in the VMI case. In *Tuan Anh Nguyen et al. v. INS* (2001) the
court upheld an immigration statute, originally dating from 1952,
governing the citizenship of children born abroad to one citizen
parent.[61] The law permits the children of unmarried citizen mothers and noncitizen fathers to be naturalized automatically. But the
law maintains several legal requirements for children born abroad

to unmarried citizen fathers and noncitizen mothers before those children can claim a right to U.S. citizenship. These requirements include providing clear and convincing evidence of paternity and verifying that the father had established a relationship with the child (through financial support and acknowledgment of paternity) before the child has reached the age of eighteen. If these requirements are not met before the child reaches the age of majority, he or she loses the right to claim U.S. citizenship.[62]

In a 5–4 decision, the majority ruled in *Nguyen* that the distinction in the policy between mothers and fathers was significantly related to two important governmental purposes: first, to verify a biological parent-child relationship (the court argued that this connection was easily confirmable in the case of mothers but not fathers); and, second, to promote an opening for a meaningful parent-child relationship to develop (the court suggested that this relationship was essential to biological motherhood but not biological fatherhood).[63] In an appeal to the notion that fathers and mothers are not "similarly situated" with regard to biological parenthood, the court upheld the law even though it placed a considerable burden of parental responsibility on foreign-born mothers in a manner that did not equally weigh on citizen-mothers or foreign-born fathers.[64]

The four justices who dissented from the decision in the *Nguyen* case included Sandra Day O'Connor, Ruth Bader Ginsburg, David Souter, and Stephen Breyer. The dissent, written by Justice O'Connor, criticized the court for upholding a law that reinforced harmful gender stereotypes of parental roles and obligations. In Justice O'Connor's words, the challenged statute is "paradigmatic of a historic regime that left women with responsibility, and freed men from responsibility, for nonmarital children."[65] The premise in the discriminatory citizenship law is that mothers are more likely than fathers to develop significant bonds with their children. By upholding the statute, Justice O'Connor maintained, the court had implicitly endorsed the notion that fatherhood is optional while motherhood is not.[66]

In *Nguyen* the court reasoned that the government's intended objective in making the statute was to confirm paternity as well as to promote impactful relationships between parents and children born overseas and outside of marriage. But, as Justice O'Connor's dissent noted, sex-neutral alternatives to the sex-specific requirements of the statute could have achieved the same purpose. If the court had used the stronger strict level of judicial review for this case, it would have needed to determine that the extralegal requirements for children born abroad to unmarried citizen fathers and noncitizen mothers were necessary for achieving a vital governmental objective. As legal expert Jessica Neuwirth explains, the availability of sex-neutral alternatives to achieving the stated purpose of the statute would have "render[ed] the sex-based discriminatory requirements of the law unnecessary and therefore impermissible under this higher standard of review." But with the less rigorous intermediate standard of review, the existence of equivalent, sex-neutral options did not preclude the court from ruling that the sex-discriminatory requirements were still substantially related to the government's purpose and were thus permissible.[67]

As the high court's decision in *Nguyen* demonstrates, the intermediate level of review that is central to the modern constitutional doctrine of gender jurisprudence has not unseated the authority of the federal government or the states to treat men and women citizens differently. On the contrary, intermediate scrutiny has held that sex-based differential treatment only needs to be substantially (not unavoidably) connected to an important legislative cause in order to be legitimate. Hence, the modern constitutional doctrine of gender jurisprudence has failed to fundamentally remove sex as a valid legal category. This failure, moreover, has allowed aspects of the common law tradition of sex-specific marital duties to persist, as historian Nancy Cott puts it, "in skeleton form."[68] In 1993, for instance, a California appeals court refused to support a wife's claim to collect assets from her husband's estate as compensation for taking care of him at home after he had suffered a stroke. According to the court, providing the widow with compensation would be distasteful and "antithetical to the institution of marriage as the Legislature has defined it." Citing precedents from 1937 and 1941, the court ruled that the wife's care of the husband was plainly part of her "marital duty of support."[69]

The Legacy of Protectionism

Complete constitutional equality continues to elude men and women citizens of the United States. Furthermore, our present practices align more closely with the protectionist mind-set than with the ethos of emancipationism. Certainly the intermediate level of judicial scrutiny embedded in the modern constitutional doctrine of gender jurisprudence has marked a significant move away from the more ineffective rational standard of review that had previously made it easier to uphold sexually discriminatory laws and customs. Even so, when the intermediate standard is not held to its most robust form, as seen in *Nguyen* and other cases, it signals the success of the protectionist belief in limited constitutional equality for men and women citizens. As most prominently displayed in the PCSW's final report, protectionists had formed the idea of intermediate constitutional sexual equality toward the end of the original ERA conflict to strengthen America's gendered citizenship. The intermediate level of judicial review is of a piece with the protectionist idea of limited sexual equality, because it fulfills the PCSW's call for a constitutional approach that recognizes women's status as full citizens through the Fourteenth Amendment while preserving the government's ability to treat citizens differently on account of sex.

To be sure, the renewed women's activism of the mid- to late 1960s and 1970s did produce several victories that have helped to alleviate the sharper limitations on women's societal position. These achievements, however, have not completely dislodged a protectionist outlook that has continued to condition our dominant cultural consensus in such a manner that we still frame women's roles around their traditional duties in the domestic sphere. This tendency ultimately perpetuates the sexual division of labor entrenched in protectionism and leads society to expect women to focus on the family so that men can be free to work outside of the home. As feminist scholar Jo Freeman describes it, "There is still a basic division of labor in which men are expected to be the 'breadwinners' and women are expected to focus their energies on the family, although each may 'help' with the other's task."[70]

In effect, the lasting influence of this protectionist belief has reinforced the subordinate position of women when they do decide to pursue activities that extend beyond their conventional roles as wives and mothers. When, for example, women enter male-dominated fields, they typically do so in junior slots where they often remain with lower salaries. Additionally, the tenacious belief that women are equipped only to perform work that mirrors their supposedly natural domestic functions has still rendered women's work outside of the home to be viewed as untrained and inferior. As a result, women continue to suffer from a significant wage gap that privileges men over women who are similarly situated but not identically employed, such as male janitors and female housekeepers.[71] Legal scholar Cynthia Grant Bowman also reminds us that public spaces still function as sexualized battle arenas. As she explains it, "The law often overlooks harms to women. One such harm is the harassment that women face when they travel along city streets and appear in other public places."[72] To elaborate on Bowman's point, historian Sandra VanBurkleo notes that when women have had to deal with random men yelling catcalls or making obscene gestures at them, it is not trivial sex play; for many women such encounters "affirm power imbalances, physical insecurity, and the sexualization of ordinary exchanges—that is to say, inequality."[73]

While the modern constitutional doctrine of gender jurisprudence has recognized both men and women as rights-bearing citizens, its failure to guarantee absolute constitutional sexual equality has allowed men to maintain their historically greater access to political, economic, and social power. Overall, the protectionist victory in the original ERA conflict created a belief in the equity of sex-specific treatment that continues to shape the dominant cultural consensus to this day. Yet, this concept of limited equality also preserves women's disadvantaged position, because it rationalizes the prejudiced attitude that sex should determine a citizen's rights.

The dominance of protectionism, however, is not everlasting. In recent years there has been significant movement to ensure that men and women citizens have equal responsibilities when it comes to the defense of the country. In 2013, for instance, the Department of Defense officially lifted the ban on women serving in combat positions. Two years later it removed all gender-based restrictions, making women eligible for every military service role. Due to these changes, a federal judge ruled in February 2019 that the Selective Service System requiring solely men to register for the draft was unconstitutional.[74] In the ruling Judge Gray H. Miller made only a declaratory judgment; he did not issue an injunction. In other words, the ruling failed to result in an immediate court order necessitating any particular change to the Selective Service male-only draft registration requirement. As of 2020 the Selective Service System has not changed its policy, and it remains unclear if Congress or the courts will decisively move to modify the system. The ruling, then, was largely a symbolic gesture.[75] Nonetheless, it does reveal the emergence of a crack in the strength of protectionism, especially with regard to equalizing the obligations of citizenship.

As seen in both ERA conflicts, significant societal and political changes do contain the potential to create openings for emancipationists to expose the limitations of protectionism. Due in part to the wave of feminist anger that resulted from the 2016 presidential election of Donald Trump, there has been a rise in anti–gender-discrimination movements, such as the #MeToo and #TimesUp initiatives. These movements have raised awareness of several ongoing problems that impact women in particular, including inadequate sexual harassment policies in educational institutions and employment practices, the prevalence of sexual assault, and the persistence of gender-based pay differences.

These campaigns have also revived calls for the ratification of the ERA. Thanks to the lobbying work of several pro-ERA groups, the amendment has received three additional ratifications in recent years. In March 2017 Nevada became the first state legislature in forty years to ratify the ERA. A little more than a year later Illinois state lawmakers followed Nevada's example and decided to ratify the ERA; that move in May 2018 left the amendment one state away from the three-fourths of the states required for ratification of a constitutional amendment.[76] After the elections of November 2019, new hope for the ERA further materialized in Virginia, as voters chose an impressive influx of pro-ERA politicians and gave Democrats control over the Virginia state legislature.[77] Shortly thereafter, in January 2020, Virginia became the thirty-eighth state to ratify the ERA, presumably giving the amendment the necessary state approvals to be added to the Constitution.[78]

Nevertheless, there are still significant ratification issues that will need to be dealt with before the ERA can be fully incorporated into the Constitution. These issues mainly concern questions over the continued viability of the 1982 deadline for state ratifications and if Congress will set aside that deadline to accept the newer state approvals.[79] A few days before Virginia proceeded to ratify the ERA, the Justice Department's Office of Legal Counsel (OLC) gave an opinion in which it asserted that the deadline established by Congress remained in effect. Because of the ratification deadline, the OLC concluded that the amendment was no longer pending before the states, which would then render the latest state ratifications inconsequential.[80] In reaction to the OLC's opinion, the archivist of the United States, David Ferriero, delivered a statement in January 2020 indicating that he would defer to the OLC's judgment and not certify Virginia's ratification or add the ERA to the Constitution unless directed otherwise by a federal court order.[81] There is also the issue of the five states that have rescinded their previous ratifications of the ERA. While the Constitution gives Congress plenary power in providing for the ratification process, it is unclear whether future court action will accept that Congress possesses dispositive authority with regard to the validity of state rescissions. Put another way, there are additional barriers to the ERA's constitutional incorporation that will require an overwhelming level of support for the amendment to surmount them.[82]

As the legal and political debates ignited by the latest state ratifications suggest, protectionism and its opposition to the ERA remain influential even with the current growth in pro-ERA activism. In a 2019 opinion piece for the *Washington Times*, for example, Rebecca Hagelin, an active ERA opponent, argued that it was "natural" to understand that "men and women are equal but different." She went on to claim that if the amendment were to pass, "every single hard-fought legal protection that women have gained over the years will vanish."[83] Once again the arguments against the ERA rest on the protectionist idea that genuine legal fairness requires the law to be free to treat men and women citizens differently. As seen before with both ERA conflicts, protectionists are not opposed to the idea of gender equity per se and they are not opposed to the idea of women being rights-bearing citizens. They are opposed to the ERA, however, because they believe that inherent differences across the sexes make it necessary for men and women to have separate and distinct rights.

In the long-running struggle for the ERA, amendment supporters have perfected the emancipationist position to show that a consistently applied, single standard of rights for men and women citizens is an essential step toward eradicating the sexual inequities embedded in our social fabric. As they have shown, passage of the ERA would raise sex discrimination cases to the highest and strictest standard of judicial review to ensure that men and women are able to participate as citizens on the same terms. Most of all they have shown that passage of the ERA would remove sex as a valid legal classification in and of itself, and it would force the law to recognize men and women citizens as functional individuals in their own right.[84]

But even with their sharpened arguments, ERA supporters have yet to effectively appreciate the strength of the protectionist stance and its confidence in the legitimacy of sex-specific rights. For ERA supporters to cut a lasting crack into the appeal of protectionism, they need to eschew the tendency to dismiss the opposition's arguments as simply being uninformed or against women's empowerment. Moreover, they need to fully address protectionists' concerns that the ERA will take indispensable rights away from women. In the end, a solid drive for complete constitutional sexual equality will be successful only when the prevalence of protectionist patterns of thought has faded from view and more people are willing to question the equity of America's gendered citizenship.

NOTES

Introduction

1. For background information on Felix Frankfurter, see Hirsch, *Enigma of Felix Frankfurter*.

2. Felix Frankfurter to Ethel Smith, August 7, 1923, reel 51, National Consumers' League papers, Manuscript Division, Library of Congress (LOC), Washington DC (hereafter NCL papers).

3. "Members of Congress Express Views on Equal Rights Amendment," *Congressional Digest* 3, no. 6 (March 1924): 197. For background information on Charles Curtis, see Unrau, "Charles Curtis."

4. U.S. Congress, Senate Judiciary Subcommittee, *Equal Rights for Men and Women: Hearings on S.J. Res. 65*, 75th Cong., 3rd sess., supplemental statement, March 7, 1938, 182 (testimony of Donald Quigley Palmer, American Newspaper Guild).

5. "If the Constitution is to continue its development in the line of its own democratic nature, the next step must be to make all men and women equal under the terms of the law . . . the logic of this step is self-evident." U.S. Congress, Senate Judiciary Subcommittee, *Equal Rights for Men and Women: Hearings on S.J. Res. 65*, 75th Cong., 3rd sess., February 7–10, 1938, 153–54 (testimony of Dr. Miriam Oatman, Brookings Institution).

6. "The Equal Rights Amendment," *Washington Post*, June 2, 1936, 8.

7. National Consumers' League, *Don't Buy a Gold Brick*, pamphlet, 1944, folder 21, box 3, Hattie Smith papers, Schlesinger Library (SL), Radcliffe Institute, Harvard University, Cambridge, Massachusetts (hereafter, Hattie Smith papers).

8. U.S. Congress, Senate Judiciary Subcommittee, *Equal Rights for Men and Women: Hearings on S.J. Res. 65*, 75th Cong., 3rd sess., February 7–10, 1938, 53 (testimony of James O. Murdock, attorney).

9. See, for example, Edith Houghton Hooker, "The Woman with Gifts to Bring," *Equal Rights* 1, no. 11 (April 1923): 85.

10. Paul, *Conversations with Alice Paul*, 401.

11. U.S. Congress, Senate Judiciary Subcommittee, *Equal Rights for Men and Women: Hearings on S.J. Res. 65*, 75th Cong., 3rd sess., February 7–10, 1938, 37 (testimony of Elizabeth Dolan, National Council of the Daughters of Isabella).

12. Mathews and De Hart, *Sex, Gender, and the Politics of* ERA, 30–32.

13. See Mathews and De Hart, *Sex, Gender, and the Politics of* ERA, 27–35; Harrison, *On Account of Sex*, 198–221; and Lichtman, *White Protestant Nation*, 320–21.

14. In 1978 Congress extended the ERA's state ratification deadline to June 30, 1982.

15. See Boles, *Politics of the Equal Rights Amendment*; Berry, *Why* ERA *Failed*; Steiner, *Constitutional Inequality*; Mansbridge, *Why We Lost the* ERA; Hoff-Wilson, *Rights of Passage*; and Spruill, *Divided We Stand*.

16. See Critchlow, *Phyllis Schlafly and Grassroots Conservatism*; and Spruill, *Divided We Stand*.

17. In *Sex, Gender, and the Politics of* ERA, Donald Mathews and Jane Sherron De Hart do provide an important examination that further expands the interpretive terrain of the ERA beyond the question of failure. They explore how the ERA ratification struggle in North Carolina illuminates the dynamic relationship between race and gender in the political arena of the 1970s.

18. Cynthia Harrison's *On Account of Sex* also moves the examination of the ERA beyond the issue of failure; her work includes a discussion of the ERA's turbulent history in the 1940s and early 1960s to help explain the evolution of social policy in the post–World War II era.

19. Joan Zimmerman's "The Jurisprudence of Equality" is an exception to the female-centric focus of previous studies. Zimmerman argues that the contentious effort to draft the ERA in the early 1920s signifies a growing divide between two structures of legal thought: sociological jurisprudence and legal formalism. Although she provides significant findings, her analysis does not fully capture the range of variations involved in the conflicting positions, because it overlooks how various ERA proponents supported welfare legislation (as long as such legislation was neutral as to sex), while many amendment opponents opposed the concept of social benefits.

20. See O'Neill, *Everyone Was Brave*; Lemons, *Woman Citizen*; Becker, *Origins of the Equal Rights Amendment*; F. Gordon, *After Winning*; and Lunardini, *From Equal Suffrage to Equal Rights*.

21. Other works that look at how the ERA sheds light on the women's movement include Chafe, *American Woman*; Cott, *Grounding of Modern Feminism*; Rupp and Taylor, *Survival in the Doldrums*; Butler, *Two Paths to Equality*; Cobble, *Other Women's Movement*; and Draper and Diamond, *Hidden History of the Equal Rights Amendment*.

22. "Equal Rights Amendment Gains Powerful Advocate," *Equal Rights* 23, no. 2 (February 1, 1937): 11.

23. Cott, *Grounding of Modern Feminism*, 134–35.

24. "Foe Tells Views on Women's Pact," *New York Times*, December 21, 1933, 18.

25. Nielsen, *Un-American Womanhood*, 4–5, 63, 105–6.

26. VanBurkleo, *"Belonging to the World"*; Ritter, *Constitution as Social Design*.

27. Mettler, *Dividing Citizens*; Cott, *Public Vows*; Kessler-Harris, *In Pursuit of Equity*.

28. Kerber, *No Constitutional Right to Be Ladies*; Siegel, "Collective Memory of the Nineteenth Amendment"; Siegel, "She the People."

1. The Radical Nineteenth Amendment

1. Commonwealth v. Genevieve Welosky, 276 Mass. 398 (1931), 415.

2. Okin, *Women in Western Political Thought*, 199–201; Pateman, *Sexual Contract*, 19–117; Clark, "Women and John Locke"; Hunt, *Inventing Human Rights*, 28–29.

3. Pateman, "Equality, Difference, Subordination," 19–20. See also Pateman, *Disorder of Women*, 4, 21; Gundersen, "Independence, Citizenship, and the American Revolution"; and Smith-Rosenberg, "Dis-Covering the Subject of the 'Great Constitutional Discussion."

4. Kann, *Republic of Men*, 1.

5. Hoff, *Law, Gender, and Injustice*, 117.

6. Blackstone, *Commentaries on the Laws of England*, 1:442–45. Linda Kerber attests to American jurists' esteem of Blackstone in Kerber, *No Constitutional Right to Be Ladies*, 14–15.

7. U.S. Congress, House Judiciary Committee, *Extending the Right of Suffrage to Women*, 48th Cong., 1st sess., April 24, 1884, 3.

8. Bushnell, *Women's Suffrage*, 71.

9. Dissolution of a marriage potentially offered independence to women, but it could also increase the possibility that women would become dependent on others in new ways. Still, for most women widowhood gave them their best chance for legally recognized independence. See Gundersen, "Independence, Citizenship, and the American Revolution," 72.

10. Hartog, *Man and Wife*, 293.

11. Cott, *Public Vows*; Hoff, *Law, Gender, and Injustice*, 87–88; Kerber, "Paradox of Women's Citizenship in the Early Republic."

12. Kerber, "Meanings of Citizenship," 838.

13. Reeve, *Law of Baron and Femme*, 73.

14. Siegel, "Home as Work"; Cott, "Marriage and Women's Citizenship."

15. Warbasse, *Changing Legal Rights of Married Women*; Stanley, "Conjugal Bonds and Wage Labor"; Basch, *In the Eyes of the Law*.

16. See Chused, "Married Women's Property Law"; Lebsocks, *Free Women of Petersburg*; Rabkin, *Fathers to Daughters*; and Salmon, *Women and the Law of Property*.

17. Siegel, "Modernization of Marital Status Law," 2140.

18. Miller v. Miller, 42 N.W. 641 (Iowa 1889), 641–42.

19. Foxworthy v. Adams, 124 S.W. 381 (Kentucky 1910), 383. For a larger discussion of these cases, see Siegel, "Modernization of Marital Status Law," 2202–5.

20. Siegel, "Modernization of Marital Status Law," 2130.

21. Bradwell v. Illinois, 83 U.S. 130 (1873), 140–41.

22. Minor v. Happersett, 88 U.S. 162 (1875).

23. Siegel, "Collective Memory of the Nineteenth Amendment," 147–49.

24. Siegel, "She the People," 981–82.

25. *Congressional Globe*, 40th Cong., 2nd sess., 1868, 39, pt. 2: 1956.

26. DuBois, "Outgrowing the Compact of the Fathers," 147–48; De Hart, "Women's History and Political History," 30.

27. Bredbenner, *Nationality of Her Own*, 6.

28. Cott, "Marriage and Women's Citizenship," 1462.

29. Cott, "Marriage and Women's Citizenship," 1462; Kerber, *No Constitutional Right to Be Ladies*, 40–43.

30. Mackenzie v. Hare, 239 U.S. 299 (1915), 313.

31. Urofsky, "State Courts and Protective Legislation during the Progressive Era," 91.

32. VanBurkleo, *"Belonging to the World,"* 221–23.

33. Foner, *Story of American Freedom*, 157–58. See also N. Erickson, "*Muller v. Oregon* Reconsidered"; Strum, *Louis D. Brandeis*, 114; and Lehrer, *Origins of Protective Legislation*, 103.

34. Ritchie v. People of Illinois, 155 Illinois 98 (1895), 102, 107–9, 111–12.

35. Zimmerman, "Jurisprudence of Equality," 196.

36. Kelley, *Some Ethical Gains*, viii, 254–55; Kelley, *Modern Industry*, 30–33; Hart, *Bound by Our Constitution*, 98; Zimmerman, "Jurisprudence of Equality," 195–200.

37. Several state courts had decided well before *Muller* that the reasoning behind *Lochner v. New York* (1905) applied only to men and need not prevent the adoption of special labor laws for women. *Lochner* had been the first case in which the U.S. Supreme Court used the doctrine of substantive due process to strike down a labor law that restricted work hours on the basis that it violated a citizen's right to contract freely. Lochner v. New York, 198 U.S. 45 (1905); VanBurkleo, *"Belonging to the World,"* 223.

38. Muller v. Oregon, 208 U.S. 412 (1908), 420–22.

39. Foner, *Story of American Freedom*, 157–58.

40. Brandeis and Goldmark, *Women in Industry*, 19, 38, 41, 49–50.

41. VanBurkleo, *"Belonging to the World,"* 221–24.

42. Chafe, *American Woman*, 80.

43. Kelley, *Women in Industry*, 153.

44. Frankfurter, foreword to *Impatient Crusader*, v. See also VanBurkleo, *"Belonging to the World,"* 224.

45. Kerber, *Women of the Republic*; Welter, "Cult of True Womanhood."

46. Skocpol, *Protecting Soldiers and Mothers*; Sklar, "Historical Foundations of Women's Power in the Creation of the American Welfare State"; Mink, *Wages of Motherhood.*

47. Flexner, *Century of Struggle*, esp. 41–52, 181–86.

48. DuBois, *Feminism and Suffrage*, 53, 58–78.

49. Stanton, Anthony, and Gage, *History of Woman Suffrage*, 1:170–73; Kerber, "From the Declaration of Independence to the Declaration of Sentiments," 115.

50. Jacobi, *"Common Sense,"* 138.

51. Stanton, "Solitude of Self," 159–60.

52. Siegel, "She the People," 987–93. See also DuBois, "Outgrowing the Compact of the Fathers."

53. Wheeler, *One Woman, One Vote*, 11–13.

54. VanBurkleo, *"Belonging to the World,"* 190–95. See also Buechler, *Transformation of the Woman Suffrage Movement.*

55. Kraditor, *Ideas of the Woman Suffrage Movement*, 44–46.

56. Kelley, *Some Ethical Gains*, 172, 184. See also Zimmerman, "Jurisprudence of Equality," 219; and Harper, *History of Woman Suffrage*, 492.

57. Evans, *Born for Liberty*, 155.

58. Wheeler, *One Woman, One Vote*, 12–13.

59. Evans, *Born for Liberty*, 156. See also Jones, *Vanguard.*

60. Suffragism had become an overwhelming force by 1900. For contemporary accounts, see Catt and Shuler, *Woman Suffrage and Politics*; Duniway, *Path Breaking*; and Irwin, *Up Hill with Banners Flying.*

61. See Fowler, *Carrie Catt*, esp. chap. 9.

62. See Van Voris, *Carrie Chapman Catt*; and Graham, *Woman Suffrage and the New Democracy.*

63. For more information, see Ford, "Alice Paul and the Triumph of Militancy"; and Adams and Keene, *Alice Paul and the American Suffrage Campaign.*

64. Wheeler, *One Woman, One Vote*, 16–17.

65. Stevens, *Jailed for Freedom.*

66. Wheeler, *One Woman, One Vote*, 16–17.

67. Ford, *Iron Jawed Angels.*

68. Siegel, "She the People," 951. See also Mathews and De Hart, *Sex, Gender, and the Politics of ERA*, 27.

69. Allen, *Only Yesterday*; O'Neill, *Everyone Was Brave*; Chafe, *American Woman*; Burnham, "Theory and Voting Research"; P. Baker, "Domestication of Politics," 620–48; Alpern and Baum, "Female Ballots," 43–67; Harvey, "Political Consequences of Suffrage Exclusion"; Ritter, *Constitution as Social Design*. For an overview of the initial representations of women in the 1920s, see Freedman, "New Woman."

70. More recent works have started to emphasize the positive impact of the Nineteenth Amendment; see Cott, "Across the Great Divide," 3; Andersen, *After Suffrage*; Smith, "One United People"; and Siegel, "She the People."

71. Quoted in Catt and Shuler, *Woman Suffrage and Politics*, 451.

72. See also "The Vote of the Women," *The Youth's Companion*, October 28, 1920, 670; and Mayme Ober Peak, "Women in Politics," *Outlook*, January 23, 1924, 148.

73. Florence Allen, "The First Ten Years," *Woman's Journal*, August 5, 1930, 5–7.

74. "Is Woman Suffrage Failing?," *Woman Citizen*, March 22, 1924, 8.

75. United States v. Hinson, 2 F. Supp. 200 (Florida 1925). See also VanBurkleo, *"Belonging to the World,"* 206.

76. VanBurkleo, *"Belonging to the World,"* 206–7.

77. Curtis v. Ashworth, 142 S.E. 111 (Georgia 1928), 113. See also Ritter, *Constitution as Social Design*, 88–89.

78. Congressional Record, 67th Cong., 2nd sess., 1922, 62, pt. 9: 9047.

79. Congressional Record, 67th Cong., 2nd sess., 1922, 62, pt. 9: 9048.

80. For text of the original Cable Act, see U.S. Congress, Senate Committee on Immigration, *American Citizenship Rights of Women*, 72nd Cong., 2nd sess., March 2, 1933, 44. For a larger discussion of the Cable Act's significance, see Cott, "Marriage and Women's Citizenship in the United States," 1464–71.

81. Breckinridge, *Marriage and the Civic Rights of Women*, 23–25; Gettys, *Law of Citizenship in the United States*, 124–25; Waltz, *Nationality of Married Women*, 43–44. For a complete history of the Cable Act, see Bredbenner, *Nationality of Her Own*.

82. Sapiro, "Women, Citizenship, and Nationality"; Cott, "Marriage and Women's Citizenship," 1463–71.

83. Cott, "Marriage and Women's Citizenship in the United States," 1464–65.

84. Congressional Record, 67th Cong., 2nd sess., June 20, 1922, 62, pt. 9: 9039–67.

85. For the text of the 1930s and 1931 changes, see U.S. Congress, Senate Committee on Immigration, *American Citizenship Rights of Women*, March 2, 1933, 44–50. For debate on the 1934 changes, see Congressional Record, 73rd Cong., 2nd sess., April 25, 1934, 78, pt. 7: 7329–59. On the campaign to improve the Cable Act, see Lemons, *Woman Citizen*, 65–68; Waltz, *Nationality of Married Women*, 51–58; Cott, "Marriage and Women's Citizenship," 1469–70; and Bredbenner, *Nationality of Her Own*, 165–71.

86. "Another Constitutional Amendment in Process of Evolution," *Baltimore Sun*, August 3, 1921, 6.

87. George Stewart Brown, "New Nationalists Proceed to Wreck the Constitution: Home Rule and Local Self-Government, Says Brown, Are Threatened with Destruction by Federal Amendment," *Baltimore Sun*, February 1, 1922, 8.

88. Sue White, "Legal Attacks on Suffrage Amendment: Last Minute Efforts to Keep Women from the Polls in November Fail," *Suffragist* 7, no. 10 (November 1920): 268, 290; VanBurkleo, *"Belonging to the World,"* 201; Ritter, *Constitution as Social Design*, 45.

89. The state that brought this case was Maryland, which, along with several other southern states, rejected the woman suffrage amendment. Many of these southern states feared that the Nineteenth Amendment would enable Black American women to vote. O'Neal, "Susan B. Anthony Amendment."

90. Siegel, "She the People," 1004–5.

91. Leser v. Garnett, 258 U.S. 130 (1922) (No. 553), brief for plaintiffs in error at 75.

92. See Marbury, "Nineteenth Amendment and After," 17.

93. "The Last Battle against the Nineteenth Amendment," *Baltimore Sun*, November 19, 1921, 6.

94. Ritter, *Constitution as Social Design*, 44–45.

95. Leser v. Garnett, 258 U.S. 130 (1922), 136. The same day the high court handed down *Leser*, it denied another challenge to the amendment, finding that the plaintiff lacked standing to sue. Fairchild v. Hughes, 258 U.S. 126 (1922).

96. While the Fifteenth and Nineteenth Amendments forbid withholding a citizen's right to vote on the basis of race or sex, respectively, both amendments left the door open for states to determine other specific qualifications for suffrage. Consequently, several states legislatures, predominantly in the South, used discriminatory practices such as literacy tests and poll taxes to disenfranchise a majority of Black Americans. The landmark Voting Rights Act of 1965 passed by Congress took major steps toward confronting the suppression of Black Americans' voting rights. Ritter, *Constitution as Social Design*, 44–46; Jones, *Vanguard*; Kousser, *Shaping of Southern Politics*; McCormick, *From Realignment to Reform*.

97. Adkins v. Children's Hospital, 261 U.S. 525 (1923), 553.

98. Radice v. New York, 264 U.S. 292 (1924), 294.

99. John Harrington, "Woman's Rights Would Become Woman's Wrongs," *New York Times*, January 22, 1922, 84.

100. August S. Beatman, "History, Civics, and Economics," *The Independent* (New York), 111, no. 3858 (December 1923): 325.

101. Catharine Waugh McCulloch, "Trial by Jury," *Woman Citizen*, October 2, 1920, 488.

102. Kerber, *No Constitutional Right to Be Ladies*, 128–220.

103. Blackstone, *Commentaries on the Laws of England*, 3:479.

104. Ritter, *Constitution as Social Design*, 100–108.

105. Elizabeth Sheridan, "Women and Jury Service," *American Bar Association Journal* 11 (1925): 794–95.

106. Florence Elizabeth Kennard, "Maryland Women Demand Jury Service," *Equal Rights* 17, no. 3 (March 7, 1931): 22–23.

107. VanBurkleo, *"Belonging to the World,"* 202; Kerber, *No Constitutional Right to Be Ladies*, 139–40; Ritter, *Constitution as Social Design*, 124–25; Cott, *Grounding of Modern Feminism*, 100–114; Young, *In the Public Interest.*

108. People v. Barltz, 180 N.W. 423 (Michigan 1920), 425.

109. Parus v. District Court, 174 P. 706 (Nevada 1918); State v. Walker, 185 N.W. 619 (Iowa 1921); Palmer v. State, 150 N.E. 917 (Indiana 1926).

110. In addition to the Supreme Court's ruling in *Neal v. Delaware*, 103 U.S. 370 (1881), the court ruled in *Strauder v. West Virginia*, 100 U.S. 303 (1880), that laws excluding Black American men from jury service violated their rights under the Equal Protection Clause of the Fourteenth Amendment. Still, state officials in many locales, particularly in southern states, evaded the rulings in *Neal* and *Strauder* by setting up practices other than explicit legal bans on account of race in order to exclude Black Americans from jury service. Marder, "Changing Composition of the American Jury."

111. Ritter, *Constitution as Social Design*, 124–26.

112. "Asking for Trouble," *The Independent* 114, no. 3905 (April 4, 1925): 368.

113. "Women as Jurors," *Central Law Journal* 93, no. 4 (July 29, 1921): 57.

114. State v. James, 114 A. 553 (New Jersey 1921), 555.

115. In re Grilli, 179 N.Y.S. 795 Kings Co. S. Ct. (New York 1920), 797.

116. People ex rel. Fyfe v. Barnett, 319 Ill. 403 (1925), 407–8, 410. This approach was also taken by Idaho in *State v. Kelley* 229 P. 659 (Idaho 1924). VanBurkleo, *"Belonging to the World,"* 202; Ritter, *Constitution as Social Design*, 124.

117. Commonwealth v. Genevieve Welosky, 276 Mass. 398 (1931), 401–2, 407.

118. Commonwealth v. Genevieve Welosky, 276 Mass. 398 (1931), 407, 414–15. See also VanBurkleo, *"Belonging to the World,"* 202.

119. Fay v. New York, 322 U.S. 261 (1947).

120. Hoyt v. Florida, 368 U.S. 57 (1961), 58–59, 62.

121. VanBurkleo, *"Belonging to the World,"* 200–206.

122. A noteworthy break from the trend against women's right to serve on juries is the ruling in *White v. Crook*, 251 F. Supp. 401 (Alabama 1966). In this case federal judges in Alabama held that a state law excluding women from jury service violated their rights under the Fourteenth Amendment. But in *State v. Hall*, 187 So. 2d 861 (Mississippi 1966), which challenged the constitutionality of a Mississippi law excluding women from jury service, the Supreme Court of Mississippi declined to apply the doctrine of *White v. Crook*, ruling that jury service was a legislative grant of privilege, not a right. VanBurkleo, *"Belonging to the World,"* 200–206, 260–62; Chiappetti, "Winning the Battle but Losing the War"; Kerber, *No Constitutional Right to Be Ladies*, 206–20.

123. Taylor v. Louisiana, 419 U.S. 522 (1975), 527. See also Freeman, "Revolution for Women in Law and Public Policy," 376–78.

124. Siegel, "She the People," 1019; Opinion of the Justices, 113 A. 614 (Maine 1921), 617.

125. Preston v. Roberts, 110 S.E. 586 (North Carolina 1922). See also Siegel, "She the People," 1019–20; and Lemons, *Woman Citizen*, 68–69.

126. Dickson v. Strickland, 265 S.W. 1012 (Texas 1924), 1023.

127. Ritter, *Constitution as Social Design*, 50–52.

128. "Ruling Bars Women from State Offices," *Baltimore Sun*, February 19, 1921, 18.

129. In re Opinion Justices, 139 A. 180 (New Hampshire 1927), 184. See also Ritter, *Constitution as Social Design*, 51–52.

130. Breckinridge, *Marriage and the Civic Rights of Women*.

131. Ritter, *Constitution as Social Design*, 89–90.

132. Albert Levitt, "The Domicile of a Married Woman II—For Divorce and Other Purposes," *Central Law Journal* 91, no. 2 (July 9, 1920): 8.

133. Siegel, "She the People," 1018.

134. Ritter, *Constitution as Social Design*, 91–92.

135. Commonwealth v. Rutherford, 169 S.E. 909 (Virginia 1933), 909.

136. Commonwealth v. Rutherford, 913.

137. Ritter, *Constitution as Social Design*, 91–94.

138. Commonwealth v. Rutherford, 922.

139. Ritter, *Constitution as Social Design*, 93.

140. Siegel, "Modernization of Marital Status Law"; Siegel, "Home as Work"; Siegel, "She the People"; Siegel, "Collective Memory of the Nineteenth Amendment."

141. Alice Paul to Caroline Spencer, October 14, 1920, folder 12, box 6, National Woman's Party papers, Manuscript Division, LOC (hereafter NWP papers); Elsie Hill to Mrs. Roberts, March 15, 1921, folder 15, box 10, NWP papers; Pardo, *National Woman's Party Papers*, 8.

142. Elsie Hill to Iris Calderhead Walker, April 1, 1921, folder 1, box 10, NWP papers. See also NWP newsletter, March 21, 1921, folder 15, box 10, NWP papers.

143. Alice Paul to Mrs. H. O. Sarrels, April 8, 1921, folder 1, box 10, NWP papers.

144. Elsie Hill to Mrs. James Swift, April 13, 1921, folder 2, box 11, NWP papers.

145. Paul to Sarrels, April 8, 1921, folder 1, box 10, NWP papers. See also Alice Paul to Ann Lord, April 9, 1921; and Hill to Walker, April 1, 1921, both in folder 1, box 10, NWP papers.

146. Alice Paul to Caroline Spencer, August 30, 1921, folder 3, box 14; Elsie Hill to Shippen Lewis, April 7, 1921, folder 1, box 10; Alice Paul to Bertha Fowler, April 8, 1921, folder 1, box 10, all in NWP papers.

147. Paul to Sarrels, April 8, 1921; Paul to Lord, April 9, 1921; Hill to Walker, April 1, 1921, all in folder 1, box 10, NWP papers.

148. Paul to Lord, April 9, 1921, folder 1, box 10, NWP papers.

149. Anita Pollitzer to Valantine Winters, April 9, 1921, folder 1, box 10, NWP papers.

150. Recalled in Anita Pollitzer to Katherine Morey, April 12, 1921, folder 2, box 11, NWP papers. See also Anita Pollitzer to Florence Bayard Hilles, April

25, 1921, folder 3, box 11; Paul to Lord, April 9, 1921, folder 1, box 10; and Anita Pollitzer to Dr. Caroline Spencer, April 9, 1921, folder 1, box 10, all in NWP papers.

151. Pollitzer to Winters, April 9, 1921; Alice Paul to Margaret Long, April 7, 1921, both in folder 1, box 10, NWP papers; Pollitzer to Hilles, April 25, 1921, folder 3, box 11, NWP papers.

152. Cott, "Across the Great Divide"; Cott, *Grounding of Modern Feminism*, 110–14.

153. Recalled in Elsie Hill to Miss Baber, April 23, 1921, folder 3, box 11, NWP papers. See also Pollitzer to Spencer, April 9, 1921, folder 1, box 10, NWP papers.

154. Elsie Hill to Shippen Lewis, May 4, 1921, folder 4, box 11, NWP papers.

155. Anita Pollitzer to Mary Winsor, May 13, 1921, folder 5, box 11, NWP papers.

156. Alice Paul to Florence Sanville, April 2, 1921, folder 1, box 10, NWP papers. See also Pollitzer to Spencer, April 9, 1921, folder 1, box 10, NWP papers.

157. Ella Clapp Thompson to Anita Pollitzer, April 1, 1921, folder 1, box 10, NWP papers.

158. Jones, *Vanguard*. See also the information provided in note 96 of this chapter.

159. For a brief professional biography of Albert Levitt, see Schwarz, *Who's Who in Law*, 550–51.

160. Joan Zimmerman is the first scholar to underscore Albert Levitt's contribution to the early equal rights campaign. See Zimmerman, "Jurisprudence of Equality."

161. Elsie Hill to Mary Winsor, May 14, 1921, folder 5, box 11, NWP papers.

162. Hill to Winsor, May 14, 1921, folder 5, box 11, NWP papers.

163. [Albert Levitt], "Suggested Amendment to the Constitution of the United States. Marked Tentative," memorandum, May 16, 1921, folder: "Drafts of the Equal Rights Amendment, 1921–1971," box 200, NWP papers; Hill to Winsor, May 14, 1921; Elsie Hill to Sarah Colvin, May 16, 1921, both in folder 5, box 11, NWP papers; Zimmerman, "Jurisprudence of Equality," 206–7.

164. Hill to Winsor, May 14, 1921, folder 5, box 11, NWP papers.

165. Hill to Colvin, May 16, 1921, folder 5, box 11, NWP papers. See also Alice Paul to Caroline Spencer, May 16, 1921; and Elsie Hill to Shippen Lewis, May 20, 1921, both in folder 5, box 11, NWP papers.

166. Albert Levitt claimed that he wrote more than seventy-five different drafts of the ERA, while Alice Paul suggested that the ERA had gone through several hundred drafts. Albert Levitt to Mildred Gordon, November 28, 1921, reel 14, National Women's Trade Union League papers, Manuscript Division, LOC (hereafter NWTUL papers); Alice Paul to John Dawson, November 1, 1922, folder 7, box 30, NWP papers.

2. "The Right to Differ"

1. Florence Kelley, "The Right to Differ," *Survey* 49 (December 1922): 374–76.

2. My analysis of the drafting period is partly informed by Joan Zimmerman's study on the ERA and its connection to the women's minimum wage struggle. See Zimmerman, "Jurisprudence of Equality."

3. Mary Burt Messer to Elsie Hill, July 7, 1921, folder 10, box 13, NWP papers.

4. Lavinia H. Egan to David Johnson, July 17, 1921, folder 11, box 13, NWP papers.

5. Elsie Hill to Isabella De Angelis, May 16, 1921, folder 5, box 11, NWP papers.

6. [Levitt], "Suggested Amendment to the Constitution of the United States. Marked Tentative," May 16, 1921; [Roscoe Pound], "Suggested Amendment to the Constitution of the United States," memorandum, May 31, 1921, both in folder: "Drafts of the Equal Rights Amendment, 1921–1971," box 200, NWP papers.

7. Roscoe Pound to Albert Levitt, May 27, 1921, folder 6, box 12, NWP papers.

8. [Roscoe Pound], "Section 2," memorandum [1922], folder: "Drafts of the Equal Rights Amendment, 1921–1971," box 200, NWP papers. This draft is based on an earlier draft also written by Pound. Zimmerman, "Jurisprudence of Equality," 206–7.

9. Albert Levitt to Roscoe Pound, May 25, 1921; Pound to Levitt, May 27, 1921, both in folder 6, box 12, NWP papers; Albert Levitt to Roscoe Pound, May 25, 1921, part 1, reel 35, Roscoe Pound papers, Manuscript Division, LOC (hereafter Roscoe Pound papers).

10. Alice Paul to Mrs. H. O. Sarrels, April 8, 1921, folder 1, box 10, NWP papers. See also Alice Paul to Felix Frankfurter, June 29, 1921, folder 9, box 12, NWP papers.

11. Elsie Hill to Caroline Spencer, June 2, 1921, folder 7, box 12, NWP papers.

12. Elsie Hill to Shippen Lewis, May 20, 1921, folder 5, box 11, NWP papers.

13. Florence Kelley to Elsie Hill, March 21, 1921, folder 15, box 10, NWP papers. See also Florence Kelley to Roscoe Pound, June 3, 1921, part 1, reel 40, Roscoe Pound papers.

14. Florence Kelley to Maud Wood Park, April 23, 1921, folder: "National Consumers League 1921," box I-24, National League of Women Voters papers, Manuscript Division, LOC (hereafter LWV papers).

15. Florence Kelley to Elsie Hill, June 3, 1921, folder 7, box 12, NWP papers.

16. Felix Frankfurter to Elsie Hill, June 7, 1921, folder 7, box 12, NWP papers.

17. Elsie Hill to Felix Frankfurter, June 9, 1921, folder 7, box 12, NWP papers.

18. Alice Paul to Elsie Hill, June 9, 1921, folder 7, box 12; Alice Paul to Mrs. John Rodgers, June 15, 1921, folder 8, box 12; Elsie Hill to Mr. John R. Shillady, July 12, 1921, folder 10, box 13, all in NWP papers.

19. Felix Frankfurter to Alice Paul, June 30, 1921, folder 9, box 12, NWP papers.

20. Alice Paul to Albert Levitt, July 11, 1921; Alice Paul to Miss Fanny T. Cochran, July 11, 1921; Alice Paul to Anita Pollitzer, July 12, 1921; Hill to Shillady, July 12, 1921, all in folder 10, box 13, NWP papers.

21. Frankfurter to Paul, June 30, 1921, folder 11, box 13, NWP papers.

22. Paul to Levitt, July 11, 1921; Alice Paul to Albert Levitt, July 13, 1921, both in folder 10, box 13, NWP papers; Alice Paul to Albert Levitt, July 18, 1921; Albert Levitt to Alice Paul, July 20, 1921; Elsie Hill to Crystal Eastman, July 21, 1921, all in folder 11, box 13, NWP papers.

23. Alice Paul to Caroline Spencer, July 12, 1921, folder 10, box 13, NWP papers.

24. Paul to Levitt, July 18, 1921, folder 11, box 13, NWP papers.

25. Levitt to Paul, July 20, 1921, folder 11, box 13, NWP papers.

26. Elsie Hill to Rhoda White, August 30, 1921, folder 3, box 14, NWP papers.

27. Alice Paul's July 1921 letter to Felix Frankfurter is discussed in the following correspondence: Hill to Shillady, July 12, 1921; Elsie Hill to Rebecca Hourwich, July 12, 1921; Paul to Levitt, July 13, 1921, all in folder 10, box 13, NWP papers; Dean Acheson to Alice Paul, July 16, 1921; Paul to Levitt, July 18, 1921, both in folder 11, box 13, NWP papers.

28. Felix Frankfurter to John R. Shillady, July 15, 1921, reel 51, NCL papers. Felix Frankfurter also sent Alice Paul another copy of his June 30, 1921, letter, which stated his concerns with the proposed amendment. See John R. Shillady to Elsie Hill, July 19, 1921; Frankfurter to Paul, June 30, 1921; and Felix Frankfurter to Alice Paul, July 21, 1921, all in folder 11, box 13, NWP papers.

29. Albert Levitt to Alice Paul, July 28, 1921, folder 11, box 13, NWP papers. See also Alice Paul to Dora Lewis, July 27, 1921, folder 11, box 13, NWP papers.

30. Felix Frankfurter, "Memorandum on the Proposed Amendment to the United States Constitution presented by the National Woman's Party," July 21, 1921, reel 51, NCL papers. See also Frankfurter to Paul, July 21, 1921, folder 11, box 13, NWP papers.

31. Paul to Levitt, July 13, 1921, folder 10; Hill to Eastman, July 21, 1921, folder 11; Elsie Hill to Mabel Vernon, July 23, 1921, folder 11, all in box 13, NWP papers.

32. Maud Younger to Ethel Smith, October 8, 1921, reel 14, NWTUL papers. See also Ethel Smith to Elsie Hill, July 27, 1921, folder 11, box 13, NWP papers.

33. Albert Levitt to Roscoe Pound, "Friday Morning," [August 5, 1921], part 1, reel 35, Roscoe Pound papers. See also Alice Paul to Mrs. William Kent, July 25, 1921; Alice Paul to Mary Winsor, July 27, 1921; Paul to Lewis, July 27, 1921; and Alice Paul to Caroline Spencer, July 27, 1921, all in folder 11, box 13, NWP papers.

34. Paul to Kent, July 25, 1921; Paul to Winsor, July 27, 1921; Paul to Lewis, July 27, 1921; Paul to Spencer, July 27, 1921, all in folder 11, box 13, NWP papers; Levitt to Pound, "Friday Morning," [August 5, 1921], part 1, reel 35, Roscoe

Pound papers; Alice Paul to Dora Lewis, August 9, 1921, folder 1; Elsie Hill to Mrs. Willard Straight, August 17, 1921, folder 2, both in box 13, NWP papers.

35. Elsie Hill to Alice Paul, August 2, 1921, folder 1, box 13, NWP papers.

36. Hill to Paul, August 2, 1921, folder 1, box 13, NWP papers.

37. Hill to Straight, August 17, 1921, folder 2, box 13, NWP papers; Roscoe Pound to Ethel Smith, August 1, 1921, reel 14, NWTUL papers; Hill to Paul, August 2, 1921, folder 1, box 13, NWP papers; Levitt to Pound, "Friday Morning," [August 5, 1921], part 1, reel 35, Roscoe Pound papers.

38. Lawyer's comment reported in Caroline Spencer to Alice Paul, August 26, 1921, folder 3, box 14, NWP papers.

39. Paul to Hill, August 2, 1921, folder 1, box 13, NWP papers. See also Alice Paul to Mrs. William Kent, August 12, 1921, folder 2, box 13; Anita Pollitzer to Alice Paul, August 13, 1921, folder 2, box 13; and Shippen Lewis to Alice Paul, August 25, 1921, folder 3, box 14, all in NWP papers.

40. Alice Paul to Mary Philbrook, August 31, 1921, folder 3, box 14, NWP papers; Alice Paul to Agnes Morey, October 7, 1921, folder 5, box 15; Shippen Lewis, "Opinion by Mr. Shippen Lewis with Regard to Adding a Second Section to the Amendment Expressly Safeguarding the Welfare Legislation for Women," statement, [November] 1921, folder 4, box 17; Maud Younger to Congressman John I. Nolan, November 28, 1921, folder 4, box 17; George Gordon Battle, "Opinion of George Gordon Battle as to Proposed Constitutional Amendment Prohibiting Political, Civil, and Legal Disabilities or Inequalities on Account of Sex or Marriage," memorandum, December 1, 1921, folder 5, box 17, all in NWP papers; Pardo, *National Woman's Party Papers*, 9–10.

41. Paul to Philbrook, August 31, 1921, folder 3, box 14, NWP papers.

42. NWP, "Opinion of Robert Kerr of Colorado Springs, Former Judge of County and Probate Court," memorandum, August 17, 1921, folder 2, box 13, NWP papers.

43. Alice Paul to Shippen Lewis, August 13, 1921, folder 2, box 13; Alice Paul to Dora Lewis, August 16, 1921, folder 2, box 13; Shippen Lewis to Alice Paul, August 25, 1921, folder 3, box 14; Alice Paul to Dora Lewis, August 27, 1921, folder 3, box 14; Alice Paul to Caroline Spencer, August 30, 1921, folder 3, box 14; Alice Paul to Mary Philbrook, August 31, 1921, folder 3, box 14, all in NWP papers.

44. Paul wrote out this intended phrasing of the amendment in the following letters: Paul to Dora Lewis, August 27, 1921; Paul to Philbrook, August 31, 1921, both in folder 3, box 14, NWP papers.

45. "Equal Rights Bill Studied by Women: Lawyers Here Confer on Draft to Be Presented to Congress as an Amendment. No Favors Are Wanted[;] Only Privileges Sought Are Those Men Now Enjoy in Law, Say Miss Laughlin. Draft Has Two Sections. For Free and Equal Basis," *New York Times*, September 16, 1921, 10; "Council Accepts Equal-Rights Bill," *Washington Post*, October 3, 1921, 2.

46. "Fixes Equal Rights Amendment Form: Draft Makes Men and Women Equal in All Political, Civil, and Legal Rights," *New York Times*, December 12, 1921, 17.

47. Hale quoted in "Fixes Equal Rights Amendment Form," 17.

48. Harry Slattery, statement, November 1921, folder 4, box 17, NWP papers.

49. Felix Frankfurter to Ethel Smith, September 8, 1921, reel 100, Felix Frankfurter papers, Manuscript Division, LOC (hereafter Felix Frankfurter papers).

50. Florence Kelley to Felix Frankfurter, October 10, 1921, reel 100, Felix Frankfurter papers. See also Florence Kelley to Felix Frankfurter, October 24, 1921, and November 28, 1921, both in reel 51, NCL papers.

51. Ethel Smith to Maud Younger, December 28, 1921, folder 7, box 17, NWP papers. See also Ethel Smith to Maud Younger, October 3, 1921, reel 51, NCL papers; and Ethel Smith to J. D. Wilkinson, December 21, 1921, folder 7, box 17, NWP papers.

52. Ethel Smith to George Gordon Battle, December 15, 1921, folder 6, box 17, NWP papers.

53. Albert Levitt to Roscoe Pound, September 29, 1921, part 1, reel 25, Roscoe Pound papers.

54. Albert Levitt to Alice Paul, December 5, 1921, folder 5, box 17, NWP papers.

55. Alice Paul to Albert Levitt, December 14, 1921, folder 6, box 17, NWP papers.

56. Albert Levitt to Alice Paul, December 18, 1921, folder 6, box 17, NWP papers (italics added for emphasis). See also Paul to Morey, October 7, 1921, folder 5, box 15, NWP papers; Florence Kelley to Miss Clara Southwick, December 17, 1921; Florence Kelley to Hon. Newton Baker, December 20, 1921, both in reel 51, NCL papers; and Anita Pollitzer to Albert Levitt, December 20, 1921, folder 6, box 17, NWP papers.

57. Florence Kelley to Alice Paul, December 2, 1921, folder 5, box 17, NWP papers.

58. NWP, "Conference Held December 4, 1921," memorandum, folder 5, box 17, NWP papers.

59. Paul to Morey, October 7, 1921, folder 5, box 15, NWP papers.

60. Kelley, however, did consent to Paul's suggestion that she refrain from publicly condemning the amendment until she had discussed possible saving clauses with the NCL's board when it met in January. Paul in return agreed to hold off on introducing the amendment until after the NCL's board meeting. Even with these apparent conciliatory moves, the NCL finalized their opposition to the amendment in January 1922. See Florence Kelley, "Conference with Representatives of the Woman's Party," memorandum, December 4, 1921, reel 51, NCL papers; NWP, "Conference Held December 4, 1921,"

folder 5; Rebecca Hourwich to Alice Paul, January 10, 1922, folder 6, both in box 17, NWP papers.

61. Frankfurter to Smith, September 8, 1921; Ethel Smith to Florence Kelley, September 6, 1921; Kelley to Frankfurter, October 24, 1921; Kelley to Frankfurter, November 28, 1921; Smith to Younger, October 3, 1921, all in reel 51, NCL papers; Florence Kelley to Maud Wood Park, November 30, 1921; Molly Dewson to Maud Wood Park, December 1, 1921, both in folder: "National Consumers' League, 1921," box I-24, LWV papers.

62. NWP, "Conference Held December 4, 1921," folder 5, box 17, NWP papers.

63. Dean Acheson to Florence Kelley, December 7, 1921, reel 51, NCL papers. See also Dean Acheson to Ethel Smith, October 13, 1921, reel 51, NCL papers.

64. Dean Acheson to Felix Frankfurter, December 7, 1921, reel 11, Felix Frankfurter papers.

65. Kelley to Southwick, December 17, 1921; Kelley to Baker, December 20, 1921, both in reel 51, NCL papers. See also Zimmerman, "Jurisprudence of Equality," 216–17.

66. Florence Kelley to Simeon D. Fess, December 16, 1921, reel 51; NCL, "Twenty Questions about the Proposed Equal Rights Amendment of the Woman's Party," pamphlet, 1923–24, folder: "Equal Rights Amendment," box J10, both in NCL papers. See also VanBurkleo, "Belonging to the World," 214.

67. Anita Pollitzer to Simeon Fess, September 10, 1920, folder 10, box 6, NWP papers; Equal Rights 1, no. 4 (March 1923): 32.

68. S. D. Fess to Ethel Smith, October 10, 1921; Ethel Smith to Florence Kelley, December 15, 1921; Kelley to Fess, December 16, 1921; S. D. Fess to Mr. M. William, December 24, 1921, all in reel 51, NCL papers.

69. Alice Paul to William Draper Lewis, December 24, 1921, folder 7, box 17, NWP papers.

70. William Draper Lewis to Alice Paul, January 10, 1922, folder 9, box 18, NWP papers.

71. NWP, National Council Meeting Minutes, December 17, 1921, January 17, 1922, folder 3, box 197; Anita Pollitzer to Mrs. M. L. Graham Bankeston, January 18, 1922, folder 10, box 18, both in NWP papers.

72. Elsie Hill to Mary Philbrook, July 8, 1921, folder 10, box 13, NWP papers.

73. Frankfurter to Paul, June 30, 1921, folder 9, box 12, NWP papers.

74. NWP, National Council Meeting Minutes, January 17, 1922, folder 3, box 197, NWP papers.

75. Burnita Shelton Matthews, Legal Research Department, "Report Number 26: Legal Discriminations against Women," 1924, folder: "Legal Reports, 1919–1969, No. 1–37," box 206, NWP papers.

76. NWP, National Council Meeting Minutes, December 17, 1921, January 17, 1922, folder 3, box 197, NWP papers. See also Pardo, National Woman's Party Papers, 197–99.

77. NWP, Legal Research Department, "Report Number 14: Husband Is the Head of the Family," 1923; NWP, Legal Research Department, "Report Number 2," February 1921, both in folder: "Legal Reports, 1919–1969, Nos. 1–37," box 206, NWP papers.

78. NWP, Legal Research Department, "Report Number 23: Fifty Points Where the Law Discriminates against Women," 1924, folder: "Legal Reports, 1919–1969, No. 1–37," box 206, NWP papers.

79. Matthews, Legal Research Department, "Report Number 26," 1924, folder: "Legal Reports, 1919–1969, No. 1–37," box 206, NWP papers.

80. NWP, Legal Research Department, "Report Number 23," 1924, folder: "Legal Reports, 1919–1969, No. 1–37," box 206, NWP papers.

81. Burnita Shelton Matthews, "Legal Discriminations against Women," report, [1927–36], folder 1020, box 76, Alice Paul papers, SL (hereafter Alice Paul papers). See also Matthews, Legal Research Department, "Report Number 26," 1924, folder: "Legal Reports, 1919–1969, No. 1–37," box 206, NWP papers.

82. Matthews, "Legal Discriminations against Women," report, [1927–36], folder 1020, box 76, Alice Paul papers.

83. Matthews, Legal Research Department, "Report Number 26," 1924, folder: "Legal Reports, 1919–1969, No. 1–37," box 206, NWP papers. See also NWP, Legal Research Department, "Report Number 35: A Monograph. The Status of Women," 1925, folder: "Legal Reports, 1919–1969, No. 1–37," box 206, NWP papers.

84. NWP, Legal Research Department, "Report Number 23," 1924, folder: "Legal Reports, 1919–1969, No. 1–37," box 206, NWP papers.

85. NWP, Legal Research Department, "Night Work for Women," report, [n.d.], folder: "Legal Reports, 1919–1969, No. 1–37," box 206, NWP papers.

86. NWP, Legal Research Department, "Is It Right That Men and Women Should Live under Different Set[s] of Laws?," report, [n.d.], folder 1021, box 76, Alice Paul papers.

87. NWP, Legal Research Department, "Do Working Women Want Special Labor Laws?," report, [n.d.]; NWP, Legal Research Department, "Women Were Dismissed from Railroads Owing to Special Labor Laws Regulating Their Hours to Work," report, [n.d.], both in folder: "Legal Reports, 1919–1969, No. 1–37," box 206, NWP papers. See also Consuelo Furman, "Is Special Legislation for Women Desirable?," *Equal Rights* 1, no. 15 (May 1923): 115.

88. NWP, Legal Research Department, "History of Common Law," report, [n.d.], folder 1021, box 76, Alice Paul papers.

89. Gail Laughlin to Members of the National Council, April 7, 1922, folder 10, box 21; NWP, National Council Meeting Minutes, April 11, 1922, folder 3, box 197; Eleanor Brannan to Sophie L.W. Clark, November 15, 1922, folder 9, box 30, all in NWP papers. See also Pardo, *National Woman's Party Papers*, 14; Zimmerman, "Jurisprudence of Equality," 217; and Hoffert, *Alva Vanderbilt Belmont*, 145.

90. NWP, "Declaration of Principles," memorandum, November 11–12, 1922, folder 3, box 197, NWP papers.

91. NWP, "Declaration of Principles," November 11–12, 1922, folder 3, box 197, NWP papers.

92. NWP, "Declaration of Principles," November 11–12, 1922, folder 3, box 197, NWP papers. See also "Declaration of Principles," *Equal Rights* 1, no. 1 (February 17, 1923): 2–3.

93. The text of the proposed amendment now read, "No distinction between the rights of the sexes shall exist within the United States or any place subject to their jurisdiction." Eleanor Brannan to Mrs. W. C. Duffus, November 13, 1922, folder 9, box 30, NWP papers.

94. Eleanor Brannan to Ellen B. Crump, November 14, 1922, folder 9, box 30; Eleanor Brannan to Gail Laughlin, November 16, 1922, folder 10, box 31; Alice Paul to Eleanor Brannan, April 2, 1923, folder 1, box 36, all in NWP papers.

95. "Boosting Liberty," *Equal Rights* 14, no. 3 (August 11, 1928): 212. See also "Greetings from Mrs. Harvey Wiley," *Equal Rights* 1, no. 42 (December 1, 1923): 333.

96. "The Freedom of Equality," *Equal Rights* 1, no. 2 (February 24, 1923): 12.

97. Emma Wold, "The Legal Status of American Women," *Equal Rights* 12, no. 9 (April 11, 1925): 69–72.

98. "Greetings from W. M. Cabell Bruce," *Equal Rights* 1, no. 1 (February 17, 1923): 2.

99. *Equal Rights* 1, no. 5 (March 17, 1923): 35.

100. NWP, National Council Meeting Minutes, June 19, 1923, folder 3, box 197, NWP papers.

101. Caroline Spencer to Alice Paul, June 29, 1923, folder 10, box 38, NWP papers. See also Caroline Spencer to Alice Paul, April 9, 1923, folder 2, box 36; and Alice Paul to Mrs. Charles McClatchy, June 25, 1923, folder 10, box 38, both in NWP papers.

102. NWP, National Council Meeting Minutes, October 25, 1922, folder 3, box 197; Alice Paul to Eleanor Brannan, March 10, 1923 folder 6, box 35; Paul to Brannan, April 2, 1923, folder 1, box 36; Alice Paul to Caroline Spencer, April 11, 1923, folder 2, box 36; Alice Paul to Jane Norman Smith, May 25, 1923, folder 7, box 37; NWP, National Council Meeting Minutes, June 19, 1923, folder 3, box 197, all in NWP papers.

103. "Women Adopt Form for Equal Rights," *New York Times*, July 22, 1923, 1; "Women Adopt Full Rights Amendment," *Baltimore Sun*, July 22, 1923; "Women Draft Equal Rights Amendment," *Chicago Daily Tribune*, July 21, 1923, 11; "Women Want Rights Put in Constitution," *Washington Post*, July 21, 1923; "Equal Rights Plan Indorsed," *Los Angeles Times*, July 22, 1923, 13; "The Seneca Falls Conference," *Equal Rights* 1, no. 24 (August 4, 1923): 195–98.

104. *The Nation* quoted in "Comments in the Press," *Equal Rights* 1, no. 30 (September 8, 1923): 246.

105. "Pilgrimage to the Grave of Susan B. Anthony," *Equal Rights* 1, no. 18 (June 16, 1923): 139; Lavinia Egan, "The Seneca Falls Conference," *Equal Rights* 1, no. 24 (August 4, 1923): 195; "Comments in the Press," *Equal Rights* 1, no. 30 (September 8, 1923): 246; Becker, *Origins of the Equal Rights Amendment*, 105–7.

106. Dean Acheson to Ethel Smith, September 8, 1921, reel 51, NCL papers. See also Kelley, "Right to Differ," 375–76; Florence Kelley to Honorable Newton B. Baker, November 14, 1922, reel 51, NCL papers; NWTUL, "Blanket Amendment Opinions," memorandum, August 10, 1923, reel 14, NWTUL papers.

107. NCL, *Why It Should Not Pass*, pamphlet, May 1922, folder 1078, box 81, Alice Paul papers.

108. Henry Bates to Florence Kelley, September 4, 1922, reel 51, NCL papers.

109. Ladd-Taylor, "Toward Defining Maternalism in U.S. History," 110. See also Koven and Michel, *Mothers of a New World*, 5–6.

110. Lichtman, *White Protestant Nation*, 19–23.

111. Nielsen, *Un-American Womanhood*, 4–5; C. Erickson, "Conservative Women and Patriotic Maternalism."

112. Elizabeth Putnam to the Editor of the *Boston Herald*, November 17, 1923, folder 455, box 27, Elizabeth Putnam papers, SL (hereafter Elizabeth Putnam papers).

113. Lichtman, *White Protestant Nation*, 24–26; Green, "From Antisuffragism to Anti-Communism," 301.

114. Nielsen, *Un-American Womanhood*, 62–63.

115. The WJCC was a confederation of independent women's groups with the purpose of promoting congressional legislation of interest to women. Congress founded the Women's Bureau in 1920 and located it within the Department of Labor. The main function of the Women's Bureau was to collect information about women workers.

116. Lemons, *Woman Citizen*, 70–73. See also Young, *In the Public Interest*.

117. Wilson, *Women's Joint Congressional Committee*, 2–3.

118. Muncy, *Creating a Female Dominion*; Sklar, "Historical Foundations of Women's Power in the Creation of the American Welfare State."

119. Mary Van Kleeck, "Is Blanket Amendment Best Method in Equal Rights Campaign? Con," *Congressional Digest* 3, no. 6 (March 1924): 198. By the 1930s she had changed the style of her surname to Mary van Kleeck.

120. Harrison, *On Account of Sex*, 13–14.

121. Alice Hamilton, "Protection for Women Workers," *Forum* 72 (August 1924): 152–60.

122. Margaret Robinson, "What Equal Rights Means," *Woman Patriot* 13, no. 9 (1929): 8.

123. James Wadsworth to Mrs. Edward Allen, January 22, 1925, folder: "Constitutional Amendments, August 27, 1918–September 17 1925," box 17,

James W. Wadsworth Jr. papers, Manuscript Division, LOC (hereafter James Wadsworth papers).

124. M. Anderson, *Woman at Work*, 157.

125. See Lemons, *Woman Citizen*, 70–73.

126. John R. Commons to the League of Women Voters, December 31, 1930, folder: "Committee Hearings," box II-221, LWV papers.

127. U.S. Congress, Senate Judiciary Subcommittee, *Equal Rights Amendment: Hearing on S.J. Res. 64*, 70th Cong., 2nd sess., February 1, 1929, 60.

128. NWP, National Council Meeting Minutes, November 6, 1923, folder 3, box 197; Alice Paul to Jane Norman Smith, November 6, 1923, folder 7, box 42, both in NWP papers. See also Zimmerman, "Jurisprudence of Equality," 223.

129. "Members of Congress Express Views on Equal Rights Amendment," *Congressional Digest* 3, no. 6 (March 1924): 197. See also Alice Paul to Daniel Read Anthony Jr., December 22, 1927, folder: "D. R. Anthony Jr. Correspondence, 1925–1928," box 259.1, Daniel Read Anthony Jr. papers, Kansas Historical Society, Topeka, Kansas.

130. During this period a subcommittee of the Senate Judiciary Committee held hearings on the ERA in 1924, 1925, 1929, and 1931. The House Judiciary Committee held hearings in 1925 and 1932. The Senate subcommittee hearings in 1924 and 1925 were unrecorded, and consequently there are no transcripts.

131. U.S. Congress, Senate Judiciary Subcommittee, *Equal Rights Amendment: Hearing on S.J. Res. 64*, February 1, 1929, 42 (testimony of Everett Fraser).

132. U.S. Congress, Senate Judiciary Subcommittee, *Equal Rights Amendment: Hearing on S.J. Res. 64*, February 1, 1929, 55 (testimony of Benjamin Loring Young).

133. U.S. Congress, Senate Judiciary Subcommittee, *Equal Rights Amendment: Hearing on S.J. Res. 64*, February 1, 1929, 56 (testimony of Florence Kelley).

134. U.S. Congress, House Committee on the Judiciary, *Equal Rights Amendment to the Constitution: Hearing on H.J. Res. 197*, 72nd Cong., 1st sess., March 16, 1932, 23–25 (testimony of Mrs. William J. Carson of the LWV).

135. U.S. Congress, House Committee on the Judiciary, *Equal Rights Amendment to the Constitution: Hearing on H.J. Res. 75*, 68th Cong., 2nd sess., February 4–5, 1925, 49 (testimony of Edgar Bancroft).

136. U.S. Congress, Senate Judiciary Subcommittee, *Equal Rights Amendment: Hearing on S.J. Res. 64*, February 1, 1929, 65–66 (testimony of Thomas Cadwalader).

137. U.S. Congress, House Committee on the Judiciary, *Equal Rights Amendment: Hearing on H.J. Res. 197*, 72nd Cong., 1st sess., March 16, 1932, 30 (testimony of Selma Borchardt).

138. U.S. Congress, House Committee on the Judiciary, *Equal Rights Amendment Hearing on H.J. Res. 75*, February 4–5, 1925, 82 (testimony of Cadwalader).

139. U.S. Congress, House Committee on the Judiciary, *Equal Rights Amendment Hearing on H.J. Res. 75*, February 4–5, 1925, 44 (testimony of Katharine Ludington).

140. U.S. Congress, Senate Judiciary Subcommittee, *Equal Rights Amendment: Hearing on S.J. Res. 64*, February 1, 1929, 66 (testimony of Cadwalader).

141. U.S. Congress, House Committee on the Judiciary, *Equal Rights Amendment: Hearing on H.J. Res. 75*, February 4–5, 1925, 43.

142. U.S. Congress, House Committee on the Judiciary, *Equal Rights Amendment: Hearing on H.J. Res. 197*, March 16, 1932, 26.

143. U.S. Congress, Senate Judiciary Subcommittee, *Equal Rights Amendment: Hearing on S.J. Res. 64*, February 1, 1929, 38–39; Benjamin Loring Young, *The Legal Status of Women in Massachusetts: A Brief Preliminary Discussion*, pamphlet, January 1923, folder 560, box 33, Elizabeth Putnam papers.

144. U.S. Congress, House Committee on the Judiciary, *Equal Rights Amendment: Hearing on II.J. Res. 75*, February 4–5, 1925, 72–73 (testimony of Agnes Regan).

145. U.S. Congress, House Committee on the Judiciary, *Equal Rights Amendment: Hearing on H.J. Res. 75*, February 4–5, 1925, 43 (testimony of Ludington).

146. U.S. Congress, House Committee on the Judiciary, *Equal Rights Amendment: Hearing on H.J. Res. 75*, February 4–5, 1925, 25–27.

147. U.S. Congress, House Committee on the Judiciary, *Equal Rights Amendment: Hearing on H.J. Res. 197*, March 16, 1932, 5.

148. U.S. Congress, House Committee on the Judiciary, *Equal Rights Amendment: Hearing on H.J. Res. 75*, February 4–5, 1925, 2 (testimony of Maud Younger).

149. U.S. Congress, Senate Judiciary Subcommittee, *Equal Rights Amendment: Hearing on S.J. Res. 64*, February 1, 1929, 18.

150. U.S. Congress, House Committee on the Judiciary, *Equal Rights Amendment to the Constitution: Hearing on H.J. Res. 75*, February 4–5, 1925, 40 (testimony of Anita Pollitzer).

151. U.S. Congress, Senate Judiciary Subcommittee, *Equal Rights Hearing on S.J. Res. 52*, 71st Cong., 3rd sess., January 6, 1931, 17.

152. "Equal Rights for Women," *Youth's Companion*, August 23, 1923, 34.

153. "Strident Sex in Politics," *Chicago Daily Tribune*, July 12, 1925, 8.

154. Silas Bent, "The Women's War," *New York Times*, January 14, 1923, SM4.

155. Lichtman, *White Protestant Nation*, 8–10.

156. Smith-Rosenberg, *Disorderly Conduct*; Rotundo, *American Manhood;* Dubbert, *Man's Place*; Dumenil, *Modern Temper*; Greenwald, *Women, War, and Work*.

157. Samuel Harden Church, "White Collar Women: Dr. Church Thinks Too Many Have Taken Jobs from Men," *New York Times*, August 3, 1933, 16.

158. See Scharf, *To Work and to Wed.*

3. "To Be Regarded as Persons"

1. U.S. Congress, House Judiciary Subcommittee, *A Bill to Provide for Equal Rights*, 75th Cong., 1st sess., May 26, 1937, 16, 20 (testimony of Elsie Hill).

2. DeWolf, "Equal Rights Amendment and the Rise of Emancipationism."

3. Marshall, *Citizenship and Social Class*, 15, 17.

4. Kessler-Harris, *In Pursuit of Equity*, 10–13.

5. Ritter, *Constitution as Social Design*, 136–37.

6. See L. Gordon, *Pitied but Not Entitled*; and L. Gordon, "Putting Children First."

7. Muncy, *Creating a Female Dominion in American Reform*; Skocpol, *Protecting Soldiers and Mothers*; Mink, *Wages of Motherhood.*

8. Cott, *Public Vows*, 174–75; Lichtman, *White Protestant Nation*, 91.

9. Ritter, *Constitution as Social Design*, 142; L. Gordon, *Pitied but Not Entitled*, 281–83; Cott, *Public Vows*, 175; Nelson, "Origins of the Two-Channel Welfare State"; Sainsbury, *Gendering Welfare States*; Kessler-Harris, "Designing Women and Old Fools."

10. Kessler-Harris, *In Pursuit of Equity*, 11; Lister, "Tracing the Contours of Women's Citizenship"; Mettler, *Dividing Citizens*, 8–10, 16–18.

11. Muna Lee, "The Woman's Party Stands Guard," *Equal Rights* 16, no. 35 (October 4, 1930): 278–79.

12. NWP, National Council Meeting Minutes, November 18, 1933, folder, 5, box 197, NWP papers.

13. NWP, "Call to Convention of the National Woman's Party," memorandum, November 16–17, 1934, folder 5, box 197, NWP papers.

14. Ruth Shallcross, "Portrait of the Working Wife," *Independent Woman* 19 (August 1940): 234–35.

15. Scharf, *To Work and to Wed*, 45.

16. "The Facts in the B&O Case," *Equal Rights* 18, no. 14 (May 7, 1932): 11.

17. Gladys Oaks, "Should Married Women Work?," *Equal Rights* 16, no. 51 (January 24, 1931): 405–6.

18. Scharf, *To Work and to Wed*, 43–45.

19. Cott, *Public Vows*, 168–79; Lemons, *Woman Citizen*, 230–32; Becker, *Origins of the Equal Rights Amendment*, 148–50.

20. NWP, National Council Meeting Minutes, September 20, 1930, folder 4, box 197, NWP papers; "Protests to Textile Men," *Equal Rights* 16, no. 40 (November 8, 1930): 317; Pardo, *National Woman's Party Papers*, 43, 50.

21. NWP, "Calendar of Events," memorandum, October 1, 1930, folder 4, box 197; Muna Lee to Mrs. Thomas C. Mirkil, February 5, 1931, folder 12, box 77; Muna Lee to Josephine Casey, April 4, 1931, folder 16, box 78, all in NWP papers; Lee, "Woman's Party Stands Guard," 278–79; "Seeking to Bar Women Workers," *Equal Rights* 16, no. 38 (1930): 300–301; "High Points in Woman's Party Activities," *Equal Rights* 17, no. 22 (July 4, 1931): 172–73; Jane

Norman Smith, "The Background of the Interstate Minimum Wage Compact," *Equal Rights* 20, no. 32 (September 8, 1934): 251–52; Pardo, *National Woman's Party Papers*, 43–51.

22. NWP, "The History of Section 213," pamphlet, 1935, folder 12, box 252, NWP papers.

23. NWP, "History of Section 213," 1935, folder 12, box 252, NWP papers; Lemons, *Woman Citizen*, 231.

24. According to historian Alice Kessler-Harris, "About 1,600 workers voluntarily or involuntarily left the civil service, at least 75 percent of them women." Kessler-Harris, *In Pursuit of Equity*, 59. See also Cott, *Public Vows*, 173; and Lemons, *Woman Citizen*, 231.

25. NWP, Business and Women's Legislative Council, Minutes, January 20, 1932, folder: "Miscellaneous Organizations," box 199; Alma Lutz, *What Price Marriage?*, pamphlet, June 9, 1934, folder 13, box 252; NWP, Executive Committee of the GWC, Minutes, May 22, 1935, folder: "National Committees," box 198; NWP, GWC, *Progress Report*, pamphlet, 1936, folder 13, box 252, all in NWP papers; Pardo, *National Woman's Party Papers*, 57–59.

26. NWP, Executive Committee of the GWC, Minutes, May 22, 1935, folder: "National Committees," box 198, NWP papers.

27. U.S. Congress, Senate Committee on Appropriations Subcommittee, *Legislative Establishment Appropriation Act for 1933, Part II*, 72nd Cong., 2nd sess., 1933, 136.

28. Pardo, *National Woman's Party Papers*, 58, 62–63.

29. Alma Lutz, *Shall Woman's Work Be Regulated by Law?*, pamphlet, September 1930, folder 12, box 252, NWP papers.

30. "Penalizing Marriage," *Equal Rights* 16, no. 40 (November 8, 1930): 317.

31. Burnita Shelton Matthews, "The Equal Rights Amendment," copy of a speech, May 1934, folder 13, box 252, NWP papers.

32. Matthews, "Equal Rights Amendment," May 1934, folder 13, box 252, NWP papers.

33. Vee Terrys Perlman, "The Minimum Wage Muddle," 1934, folder 13, box 252, NWP papers.

34. Chairman [Anna Kelton Wiley] to Elisabeth Long, February 25, 1931, folder 13, box 77, NWP papers (original emphasis).

35. Democratic senator Hugo L. Black of Alabama and Democratic representative William P. Connery of Massachusetts had introduced the legislation. Even though the Black-Connery bill failed to pass Congress, it did provide a blueprint for the FLSA of 1938. Perlman, "Minimum Wage Muddle," 1934, folder 13, box 252, NWP papers; Pardo, *National Woman's Party Papers*, 62–63; Figart, Mutari, and Power, *Living Wages, Equal Wages*, 101–5.

36. U.S. Congress, House Committee on Labor, *Thirty-Hour Week Bill*, 73rd Cong., 1st sess., April and May 1933, 744–45 (testimony of Maud Younger).

37. Perlman, "Minimum Wage Muddle," 1934, folder 13, box 252, NWP papers (original emphasis).

38. Maud Younger, "The NRA and Protective Laws for Women," *Equal Rights* (July 28, 1934): 204–5. See also "Maud Younger Addresses Recovery Administration," *Equal Rights* 19, no. 23 (1933): 180; and "At Women's Expense," *Equal Rights* 19, no. 28 (1933): 221.

39. Administering the NRA was a nightmare, because the act had failed to establish uniformity in the minimum-wage codes. Many women lost the chance to acquire minimum wages, as their industries were slow to adapt codes. Other women were paid lower wages than their male counterparts due to sex-based wage differentials. Even though many NRA industry codes mandated a forty-cent-per-hour minimum wage, about one-quarter of the codes provided for lower rates for women. Mettler, *Dividing Citizens*, 179n9; Bernstein, *Caring Society*, 119–20; Kessler-Harris, *Out to Work*, 262.

40. J. Smith, "Background of the Interstate Minimum Wage Compact," 252.

41. Anita Pollitzer to Donald Richberg, September 1934, folder 5, box 92; Hugh Johnson to Florence Bayard Hilles, September 11, 1934, folder 5, box 92; Anita Pollitzer to Frances Perkins, September 30, 1934, folder 5, box 92; Donald Richberg to Anita Pollitzer, October 5, 1934, folder 6, box 93, all in NWP papers. See also Ruby Black, "Recovery Administration Favors Equal Pay," *Equal Rights* 19, no. 22 (1933): 172; "The Industrial Codes and Equal Rights," *Equal Rights* 19, no. 26 (1933): 204–5; and "Donald Richberg Favors Equality," *Equal Rights* 20, no. 45 (1934): 356.

42. VanBurkleo, *"Belonging to the World,"* 217; see also 226–27.

43. Cott, *Grounding of Modern Feminism*, 141. See also Lemons, *Woman Citizen*, viii, 182–91; Becker, *Origins of the Equal Rights Amendment*, 10–11; and Draper and Diamond, *Hidden History of the Equal Rights Amendment*, 21–42.

44. "The Forgotten Woman," *Equal Rights* 19, no. 26 (July 29, 1933): 202.

45. Muna Lee, "Fight Ouster of Women from Night Textile Jobs as Sex Discrimination," memorandum, March 14, 1931, reel 51, NCL papers.

46. Alice Paul, for example, described herself as someone who leaned more toward conservative economic policies. Paul, *Conversations with Alice Paul*, 436–37.

47. U.S. Congress, House Committee on the Judiciary, *Equal Rights Amendment to the Constitution: Hearing on H.J. Res. 197*, 72nd Cong., 1st sess., March 16, 1932, 12.

48. Perlman, "Minimum Wage Muddle," 1934, folder 13, box 252, NWP papers.

49. Lee, "Woman's Party Stands Guard," 278–79.

50. NWP, National Council Meeting Minutes, November 18, 1933, folder 5, box 197, NWP papers. See also Grace Brewer to Council Member, October 11, 1934, folder 6, box 93, NWP papers.

51. "Open Season for Venting Past Prejudices," *Equal Rights* 18, no. 28 (August 13, 1932): 222–23; Scharf, *To Work and to Wed*, 47.

52. NWP, National Council Meeting Minutes, April 9, 1933, folder 5, box 197, NWP papers; "Budget Head Hears Protest," *Equal Rights* 19, no. 11 (1933): 83–85; Pardo, *National Woman's Party Papers*, 62.

53. [Grace Brewer] to Mrs. Withrow, October 23, 1934, folder 6, box 93; Edith Horton Hooker to Edwina Austin Avery, October 2, 1934, folder 6, box 93; Grace Brewer to Mrs. Bowman, December 17, 1934, folder 8, box 93; NWP, *Bills before Congress of Interest to Feminists*, pamphlet, January 11, 1936, folder 11, box 252; NWP, *Progress Report*, pamphlet, 1936, folder 13, box 252, all in NWP papers; Harriet Sheppard, "Committee Reports Bill for Equality in Government Service," *Equal Rights* 21, no. 12 (1935): 4; Pardo, *National Woman's Party Papers*, 73–74.

54. Scharf, *To Work and to Wed*, 59–60.

55. U.S. Congress, House Committee on Civil Service, *To Amend Married Persons' Clause*, 74th Cong., 1st sess., April 18–19 and 23–24, 1935, 22–23 (testimony of Dorothy Dunn).

56. U.S. Congress, House Committee on Civil Service, *To Amend Married Person's Clause*, April 18–19 and 23–24, 1935, 30 (testimony of Anita Pollitzer).

57. U.S. Congress, House Committee on Civil Service, *To Amend Married Person's Clause*, April 18–19 and 23–24, 1935, 13–15 (testimony of Mrs. Harris Baldwin). See also Scharf, *To Work and to Wed*, xii–xiii.

58. Despite the 1935 hearing, Congress did not vote to repeal Section 213 until 1937. See NWP, "The History of Section 213," 1935, folder 12; NWP, "Progress Report," 1936, folder 13, both in box 252, NWP papers; and Pardo, *National Woman's Party Papers*, 74.

59. U.S. Congress, Senate Committee on the Judiciary Subcommittee, *Equal Rights for Men and Women: Hearing on S.J. Res. 1*, 73rd Cong., 1st sess., May 27, 1933, 2.

60. U.S. Congress, Senate Committee on the Judiciary Subcommittee, *Equal Rights for Men and Women Hearing on S.J. Res. 1*, May 27, 1933, 17 (testimony of Rebekah Greathouse). Few protectionists testified at the 1933 hearing. Prominent liberal protectionist Mary Anderson, head of the Women's Bureau, later explained that ERA opponents deliberately avoided the 1933 hearing to "not give them [ERA proponents] a chance to put on their usual act." M. Anderson, *Woman at Work*, 164–65.

61. "Lawyers Press for Early Passage of the Equal Rights Amendment," *Equal Rights* 21, no. 14 (September 1, 1935): 1–2; "Business and Professional Women for Equal Rights," *Equal Rights* 23, no. 14 (1937): 110–12; [Alice Paul] to Lois, October 31, 1934, folder 6, box 93, NWP papers; Anita Pollitzer to Louis Ludlow, December 21, 1934, folder 8, box 93, NWP papers; Eleanor James Ottaway to Mrs. John Winant, January 30, 1936, reel 51, NCL papers; Pardo, *National Woman's Party Papers*, 67, 78.

62. For an in-depth analysis of women's nationality rights, see Bredbenner, *Nationality of Her Own.*

63. Wilson, *Women's Joint Congressional Committee*; Lemons, *Woman Citizen*, 68.

64. The 1930 and 1931 revisions to the Cable Act repealed the ineligible-spouse disqualification for naturalization, rescinded the presumptive loss of citizenship for residence abroad, and removed the barriers to repatriation to women who had already lost their nationality status for those reasons. Waltz, *Nationality of Married Women*, 51–58; Bredbenner, *Nationality of Her Own*, 165–71, 227; Cott, "Marriage and Women's Citizenship," 1468–70.

65. Pardo, *National Woman's Party Papers*, 44–48; Bredbenner, *Nationality of Her Own*, 7–9, 199–201; Becker, *Origins of the Equal Rights Amendment*, 161–87.

66. Doris Stevens, *The International Road to Equality*, pamphlet, July 5, 1934, folder 12, box 252, NWP papers.

67. The text of the proposed treaty is provided in "The First Treaty Giving Complete Equality to Women in the History of the World Signed at Montevideo," *Equal Rights* 20, no. 23 (1934): 179–81. See also Bredbenner, *Nationality of Her Own*, 204.

68. "U.S. Move to Block a Feminism Treaty Laid to Strife Here," *New York Times*, December 18, 1933, 1; Bredbenner, *Nationality of Her Own*, 233–34.

69. "Foe Tells Views on Women's Pact," *New York Times*, December 21, 1933, 18.

70. "Pact Action Denied by Mrs. Roosevelt," *New York Times*, December 27, 1933, 10.

71. "Foe Tells Views on Women's Pact," 18. See also "Topic of the Times," *New York Times*, December 20, 1933, 20.

72. "Comment by Miss Dorothy Straus on the Proposed 'Equal Rights' Treaty," memorandum, n.d., folder: "International Co-Operation Dept," box II-295, LWV papers. See also Mildred Adams, "Again Controversy Arises over Equality for Women," *New York Times*, December 24, 1933, 4.

73. Bredbenner, *Nationality of Her Own*, 217. However, not all liberal protectionists disapproved of the Equal-Nationality Treaty, as some of them actively supported it. For instance, Democratic senator Robert Wagner sent cables to Secretary of State Cordell Hull urging him to back the measure. See "U.S. Move to Block a Feminism Treaty Laid to Strife Here," 1.

74. "Lawyers Press for Early Passage of the Equal Rights Amendment," 1–2; Bredbenner, *Nationality of Her Own*, 234.

75. Kendall Foss, "Women Insist U.S. Sign Pact at Montevideo," *Washington Post*, December 20, 1933, 2.

76. Kendall Foss, "U.S. to Sign Equality Pact for Women: Montevideo Treaty to Be Made," *Washington Post*, December 21, 1933, 1. See also "U.S. Move to Block a Feminism Treaty Laid to Strife Here," 1; "Equal Nationality Rights," *Washington Post*, December 22, 1933, 6; Frances Mangum, "Representative Jenckes Calls It a Great Step Forward," *Washington Post*, December 22, 1933, 15.

77. NWP, National Council Meeting Minutes, May 5–6, 1934, folder 5, box 197, NWP papers; "First International Equal Rights Convention to Be Signed at Montevideo," *Equal Rights* 19, no. 47 (December 23, 1933): 363–65. See also Bredbenner, *A Nationality of Her Own*, 235–38.

78. NWP, National Council Meeting Minutes, April 9, 1933; NWP, National Council Meeting Minutes, May 7, 1933; NWP, National Council Meeting Minutes, May 5–6, 1934, all in folder 5, box 197, NWP papers; Pardo, *National Woman's Party Papers*, 56–57.

79. Vice Chairman to Party Member, October 19, 1934, folder 6, box 93, NWP papers; Pardo, *National Woman's Party Papers*, 56–57, 61, 67–68.

80. U.S. Congress, House Committee on Immigration and Naturalization, *Provide Equality in Matters of Citizenship*, 73rd Cong., 1st sess., May 15, 1933, H. Rep. No. 131, 2.

81. *Congressional Record*, 73rd Cong., 2nd sess., April 25, 1934, 78, pt. 7: 7329.

82. U.S. Congress, House Committee on Immigration and Naturalization, *Relating to Naturalization and Citizenship Status of Children*, 73rd Cong., 1st sess., March 28, 1933, 15–17, 44, 51. See also Bredbenner, *Nationality of Her Own*, 239–40.

83. For a copy of the letter from Cordell Hull to William Bankhead, dated March 24, 1934, see U.S. Congress, House Committee on Rules, *To Amend the Law Relative to Citizenship and Naturalization*, 73rd Cong., 2nd sess., March 24, 1934, 2. See also Cordell Hull to William Bankhead, March 24, 1934, folder 12, box 91, NWP papers.

84. For a copy of the letter from Cordell Hull to Samuel Dickstein, dated March 27, 1933, see U.S. Congress, House Committee on Immigration and Naturalization, *Relating to Naturalization and Citizenship Status of Children*, March 28, 1933, 8.

85. For a copy of the letter from Wilbur Carr to Samuel Dickstein, dated February 10, 1933, see U.S. Congress, House Committee on Immigration and Naturalization, *Relating to Naturalization and Citizenship Status of Children*, March 28, 1933, 9–11. See also Bredbenner, *Nationality of Her Own*, 230–32.

86. Frances Perkins to William Bankhead, March 26, 1934; Helen Hill Weed, "Deputation of Democratic Women to the White House," memorandum, March 26, 1934, both in folder 12, box 91, NWP papers; Bredbenner, *Nationality of Her Own*, 238–40.

87. Myrtle Patterson to Sarah Colvin, March 29, 1934, folder 12, box 91, NWP papers.

88. J. A. Latimer to James Farley, March 23, 1934; [Doris Stevens] to Cordell Hull, March 24, 1934; Weed, "Deputation of Democratic Women to the White House," March 26, 1934; Alice Paul to Cecile Maurer, March 28, 1934; Patterson to Colvin, March 29, 1934, all in folder 12, box 91, NWP papers.

89. Marguerite Dugan Bodziak to James Farley, March 25, 1934; Molly Dewson to Mrs. Stanley Hodge, March 27, 1934, both in folder 12, box 91, NWP papers; Bredbenner, *Nationality of Her Own*, 241.

90. For copies of the letters from Cordell Hull to William Bankhead, dated March 26, 1934, and Frances Perkins to William Bankhead, dated March 26, 1934, see U.S. Congress, Senate Committee on Immigration, *To Provide Equality in Matter of Citizenship*, 73rd Cong., 2nd sess., April 26, 1934, S. Rep. No. 865, 2–3. See also *Congressional Record*, 73rd Cong., 2nd sess., April 25, 1934, 78, pt. 7: 7333.

91. "Senate Votes Women Nationality Rights: Bill Ends All Discriminations in Old Laws," *New York Times*, May 11, 1934, 1; "Equality in Nationality Becomes Law of the Land," *Equal Rights* 20, no. 18 (June 2, 1934): 139–40.

92. U.S. Congress, House Committee on Immigration and Naturalization, *Provide Equality in Matters of Citizenship*, May 15, 1933, H. Rep. No. 131, 2. See also Cott, "Marriage and Women's Citizenship," 1469; and Bredbenner, *Nationality of Her Own*, 240–41.

93. Title 8, U.S.C. section 1409, originally dating from 1952, Immigration and Nationality Act, 8 U.S.C. 1409 (a) (2006); Kitch, *Specter of Sex*, 178–79; Neuwirth, *Equal Means Equal*, 73–76.

94. Bredbenner, *Nationality of Her Own*, 241.

95. Louis Ludlow to Anita Pollitzer, December 21, 1934, folder 8, box 93, NWP papers.

96. Madison, *Indiana through Tradition and Change*, 371.

97. Louis Ludlow to Anita Pollitzer, December 26, 1934, folder 8, box 93, NWP papers. See also "The Equal Rights Amendment," *Washington Post*, June 2, 1936, 8.

98. "Letters Favoring Amendment," *Equal Rights* 21, no. 3 (March 15, 1935): 3–4.

99. NWP, Congressional Committee Meeting Minutes, June 9, 1934, folder: "National Committee Minutes," box 198, NWP papers.

100. Anna Milburn to Congressman Marion Zioncheck, September 3, 1934, folder 5, box 92, NWP papers.

101. Betty Gram Swing was married to Raymond Gram Swing, a popular print and broadcast journalist who was also a vocal proponent of the ERA in his own right. Raymond Gram Swing, "Speech before the National Conference, National Woman's Party," December 1934, folder 8, box 93, NWP papers.

102. NWP, "Proceedings Biennial Convention of the National Woman's Party," memorandum, November 14, 1936, folder: "National Woman's Party Proceedings, November 1934, November 1936," box 199, NWP papers. See also "Report of the Congressional Committee," *Equal Rights* 22, no. 3 (February 1, 1936): 1–2.

103. Anita Pollitzer, "Congressional," *Equal Rights* 21, no. 21 (December 15, 1935): 3.

104. NWP, Congressional Committee, "Report of the Congressional Committee," memorandum, January 1–April 17, 1935, folder 5, box 197, NWP papers. See also Edwina Austin Avery to Jane Norman Smith, May 26, 1934, folder 1, box 91, NWP papers.

105. Anita Pollitzer claimed that at least ten representatives had expressed support for the amendment. NWP, National Council Meeting Minutes, April 14, 1935, folder 5, box 197, NWP papers.

106. "The Amendment Advances Politically," *Equal Rights* 21, no. 6 (May 1, 1935): 1.

107. "Status of Bill When Congress Adjourned," *Equal Rights* 21, no. 5 (September 15, 1935): 1–2.

108. "Congressional Outlook Encouraging," *Equal Rights* 22, no. 2 (January 15, 1936): 1.

109. The subcommittee did not issue a written report. Instead, it voted to favorably recommend the ERA. See NWP, *Equal Rights Amendment: Questions and Answers on the Equal Rights Amendment*, pamphlet, 1943, folder: "National Woman's Party," box 56, Republican National Committee papers: News clippings and publications, 1932–65, Dwight David Eisenhower Library (DDEL), Abilene, Kansas (hereafter RNC papers); Betty Gram Swing, "Amendment Receives Favorable Action: Subcommittee Favorably Votes Equal Rights Amendment Out to Main Judiciary Committee," *Equal Rights* 22, no. 12 (June 15, 1936): 1.

110. "Subcommittee O.K. Given Proposed Equal Rights Amendment," *Chicago Daily Tribune*, May 31, 1936, 1.

111. Swing, "Amendment Receives Favorable Action," 1 (original emphasis).

112. U.S. Congress, House Judiciary Subcommittee, *Bill to Provide for Equal Rights*, May 26, 1937, 1–4.

113. U.S. Congress, House Judiciary Subcommittee, *Bill to Provide for Equal Rights*, May 26, 1937, 21 (testimony of Elsie Hill).

114. U.S. Congress, House Judiciary Subcommittee, *Bill to Provide for Equal Rights*, May 26, 1937, 8 (testimony of Emma Wold).

115. U.S. Congress, House Judiciary Subcommittee, *Bill to Provide for Equal Rights*, May 26, 1937, 7.

116. U.S. Congress, House Judiciary Subcommittee, *Bill to Provide for Equal Rights*, May 26, 1937, 9–10 (testimony of Rebekah Greathouse).

117. U.S. Congress, House Judiciary Subcommittee, *Bill to Provide for Equal Rights*, May 26, 1937, 16. See also testimony from the same hearing, 18–20.

118. NWP, "Equal Rights Amendment: Questions and Answers on the Equal Rights Amendment," 1943, folder: "National Woman's Party," box 56, RNC papers.

119. "Equal Rights Amendment Gains Powerful Advocate," *Equal Rights* 23, no. 2 (February 1, 1937): 11.

120. Royal Copeland, "Adoption of Equal Rights Amendment Vital," *Equal Rights* 23, no. 3 (February 15, 1937): 15.

121. Alice Paul, "The History of These Proposed Modifications and the Reasons Therefore [*sic*]," notes, [1941–42], folder 1050, box 79, Alice Paul papers; Pardo, *National Woman's Party Papers*, 100–102; Patterson, *Congressio-*

nal Conservatism, 46–49, 201–2, 274; Harrison, *On Account of Sex,* 20–21; Dunn, *Roosevelt's Purge,* 53, 77, 81–89.

122. Lichtman, *White Protestant Nation,* 58, 82.

123. L. Gordon, "Black and White Visions of Welfare," 559–90; Ware, *Beyond Suffrage,* 1–18, 60. See also L. Gordon, *Pitied but Not Entitled,* 67–111, 183–209.

124. Cott, *Public Vows,* 178.

125. Eleanor Roosevelt, "Is Woman's Place in the Home?," text of a radio speech, March 1, 1935, folder: "Is Woman's Place in the Home?," box 1401, Eleanor Roosevelt papers, Franklin D. Roosevelt Presidential Library (FDRL), Hyde Park, New York (hereafter Eleanor Roosevelt papers). See also L. Gordon, *Pitied but Not Entitled,* 55, 107, 195–96; and Mink, *Wages of Motherhood,* 123–50.

126. In 1933 the New Deal women's network pushed the Federal Emergency Relief Administration to sponsor a White House conference on the emergency needs of women. In addition, in 1934 these women considered forming a coordinating consultant commission on the economic welfare of women. That program, however, failed to take off. L. Gordon, *Pitied but Not Entitled,* 195.

127. Anderson, *Woman at Work,* 152–56.

128. Under Mary Anderson's leadership, the Women's Bureau conducted an extensive investigation into the injurious effects of Section 213 and reported them to Congress as well as the Civil Service Commission. M. Anderson, *Woman at Work,* 155–56.

129. Kessler-Harris, *In Pursuit of Equity,* 60–63; Hartman, *Home Front and Beyond,* 16–21.

130. Eleanor Roosevelt, "Married Women Working," text of a radio speech, February 2, 1933, folder: "Married Women Working," box 1398, Eleanor Roosevelt papers.

131. Helen Hill Weed, "The Menace of Interstate Compacts," *Equal Rights* 20, no. 42 (March 10, 1934): 323–33; Becker, *Origins of the Equal Rights Amendment,* 149–50.

132. For emancipationists' arguments against the interstate compacts, see Perlman, "Minimum Wage Muddle," 1934; Alma Lutz, *Women and Wages,* pamphlet, October 17, 1934, both in folder 13, box 252, NWP papers; and Jane Norman Smith, "Minimum Wage Legislation: Law[s] Applying to Women Only Are Found to Have Ill Effects," reprint of a *New York Times* article, December 30, 1935, reel 51, NCL papers.

133. See Elinore Morehouse Herrick, "Mrs. Herrick Sees and Clarifies Some Erroneous Conclusions," reprint of a *New York Times* article, January 2, 1936; Elmer Andrews, "Wage Laws for Women," reprint of a *New York Times* article, January 8, 1936; Rose Schneiderman, "Women's Trade Union League Disputes Mrs. Smith's Statements," reprint of a *New York Times* article, January 10, 1936, all in reel 51, NCL papers.

134. Robert Wagner, "Wagner Speech," February 3, 1938, reel 51, NCL papers.

135. Faue, *Community of Suffering and Struggle*, 83; Kessler-Harris, *Out to Work*, 257; Scharf, *To Work and to Wed*, 43–65.

136. Mary C. Wing to Senator Pat McCarran, January 27, 1938, reel 51, NCL papers.

137. "Women in Industry: Address of Hon. Robert F. Wagner of New York on the Occasion of the Public Affairs Dinner of the Institute of Women's Professional Relations," May 7, 1935, reel 51, NCL papers.

138. M. Anderson, "Economic Status of Wage-Earning Homemakers," 865.

139. See Kessler-Harris, *In Pursuit of Equity*, 39; Cott, *Grounding of Modern Feminism*, 205–6; Harrison, *On Account of Sex*, 14–15; Hartman, *Home Front and Beyond*, 16–21; and Hart, "Minimum-Wage Policy and Constitutional Inequality."

140. M. Anderson, *Woman at Work*, 210–11.

141. M. Anderson, *Woman at Work*, 210–12; Women's Charter Group, Joint Conference Group of Women, Meeting Minutes, December 2, 1936, reel 54, NCL papers; Pardo, *National Woman's Party Papers*, 83–84.

142. M. Anderson, *Woman at Work*, 211.

143. Mary van Kleeck to Felix Frankfurter, October 16, 1936, reel 54, NCL papers.

144. Mary van Kleeck to Lucy Mason, December 21, 1936, reel 54, NCL papers.

145. Women's Charter Group, Joint Conference Group of Women, Meeting Minutes, December 2, 1936, reel 54, NCL papers.

146. Joint Conference Group in the United States for the Women's Charter, "The Women's Charter—What and Why," memorandum, December 21, 1936, reel 54, NCL papers.

147. Van Kleeck to Mason, December 21, 1936, reel 54, NCL papers.

148. Elinore Morehouse Herrick, "Women's Charter," statement, April 30, 1937, reel 54, NCL papers.

149. Blanch Freedman to Friend, January 22, 1938, reel 54, NCL papers.

150. M. Anderson, *Woman at Work*, 212.

151. Women's Charter Group, Joint Conference Group of Women, Meeting Minutes, December 2, 1936; Mary Anderson to Lucy Mason, December 8, 1936, December 10, 1938, all in reel 54, NCL papers.

152. Lucy Mason to Ruth Hanna, May 13, 1937, reel 54, NCL papers.

153. Mary Anderson to Lucy Mason, May 15, 1937, reel 54, NCL papers.

154. Lucy Mason to Mary Anderson, January 27, 1937, reel 54, NCL papers. See also Felix Frankfurter to Mary van Kleeck, October 27, 1936, reel 54, NCL papers.

155. Ruth Hanna to Lucy Mason, April 29, 1937, reel 54, NCL papers.

156. Dorothy Straus to Molly Dewson, January 4, 1938, folder: "Equal Rights Amendment," box 8, Molly Dewson papers, FDRL (hereafter Molly Dewson papers).

4. "We Women Want to Be Persons Now"

1. U.S. Congress, Senate Judiciary Subcommittee, *Equal Rights Amendment Hearings on S.J. Res. 61*, 79th Cong., 1st sess., September 28, 1945, 4.

2. Sicherman and Green, *Notable American Women*, 477.

3. DeWolf, "Equal Rights Amendment and the Rise of Emancipationism."

4. Dorothy Straus to Molly Dewson, January 25, 1938, folder: "Equal Rights Amendment, 1937–1949," box 8, Molly Dewson papers; Anne Petersen, "Lines Sharply Split on Eve of Equal Rights Amendment," *New York Times*, February 6, 1938, 85.

5. U.S. Congress, Senate Judiciary Subcommittee, *Equal Rights for Men and Women: Hearings on S.J. Res. 65*, 75th Cong., 3rd sess., February 7–10, 1938, 1.

6. Dorothy Straus to Molly Dewson, January 4, 1938, folder: "Equal Rights Amendment, 1937–1949," box 8, Molly Dewson papers.

7. Straus to Dewson, January 25, 1938, folder: "Equal Rights Amendment, 1937–1949," box 8, Molly Dewson papers.

8. Straus to Dewson, January 4, 1938, folder: "Equal Rights Amendment, 1937–1949," box 8, Molly Dewson papers. See also Straus to Dewson, January 25, 1938; and Molly Dewson to Robert Wagner, January 26, 1938, both in folder: "Equal Rights Amendment, 1937–1949," box 8, Molly Dewson papers.

9. William E. Borah to Pauline Newman, February 9, 1938, folder 136, box 8, Pauline Newman papers, SL (hereafter Pauline Newman papers).

10. Straus to Dewson, January 4, 1938, folder: "Equal Rights Amendment, 1937–1949," box 8, Molly Dewson papers. See also Straus to Dewson, January 25, 1938, folder: "Equal Rights Amendment, 1937–1949," box 8, Molly Dewson papers.

11. U.S. Congress, Senate Judiciary Subcommittee, *Equal Rights for Men and Women: Hearings on S.J. Res. 65*, February 7–10, 1938, 3 (testimony of Dorothy Straus).

12. U.S. Congress, Senate Judiciary Subcommittee, *Equal Rights for Men and Women: Hearings on S.J. Res. 65*, February 7–10, 1938, 70 (testimony of Edgar Bronson Tolman; statement of William Millard).

13. U.S. Congress, Senate Judiciary Subcommittee, *Equal Rights for Men and Women: Hearings on S.J. Res. 65*, February 7–10, 1938, 70 (statement of Millard).

14. U.S. Congress, Senate Judiciary Subcommittee, *Equal Rights for Men and Women: Hearings on S.J. Res. 65*, February 7–10, 1938, 49 (testimony of Dean Acheson).

15. U.S. Congress, Senate Judiciary Subcommittee, *Equal Rights for Men and Women: Hearings on S.J. Res. 65*, February 7–10, 1938, 91–92 (testimony of Mrs. Rufus M. Gibbs).

16. U.S. Congress, Senate Judiciary Subcommittee, *Equal Rights for Men and Women: Hearings on S.J. Res. 65*, February 7–10, 1938, 86 (statement of Ethel Smith).

17. U.S. Congress, Senate Judiciary Subcommittee, *Equal Rights for Men and Women: Hearings on S.J. Res. 65*, February 7–10, 1938, 42 (testimony of Mrs. John Hader).

18. U.S. Congress, Senate Judiciary Subcommittee, *Equal Rights for Men and Women: Hearings on S.J. Res. 65*, February 7–10, 1938, 34 (testimony of Straus).

19. U.S. Congress, Senate Judiciary Subcommittee, *Equal Rights for Men and Women: Hearings on S.J. Res. 65*, February 7–10, 1938, 100–101; "Five Women Sponsor Equal Rights," *New York Times*, February 25, 1938, 11; Fry, "Alice Paul and the Equal Rights Amendment," 18.

20. U.S. Congress, Senate Judiciary Subcommittee, *Equal Rights for Men and Women: Hearings on S.J. Res. 65*, February 7–10, 1938, 14 (testimony of Senator Warren Austin).

21. NWP, National Council Meeting Minutes, March 12, 1938, folder 5, box 197, NWP papers; U.S. Congress, Senate Judiciary Subcommittee, *Equal Rights for Men and Women: Hearings on S.J. Res. 65*, February 7–10, 1938, 169.

22. U.S. Congress, Senate Judiciary Subcommittee, *Equal Rights for Men and Women: Hearings on S.J. Res. 65*, February 7–10, 1938, 119 (testimony of Dorothy Ashby Moncure).

23. Hartman, *Home Front and Beyond*, 18–21. See also Ritter, *Constitution as Social Design*, 143–45.

24. Lemons, *Woman Citizen*, 231–32; Becker, *Origins of the Equal Rights Amendment*, 146–48.

25. Hartman, *Home Front and Beyond*, 18–19.

26. U.S. Congress, Senate Judiciary Subcommittee, *Equal Rights for Men and Women: Hearings on S.J. Res. 65*, February 7–10, 1938, 97 (testimony of Miller).

27. U.S. Congress, Senate Judiciary Subcommittee, *Equal Rights for Men and Women: Hearings on S.J. Res. 65*, February 7–10, 1938, 139 (testimony of Sarah Gibbs Pell).

28. Dean Acheson to Elisabeth Christman, February 17, 1938, folder: "Equal Rights Amendment, 1938–1943," box 5, Dean Acheson papers, Harry S. Truman Library (HSTL), Independence, Missouri (hereafter Dean Acheson papers).

29. Mary Dublin to Mrs. John C. Hader, April 18, 1938, reel 51, NCL papers.

30. Anne Petersen, "'Fight to Last Ditch' Mapped against Equal Rights Proposal," *New York Times*, February 27, 1938, 77.

31. U.S. Congress, Senate Judiciary Committee, *Equal Rights Amendment: Report to Accompany S.J. Res. 65*, 75th Cong., 3rd sess., April 20, 1938, S. Rep. No. 1641.

32. "Equal Rights Amendment Now before the Senate," *Equal Rights* 24, no. 7 (April 1938): 235. See also "Equal Rights Bill Gets Senate Test," *New York Times*, March 22, 1938, 3.

33. Borah to Newman, February 9, 1938, folder 136, box 8, Pauline Newman papers; "The Amendment Moves," *Equal Rights* 24, no. 12 (June 1938):

274; Dorothy Ashby Moncure, "Status of Equal Rights Amendment," *Women Lawyers Journal* 28 (1938): 28–30.

34. Carter v. Carter, 298 U.S. 238 (1936); Morehead v. New York ex rel. Tipaldo, 298 U.S. 587 (1936).

35. Perkins, *Roosevelt I Knew,* 255–56; Bernstein, *Caring Society,* 132; Mettler, *Dividing Citizens,* 182; Ritter, *Constitution as Social Design,* 135–42.

36. Ritter, *Constitution as Social Design,* 136.

37. West Coast Hotel Co. v. Parrish, 330 U.S. 379 (1937), 391. See also Ritter, *Constitution as Social Design,* 139–41.

38. West Coast Hotel Co. v. Parrish, 400.

39. Ritter, *Constitution as Social Design,* 141.

40. United States v. Darby Lumber Co., 312 U.S. 100 (1941). See also Ritter, *Constitution as Social Design,* 141–42; and, Mettler, *Dividing Citizens,* 181–83.

41. National Labor Relations Board v. Jones and Laughlin Steel Corporation, 301 U.S. 1 (1937), 37.

42. Mettler, *Dividing Citizens,* 183.

43. Kessler-Harris, *In Pursuit of Equity,* 102–3, 105; Figart, Mutari, and Power, *Living Wages,* 115.

44. Chafe, *American Woman,* 81.

45. U.S. Congress, Senate Committee on Education and Labor, *Joint Hearings on the Fair Labor Standards Act,* 75th Cong., 1st sess., June 2–15, 1937, 174–75, 406.

46. Steinberg, *Wages and Hours,* 109–14; Kessler-Harris, *In Pursuit of Equity,* 105–6.

47. Hart, *Bound by Our Constitution,* 165–66; Mettler, *Dividing Citizens,* 195.

48. The FLSA also excluded most Black American men, who constituted 80 percent of agricultural workers. Kessler-Harris, *In Pursuit of Equity,* 105–6.

49. Mettler, *Dividing Citizens,* 187.

50. Perkins, *Roosevelt I Knew,* 256–67; Kessler-Harris, *In Pursuit of Equity,* 101–2.

51. Kessler-Harris, *In Pursuit of Equity,* 113; Hart, *Bound by Our Constitution,* 165.

52. U.S. Congress, Senate Committee on Education and Labor, *Joint Hearings on the Fair Labor Standards Act,* June 2–15, 1937, 196, 403–10.

53. L. Baker, *Felix Frankfurter,* 114–15; Thomas, *Felix Frankfurter,* 315–19, 324–25; Parrish, "Felix Frankfurter and American Federalism," 27–35; Mettler, *Dividing Citizens,* 187.

54. U.S. Congress, House Judiciary Subcommittee, *Amend the Constitution Relative to Equal Rights,* 79th Cong., 1st sess., February 21–March 31, 1945, 88 (testimony of Frances Perkins).

55. Kessler-Harris, *In Pursuit of Equity,* 115.

56. Franklin Roosevelt, Presidential Press Conferences, April 8, 1938, vol. 9, 297, quoted in Hart, *Bound by Our Constitution,* 166, 240n81.

57. Kerber, "Separate Spheres," 9–39.

58. U.S. Congress, Senate Committee on Education and Labor, *Joint Hearings on the Fair Labor Standards Act,* June 2–15, 1937, 275 (testimony of John Lewis).

59. U.S. Congress, House Judiciary Subcommittee, *Amend the Constitution Relative to Equal Rights,* February 21–March 31, 1945, 88 (testimony of Frances Perkins).

60. Mettler, *Dividing Citizens,* 189–90.

61. United States v. Darby Lumber Co., 125.

62. Helen Elizabeth Brown, *Unequal Justice under Law: Women and the Constitution,* pamphlet, August 6, 1942, folder: "Equal Rights Amendment," box 601, Robert A. Taft papers, LOC (hereafter Robert A. Taft papers). See also Ritter, *Constitution as Social Design,* 136–48.

63. "Should Congress Approve the Proposed Equal Rights Amendment, Pro.," *Congressional Digest* 22, no. 4 (April 1943): 111.

64. See Industrial League for Equality, *Industrial Workers and the Equal Rights Amendment,* pamphlet, 1941, folder 1079, box 81, Alice Paul papers.

65. "Should Congress Approve the Proposed Equal Rights Amendment, Pro.," 116.

66. Dorothy Ashby Moncure, *The Equal Rights Amendment in the Light of the Fair Labor Standards Act,* pamphlet, n.d., folder 5, box 119, Carl Hayden papers, Hayden Library, Arizona State University (ASU), Tempe, Arizona (hereafter Carl Hayden papers); "Should Congress Approve the Proposed Equal Rights Amendment, Pro.," 116.

67. "The National Woman's Party Explains Its Proposal for an Equal-Rights Amendment," *Congressional Digest* 22, no. 4 (April 1943): 104.

68. Nora Stanton Barney, *Women as Human Beings,* pamphlet, 1946, folder 1, box 43, Carl Hayden papers.

69. "The National Woman's Party Explains Its Proposal for an Equal-Rights Amendment," 104. See also Helen Robbins Bittermann, *Protective Laws for Women Only,* pamphlet, October 25, 1941, folder 17, box 18, Dorothy Shipley Granger papers, SL (hereafter Dorothy Shipley Granger papers).

70. "Should Congress Approve the Proposed Equal Rights Amendment, Pro.," 114.

71. Anna Kelton Wiley and Lucy Dickinson to Congressmen, March 24, 1947, folder 1, box 43, Carl Hayden papers.

72. Marie Moore Forrest to Caroline Lexow Babcock, June 28, 1940; Mrs. Herron to Caroline Babcock, June 28, 1940; Alice Paul to Caroline Babcock, June 29, 1940, all in folder 6, box 116, NWP papers; Pardo, *National Woman's Party Papers,* 101–2.

73. Harrison, *On Account of Sex,* 20–21.

74. NWP, National Council Meeting Minutes, July 10, 1940, folder 5, box 197, NWP papers; Alice Paul, "The History of These Proposed Modifications and the Reasons Therefore [*sic*]," [1941–42], folder 1050, box 79, Alice Paul

papers; Kathleen McLaughlin, "Equal Job Rights for Women Backed," *New York Times*, June 27, 1940, 1; Pardo, *National Woman's Party Papers*, 101–3.

75. The text of the radio discussion can be found in "Should Congress Approve the Proposed Equal Rights Amendment, Pro.," 108.

76. Hartman, *Home Front and Beyond*, ix, 34, 123.

77. Even though women's wages went up during the war, they failed to reach the level of men's wages. Also, a number of child-care facilities did not have the capacity or staff to meet demand. Harrison, *On Account of Sex*, 3–4; Ritter, *Constitution as Social Design*, 145–46.

78. Harrison, *On Account of Sex*, 3–4. See also Chafe, *American Woman*, esp. chaps. 6 and 7; Schweitzer, "World War II and Female Labor Participation Rates," 89–95; K. Anderson, *Wartime Women*, 3–22; and Evans, *Born for Liberty*, 221–27, 239–41.

79. Rupp, *Mobilizing Women for War*; Honey, *Creating Rosie the Riveter*; Westbrook, "Fighting for the American Family."

80. Honey, *Creating Rosie the Riveter*, 7.

81. Harrison, *On Account of Sex*, 4; Hartman, *Home Front and Beyond*, 86; Oppenheimer, *Female Labor Force in the United States*, 8.

82. Greathouse, "Effect of Constitutional Equality on Working Women," 228.

83. "Should Congress Approve the Proposed Equal Rights Amendment, Pro.," 107, 110.

84. "Should Congress Approve the Proposed Equal Rights Amendment, Pro.," 112.

85. "Should Congress Approve the Proposed Equal Rights Amendment, Pro.," 107.

86. "Equality before the Law," copy of a *New York Herald Tribune* article, September 20, 1943, folder 1079, box 81, Alice Paul papers.

87. "Editorial Support and Nationwide Publicity for the Equal Rights Amendment," *Equal Rights* 30, no. 1 (January 1944): 3; NWP, *National Woman's Party— The Present Campaign for Equality of Rights for Women*, pamphlet, 1945, folder, 13, box 252, NWP papers; Pardo, *National Woman's Party Papers*, 115–16.

88. "Equal Rights Bill Sent On to Senate: Judiciary Committee Favors 9 to 3," *New York Times*, May 12, 1942, 22.

89. "Equal Rights Bill No. 1 in the House, Ludlow Offers Measure Which Has Been in Congress Continually since 1923," *New York Times*, January 6, 1943, 12; "Equal Rights Plan Up Again in Senate: Gillette and 23 others Sponsor Joint Resolution," *New York Times*, January 22, 1943, 23.

90. NWP, "Equal Rights Amendment: Questions and Answers on the Equal Rights Amendment," 1943, folder: "National Woman's Party," box 56, RNC papers; "Amendment Receives Unanimous Favorable Report from Both Judiciary Sub-Committees of Congress," *Equal Rights* 29, no. 3 (March 1943): 17; "The Legislative Journey of the Equal Rights Amendment, 1923–1943," *Congressional Digest* 22, no. 4 (April 1943): 105–6.

91. Stephen Rice, copy of memorandum, August 15, 1941; Paul, "History of These Proposed Modifications and the Reasons Therefore," [1941–42], both in folder 1050, box 79, Alice Paul papers; Pardo, *National Woman's Party Papers*, 104–6.

92. Alice Paul, "Memorandum for Senator Hughes on the Equal Rights Amendment," [1941–42]; Paul, "History of These Proposed Modifications and the Reasons Therefore," [1941–42], both in folder 1050, box 79, Alice Paul papers; Pardo, *National Woman's Party Papers*, 110–17.

93. NWP, National Council Meeting Minutes, January 20, 1943, January 24, 1943, March 20, 1943, all in folder 6, box 198, NWP papers.

94. "The Amendment Advances in Senate," *Equal Rights* 29, no. 5 (May 1943): 37, 44; Pardo, *National Woman's Party Papers*, 116–18.

95. The five senators who opposed the amendment in the Senate committee were Tom Connally (D-TX), Abe Murdock (D-UT), Pat McCarran (D-NV), Charles O. Andrews (D-FL), and John Danaher (R-CT). "For Equal Rights Bill: Senate Committee Approves Women's Amendment," *New York Times*, May 25, 1943, 21; Anna Kelton Wiley, "Another Milestone Passed," *Equal Rights* 29, no. 6 (June 1943): 45–46, 50.

96. The text of the 1940s rephrasing for the ERA can be found in NWP, *The Case for the Equal Rights Amendment*, pamphlet, 1944, folder 11, box 252, NWP papers. See also Jo Freeman, "What's in a Name? Does It Matter How the Equal Rights Amendment Is Worded?," *Women, Law, and Public Policy* (blog), June 1996, https://www.jofreeman.com/lawandpolicy/eraname.htm; Paul, *Conversations with Alice Paul*, 266, 269; Fry, "Alice Paul and the Equal Rights Amendment"; and Pardo, *National Woman's Party Papers*, 110–20.

97. Peter Seitz to Mary Anderson, June 11, 1943, reel 51, NCL papers. See also Mary Anderson to Dean Acheson, June 8, 1943; and Dean Acheson to Mary Anderson, June 18, 1943, both in folder: "Equal Rights Amendment, 1938–1943," box 5, Dean Acheson papers.

98. Wiley, "Another Milestone Passed."

99. NWP, "Equal Rights Amendment: Questions and Answers on the Equal Rights Amendment," 1943, folder: "National Woman's Party," box 56, RNC papers.

100. Jane Todd, "Material Pertaining to Equal Rights Amendment," memorandum, December 28, 1943, folder: "Core Nat'l Fed. Eq. Rights Briefs," box 148, National Federation of Republican Women papers, DDEL; "Clubs of the General Federation Endorse Equal Rights Amendment," *Equal Rights* 30, no. 5 (May 1944): 38; "N.E.A. Supports Equal Rights Amendment," *Equal Rights* 20, no. 7 (August–September 1944): 54; Pardo, *National Woman's Party Papers*, 114–15, 121–22, 139.

101. Mary Frank Rhoads, "Formation of Women's Joint Legislative Committee for Equal Rights," *Equal Rights* 29, no. 5 (1943 May): 40; Harrison, *On Account of Sex*, 17; Pardo, *National Woman's Party Papers*, 114–15, 139; Rupp and Taylor, *Survival in the Doldrums*, 73–76.

102. "Should Congress Approve the Proposed Equal Rights Amendment, Pro.," 107–17; NWP, *Men Speak for Equal Rights Amendment*, pamphlet, [1943], folder 6, box 19, Dorothy Shipley Granger papers; Alice Paul, "On Record in Support of the Equal Rights Amendment in Addition to Its Congressional Sponsors," memorandum, [1945–47], folder 1080, box 81, Alice Paul papers; NWP, "National Woman's Party—The Present Campaign for Equality of Rights for Women," 1945, folder 13, box 252, NWP papers.

103. Paul, "On Record in Support of the Equal Rights Amendment in Addition to Its Congressional Sponsors," memorandum, [1945–47], folder 1080, box 81, Alice Paul papers.

104. These governors included Earl Warren of California, Sidney Osborn of Arizona, John Vivian of Colorado, Walter Bacon of Delaware, and Henry Schricker of Indiana. NWP, *Governors Endorse Equal Rights Amendment*, pamphlet, 1944, folder 22, box 2, Alma Lutz papers, SL (hereafter Alma Lutz papers); NWP, "National Woman's Party—The Present Campaign for Equality of Rights for Women," 1945, folder 13, box 252, NWP papers; "Governors Endorse Amendment," *Equal Rights* 20, no. 7 (August–September 1944): 55; Pardo, *National Woman's Party Papers*, 121–22.

105. Republican representative Clare Boothe Luce of Connecticut too expressed tentative support for the amendment by announcing that she favored congressional submission of the amendment to the states. "For the Equal Rights Amendment," *New York Times*, February 22, 1943, 14; "Should Congress Approve the Proposed Equal Rights Amendment to the Constitution, Pro.," 107–17.

106. "Should Congress Approve the Proposed Equal Rights Amendment, Pro.," 107–17; Pardo, *National Woman's Party Papers*, 120–23.

107. Henry Wallace to Emma Guffey Miller, January 27, 1944, file 1079, box 81, Alice Paul papers (original emphasis). See also "Vice President Wallace Endorses Equal Rights Amendment," reprint of a *New York Times* article, January 27, 1944, folder 6, box 19, Dorothy Shipley Granger papers; Ruth Young to Henry Wallace, February 8, 1944, reel 52, NCL papers; and Ruth Young to Henry Wallace, February 9, 1944, reel 52, NCL papers.

108. Harry Truman to Emma Guffey Miller, April 20, 1944, folder 120-A, box 653, White House Central Files, Official File, HSTL. See also "Truman Reaffirms Equal Rights Backing," *New York Times*, September 22, 1945, 14.

109. While the New Deal women, especially Eleanor Roosevelt and Molly Dewson, openly proclaimed their disdain for the ERA, President Roosevelt was more tactful. He never publicly committed himself as opposed to or in favor of the amendment. Throughout all his years in office, however, he refused to meet with amendment supporters in person; he was the only president not to do so. Serena Foley Davis to Franklin D. Roosevelt, July 17, 1940; William Langer to Edwin Watson, August 4, 1943; Edwin Watson to Claude Pepper, October 4, 1943, all in folder: "Equal Rights Amendment," box 1-2-2, White House Official File, Office File 120, FDRL.

110. Paul, *Conversations with Alice Paul*, 511.

111. "Equal Rights Victory at GOP Convention," *Equal Rights* 30, no. 7 (August–September 1944): 56–58; Paul, *Conversations with Alice Paul*, 516; Kathleen McLaughlin, "Platform Victory Is Won by Women," *New York Times*, June 27, 1944, 15.

112. George Gordon Battle, "Excerpts from Brief in Support of the Equal Rights for Women Amendment," memorandum, n.d., folder 1081, box 81, Alice Paul papers; Anita Pollitzer, "Democrats Adopt Equal Rights Amendment Plank," *Equal Rights* 30, no. 7 (August–September 1944): 58–60.

113. Kathleen McLaughlin, "Contest Develops on Equal Rights," *New York Times*, July 19, 1944, 13; Kathleen McLaughlin, "Democrats Yield on Equal Rights Plank," *New York Times*, July 21, 1944, 12.

114. Pollitzer, "Democrats Adopt Equal Rights Amendment Plank," 58–60; McLaughlin, "Democrats Yield on Equal Rights Plank," 12.

115. Copy of a statement from Eleanor Roosevelt, memorandum, July 9, 1944; Dorothy McAllister to Mrs. W. T. Boost, July 11, 1944, both in reel 52, NCL papers; McLaughlin, "Contest Develops on Equal Rights," 13.

116. Eleanor Roosevelt did offer support for the ERA in May 1951, but this was a tentative endorsement at best. Eleanor Roosevelt, "On the Status of Women," copy of a syndicated column, June 1, 1946, reel 52, NCL papers; Eleanor Roosevelt, "My Day," copies of syndicated columns, May 24, 1951, June 6, 1951, both in folder: "My Day, May–June 1951," box 1444, Eleanor Roosevelt papers.

117. Harrison, *On Account of Sex*, 118–20.

118. Pollitzer, "Democrats Adopt Equal Rights Amendment Plank," 58–60; McLaughlin, "Contest Develops on Equal Rights," 13; McLaughlin, "Democrats Yield on Equal Rights Plank," 12; Paul, *Conversations with Alice Paul*, 516–18; Gould Lincoln, "The Political Mill," copy of a column from the *Evening Star* (Washington DC), August 1, 1944, folder 16, box 18, Dorothy Shipley Granger papers.

119. Harrison, *On Account of Sex*, 19–21.

120. "Asks Equal Rights Votes: Ludlow Tells House 74 Members Are for the Amendment," *New York Times*, February 1, 1945, 17.

121. "New York Legislature Memorializes Congress to Pass Equal Rights Amendment," *Equal Rights* 31, no. 2 (1945): 13.

122. Due to wartime restrictions on transportation, the House Judiciary's subcommittee decided not to hold a formal hearing on the amendment. It instead asked amendment opponents and proponents to submit written statements that outlined their arguments. See House Judiciary Subcommittee, *Amend the Constitution Relative to Equal Rights*, February 21–March 31, 1945.

123. U.S. Congress, House Judiciary Committee, *Equal Rights Amendment: Report to Accompany H.J. Res. 49*, 79th Cong., 1st sess., July 12, 1945, H. Rep. No. 907, 204. The committee reported the amendment favorably with a 15-to-7 vote.

124. Amelia Himes Walker, "House Judiciary Committee Reports Equal Rights Amendment First Time in History of Amendment," *Equal Rights* 31, no. 4 (July–August 1945): 41.

125. U.S. Congress, Senate Judiciary Subcommittee, *Equal Rights Amendment Hearings on S.J. Res. 61*, September 28, 1945, 6.

126. U.S. Congress, Senate Judiciary Subcommittee, *Equal Rights Amendment Hearings on S.J. Res. 61*, September 28, 1945, 3 (testimony of Senator George Radcliffe).

127. U.S. Congress, Senate Judiciary Subcommittee, *Equal Rights Amendment Hearings on S.J. Res. 61*, September 28, 1945, 24–27, 28.

128. U.S. Congress, Senate Judiciary Subcommittee, *Equal Rights Amendment Hearings on S.J. Res. 61*, September 28, 1945, 4 (testimony of Emma Guffey Miller).

129. U.S. Congress, Senate Judiciary Subcommittee, *Equal Rights Amendment Hearings on S.J. Res. 61*, September 28, 1945, 80–81 (testimony of Frank Donner).

130. U.S. Congress, Senate Judiciary Subcommittee, *Equal Rights Amendment Hearings on S.J. Res. 61*, September 28, 1945, 58, 80 (testimony of Marvin Harrison).

131. U.S. Congress, Senate Judiciary Committee, *Equal Rights Amendment to Accompany S.J. Res. 61*, 79th Cong., 2nd sess., March 5, 1946, S. Rep. No. 1013, 14.

132. U.S. Congress, Senate Judiciary Committee, *Equal Rights Amendment to Accompany S.J. Res. 61*, March 5, 1946, S. Rep. No. 1013, 1.

133. "Senate Judiciary Committee Victory," *Equal Rights* 32, no. 1 (January–February 1946): 1.

5. "Motherhood Cannot Be Amended"

1. "Equal Rights Amendment," *New York Times*, July 20, 1946, 12.

2. The WJLC had recruited Senator Barkley to the emancipationist cause earlier that summer. See Katharine Norris, "Senate Majority Leader Barkley Receives Women's Joint Legislative Committee for Equal Rights," *Equal Rights* 32, no. 3 (May–June, 1946): 24, 30.

3. Congressional Record, 79th Cong., 2nd sess., July 17, 1946, 92, pt. 7: 9219.

4. Congressional Record, 79th Cong., 2nd sess., July 19, 1946, 92, pt. 8: 9403.

5. "Equal Rights Amendment Reaches Vote in Senate," *Equal Rights* 32, no. 4 (July–August, 1946): 33, 35, 40.

6. Pardo, *National Woman's Party Papers*, 133–34.

7. See Danese, *Claude Pepper and Ed Ball.*

8. See Halt, "Joseph F. Guffey, New Deal Politician from Pennsylvania."

9. Pederson, *Presidential Profiles*, 43.

10. Congressional Record, 79th Cong., 2nd sess., July 18, 1946, 92, pt. 7: 9310.

11. Congressional Record, 79th Cong., 2nd sess., July 18, 1946, 92, pt. 7: 9324.

12. Congressional Record, 79th Cong., 2nd sess., July 18, 1946, 92, pt. 7, 9302.

13. Pardo, *National Woman's Party Papers*, 133–34.

14. See Huthmacher, *Senator Robert F. Wagner*.

15. See Patterson, *Congressional Conservatism*.

16. See Price, "Stalwart Conservative in the Senate."

17. Congressional Record, 79th Cong., 2nd sess., July 18, 1946, 92, pt. 7: 9293.

18. Congressional Record, 79th Cong., 2nd sess., July 18, 1946, 92, pt. 7: 9311.

19. Congressional Record, 79th Cong., 2nd sess., July 18, 1946, 92, pt. 7: 9316.

20. "Equal Rights Amendment Reaches Vote in Senate," 33, 35, 40; Pardo, *National Woman's Party Papers*, 133–34.

21. "Senate Rejects Women's Equal Rights Measure," *Chicago Daily Tribune*, July 20, 1946, 9.

22. Paul, *Conversations with Alice Paul*, 517–18; "Equal Rights Amendment Reaches Vote in Senate," 1, 35, 40.

23. "Equal Rights Amendment Reaches Vote in Senate," 33; see also 35, 40.

24. Bess Furman, "Equal Rights Fails to Get Two Thirds," *New York Times*, July 20, 1946, 1.

25. "Equal Rights Amendment," 12.

26. Mary Anderson to Hattie Smith, October 30, 1944, folder 20, box 3, Hattie Smith papers.

27. National Committee to Defeat the Un-Equal Rights Amendment (hereafter NCDURA), National Directing Committee Meeting Minutes, September 28, 1944, folder 21, box 3, Hattie Smith papers.

28. NCDURA, press release, October 1944, reel 52, NCL papers.

29. Dorothy McAllister to Dr. Alice Hamilton, November 3, 1944, reel 53, NCL papers.

30. Anderson to Smith, October 30, 1944, folder 20, box 3, Hattie Smith papers.

31. McAllister to Hamilton, November 3, 1944, reel 53, NCL papers.

32. Dorothy McAllister to Hattie Smith, February 8, 1945, folder 20, box 3, Hattie Smith papers.

33. Dorothy McAllister to Elizabeth Magee, December 11, 1944, reel 53, NCL papers. See also NCDURA, memorandum, June 29, 1945, folder 20, box 3, Hattie Smith papers.

34. NCDURA, National Directing Committee Meeting Minutes, September 28, 1944, folder 21, box 3, Hattie Smith papers; McAllister to Magee, December 11, 1944, reel 53, NCL papers; Harrison, *On Account of Sex*, 20.

35. Anderson to Smith, October 30, 1944, folder 20, box 3, Hattie Smith papers. See also McAllister to Smith, February 8, 1945, folder 20; and Dorothy McAllister to Member, March 1, 1945, folder 21, both in box 3, Hattie Smith papers.

36. NCDURA, Meeting Notes, April 26, 1945; Rose Glick to Elizabeth Magee, April 28, 1945; Margaret Stone to Elizabeth Magee, April 30, 1945, all in reel 53, NCL papers.

37. Stone to Magee, April 30, 1945, reel 53, NCL papers.

38. NCDURA, Meeting Notes, April 26, 1945; Glick to Magee, April 28, 1945, both in reel 53, NCL papers.

39. NCDURA, Meeting Notes, April 26, 1945, reel 53, NCL papers.

40. Glick to Magee, April 28, 1945, reel 53, NCL papers. See also Stone to Magee, April 30, 1945, reel 53, NCL papers; and Dorothy McAllister to Hattie Smith, May 8, 1945, folder 20, box 3, Hattie Smith papers.

41. NCDURA, Meeting Notes, April 26, 1945; Glick to Magee, April 28, 1945; Stone to Magee, April 30, 1945; Dorothy McAllister to Elizabeth Magee, May 5, 1945; Massachusetts Committee to Defeat the Un-Equal Rights Amendment, "Notice," memorandum, [July 1945]; Dorothy McAllister to Jeanette Studley, January 16, 1946, all in reel 53, NCL papers; Pardo, *National Woman's Party Papers*, 129–32.

42. NCDURA, *Warning! Look Out for the So-Called Equal Rights Amendment*, pamphlet, [1945], folder 21, box 3, Hattie Smith papers.

43. This pamphlet was an older NCL leaflet that the NCDURA redistributed. NCDURA, "Don't Buy a Brick," memorandum, November 11, 1944, reel 52, NCL papers; NCL, *Don't Buy a Gold Brick*, pamphlet, 1944, folder 21, box 3, Hattie Smith papers.

44. "Illusory Women's Rights," *Washington Post*, July 19, 1945, 6.

45. "Illusory Women's Rights," *Washington Post*, July 27, 1945, 8.

46. NCDURA, National Directing Committee Meeting Minutes, September 28, 1944, folder 21, box 3, Hattie Smith papers.

47. NCDURA, "Women Leaders Protest Equal Rights Amendment," press release, June 11, 1945, reel 53, NCL papers. See also NCDURA, memorandum, June 29, 1945, folder 20, box 3, Hattie Smith papers.

48. NCDURA, memorandum, June 29, 1945, folder 20, box 3, Hattie Smith papers; ACLU, "On Women's Rights," memorandum, July 1945, folder: "Equal Rights Amendment, 1943–1945," box 601, Robert A. Taft papers; Pardo, *National Woman's Party Papers*, 124–26.

49. NCDURA, "Call to National Committee," memorandum, February 6, 1946, reel 53, NCL papers.

50. McAllister to Studley, January 16, 1946, reel 53, NCL papers.

51. Elizabeth Magee to Alice Hamilton, February 25, 1946, reel 53, NCL papers.

52. Robert Taft to Alice Hamilton, May 27, 1946, reel 52, NCL papers. See also NCDURA, "Legislation That Will Be Jeopardized by Passage of the So-Called Equal Rights Amendment," memorandum, March 1, 1946, folder: "Equal Rights Amendment, 1943–1945," box 601, Robert A. Taft papers.

53. Mary Anderson to Matthew J. Connelly, April 19, 1945, folder 120-A, box 653, White House Central Files, Official File, HSTL; Stone to Magee, April 30, 1945, reel 53, NCL papers; Francis Perkins to Matthew J. Connelly, June 19, 1945, file 120-A, box 653, White House Central Files, Official File, HSTL.

54. Dorothy McAllister to President Truman, February 13, 1946, file 120-A, box 653, White House Central Files, Official File, HSTL.

55. William Hassett to David Niles, February 14, 1946, file 120-A, box 653, White House Central Files, Official File, HSTL.

56. David Niles to William Hassett, February 18, 1946, file 120-A, box 653, White House Central Files, Official File, HSTL.

57. Matthew J. Connelly to Dorothy McAllister, February 18, 1946, file 120-A, box 653, White House Central Files, Official File, HSTL. See also "A.W." to Mr. Hassett, April 1, 1949, file 120-A, box 654, White House Central Files, Official File, HSTL.

58. By the early 1950s President Truman was privately critical of the amendment. In the summer of 1950, for example, President Truman wrote to Emma Guffey Miller that he no longer saw a need for the amendment, because "men are just slaves and I suppose they will always continue to be." President Truman to Emma Guffey Miller, August 12, 1950, folder: "Correspondence, Harry Truman," box 1, India Edwards papers, HSTL (hereafter India Edwards papers). See also Emma Guffey Miller to India Edwards, August 17, 1950, folder: "Correspondence, Harry Truman," box 1, India Edwards papers.

59. NCDURA, "Urgent," memorandum, June 19, 1946, folder: "National Committee to Defeat the Un-Equal Rights Amendment," box III-225, LWV papers.

60. NCDURA, *These Lawyers and Legal Scholars Oppose the So-Called Equal Rights Amendment*, pamphlet, n.d., folder: "National Committee to Defeat the Un-Equal Rights Amendment," box III-225, LWV papers; NCDURA, "Suggested Plan of Action," memorandum, July 1946, reel 53; Dorothy McAllister, "Senators Who Have Said They Will Be Leaders in the Fight against the Amendment," memorandum, July 1946, reel 53; National Committee on the Status of Women, "Report," memorandum, April 15, 1947, reel 52, all in NCL papers.

61. NCDURA, "Suggested Plan of Action," memorandum, July 1946; Dorothy McAllister to Irene [Silverly], July 16, 1946, both in reel 53, NCL papers.

62. NCDURA, "Suggested Plan of Action," memorandum, July 1946, reel 53, NCL papers.

63. Eleanor Roosevelt, "On the Status of Women," syndicated column, June 1, 1946, reel 52, NCL papers.

64. NCDURA, "A Joint Statement Headed by Mrs. Roosevelt," press release, July 18, 1946, reel 53, NCL papers. See also NCDURA, "Victory Bulletin," memorandum, July 31, 1946, folder 20, box 3, Hattie Smith papers.

65. Harrison, *On Account of Sex*, 6. See also Hartman, *Home Front and Beyond*, 25.

66. Chafe, *American Woman*, 176–77. See also his later work: Chafe, *Paradox of Change*, 154–72.

67. Anderson, *Wartime Women*, 153–54.

68. Eleanor Roosevelt, "For Click Magazine," draft, April 1944, folder, "Women's Place after the War," box 1415, Eleanor Roosevelt papers.

69. Frieda Miller, "What's Ahead for Women Workers," Women's Bureau press release, January 6, 1946, folder 169, box 8, Frieda Miller papers, SL (hereafter Frieda Miller papers).

70. The Selective Service Act gave veterans priority over wartime workers in the competition for their old jobs. Chafe, *American Women*, 179; Harrison, *On Account of Sex*, 4–5; VanBurkleo, *"Belonging to the World,"* 235.

71. This discrepancy is because the 350,000 women who volunteered for the armed services represented only about 2 percent of all military personnel. Hartman, *Home Front and Beyond*, 25–26.

72. Several scholars argue that since the original calls for women to do war work never fully challenged the core ideas of femininity, it was an easy return to conventional sex boundaries in the postwar era. Rupp, *Mobilizing Women for War*; Honey, *Creating Rosie the Riveter*; Harrison, *On Account of Sex*, 4–6.

73. Hartman, "Prescriptions for Penelope," 223–39. See also Anderson, *Wartime Women*, 174–77.

74. Works from this genre include Waller, *Veteran Comes Back*; Kitching, *Sex Problems of the Returned Veteran*; Mariano, *Veteran and His Marriage*; and Kupper, *Back to Life*. See Hartman, "Prescriptions for Penelope," 223–25, 237; and Hartman, *Home Front and Beyond*, 24–25, 29.

75. A growing number of sociologists and anthropologists were also moving away from the biological determinism that had shaped the work of Ferdinand Lundberg, who was a journalist, and Marynia Farnham, a psychiatrist. These scholars included Margaret Mead, Peter Berger, Elizabeth Nottingham, Mirra Komarovsky, and Florence Kluckhohn. Chafe, *American Woman*, 210–13; Anderson, *Wartime Women*, 174–77.

76. Chafe, *American Woman*, 202–8.

77. Lundberg and Farnham, *Modern Woman*, 8–11, 234–37, 355–57.

78. At its 1949 convention the International Union of Hotel and Restaurant Employees and Bartenders claimed that it had been victorious in seventeen states by winning the passage of various pieces of exclusionary legislation against women bartenders. Union men justified such legislation by claiming that the measures protected the morals of American women. Critics of the legislative efforts, in contrast, described the moves as an attempt to eliminate competition from women for bartending jobs. Hartman, *Home Front and Beyond*, 131–32.

79. Babcock et al., *Sex Discrimination and the Law*, 142–47.

80. Goesaert v. Cleary, 335 U.S. 464 (1948), 464–67.

81. In an earlier case, *Breedlove v. Suttles* (1937), judicial authorities had previously denied women access to all the rights and responsibilities that came from being "persons" under the Fourteenth Amendment. The U.S. Supreme Court ruled that a state could exempt women from certain taxes on

the grounds that a "tax being on persons, women may be exempted on the basis of special considerations to which they are naturally entitled." According to that ruling, women still occupied a special legal status that the law had based on traditional ideas about women's "natural" capabilities. Breedlove v. Suttles, 302 U.S. 277 (1937), 282.

82. Hartman, *Home Front and Beyond*, 24.

83. Harrison, *On Account of Sex*, 6, 25 See also Hartman, *Home Front and Beyond*, 24, 164–65; and Rupp, *Mobilizing Women for War*, 186.

84. It should be noted that 36 percent of the respondents said they believed that women would gain equal job opportunities with men in the "near future." Roper/Fortune Survey question, "Do you think women actually will be allowed an equal chance with men for any job in business and industry in the near future or do you think it will be a long time before that happens?," April 12–30, 1946. Poll data come from the collection of the Roper Center for Public Opinion Research, University of Connecticut, available through Lexis-Nexis.

85. Hartman, *Home Front and Beyond*, 24–25, 92–93.

86. Chafe, *American Woman*, 182–83.

87. Hartman, *Home Front and Beyond*, 24–25. See also Figart, Mutari, and Power, *Living Wages*, 18–21; Chafe, *American Woman*, 182, 191; and Hartman, *Home Front and Beyond*, 23–24, 92–93, 214.

88. Hartman, *Home Front and Beyond*, 92–93.

89. Chafe, *American Woman*, 182–83. See also Hartman, *Home Front and Beyond*, 24–25; Figart, Mutari, and Power, *Living Wages*, 23–25; and Oppenheimer, *Female Labor Force in the United States*, 10–11.

90. Chafe, *American Woman*, 182–83. See also Oppenheimer, *Female Labor Force in the United States*, 64–95; Hartman, *Home Front and Beyond*, 92–93.

91. Figart, Mutari, and Power, *Living Wages*, 22–23; Chafe, *American Woman*, 183, 191–93; Hartman, *Home Front and Beyond*, 93.

92. Gertrude Samuels, "Why Do Twenty Million Women Work?," *New York Times Magazine*, September 9, 1951, 35.

93. Chafe, *American Woman*, 191–92.

94. Harrison, *On Account of Sex*, 5. See also Hartman, *Home Front and Beyond*, 24, 94.

95. Harrison, *On Account of Sex*, 4–6, 24–25. See also Hartman, *Home Front and Beyond*, 24, 94; and Milkman, *Gender at Work*, chaps. 7 and 8.

96. Chafe, *American Woman*, 195. See also Hartman, *Home Front and Beyond*, 94–95.

97. Harry Truman, "Statement by the President," copy of transcript, October 17, 1945, folder 63, box 145, White House Central Files, President's Personal File, HSTL.

98. *New York Times*, January 10, 1947; Pardo, *National Woman's Party Papers*, 147.

99. Up until the early 1960s the parties continued to officially back the amendment in their platforms. Rupp and Taylor, *Survival in the Doldrums*, 63; Freeman, *Room at a Time*, 211–12.

100. Fry, "Alice Paul and the Equal Rights Amendment," 15; Pardo, *National Woman's Party Papers*, 147–50.

101. U.S. Congress, Senate Judiciary Committee, *"Equal Rights": Report to Accompany S.J. Res. 25*, 81st Cong., 1st sess., March 22, 1949, S. Rep. No. 137, 1.

6. "Socially Desirable Concepts"

1. Women's Bureau, Labor Advisory Committee, Meeting Minutes, January 9, 1947, folder 140, box 6, Frieda Miller papers.

2. Sicherman and Green, *Notable American Women*, 479.

3. Women's Bureau, Labor Advisory Committee, Meeting Minutes, January 9, 1947, folder 140, box 6, Frieda Miller papers.

4. Louise Young to Kathryn Stone, November 20, 1947, folder: "National Committee on the Status of Women," box III-225, LWV papers.

5. Rachel Conrad Nason to Elizabeth Magee, December 18, 1946; Rachel Conrad Nason to Dorothy Kenyon, December 20, 1946, both in reel 53, NCL papers; Mary Anderson to Hattie Smith, March 14, 1947, folder 21, box 3, Hattie Smith papers.

6. Dorothy McAllister to Frieda Miller, January 15, 1947, reel 53, NCL papers.

7. Peter Seitz, "A Bill to Eliminate Unfair Discriminations," memorandum, February 10, 1947, folder: "Equal Rights for Women," box 601, Robert A. Taft papers. See also Harrison, *On Account of Sex*, 26.

8. Nason to Kenyon, December 20, 1946; Mary Anderson, "Confidential: To the National Committee to Defeat the Un-Equal Rights Amendment," memorandum, January 8, 1947, both in reel 53, NCL papers.

9. NCDURA, "To the Presidents and Representatives of Member Organizations of the NCDURA," memorandum, January 18, 1947, reel 53, NCL papers. See also McAllister to Miller, January 15, 1947; Anderson, "Confidential: To the National Committee to Defeat the Un-Equal Rights Amendment," January 8, 1947; and Nason to Kenyon, December 20, 1946, all in reel 53, NCL papers.

10. Seitz, "Bill to Eliminate Unfair Discriminations," February 10, 1947, folder: "Equal Rights for Women," box 601, Robert A. Taft papers.

11. NCDURA, "Confidential: Supporting Comment on Proposed Joint Resolution on the Status of Women," memorandum, January 21, 1947, folder 21, box 3, Hattie Smith papers. See also Harrison, *On Account of Sex*, 27.

12. Women's Bureau, Labor Advisory Committee, Meeting Minutes, January 9, 1947, folder 140, box 6, Frieda Miller papers.

13. NCSW, memorandum, October 15, 1947, reel 52, NCL papers. See also Anderson to Smith, March 14, 1947, folder 21, box 3, Hattie Smith papers; NCSW, "Report," memorandum, April 15, 1947, reel 52, NCL papers; and Dorothy McAllister to Mrs. James Austin Stone, April 2, 1947, reel 53, NCL papers.

14. Louise Young to Friends of the National Committee on the Status of Women, July 6, 1948, folder 21, box 3, Hattie Smith papers; NCSW, press release, February 18, 1947, reel 52, NCL papers.

15. Mrs. Robert Macauley, "Confidential: Proposed Joint Resolution on the Status of Women," memorandum, January 21, 1947; Seitz, "Bill to Eliminate Unfair Discriminations," February 10, 1947; "A Bill on the Status of Women," memorandum, February 17, 1947, all in folder: "Equal Rights for Women," box 601, Robert A. Taft papers; James Wadsworth to Hon W. C. Andrews, April 16, 1947, folder: "Equal Rights Amendment, March 8–April 16, 1947," box 24, James Wadsworth papers; Anderson to Smith, March 14, 1947, folder 21, box 3, Hattie Smith papers; NCSW, "Second Report," memorandum, April 15, 1947, reel 52, NCL papers.

16. Patterson, *Congressional Conservativism*; Patterson, *Mr. Republican.*

17. Robert Taft to Alice Hamilton, May 27, 1946, reel 52, NCL papers.

18. James Wadsworth to Jane Todd, March 20, 1947, folder: "Equal Rights Amendment, March 8–April 16, 1947," box 24, James Wadsworth papers. See also James Wadsworth to Mrs. Vernon Howe, February 1, 1949, folder: "Equal Rights Amendment, January 31, 1949–February 22, 1950," box 24, James Wadsworth papers.

19. Anderson to Smith, March 14, 1947, folder 21, box 3, Hattie Smith papers. See also NCSW, "Second Report," memorandum, April 15, 1947, reel 52, NCL papers.

20. "Bill on the Status of Women," February 17, 1947, folder: "Equal Rights for Women," box 601, Robert A. Taft papers.

21. Seitz, "Bill to Eliminate Unfair Discriminations," February 10, 1947, folder: "Equal Rights for Women," box 601, Robert A. Taft papers. See also "H.R. 2007," copy of the bill, February 17, 1947, folder: "Equal Rights Amendment, Nov. 15 1944–Feb. 1 1947," box 24, James Wadsworth papers.

22. "Bill on the Status of Women," February 17, 1947, folder: "Equal Rights for Women," box 601, Robert A. Taft papers.

23. Seitz, "Bill to Eliminate Unfair Discriminations," February 10, 1947, folder: "Equal Rights for Women," box 601, Robert A. Taft papers. See also NCDURA, "Confidential: Supporting Comment on Proposed Joint Resolution on the Status of Women," January 21, 1947, folder 21, box 3, Hattie Smith papers.

24. Seitz, "Bill to Eliminate Unfair Discriminations," February 10, 1947, folder: "Equal Rights for Women," box 601, Robert A. Taft papers. See also "Bill on the Status of Women," February 17, 1947, folder: "Equal Rights for Women," box 601, Robert A. Taft papers.

25. Women's Bureau Labor Advisory Committee, Meeting Minutes, January 9, 1947, folder 140, box 6, Frieda Miller papers.

26. NCSW, "Questions and Answers on Women's Bill," memorandum, April 10, 1947, folder, 1, box 43, Carl Hayden papers.

27. Felix Frankfurter to Alice Paul, June 30, 1921, folder 9, box 12, NWP papers.

28. Lawson, *To Secure These Rights.*

29. Cobble, *Other Women's Movement,* 64–65.

30. NCSW, press release, February 18, 1947, reel 52, NCL papers.

31. Wadsworth to Andrews, April 16, 1947, folder: "Equal Rights Amendment, March 8–April 16, 1947," box 24, James Wadsworth papers.

32. NCSW, "Statement by Eleanor Roosevelt Regarding Bill on the Status of Women," press release, February 18, 1947, reel 52, NCL papers.

33. "Women Protected in New Rights Bill," *New York Times,* February 18, 1947, 28.

34. "Road to Equality," *Washington Post,* reprint, February 25, 1947, folder 1, box 43, Carl Hayden papers.

35. NCSW, press release, February 18, 1947, reel 52, NCL papers.

36. Lucy Mason to Mary Anderson, May 11, 1937; Mary Anderson to Lucy Mason, May 15, 1937, both in reel 54, NCL papers. See also Anderson, *Woman at Work,* 210–12.

37. Natalie Linderholm to Anna Lord Strauss, March 11, 1947, folder: "National Committee on the Status of Women"; NCSW, "Preliminary Draft," March 24, 1947, folder: "National Committee to Defeat the Un-Equal Rights Amendment"; Dorothy McAllister to Kathryn Stone, April 5, 1947, folder: "National Committee to Defeat the Un-Equal Rights Amendment"; Young to Stone, November 20, 1947, folder: "National Committee on the Status of Women," all in box III-225, LWV papers; LWV, *Brief for Action: The Status of Women,* pamphlet, April 1, 1947, folder: "Equal Rights for Women," box 601, Robert A. Taft papers.

38. McAllister to Stone, April 5, 1947, folder: "National Committee to Defeat the Un-Equal Rights Amendment," box III-225, LWV papers.

39. LWV, *Brief for Action: The Status of Women,* pamphlet, April 1, 1947, folder: "Equal Rights for Women," box 601, Robert A. Taft papers.

40. Alma Lutz, "Only One Choice," *Independent Woman,* copy of an article, July 1947, folder 35, box 2, Alma Lutz papers.

41. Jane Todd to Congressman Wadsworth, March 18, 1947, folder: "Equal Rights Amendment, March 8–April 16, 1947," box 24, James Wadsworth papers.

42. "Celler Biological Status Bill," *Equal Rights* 39, no. 4 (1953): 6.

43. Representative Emanuel Celler (D-NY) became the main congressional supporter of the Women's Status Bill in the early to mid-1950s, when it was commonly referred to as the "Celler Biological Status Bill." For the most part the form of the bill remained the same: it included a policy statement that permitted presumably reasonable sex-based distinctions, and it called for the establishment of a presidential commission on the status of women. Alma Lutz, *Equal Rights Amendment versus Status of Women Bills,* pamphlet, n.d., folder 35, box 2, Alma Lutz papers; Cobble, *Other Women's Movement,* 67.

44. Excerpt from William S. Roach to the NCSW, March 24, 1947, attached to a letter from Dorothy McAllister to Margaret Stone, April 5, 1947, folder: "National Committee to Defeat the Un-Equal Rights Amendment," box III-225, LWV papers.

45. Dorothy McAllister reported that previously pro-ERA senators Carl Hatch (D-NM) and Alben Barkley (D-KY) had expressed interest in the Women's Status Bill and that they had privately pledged to support the new measure. "Women Protected in New Rights Bill," 28; McAllister to Miller, January 15, 1947, reel 53, NCL papers; Pardo, *National Woman's Party Papers*, 126–27; "Should Congress Approve the Proposed Equal Rights Amendment, Pro.," *Congressional Digest* 22, no. 4 (April 1943): 110.

46. "Legal Status of Women," *New York Herald Tribune*, transcription, April 2, 1947, folder 1, box 43, Carl Hayden papers.

47. Harrison, *On Account of Sex*, 28–30.

48. Harrison, *On Account of Sex*, 30–31, 248.

49. Congressional Record, 81st Cong., 2nd sess., 23 January 1950, 96, pt. 1: 761.

50. Congressional Record, 81st Cong., 2nd sess., 25 January 1950, 96, pt. 1: 869.

51. Congressional Record, 81st Cong., 2nd sess., 25 January 1950, 96, pt. 1: 868–69.

52. Rupp and Taylor, *Survival in the Doldrums*, 63.

53. Carl Hayden, "Equal Rights Amendment," statement, January 13, 1959, folder 5, box 268, Carl Hayden papers.

54. Carl Hayden to Senator, June 30, 1960, folder 5, box 268, Carl Hayden papers. See also Carl Hayden, "Equal Rights Amendment," notes, [n.d.], folder 5, box 119; Carl Hayden to Kay Walters, November 29, 1960, folder 4, box 268, both in Carl Hayden papers.

55. Harrison, *On Account of Sex*, 30–31.

56. Margaret Stone to Miss R. St. George, February 6, 1950, reel 14, NWTUL papers. See also Margaret Stone to Bess Kaye, February 8, 1950; Margaret Stone to Florence Burton, February 10, 1950; and Margaret Stone to Helen Couniban, March 17, 1950, all in reel 14, NWTUL papers.

57. Katherine Ellickson to Congressman, April 13, 1950, folder: "Older Material from CIO–Equal Rights, 1950–1951," box 3, Katherine Ellickson papers, FDRL (hereafter Katherine Ellickson papers).

58. Congressional Record, 81st Cong., 2nd sess., January 25, 1950, 96, pt. 1: 869.

59. "Equal Rights Fight in House Is Mapped: Proponents Hope for Backing of Amendment by Judiciary Body Minus Hayden Rider," *New York Times*, January 27, 1950, 19.

60. Pardo, *National Woman's Party Papers*, 157–58; Harrison, *On Account of Sex*, 32.

61. Richard Lyons, "Former Rep. Emanuel Celler Dies," *Washington Post*, January 16, 1981.

62. Emanuel Celler, "The Equal Rights Amendment," essay draft, 1954, folder: "Legal Status of Women," box 408, Emanuel Celler papers, LOC (hereafter Emanuel Celler papers).

63. Stone to Kaye, February 8, 1950; Stone to Burton, February 10, 1950, both in reel 14, NWTUL papers. See also Stone to Couniban, March 17, 1950, reel 14, NWTUL papers.

64. In 1970 Representative Martha Griffiths (D-MI) successfully used a discharge petition with 218 signatures to move the amendment out of the House Judiciary Committee to the House floor. Mathews and De Hart, *Sex, Gender, and the Politics of ERA*, 36.

65. Stone to Burton, February 10, 1950, reel 54, NWTUL papers; Katherine Ellickson, "Special Meeting to Discuss Equal Rights Amendment to Constitution," Meeting Minutes, May 28, 1951, folder: "Older Material from CIO–Equal Rights, 1950–1951," box 3, Katherine Ellickson papers; Walter Reuther, *15th Constitutional Convention cio*, report, 1953, folder 1083, box 81, Alice Paul papers; David Dubinsky to Carl Hayden, June 11, 1953, folder 8, box 457, Carl Hayden papers; Carl Hayden to John Edelman, May 19, 1953, folder: "Older Material from CIO–Equal Rights, 1953–1959," box 3, Katherine Ellickson papers.

66. The Senate Judiciary Committee voted to attach the Hayden rider in 1951. In 1953 the Senate passed the ERA with the Hayden rider attached. Carl Hayden to Dorothy Ferebee, May 19, 1953, folder 8, box 119; Carl Hayden to Helen Toland, July 1, 1953, folder 8, box 119; Carl Hayden to Honorable Lorena Lockwood, June 1, 1959, folder 4, box 268, all in Carl Hayden papers; Pardo, *National Woman's Party Papers*, 157–58; Hoff-Wilson, *Rights of Passage*, 15.

67. Reuther, *15th Constitutional Convention cio*, 1953, folder 1083, box 81, Alice Paul papers.

68. Eleanor Roosevelt, "My Day," draft, May 24, 1951, folder: "My Day May–June 1951," box 144, Eleanor Roosevelt papers.

69. Harrison, *On Account of Sex*, 32–35.

70. Eleanor Roosevelt, "My Day," draft, June 6, 1951, folder: "My Day May–June 1951," box 144, Eleanor Roosevelt papers; Elizabeth Magee to Katherine Ellickson, June 1, 1954; Joan and David Landman, "Do Women Really Want Equal Rights," *Today's Woman*, copy, February 1953, both in folder: "Older Material from CIO–Equal Rights, 1950–1951," box 3, Katherine Ellickson papers; Harrison, *On Account of Sex*, 32–33, 94–112.

71. Mary Anderson to James Mitchell, February 1955, folder: "Older Material from CIO–Equal Rights, 1950–1951," box 3, Katherine Ellickson papers; Elinore Herrick to James Mitchell, October 30, 1953; Department of Labor press release, November 17, 1953, both in folder: "1953, Women's Bureau,

Personnel Alice Leopold," box 62, James Mitchell papers DDEL (hereafter
James Mitchell papers).

72. "Excerpts from Address Delivered by the President at Madison Square
Garden," press release, October 25, 1956, folder: "136-A Equal Rights Amendment," box 1059, White House Central Files, General File, DDEL. See also
Gerald D. Morgan to Alice Paul, December 19, 1955; Mary Lord to Eileen
Slater, May 4, 1956; and James Hagerty to Gretchen Fisher, October 26, 1956,
all in folder: "136-A Equal Rights Amendment," box 1059, White House Central Files, General File, DDEL.

73. L. Arthur Minnich, "Legislative Meeting Notes, L 13," April 12, 1954,
folder: "L-13 [April 12 and 26, 1954]," box 2, White House Office, Office of
the Staff Secretary, L. Arthur Minnich Series, DDEL.

74. James Mitchell to Gerald Morgan, February 9, 1956, folder, "136-A Equal
Rights Amendment," box 1059, White House Central Files, General File, DDEL.

75. James Mitchell, "Policy Meeting 2–4, 258," notes, February 4, 1957,
folder: "Secretary's Policy Committee Chronological, meetings 258–77," box
75, James Mitchell Papers.

76. "Still a Burning Issue?," Los Angeles Times, clipping, July 23, 1957, folder:
"News Clippings, Women, Equal Rights," box 639, RNC papers.

77. Rupp and Taylor, Survival in the Doldrums, 32–37, 201; Pardo, National
Woman's Party Papers, 154–55.

78. Fry, "Alice Paul and the Equal Rights Amendment."

79. The Democratic Party removed specific approval of the ERA from its
platform in 1960, while an open endorsement of the ERA disappeared from
the Republican Party platform in 1964. Explicit support for the ERA did not
reappear in the party platforms until 1972. Freeman, Room at a Time, 209–12.

80. Darden, Best of the Southern Conservative, 160–61.

81. V. L. Hash to Paul Eaton, February 13, 1950, folder 7, box 119, Carl
Hayden papers.

82. Lichtman, White Protestant Nation, 184–85.

83. Lichtman, White Protestant Nation, 223–24.

84. Harrison, On Account of Sex, 86

85. Marie Smith, "Solving Battle of the Sexes," Washington Post, April 16,
1961, F14.

86. Peterson to Myer Feldman, May 12, 1961, folder: "ERA. 1960–61," box:
"Women," Esther Peterson papers, SL (hereafter Esther Peterson papers),
quoted in Harrison, On Account of Sex, 119, 276n32.

87. Cynthia Harrison uncovered this sequence of events. See Harrison,
On Account of Sex, 118–19.

88. Marian Dennehy to Mike Feldman, September 23, 1960; John Kennedy
to Emma Guffey Miller, September 28, 1960; Esther Peterson, "Senator John
Kennedy recently sent the following message to Mrs. Guffey Miller," notes,

October 21, 1960; "Memo by archivist Katherine Kraft," May 17, 1975, all in folder 1057, box 54, Esther Peterson papers; Harrison, *On Account of Sex*, 118–19.

89. Emma Guffey Miller continued to irritate Esther Peterson, especially when Miller tried to organize a movement to prevent President Kennedy from selecting Peterson as head of the Women's Bureau. Harrison, *On Account of Sex*, 118–21.

90. Freeman, "From Suffrage to Women's Liberation," 512.

91. Harrison, "New Frontier for Women," 633–36; Cobble, *Other Women's Movement*, 159–64.

92. Cobble, "Labor Feminists and President Kennedy's Commission," 154–61.

93. Esther Peterson, "February 28 Discussion with Trade Union Women," notes, March 3, 1961, folder 833, box 41, Esther Peterson papers; Cobble, *Other Women's Movement*, 159.

94. Cobble, *Other Women's Movement*, 160–61.

95. Cobble, *Other Women's Movement*, 64, 121.

96. Peterson, "February 28 Discussion with Trade Union Women," March 3, 1961, folder 833, box 41, Esther Peterson papers; Cobble, "Labor Feminists and President Kennedy's Commission," 156–57.

97. Cobble, "Labor Feminists and President Kennedy's Commission," 157.

98. Esther Peterson to Arthur Goldberg, June 2, 1961, folder 833, box 41, Esther Peterson papers.

99. Cynthia Harrison offers the most thorough analysis of the connection between the PCSW and the ERA. Harrison, *On Account of Sex*, chap. 7.

100. Peterson, "February 28 Discussion with Trade Union Women," March 3, 1961, folder 833, box 41, Esther Peterson papers.

101. [Esther Peterson], "The Legal Status of Women," letter draft, March 28, 1961, file 833, box 41, Esther Peterson papers.

102. [Esther Peterson], "The Legal Status of Women," letter draft, April 4, 1961, file 833, box 41, Esther Peterson papers.

103. "Need for a Commission on the Status of Women," memorandum, May 1, 1961, folder 833, box 41, Esther Peterson papers.

104. Harrison, *On Account of Sex*, 110.

105. Cobble, *Other Women's Movement*, 158–60.

106. Katherine Ellickson, "Tentative and Confidential: More Detailed Explanation of Background and Function," memorandum, July 13, 1961, folder 835, box 41, Esther Peterson papers.

107. "Outline of the Proposal," draft, July 1961, folder 835, box 41, Esther Peterson papers.

108. Cobble, "Labor Feminists and President Kennedy's Commission," 160–61; Harrison, *On Account of Sex*, 159; Kessler-Harris, *In Pursuit of Equity*.

109. U.S. President's Commission on the Status of Women (hereafter PCSW), *American Women*, 76.

110. Smith, "Solving Battle of the Sexes," F14.

111. PCSW, *Full Partnership of Women*, pamphlet, 1962, folder: "Presidential Commission on the Status of Women," box 4644, Eleanor Roosevelt papers; Harrison, "New Frontier," 638–39; Cobble, "Labor Feminists and President Kennedy's Commission," 157–58.

112. Cobble, "Labor Feminists and President Kennedy's Commission," 158–59; Kessler-Harris, *In Pursuit of Equity*, 217.

113. Apart from conducting meetings, Eleanor Roosevelt did little of the actual work of the commission. She did, however, serve as an advisor, and she made herself available for publicity purposes. Cobble, "Labor Feminists and President Kennedy's Commission," 157; Harrison, *On Account of Sex*, 112.

114. Commission member Margaret Hickey, the public affairs editor of *Ladies' Home Journal*, had been president of the pro-ERA BPWC, but it was only Marguerite Rawalt who had openly endorsed the amendment before the creation of the commission. Harrison, *On Account of Sex*, 113; Harrison, "New Frontier for Women," 638–39; Evans, *Born for Liberty*, 274–75.

115. President Kennedy did not select a new chair after Eleanor Roosevelt's death, because he considered her irreplaceable. Marjorie Hunter, "U.S. Panel Urges Women to Sue for Equal Rights," *New York Times*, October 12, 1963, 1; Cobble, "Labor Feminists and President Kennedy's Commission," 157; Harrison, "New Frontier for Women," 638–39.

116. For a more basic and accessible version of the report, see Mead and Kaplan, *American Women*.

117. PCSW, *American Women*, 46–48.

118. PCSW, *American Women*, 47–48.

119. PCSW, *American Women*, 31–32.

120. Harrison, *On Account of Sex*, 174, 184; Laughlin, *Women's Work and Public Policy*, 70.

121. Kessler-Harris, *Woman's Wage*, 84; Figart, Mutari, and Power, *Living Wages*, 164–66.

122. Figart, Mutari, and Power, *Living Wages*, 143–63.

123. Figart, Mutari, and Power, *Living Wages*, 156; Cobble, "Recapturing Working-Class Feminism"; Kessler-Harris, *In Pursuit of Equity*, 233–35; Steinberg, *Wages and Hours*.

124. Figart, Mutari, and Power, *Living Wages*, 161–62.

125. Harrison, *On Account of Sex*, 102–5; Figart, Mutari, and Power, *Living Wages*, 159–63; Kessler-Harris, *In Pursuit of Equity*, 233–36.

126. Kessler-Harris, *In Pursuit of Equity*, 235.

127. Cobble, *Other Women's Movement*, 166–67; Ritter, *Constitution as Social Design*, 220.

128. Marie Smith, "President Kennedy Signs Equal Pay Bill into Law," *Washington Post*, June 12, 1963, D1.

129. John Grimes, "Kennedy Signs' Equal Pay for Women Bill," *Wall Street Journal*, June 11, 1963, 10; "Kennedy Signs Equal Pay for Women Bill," *Los Angeles Times*, June 11, 1963, 3.

130. PCSW, *Report of the Committee on Home and Community*, 9; Harrison, *On Account of Sex*, 140.

131. PCSW, *Report of the Committee on Education*, 31; Harrison, *On Account of Sex*, 154.

132. PCSW, *American Women*, 16.

133. Harrison, *On Account of Sex*, 139–40, 159. See also Cobble, "Labor Feminists and President Kennedy's Commission," 160–61.

134. PCSW, *American Women*, 36; Harrison, *On Account of Sex*, 153.

135. PCSW, *American Women*, 30.

136. Kessler-Harris, *In Pursuit of Equity*, 225.

137. Harrison, "New Frontier," 638–40; Evans, *Born for Liberty*, 274–75.

138. Harrison, *On Account of Sex*, 121–23.

139. Voss, *Women Politicking Politely*, 21.

140. Harrison, *On Account of Sex*, 124–25; Harrison, "New Frontier," 638–40.

141. Harrison, *On Account of Sex*, 124–26.

142. PCSW, *Report of the Committee on Civil and Political Rights*, iii; PCSW, *American Women*, 77–78.

143. PCSW, *American Women*, 45.

144. PCSW, *Report of the Committee on Civil and Political Rights*, 1–2, 33–35; Harrison, *On Account of Sex*, 126–34.

145. Harrison, "Constitutional Equality for Women," 186–87; Harrison, *On Account of Sex*, 126–30; Kessler-Harris, *In Pursuit of Equity*, 229–32.

146. Harrison, *On Account of Sex*, 127.

147. VanBurkleo, *"Belonging to the World,"* 266; Harrison, *On Account of Sex*, 126–28; Rosenberg, *Jane Crow*, 255–56.

148. Mayeri, "Constitutional Choices"; Mayeri, "Pauli Murray and the Twentieth-Century Quest for Legal and Social Equality"; and Rosenberg, *Jane Crow*, 338–40.

149. Mayeri, *Reasoning from Race*, 16–19; Harrison, *On Account of Sex*, 127; Kessler-Harris, *In Pursuit of Equity*, 230.

150. PCSW, *American Women*, 45.

151. Esther Peterson to Carl Hayden, October 10, 1963, folder 3, box 268, Carl Hayden papers.

152. Carl Hayden, "Equality of Rights for Men and Women," statement, [1963], folder 3, box 268, Carl Hayden papers.

153. Harrison, *On Account of Sex*, 120–24, 130–37, 160–61; Harrison, "Constitutional Equality for Women," 186–87; Harrison, "New Frontier," 638–40; Evans, *Born for Liberty*, 274–75.

Epilogue

1. Rupp and Taylor, *Survival in the Doldrums*, 161–65, 176–77.
2. Harrison, *On Account of Sex*, 182.
3. Harrison, *On Account of Sex*, 187–91.
4. Harrison, *On Account of Sex*, 184–85, 192–96.
5. Mathews and De Hart, *Sex, Gender, and the Politics of ERA*, 32; Harrison, *On Account of Sex*, 192–98.
6. Harrison, *On Account of Sex*, 207, 217.
7. Mathews and De Hart, *Sex, Gender, and the Politics of ERA*, 34–35.
8. Hoyt v. Florida 368 U.S. 57 (1961), 62.
9. Mathews and De Hart, *Sex, Gender, and the Politics of ERA*, 28–35.
10. Harrison, *On Account of Sex*, 198–99.
11. Harrison, *On Account of Sex*, 199–200.
12. Harrison, *On Account of Sex*, 199–200, 217–21; Mathews and De Hart, *Sex, Gender, and the Politics of ERA*, 31.
13. Friedan, *Feminine Mystique*, 270 (quote), 269–82.
14. Mathews and De Hart, *Sex, Gender, and the Politics of ERA*, 31–32.
15. Harrison, *On Account of Sex*, 219–21.
16. Harrison, *On Account of Sex*, 199–201, 207–9, 211–21.
17. Freeman, "Feminist Organizations and Activities from Suffrage to Women's Liberation," 546–47.
18. Harrison, *On Account of Sex*, 207–9, 215–21.
19. Freeman, "Feminist Organizations and Activities from Suffrage to Women's Liberation," 545–51.
20. Harrison, *On Account of Sex*, 208.
21. Freeman, "Feminist Organizations and Activities from Suffrage to Women's Liberation," 547–54; Harrison, *On Account of Sex*, 208–9.
22. Harrison, *On Account of Sex*, 208–9.
23. Babcock et al., *Sex Discrimination and the Law*, 1186–87; Cott, *Public Vows*, 205–6.
24. Roe v. Wade, 410 U.S. 113 (1973).
25. Mayeri, "Constitutional Choices," 784–93; Harrison, *On Account of Sex*, 199–207.
26. Mayeri, "Constitutional Choices," 794–96.
27. Mathews and De Hart, *Sex, Gender, and the Politics of ERA*, 28–35; Mayeri, "Constitutional Choices," 797–800.
28. Rosenberg, *Jane Crow*, 338–40.
29. Mayeri, "Constitutional Choices," 800–801.

30. Harrison, *On Account of Sex*, 217–21; Mathews and De Hart, *Sex, Gender, and the Politics of ERA*, 31–35; Cobble, *Other Women's Movement*, 193–95.

31. U.S. Congress, Senate Judiciary Subcommittee, *Equal Rights Amendment: Hearings before the Subcommittee on Constitutional Amendments*, 91st Cong., 2nd sess., May 6, 1970, 333, 336. See also Brown et al., "Equal Rights Amendment," 872–981.

32. Jo Freeman "What's in a Name? Does It Matter How the Equal Rights Amendment Is Worded?," *Women, Law and Public Policy* (blog), June 1996, https://www.jofreeman.com/lawandpolicy/eraname.htm; Paul, *Conversations with Alice Paul*, 266, 269.

33. Evans, *Born for Liberty*, 290–307; Hoff-Wilson, *Rights of Passage*.

34. Evans, *Born for Liberty*, 290–309.

35. Mansbridge, *Why We Lost the ERA*; Berry, *Why ERA Failed*; Boles, *Politics of the Equal Rights Amendment*; Hoff-Wilson, *Rights of Passage*, esp. 39–106; Steiner, *Constitutional Inequality*; Spruill, *Divided We Stand*.

36. Mansbridge, *Why We Lost the ERA*, 3, 122–28; Steiner, *Constitutional Inequality*, 50–51, 56–66, 88–90, 96–107.

37. Critchlow, *Phyllis Schlafly and Grassroots Conservatism*, 14–19, 219; Freeman, "Feminist Organizations and Activities from Suffrage to Women's Liberation," 552–53; Spruill, *Divided We Stand*.

38. Lichtman, *White Protestant Nation*, 320–23.

39. Evans, *Born for Liberty*, 303–5.

40. Freeman, "Feminist Organizations and Activities from Suffrage to Women's Liberation," 552–53.

41. Schlafly, *Power of the Positive Woman*, 11, 87; Marshall, "Keep Us on the Pedestal," 547–60.

42. Phyllis Schlafly, "How ERA Would Change Federal Laws," *Phyllis Schlafly Report* 15, no. 4 (1981).

43. Phyllis Schlafly, "The Fraud of the Equal Rights Amendment," *Phyllis Schlafly Report* 5, no. 7 (February 1972).

44. Mayeri, "Constitutional Choices," 803–6, 816–25, 839.

45. Mayeri, "Constitutional Choices," 804–5, 814–25; Freeman, "Revolution for Women in Law and Public Policy," 374–75; Babcock et al., *Sex Discrimination and the Law*, 161–67.

46. Mayeri, "Constitutional Choices," 814–16, 826–27.

47. Reed v. Reed, 404 U.S. 71 (1971), 77. See also Freeman, "Revolution for Women in Law and Public Policy," 374–75; Ritter, *Constitution as Social Design*, 247–51; and Babcock et al., *Sex Discrimination and the Law*, 161–67.

48. Mayeri, "Constitutional Choices," 815–17.

49. Neuwirth, *Equal Means Equal*, 79–80; Freeman, "Revolution for Women in Law and Public Policy," 374–75.

50. Justices William Douglas, Byron White, and Thurgood Marshall agreed with Justice William Brennan Jr.'s plurality opinion and endorsed applying

the strictest level of judicial review for sex discrimination cases. Justices Harry Blackmun, Lewis F. Powell Jr., and Chief Justice Warren E. Burger had concurred in the decision, but in an opinion authored by Justice Powell they declined to hold sex to the strict scrutiny level. Justice Potter Stewart concurred only in the plurality's judgment. Justice William Rehnquist dissented in the case. Freeman, "Revolution for Women in Law and Public Policy," 374–75; Mayeri, "Constitutional Choices," 817–19.

51. Frontiero v. Richardson, 411 U.S. 677 (1973), 687.

52. Mayeri, "Constitutional Choices," 826.

53. Neuwirth, *Equal Means Equal*, 78–84; Babcock et al., *Sex Discrimination and the Law*, 161–80; Freeman, "Revolution for Women in Law and Public Policy," 374–76; Mayeri, "Constitutional Choices," 828–29.

54. Kahn v. Shevin, 416 U.S. 351 (1974), 355.

55. Freeman, "Revolution for Women in Law and Public Policy," 381.

56. Schlesinger v. Ballard, 419 U.S. 498 (1975), 508 (original emphasis).

57. California would later change its law to make unlawful sexual intercourse with a person under eighteen a gender-neutral crime. Michael M. v. Superior Court of Sonoma County, 450 U.S. 464 (1981), 471–73; Freeman, "Revolution for Women in Law and Public Policy," 381.

58. Craig v. Boren, 429 U.S. 190 (1976), 197–98, 204.

59. Mayeri, "Constitutional Choices," 828–29.

60. United States v. Virginia, 518 U.S. 515 (1996), 524; Mayeri, "Constitutional Choices," 829–30.

61. Immigration and Nationality Act, 8 U.S.C. 1409 (a) (2006); Mayeri, "Constitutional Choices," 830.

62. Neuwirth, *Equal Means Equal*, 73–76; Mayeri, "Constitutional Choices," 830–31.

63. Mayeri, "Constitutional Choices," 830.

64. In *Sessions v. Morales-Santana* (2017), the court invalidated a gender-based distinction in the immigration statute that had held different physical presence requirements for conveying citizenship to a child born abroad to an unwed citizen parent and a noncitizen parent. Under the rules, a child born overseas to an unwed citizen mother and a noncitizen father acquired citizenship at birth so long as the mother had been present in the United States for a continuous period of at least one year at some point prior to the child's birth. But a child born abroad to an unwed citizen father and a noncitizen mother could acquire citizenship only if the father had been present in the United States prior to the child's birth for a period of five years. The court ruled that this statutory gender-based distinction in the requirements for transfer of derivative citizenship violated the Equal Protection Clause of the Fifth Amendment. The court concluded, however, that it was up to Congress to resolve the issue. See Tuan Anh Nguyen et al. v. INS, 533 U.S. 53

(2001), 62–65; Mayeri, "Constitutional Choices," 830–32; Sessions v. Morales-Santana 582 U.S. (2017); 137 S. Ct. 1678 (2017).

65. Tuan Anh Nguyen v. INS, 92.

66. Neuwirth, *Equal Means Equal,* 76–77.

67. Neuwirth, *Equal Means Equal,* 78–79.

68. Cott, *Public Vows,* 205, 210.

69. Borelli v. Brusseau, 12 Cal. App. 4th 647 (1993), 654–55; Cott, *Public Vows,* 209–11.

70. Freeman, "Feminist Organizations and Activities from Suffrage to Women's Liberation," 555.

71. VanBurkleo, *"Belonging to the World,"* ix–x.

72. Bowman, "Street Harassment and the Informal Ghettoization of Women," 517.

73. VanBurkleo, *"Belonging to the World,"* 314.

74. The Supreme Court had ruled in *Rostker v. Goldberg,* 453 U.S. 57 (1981), that Congress had a legitimate basis for excluding women from the draft, since women were not eligible for combat positions. Because the Department of Defense has changed that policy, Judge Gray H. Miller ruled in *National Coalition for Men v. Selective Service System,* 355 F. Supp. 3d 568 (2019), that men and women citizens were now similarly situated for purposes of registering for the draft, making the male-only requirement unconstitutional. See Tyler Pager, "Judge Rules That a Military Draft of Only Men Is Unconstitutional," *New York Times,* February 25, 2019, A13.

75. Gregory Korte, "Q&A: A Judge Has Ruled the Male-Only Military Draft Unconstitutional; What Happens Now?," *USA Today,* February 25, 2019, https://www.usatoday.com/story/news/nation/2019/02/25/federal-judge-all-male-draft-unconstitutional-now-what-selective-service/2979346002/.

76. Lisa Murkowski and Ben Cardin, "It's Time to Finally Pass the Equal Rights Amendment," *Washington Post,* January 25, 2019, https://www.washingtonpost.com/opinions/its-time-to-finally-pass-the-equal-rights-amendment/2019/01/25/54b3626e-20d0-11e9-9145-3f74070bbdb9_story.html.

77. Maggie Astor, "The Equal Rights Amendment May Pass Now; It's Only Been 96 Years," *New York Times,* November 6, 2019, https://www.nytimes.com/2019/11/06/us/politics/virginia-ratify-equal-rights-amendment.html.

78. Alex Cohen and Wilfred U. Codrington III, "The Equal Rights Amendment Explained," Brennan Center for Justice, January 23, 2020, https://www.brennancenter.org/our-work/research-reports/equal-rights-amendment-explained.

79. Despite the lack of legal consensus regarding whether Congress actually retains the power to nullify the previous ratification deadline, the House of Representatives pushed forward in February 2020 and voted to remove the deadline. As of July 2020 the Senate has neglected to take up the issue in a decisive manner. See Danielle Kurtzleben, "House Votes to

Revive Equal Rights Amendment, Removing Ratification Deadline," NPR, February 13, 2020, https://www.npr.org/2020/02/13/805647054/house-votes-to-revive-equal-rights-amendment-removing-ratification-deadline; "E.R.A. Ratification: Likely Dead on Arrival in the Senate COMMENTARY," *Baltimore Sun* (editorial), February 13, 2020, https://www.baltimoresun.com/opinion/editorial/bs-ed-0216-era-ratification-20200213-kzp6yfftunbxrai42wdykwdt5i-story.html.

80. The OLC's opinion also casts doubt on the conclusion of the 1977 OLC opinion that had backed the earlier extension of the ERA's ratification deadline. Cohen and Codrington, "Equal Rights Amendment Explained."

81. Ferriero had previously acknowledged the validity of Nevada's and Illinois's state ratifications. David Ferriero, "NARA Press Statement on the Equal Rights Amendment," press release, National Archives, January 8, 2020, https://www.archives.gov/press/press-releases-4; Cohen and Codrington, "Equal Rights Amendment Explained."

82. The states that have rescinded their ratifications are Nebraska, Tennessee, Idaho, Kentucky, and South Dakota. Rebecca Woodward-Burns, "The Equal Rights Amendment Is One State from Ratification; Now What?" *Washington Post*, June 20, 2018, https://www.washingtonpost.com/news/monkey-cage/wp/2018/06/20/the-equal-rights-amendment-is-one-state-from-ratification-now-what/; Thomas H. Neale, "The Proposed Equal Rights Amendment: Contemporary Ratification Issues," Congressional Research Service, updated December 23, 2019, https://fas.org/sgp/crs/misc/R42979.pdf.

83. Rebecca Hagelin, "Schlafly's Legacy Marches On against Latest Push for ERA," *Washington Times*, January 13, 2019, https://www.washingtontimes.com/news/2019/jan/13/phyllis-schafly-fights-era-again-through-legacy-po/. See also Victoria Cobb, "Modern Feminism Commands Respect—without the ERA," *Richmond Times-Dispatch*, March 4, 2018, https://www.richmond.com/opinion/their-opinion/guest-columnists/victoria-cobb-column-modern-feminism-commands-respect—without/article_8b488623-5398-58c6-b91d-b3a34af5a8ec.html.

84. Grabenhofer and Erickson, "Is the Equal Rights Amendment Relevant in the Twenty-First Century?" 27–40; Susan Chira, "Do American Women Still Need an Equal Rights Amendment?," *New York Times*, February 17, 2019, SR3.

BIBLIOGRAPHY

The following source materials are organized into three sections: archival collections, court cases, and published works.

Archival and Manuscript Collections

Belmont-Paul Women's Equality National Monument, Washington DC
National Woman's Party's *Equal Rights* Publication Collection
Dwight David Eisenhower Library, Abilene, Kansas
James Mitchell papers
National Federation of Republican Women papers
Republican National Committee: News clippings and publications, 1932–65
White House Central Files, General File
White House Central Files, Official File
White House Central Files, Office of the Staff Secretary, L. Arthur Minnich Series
Franklin D. Roosevelt Presidential Library, Hyde Park, New York
Eleanor Roosevelt papers
Katherine Ellickson papers
Molly Dewson papers
White House Official File, Office File 120
Harry S. Truman Library, Independence, Missouri
Dean Acheson papers
India Edwards papers
White House Central Files, Official File
White House Central Files, President's Personal File
Hayden Library, Arizona State University, Tempe, Arizona
Carl Hayden papers
Kansas Historical Society, Topeka, Kansas
Charles and Anna E. Curtis papers

Daniel Read Anthony Jr. papers
Library of Congress, Washington DC
  Emanuel Celler papers
  Felix Frankfurter papers
  James W. Wadsworth Jr. papers
  League of Women Voters papers
  National Consumers' League papers
  National Woman's Party papers
  National Women's Trade Union League of America papers
  Robert A. Taft papers
  Roscoe Pound papers
Schlesinger Library, Radcliffe Institute, Harvard University, Cambridge,
  Massachusetts
  Alice Paul papers
  Alma Lutz papers
  Dorothy Shipley Granger papers
  Elizabeth Putnam papers
  Esther Peterson papers
  Frieda Miller papers
  Hattie Smith papers
  Pauline Newman papers

Court Cases

Adkins v. Children's Hospital, 126 U.S. 525 (1923)
Borelli v. Brusseau, 12 Cal. App. 4th 647 (1993)
Bradwell v. Illinois, 83 U.S. 130 (1873)
Breedlove v. Suttles, 302 U.S. 277 (1937)
Brown v. Board of Education, 347 U.S. 483 (1954)
Carter v. Carter, 298 U.S. 238 (1936)
Commonwealth v. Genevieve Welosky, 276 Mass. 398 (1931)
Commonwealth v. Rutherford, 169 S.E. 909 (1933)
Craig v. Boren, 429 U.S. 190 (1976)
Curtis v. Ashworth, 142 S.E. 111 (1928)
Dickson v. Strickland, 265 S.W. 1012 (1924)
Fairchild v. Hughes, 258 U.S. 126 (1922)
Fay v. New York, 322 U.S. 261 (1947)
Foxworthy v. Adams, 124 S.W. 381 (1910)
Frontiero v. Richardson, 411 U.S. 677 (1973)
Goesaert v. Cleary, 335 U.S. 464 (1948)
Hoyt v. Florida, 368 U.S. 57 (1961)
In re Grilli, 179 N.Y.S. 795 Kings Co. S. Ct. (1920)

In re Opinion Justices, 139 A. 180 (1927)

Kahn v. Shevin, 416 U.S. 351 (1974)

Leser v. Garnett, 258 U.S. 130 (1922)

Lochner v. New York, 198 U.S. 45 (1905)

Mackenzie v. Hare, 239 U.S. 299 (1915)

Michael M. v. Superior Court of Sonoma County, 450 U.S. 464 (1981)

Miller v. Miller, 42 N.W. 641 (1889)

Minor v. Happersett, 88 U.S. 162 (1875)

Morehead v. New York ex rel. Tipaldo, 298 U.S. 587 (1936)

Muller v. Oregon, 208 U.S. 412 (1908)

National Coalition for Men v. Selective Service System, 355 F. Supp. 3d 568 (2019)

National Labor Relations Board v. Jones and Laughlin Steel Corporation, 301 U.S. 1 (1937)

Neal v. Delaware, 103. U.S. 370 (1881)

Opinion of the Justices, 113 A. 614 (1921)

Palmer v. State, 150 N.E. 917 (1926)

Parus v. District Court, 174 P. 706 (1918)

People v. Barltz, 180 N.W. 423 (1920)

People ex rel. Fyfe v. Barnett, 319 Ill. 403 (1925)

Preston v. Roberts, 110 S.E. 586 (1922)

Radice v. New York, 264 U.S. 292 (1924)

Reed v. Reed, 404 U.S. 71 (1971)

Ritchie v. People of Illinois, 155 Illinois 98 (1895)

Roe v. Wade, 410 U.S. 113 (1973)

Rostker v. Goldberg, 453 U.S. 57 (1981)

Schlesinger v. Ballard, 419 U.S. 498 (1975)

Sessions v. Morales-Santana 582 U.S. (2017); 137 S. Ct. 1678 (2017)

State v. Hall, 187 So. 2d 861 (1966)

State v. Kelley, 229 P. 659 (1924)

State v. James, 114 A. 553 (1921)

State v. Walker, 185 N.W. 619 (1921)

Strauder v. West Virginia, 100 U.S. 303 (1880)

Taylor v. Louisiana, 419 U.S. 522 (1975)

Tuan Anh Nguyen et al. v. ins, 533 U.S. 53 (2001)

West Coast Hotel Co. v. Parrish, 330 U.S. 379 (1937)

White v. Crook, 251 F. Supp. 401 (1966)

United States v. Darby Lumber Co., 312 U.S. 100 (1941)

United States v. Virginia, 518 U.S. 515 (1996)

United States v. Hinson, 2 F. Supp. 200 (1925)

Published Works

Adams, Katherine H., and Michael L. Keene. *Alice Paul and the American Suffrage Campaign.* Urbana: University of Illinois Press, 2008.

Allen, Fredrick Lewis. *Only Yesterday: An Informal History of the 1920s.* New York: Harper and Row, 1931.

Alpern, Sara, and Dale Baum. "Female Ballots: The Impact of the Nineteenth Amendment." *Journal of Interdisciplinary History* 16, no. 1 (1985): 43–67.

Andersen, Kristi. *After Suffrage: Women in Partisan and Electoral Politics before the New Deal.* Chicago: University of Chicago Press, 1996.

Anderson, Karen. *Wartime Women: Sex Roles, Family Relations, and the Status of Women during World War II.* Westport CT: Greenwood, 1981.

Anderson, Mary. "The Economic Status of Wage-Earning Homemakers." *Journal of Home Economics* 24, no. 10 (1932): 865–66.

———. *Woman at Work: The Autobiography of Mary Anderson as Told to Mary Winslow.* Minneapolis: University of Minnesota Press, 1951.

Babcock, Barbara, Ann Freedman, Susan Deller Ross, Wendy Webster Williams, Rhonda Copelon, Deborah L. Rhode, and Nadine Taub. *Sex Discrimination and the Law: History, Practice, and Theory.* 2nd ed. Boston: Little, Brown, 1996.

Baker, Liva. *Felix Frankfurter.* New York: Coward-McCann, 1969.

Baker, Paula C. "The Domestication of Politics: Women and American Political Society, 1780–1920." *American Historical Review* 89 (June 1984): 620–48.

Basch, Norma. *In the Eyes of the Law: Women, Marriage, and Property in Nineteenth-Century New York.* Ithaca NY: Cornell University Press, 1982.

Becker, Susan. *The Origins of the Equal Rights Amendment: American Feminism between the Wars.* Westport CT: Greenwood, 1981.

Bernstein, Irving. *A Caring Society.* Boston: Houghton Mifflin, 1985.

Berry, Mary Frances. *Why ERA Failed: Politics, Women's Rights, and the Amending Process of the Constitution.* Bloomington: Indiana University Press, 1986.

Blackstone, William. *Commentaries on the Laws of England.* Vol. 1, *1765–1769.* A facsimile of the first edition with an introduction by Stanley N. Katz. Chicago: University of Chicago Press, 1979.

———. *Commentaries on the Laws of England.* Vol. 3, *1765–1769.* Reprint. San Francisco: Bancroft-Whitney, 1890.

Bloch, Ruth. "Gendered Meanings of Virtue in Revolutionary America." *Signs* 13, no. 1 (1987): 37–58.

Boles, Janet. *The Politics of the Equal Rights Amendment: Conflict and the Decision Process.* New York: Longman, 1979.

Bowman, Cynthia Grant. "Street Harassment and the Informal Ghettoization of Women." *Harvard Law Review* 106, no. 3 (1993): 517–80.

Brandeis, Louis, and Josephine Goldmark. *Women in Industry.* New York: Arno, 1908.

Breckinridge, Sophia. *Marriage and the Civic Rights of Women.* Chicago: University of Chicago Press, 1931.

Bredbenner, Candice Lewis. *A Nationality of Her Own: Women, Marriage, and the Law of Citizenship.* Berkeley: University of California Press, 1998.

Brown, Barbara, Thomas Emerson, Gail Falk, and Ann Freedman. "The Equal
    Rights Amendment: A Constitutional Basis for Equal Rights for Women."
    Yale Law Journal 80, no. 5 (1971): 871–985.
Buechler, Steven Michael. *The Transformation of the Woman Suffrage Move-
    ment: The Case of Illinois, 1850–1920.* New Brunswick NJ: Rutgers Univer-
    sity Press, 1986.
Burnham, Walter Dean. "Theory and Voting Research." *American Political Sci-
    ence Review* 68 (September 1974): 1002–23.
Bushnell, Horace. *Women's Suffrage: The Reform against Nature.* New York: Charles
    Scribner and Company, 1869.
Butler, Amy. *Two Paths to Equality: Alice Paul and Ethel Smith in the ERA Debate,
    1921–1929.* Albany: State University of New York Press, 2002.
Catt, Carrie Chapman, and Nettie Rogers Shuler. *Woman Suffrage and Poli-
    tics: The Inner Story of the Suffrage Movement.* New York: C. Scribner, 1923.
Chafe, William H. *The American Woman: Her Changing Social, Economic, and
    Political Roles, 1920–1970.* New York: Oxford University Press, 1972.
———. *The Paradox of Change: American Women in the Twentieth Century.* New
    York: Oxford University Press, 1991.
———. "Women's History and Political History: Some Thoughts on Progres-
    sivism and the New Deal." In *Visible Women: New Essays in American Activ-
    ism,* edited by Nancy Hewitt and Suzanne Lebsock. Urbana: University
    of Illinois Press, 1993.
Chiappetti, Caroline. "Winning the Battle but Losing the War: The Birth
    and Death of Intersecting Notions of Race and Sex Discrimination in
    White v. Crook." *Harvard Civil Rights-Civil Liberties Law Review* 52, no. 2
    (2017): 469–99.
Chused, Richard. "Married Women's Property Law: Reception of the Early
    Married Women's Property Acts by Courts and Legislatures." *American
    Journal of Legal History* 29, no. 1 (1985): 3–35.
Clark, Lorenne M. G. "Women and John Locke: Who Owns the Apples in
    the Garden of Eden?" In *The Sexism of Social and Political Theory: Women
    and Reproduction from Plato to Nietzsche,* edited by Lorenne M. G. Clark
    and Lynda Lange, 16–40. Toronto: University of Toronto Press, 1979.
Cobble, Dorothy Sue. "Labor Feminists and President Kennedy's Commission
    on Women." In *No Permanent Waves: Recasting Histories of U.S. Feminism,*
    edited by Nancy Hewitt, 144–67. New Brunswick NJ: Rutgers University
    Press, 2010.
———. *The Other Women's Movement: Workplace Justice and Social Rights in Mod-
    ern America.* Princeton: Princeton University Press, 2004.
———. "Recapturing Working-Class Feminism: Union Women in the Postwar
    Era." In *Not June Cleaver: Women and Gender in Postwar America, 1945–1960,*
    edited by Joanne Meyerowitz, 57–83. Philadelphia: Temple University
    Press, 1994.

Cott, Nancy. "Across the Great Divide: Women in Politics before and after 1920." In *One Woman, One Vote: Rediscovering the Woman Suffrage Movement*, edited by Marjorie Spruill Wheeler, 252–373. Troutdale OR: New Sage Press, 1995.

———. "Feminist Politics in the 1920s: The National Woman's Party." *Journal of American History* 71, no. 1 (June 1984): 43–68.

———. *The Grounding of Modern Feminism.* New Haven: Yale University Press, 1987.

———. "Marriage and Women's Citizenship in the United States, 1830–1934." *American Historical Review* 103, no. 5 (1998): 1440–74.

———. *Public Vows: A History of Marriage and the Nation.* Cambridge MA: Harvard University Press, 2000.

Critchlow, Donald. *Phyllis Schlafly and Grassroots Conservatism: A Woman's Crusade.* Princeton: Princeton University Press, 2005.

Danese, Tracy E. *Claude Pepper and Ed Ball: Politics, Purpose, and Power.* Gainesville: University Press of Florida, 2000.

Darden, Ida Mercedes. *The Best of the Southern Conservative.* N.p.: published by the author, 1963.

De Hart, Jane Sherron. "Women's History and Political History: Bridging Old Divides." In *American Political History: Essays on the State of the Discipline*, edited by John F. Marszalek and Wilson D. Miscamble, 25–53. Notre Dame IN: University of Notre Dame Press, 1997.

DeWolf, Rebecca. "The Equal Rights Amendment and the Rise of Emancipationism, 1932–1946." *Frontiers* 38, no. 2 (2017): 47–80.

Draper, Hal, and Stephen Diamond. *The Hidden History of the Equal Rights Amendment.* Alameda CA: Center for Socialist History, 2013.

Dubbert, Joe L. *A Man's Place: Masculinity in Transition.* Englewood Cliffs NJ: Prentice-Hall, 1979.

DuBois, Ellen Carol. *Feminism and Suffrage: The Emergence of an Independent Women's Movement in America, 1848–1869.* Ithaca NY: Cornell University Press, 1978.

———. "Outgrowing the Compact of the Fathers: Equal Rights, Woman Suffrage, and the United States Constitution, 1820–1878." *Journal of American History* 74, no. 3 (1987): 836–62.

Dumenil, Lynn. *The Modern Temper: American Culture and Society in the 1920s.* New York: Hill and Wang, 1995.

Duniway, Abigail Scott. *Path Breaking: An Autobiographical History of the Equal Suffrage Movement in the Pacific Coast States.* Portland OR: James, Kerns, & Abbott, 1914.

Dunn, Susan. *Roosevelt's Purge: How FDR Fought to Change the Democratic Party.* Cambridge MA: Harvard University Press, 2010.

Eastwood, Mary O., and Pauli Murray. "Jane Crow and the Law: Sex Discrimination and Title VII." *George Washington Law Review* 34 (December 1965): 232–65.

Edwards, Rebecca. *Angels in the Machinery: Gender in American Party Politics from the Civil War to the Progressive Era.* New York: Oxford University Press, 1997.

Erickson, Christine. "Conservative Women and Patriotic Maternalism: The Beginnings of a Gendered Conservative Tradition in the 1920s and 1930s." PhD diss., University of California, Santa Barbara, 1999.

Erickson, Nancy. "*Muller v. Oregon* Reconsidered: The Origin of Sex-Based Doctrine of Liberty of Contract." *Labor History* 30 (Spring 1989): 228–50.

Evans, Sara. *Born for Liberty: A History of Women in America.* New York: Simon and Schuster, 1997.

Faue, Elizabeth. *Community of Suffering and Struggle: Women, Men, and the Labor Movement in Minneapolis, 1915–1945.* Chapel Hill: University of North Carolina Press, 1991.

Figart, Deborah M., Ellen Mutari, and Marilyn Power. *Living Wages, Equal Wages: Gender and Labor Market Policies in the United States.* New York: Routledge, 2002.

Flexner, Eleanor. *Century of Struggle: The Woman's Rights Movement in the United States.* Cambridge MA: Belknap Press of Harvard University Press, 1959.

Ford, Linda. "Alice Paul and the Triumph of Militancy." In *One Woman, One Vote: Rediscovering the Woman Suffrage Movement,* edited by Marjorie Spruill Wheeler, 277–94. Troutdale OR: New Sage Press, 1995.

———. *Iron Jawed Angels: The Suffrage Militancy of the National Woman's Party, 1912–1920.* Lanham MD: University Press of America, 1991.

Foner, Eric. *The Story of American Freedom.* New York: Norton, 1998.

Fowler, Robert Booth. *Carrie Catt: Feminist Politician.* Boston: Northeastern University Press, 1986.

Frankel, Noralee, and Nancy Dye. *Gender, Class, Race and Reform in the Progressive Era.* Lexington: University Press of Kentucky, 1991.

Frankfurter, Felix. Foreword to *Impatient Crusader: Florence Kelley's Life Story,* by Josephine Goldmark. Urbana: University of Illinois Press, 1953.

Freedman, Estelle B. "The New Woman: Changing Views of Women in the 1920s." *Journal of American History* 61, no. 2 (1974): 372–93.

Freeman, Jo. "Feminist Organizations and Activities from Suffrage to Women's Liberation." In *Women: A Feminist Perspective,* edited by Jo Freeman. 4th ed. Mountain View CA: Mayfield, 1989.

———. "From Suffrage to Women's Liberation: Feminism in Twentieth-Century America." In *Women: A Feminist Perspective,* edited by Jo Freeman. 5th ed. Mountain View CA: Mayfield, 1995.

———. "The Revolution for Women in Law and Public Policy." In *Women: A Feminist Perspective,* edited by Jo Freeman. 5th ed. Mountain View CA: Mayfield, 1995.

———. *A Room at a Time: How Women Entered Party Politics.* Lanham MD: Rowman and Littlefield, 2002.

Friedan, Betty. *The Feminine Mystique.* In *The Essential Feminist Reader,* edited by Estelle B. Freedman. New York: Modern Library, 2007.

Fry, Amelia R. "Alice Paul and the Equal Rights Amendment." In *Rights of Passage: The Past and Future of the ERA,* edited by Joan Hoff-Wilson, 8–23. Bloomington: Indiana University Press, 1986.

Gettys, Luella. *The Law of Citizenship in the United States.* Chicago: University of Chicago Press, 1936.

Gordon, Felice. *After Winning: The Legacy of the New Jersey Suffragists, 1920–1947.* New Brunswick NJ: Rutgers University Press, 1986.

Gordon, Linda. "Black and White Visions of Welfare: Women's Welfare Activism, 1890–1945." *Journal of American History* 78, no. 2 (1991): 559–90.

———. *Pitied But Not Entitled: Single Mothers and the History of Welfare, 1890–1935.* Cambridge MA: Harvard University Press, 1994.

———. "Putting Children First: Women, Maternalism, and Welfare in the Early Twentieth Century." In *U.S. History as Women's History,* edited by Linda Kerber, Alice Kessler-Harris, and Kathryn Kish Sklar. Chapel Hill: University of North Carolina Press, 1995.

Gordon, Linda, ed. *Women, the State, and Welfare.* Madison: University of Wisconsin Press, 1990.

Grabenhofer, Bonnie, and Jan Erickson. "Is the Equal Rights Amendment Relevant in the Twenty-First Century?" *Frontiers* 38, no. 2 (2017): 27–40.

Graham, Sara Hunter. *Woman Suffrage and the New Democracy.* New Haven: Yale University Press, 1996.

Greathouse, Rebekah. "The Effect of Constitutional Equality on Working Women." *American Economic Review* 34, no. 1 (1944): 227–36.

Green, Elna. "From Antisuffragism to Anti-Communism: The Conservative Career of Ida M. Darden." *Journal of Southern History* 65, no. 2 (1999): 287–316.

Greenwald, Maurine. *Women, War, and Work: The Impact of World War I on Women Workers in the United States.* Westport CT: Greenwood, 1980.

Gundersen, Joan. "Independence, Citizenship, and the American Revolution." *Signs* 13, no. 1 (1987): 59–77.

Halt, Charles Eugene. "Joseph F. Guffey, New Deal Politician from Pennsylvania." PhD diss., Syracuse University Library, 1965.

Harper, Ida Husted, ed. *History of Woman Suffrage.* Vol. 5. New York: J. J. Little and Ives, 1922.

Harrison, Cynthia. "Constitutional Equality for Women." In *Constitutionalism and American Culture: Writing the New Constitutional History,* edited by Sandra VanBurkleo, Kermit Hall, and Robert Kaczorowski, 174–210. Lawrence: University Press of Kansas, 2002.

———. "A New Frontier for Women: The Public Policy of the Kennedy Administration." *Journal of American History* 67, no. 3 (1980): 630–46.

———. *On Account of Sex: The Politics of Women's Issues, 1945–1968.* Berkeley: University of California Press, 1989.

Hart, Vivien. *Bound by Our Constitution: Women, Workers, and the Minimum Wage.* Princeton: Princeton University Press, 1994.

———. "Minimum-Wage Policy and Constitutional Inequality: The Paradox of the Fair Labor Standards Act of 1938." *Journal of Policy History* 1, no. 3 (1989): 319–43.

Hartman, Susan. *The Home Front and Beyond: American Women in the 1940s.* Boston: Twayne, 1982.

———. "Prescriptions for Penelope: Literature on Women's Obligations to Returning World War II Veterans." *Women's Studies* 5 (1978): 223–39.

Hartog, Henrik. *Man and Wife: A History.* Cambridge MA: Harvard University Press, 2000.

Harvey, Anna. "The Political Consequences of Suffrage Exclusion: Organizations, Institutions, and the Electoral Mobilization of Women." *Social Science History* 20, no. 1 (1996): 97–132.

Hirsch, H. N. *The Enigma of Felix Frankfurter.* New Orleans: Quid Pro Books, 1981.

Hoff, Joan. *Law, Gender, and Injustice: A Legal History of U.S. Women.* New York: New York University Press, 1991.

Hoffert, Sylvia D. *Alva Vanderbilt Belmont: Unlikely Champion of Women's Rights.* Bloomington: Indiana University Press, 2012.

Hoff-Wilson, Joan, ed. *Rights of Passage: The Past and Future of the ERA.* Bloomington: Indiana University Press, 1986.

Honey, Maureen. *Creating Rosie the Riveter: Class, Gender, and Propaganda during World War II.* Amherst: University of Massachusetts Press, 1984.

Hunt, Lynn. *Inventing Human Rights: A History.* New York: Norton, 2007.

Huthmacher, Joseph. *Senator Robert F. Wagner and the Rise of Urban Liberalism.* New York: Atheneum, 1968.

Irwin, Inez Haynes. *Up Hill with Banners Flying: The Story of the Woman's Party.* New York: Harcourt Brace, 1921.

Jacobi, Mary Putnam. *"Common Sense," Applied to Woman Suffrage: A Statement of the Reasons which Justify the demand to Extend the Suffrage to Women, with Consideration of the Arguments Against Such Enfranchisement, and with Special References to the Issue Presented to the New York State Convention of 1894.* New York: G. P. Putnam's Sons, 1894.

James, Susan. "The Good Enough Citizen: Citizenship and Independence." In *Beyond Equality and Difference: Citizenship, Feminist Politics, and Female Subjectivity,* edited by Gisela Bock and Susan James. New York: Routledge, 1992.

Jones, Martha. *Vanguard: How Black Women Broke Barriers, Won the Vote, and Insisted on Equality for All.* New York: Basic Books, 2020.

Kann, Mark. *A Republic of Men: The American Founders, Gendered Language, and Patriarchal Politics.* New York: New York University Press, 1998.

Kelley, Florence. *Modern Industry: In Relation to the Family, Health, Education, Morality.* New York: Macmillan, 1914.

———. "The Right to Differ." *Survey* 49 (December 1922): 374–76.

———. *Some Ethical Gains through Legislation.* New York: Macmillan, 1905.

———. *Women in Industry: The Eight Hours Day and Rest at Night.* New York: National Consumers League, 1916. Reprinted as "Women in Industry and the Eight-Hour Day," in *Documents for America's History: Volume 2, since 1865,* edited by James A. Henretta, Rebecca Edwards, Robert O. Self, and Kevin J. Fernlund, 152–54. Boston: Bedford/St. Martin's, 2011.

Kerber, Linda. "A Constitutional Right to Be Treated Like American Ladies: Women and the Obligations of Citizenship." In *U.S. History as Women's History,* edited by Linda Kerber, Alice Kessler-Harris, and Kathryn Kish Sklar. Chapel Hill: University of North Carolina Press, 1995.

———. "From the Declaration of Independence to the Declaration of Sentiments: The Legal Status of Women in the Early Republic, 1776–1848." *Human Rights* 6 (1977): 115–24.

———. "The Meanings of Citizenship." *Journal of American History* 84, no. 3 (1997): 833–54.

———. *No Constitutional Right to Be Ladies: Women and the Obligations of Citizenship.* New York: Hill and Wang, 1998.

———. "The Paradox of Women's Citizenship in the Early Republic: The Case of *Martin vs. Massachusetts,* 1805." *American Historical Review* 97, no. 2 (1992): 349–78.

———. "Separate Spheres, Female Worlds, Woman's Place: The Rhetoric of Women's History." *Journal of American History* 75 (June 1988): 9–39.

———. *Women of the Republic: Intellect and Ideology in Revolutionary America.* Chapel Hill: University of North Carolina Press, 1980.

Kessler-Harris, Alice. "Designing Women and Old Fools: The Construction of the Social Security Amendments of 1939." In *U.S. History as Women's History,* edited by Linda Kerber, Alice Kessler-Harris, and Kathryn Kish Sklar, 87–106. Chapel Hill: University of North Carolina Press, 1995.

———. "Laws and a Living: The Gendered Content of 'Free Labor." In *Gender, Class, Race, and Reform in the Progressive Era,* edited by Noralee Frankel and Nancy Dye. Lexington: University Press of Kentucky, 1991.

———. *Out to Work: A History of Wage-Earning Women in the United States.* New York: Oxford University Press, 1982.

———. *In Pursuit of Equity: Women, Men, and the Quest for Economic Citizenship in 20th-Century America.* New York: Oxford University Press, 2001.

———. *A Woman's Wage: Historical Meanings and Social Consequences.* Lexington: University Press of Kentucky, 1990.

Kitch, Sally. *The Specter of Sex: Gendered Foundations of Racial Formation in the United States.* Albany: State University of New York Press, 2009.

Kitching, Howard. *Sex Problems of the Returned Veteran*. New York: Emerson Books, 1946.

Kousser, J. Morgan. *The Shaping of Southern Politics: Suffrage Restriction and the Establishment of the One-Party South, 1880–1910*. New Haven: Yale University Press, 1974.

Koven, Seth, and Sonya Michel, eds. *Mothers of a New World: Maternalist Politics and the Origins of the Welfare State*. New York: Routledge, 1993.

Kraditor, Aileen. *The Ideas of the Woman Suffrage Movement, 1890–1920*. New York: Norton Press, 1981.

Kupper, Herbert. *Back to Life: The Emotional Adjustment of Our Veterans*. New York: I. B. Fischer, 1945.

Ladd-Taylor, Molly. "Toward Defining Maternalism in U.S. History." *Journal of Women's History* 5, no. 2 (1993): 110–13.

Laughlin, Kathleen. *Women's Work and Public Policy: A History of the Women's Bureau*. Boston: Northeastern University Press, 2000.

Lawson, Steven, ed. *To Secure These Rights: The Report of President Harry S. Truman's Committee on Civil Rights*. Boston: St. Martin's Press, 2004.

Lebsocks, Suzanne. *The Free Women of Petersburg: Status and Culture in a Southern Town, 1784–1860*. New York: Norton, 1985.

Lehrer, Susan. *Origins of Protective Legislation for Women, 1905–1925*. Albany: State University of New York, 1987.

Lemons, Stanley J. *The Woman Citizen: Social Feminism in the 1920s*. Urbana: University of Illinois Press, 1973.

Lichtman, Allan. *White Protestant Nation: The Rise of American Conservative Movement*. New York: Grove Press, 2008.

Lister, Ruth. *Citizenship: Feminist Perspectives*. 2nd ed. New York: New York University Press, 2003.

———. "Tracing the Contours of Women's Citizenship." *Policy and Politics* 21, no. 1 (1993): 3–16.

Lloyd, Genevieve. *The Man of Reason: "Male" and "Female" in Western Philosophy*. Minneapolis: University of Minnesota Press, 1993.

Lunardini, Christine. *From Equal Suffrage to Equal Rights: Alice Paul and the National Woman's Party, 1910–1928*. New York: New York University Press, 1986.

Lundberg, Ferdinand, and Marynia Farnham. *Modern Woman: The Lost Sex*. New York: Harper and Brothers, 1947.

Madison, James H. *Indiana through Tradition and Change: A History of the Hoosier State and Its People, 1920–1945*. Indianapolis: Indiana Historical Society Press, 1982.

Mansbridge, Jane. *Why We Lost the ERA*. Chicago: University of Chicago Press, 1986.

Marbury, William L. "The Nineteenth Amendment and After." *Virginia Law Review* 7, no. 1 (1920): 1–29.

Marder, Nancy S. "The Changing Composition of the American Jury." *125th Anniversary Materials* 5 (February 2013): 66–74. http://scholarship.kentlaw.iit.edu/docs_125/5.

Mariano, John H. *The Veteran and His Marriage.* New York: Council on Marriage Relations, 1945.

Marshall, Susan. "Keep Us on the Pedestal: Women against Feminism in Twentieth-Century America." In *Women: A Feminist Perspective*, edited by Jo Freeman. 5th ed. Mountain View CA: Mayfield, 1995.

Marshall, T. H. *Citizenship and Social Class and Other Essays.* New York: Cambridge University Press, 1950.

Mathews, Donald G., and Jane Sherron De Hart. *Sex, Gender, and the Politics of ERA: A State and the Nation.* New York: Oxford University Press, 1990.

Mayeri, Serena. "Constitutional Choices: Legal Feminism and the Historical Dynamics of Change." *California Law Review* 92, no. 3 (2004): 757–839.

———. "Pauli Murray and the Twentieth-Century Quest for Legal and Social Equality." *Indiana Journal of Law and Social Equality* 2, no. 1 (2014): 80–90.

———. *Reasoning from Race: Feminism, Law, and the Civil Rights Revolution.* Cambridge MA: Harvard University Press, 2011.

McCormick, Richard L. *From Realignment to Reform: Political Change in New York State, 1893–1910.* Ithaca NY: Cornell University Press, 1981.

Mead, Margaret, and Frances B. Kaplan, eds. *American Women.* New York: Scribner, 1965.

Mehta, Uday. "Liberal Strategies of Exclusion." *Politics and Society* 18 (December 1990): 436–37.

Mettler, Suzanne. *Dividing Citizens: Gender and Federalism in New Deal Public Policy.* Ithaca NY: Cornell University Press, 1998.

Milkman, Ruth. *Gender at Work: The Dynamics of Job Segregation by Sex during World War II.* Urbana: University of Illinois Press, 1987.

Mink, Gwendolyn. *The Wages of Motherhood: Inequality in the Welfare State, 1917–1942.* Ithaca NY: Cornell University Press, 1995.

Muncy, Robyn. *Creating a Female Dominion in American Reform, 1890–1935.* Oxford: Oxford University Press, 1991.

Nelson, Barbara J. "The Origins of the Two-Channel Welfare State: Workmen's Compensations and Mothers' Aid." In *Women, the State, and Welfare*, edited by Linda Gordon, 249–81. Madison: University of Wisconsin Press, 1990.

Neuwirth, Jessica. *Equal Means Equal: Why the Time for an Equal Rights Amendment Is Now.* New York: New Press, 2015.

Nielsen, Kim. *Un-American Womanhood: Antiradicalism, Antifeminism, and the First Red Scare.* Columbus: Ohio State University Press, 2001.

Okin, Susan Moller. *Women in Western Political Thought.* Princeton: Princeton University Press, 1979.

O'Neal, Emmet. "The Susan B. Anthony Amendment: Effect of Its Ratification on the Rights of the States to Regulate and Control Suffrage Elections." *Virginia Law Review* 6, no. 5 (February 1920): 338–60.

O'Neill, William. *Everyone Was Brave: The Rise and Fall of Feminism in America.* Chicago: Quadrangle Books, 1969.

Oppenheimer, Valerie. *The Female Labor Force in the United States: Demographic and Economic Factors Governing Its Growth and Changing Composition.* Westport CT: Greenwood, 1976.

Pardo, Thomas. *The National Woman's Party Papers, 1913–1974: A Guide to the Microfilm Edition.* Sanford NC: Microfilm Corporation of America, 1979.

Parrish, Michael. "Felix Frankfurter and American Federalism." In *Federalism Studies in History, Law, and Policy: Papers from the Second Berkeley Seminar on Federalism,* edited by Harry N. Scheiber. Berkeley: University of California, 1988.

Pateman, Carole. *The Disorder of Women: Democracy, Feminism, and Political Theory.* Stanford: Stanford University Press, 1989.

———. "Equality, Difference, Subordination: The Politics of Motherhood and Women's Citizenship." In *Beyond Equality and Difference: Citizenship, Feminist Politics, and Female Subjectivity,* edited by Gisela Bock and Susan James. New York: Routledge, 1992.

———. *The Sexual Contract.* Cambridge: Polity, 1988.

Patterson, James T. *Congressional Conservatism and the New Deal.* Lexington: University of Kentucky Press, 1967.

———. *Mr. Republican: A Biography of Robert A. Taft.* Boston: Houghton Mifflin, 1972.

Paul, Alice. *Conversations with Alice Paul: Woman Suffrage and the Equal Rights Amendment; An Interview conducted by Amelia R. Fry.* Berkeley: Regional Oral History Office, University of California, Berkeley, 1976.

Pederson, William D. *Presidential Profiles: The FDR Years.* New York: Facts on File, 2006.

Perkins, Frances. *The Roosevelt I Knew.* New York: Viking, 1946.

Price, Samuel Worth, Jr. "A Stalwart Conservative in the Senate: William Chapman Revercomb." MA thesis, Marshall University, 1978.

Rabkin, Peggy. *Fathers to Daughters: The Legal Foundations of Female Emancipation.* Westport CT: Greenwood, 1980.

Reeve, Tapping. *The Law of Baron and Femme, Parent, and Child, Guardian and Ward, Master and Servant, and the Powers of the Courts of Chancery, with an Essay on the Terms, Heri, Heris, and Heirs of the Body.* New Haven CT: Oliver Steele, 1816.

Ritter, Gretchen. *The Constitution as Social Design: Gender and Civic Membership in the American Constitutional Order.* Stanford: Stanford University Press, 2006.

———. "Gender and Citizenship after the Nineteenth Amendment." *Polity* 32, no. 3 (2000): 345–75.

Rosenberg, Rosalind. *Jane Crow: The Life of Pauli Murray.* New York: Oxford University Press, 2017.

Rotundo, E. Anthony. *American Manhood: Transformations in Masculinity from the Revolution to the Modern Era.* New York: Basic Books, 1993.

Rupp, Leila J. *Mobilizing Women for War: German and American Propaganda, 1939–1945.* Princeton: Princeton University Press, 1978.

Rupp, Leila J., and Verta A. Taylor. *Survival in the Doldrums: The American Women's Rights Movement, 1945 to the 1960s.* New York: Oxford University Press, 1987.

Ryan, Mary. *Womanhood in America.* New York: Franklin Watts, 1975.

Sainsbury, Diane, ed. *Gendering Welfare States: Combining Insights of Feminist and Mainstream Research.* Thousand Oaks CA: SAGE, 1994.

Salmon, Marylynn. *Women and the Law of Property in Early America.* Chapel Hill: University of North Carolina Press, 1986.

Sapiro, Virginia. "Women, Citizenship, and Nationality: Immigration and Naturalization Policies in the United States." *Politics and Society* 13, no. 1 (1984): 13–16.

Scharf, Lois. *To Work and to Wed: Female Employment, Feminism, and the Great Depression.* Westport CT: Greenwood, 1980.

Schlafly, Phyllis. *The Power of the Positive Woman.* New York: Jove HBJ, 1977.

Schwarz, J. C., ed. *Who's Who in Law.* New York: J. C. Schwarz, 1937.

Schweitzer, Mary. "World War II and Female Labor Participation Rates." *Journal of Economic History* 40 (March 1980): 89–95.

Scott, Anne Firor. *The Southern Lady: From Pedestal to Politics.* Chicago: University of Chicago Press, 1970.

Scott, Joan W. "Gender: A Useful Tool for Historical Analysis." *American Historical Review* 91, no. 5 (1986): 1053–75.

Sicherman, Barbara, and Carol Hurd Green, eds. *Notable American Women: The Modern Period.* Cambridge MA: Harvard University Press, 1980.

Siegel, Reva. "Collective Memory of the Nineteenth Amendment: Reasoning about 'The Woman Question' in the Discourse of Sex Discrimination." In *History, Memory, and the Law,* edited by Austin Sarat and Thomas Kearns, 131–82. Ann Arbor: University of Michigan Press, 1999.

———. "Home as Work: The First Woman's Rights Claims Concerning Wives' Household Labor, 1850–1880." *Yale Law School Review* 103 (1994): 1073–1217.

———. "The Modernization of Marital Status Law: Adjusting Wives' Rights to Earnings, 1860–1930." *Georgetown Law Journal* 82 (1994): 2127–211.

———. "She the People: The Nineteenth Amendment, Sex, Equality, Federalism, and the Family." *Harvard Law Review* 115, no. 4 (2002): 948–1045.

Sklar, Kathryn Kish. "The Historical Foundations of Women's Power in the Creation of the American Welfare State, 1830–1930." In *Mothers of a New*

World: Maternalist Politics and the Origins of Welfare States, edited by Seth Koven and Sonya Michel, 43–93. New York: Routledge, 1993.

Skocpol, Theda. *Protecting Soldiers and Mothers: The Political Origins of Social Policy in the United States.* Cambridge MA: Harvard University Press, 1992.

Skocpol, Theda, and Kenneth Finegold. *State and Party in America's New Deal.* Madison: University of Wisconsin Press, 1995.

Smith, Rogers M. "One United People: Second-Class Female Citizenship and the American Quest for Community." *Yale Journal of Law and Humanities* 1, no. 2 (1989): 229–93.

Smith-Rosenberg, Carroll. "Dis-Covering the Subject of the 'Great Constitutional Discussion,' 1786–1789." *Journal of American History* 79, no. 3 (1992): 841–73.

———. *Disorderly Conduct: Visions of Gender in Victorian America.* New York: Oxford University Press, 1985.

Smith-Rosenberg, Carroll, and Charles Rosenberg. "The Female Animal: Medical and Biological Views of Woman and Her Role in Nineteenth-Century America." *Journal of American History* 60, no. 2 (1973): 332–56.

Spruill, Marjorie J. *Divided We Stand: The Battle over Women's Rights and Family Values That Polarized American Politics.* New York: Bloomsbury, 2017.

Stanley, Amy Dru. "Conjugal Bonds and Wage Labor: Rights of Contract in the Age of Emancipation." *Journal of American History* 75, no. 2 (1988): 471–500.

———. "Home Life and the Morality of the Market." In the *Market Revolution in America: Social, Political, and Religious Expressions, 1800–1880*, edited by Melvyn Stokes and Stephen Conway, 74–96. Charlottesville: University Press of Virginia, 1996.

Stanton, Elizabeth Cady. "The Solitude of Self." 1892. Reprinted in *The Search for Self-Sovereignty: The Oratory of Elizabeth Cady Stanton*, edited by Beth Waggenspack, 159–60. New York: Greenwood, 1989.

Stanton, Elizabeth Cady, Susan B. Anthony, and Matilda Joslyn Gage, eds. *History of Woman Suffrage.* Vol. 1. New York: Fowler & Wells, 1881.

———. *History of Woman Suffrage.* Vol. 2. New York: E. O. Jenkins, 1881.

Steinberg, Ronnie. *Wages and Hours: Labor Reform in Twentieth-Century America.* New Brunswick NJ: Rutgers University Press, 1982.

Steiner, Gilbert Yale. *Constitutional Inequality: The Political Fortunes of the Equal Rights Amendment.* Washington DC: Brookings Institution Press, 1985.

Steinfeld, Robert. "Property and Suffrage in the Early American Republic." *Stanford Law Review* 41, no. 2 (1989): 335–76.

Stevens, Doris. *Jailed for Freedom.* New York: Boni and Liveright, 1920.

Strum, Philippa. *Louis D. Brandeis: Justice for the People.* Cambridge MA: Harvard University Press, 1984.

Thomas, Helen Shirley. *Felix Frankfurter: Scholar on the Bench.* Baltimore: Johns Hopkins Press, 1960.

U.S. Congress. House Committee on Civil Service. *To Amend Married Persons'*
     Clause. 74th Cong., 1st sess., April 18–19 and 23–24, 1935. Washington
     DC: Government Printing Office.

U.S. Congress. House Committee on Immigration and Naturalization. *Pro-*
     vide Equality in Matters of Citizenship between American Men and American
     Women and to Clarify Status of Their Children. 73rd Cong., 1st sess., May
     15, 1933. H. Rep. No. 131. Washington DC: Government Printing Office.

———. *Relating to Naturalization and Citizenship Status of Certain Children of*
     Mothers Who Are Citizens of the United States, and Relating to the Removal of
     Certain Distinctions in Matters of Nationality. 72nd Cong., 1st sess., January
     7, 1932. Washington DC: Government Printing Office.

———. *Relating to Naturalization and Citizenship Status of Children Whose Moth-*
     ers Are Citizens of the U.S., and Relating to the Removal of Certain Inequalities
     in Matters of Nationality: Hearing before the Committee on Immigration and
     Naturalization on H.R. 3674. 73rd Cong., 1st sess., March 28, 1933. Wash-
     ington DC: Government Printing Office.

U.S. Congress. House Committee on the Judiciary. *Equal Rights Amendment to*
     the Constitution: Hearing on H.J. Res. 75. 68th Cong., 2nd sess., February
     4–5, 1925. Washington DC: Government Printing office.

———. *Equal Rights Amendment to the Constitution: Hearing on H.J. Res. 197,*
     Proposing an Amendment to the Constitution of the United States Relative to
     Equal Rights for Men and Women. 72nd Cong., 1st sess., March 16, 1932.
     Washington DC: Government Printing Office.

———. *Equal Rights Amendment: Report to Accompany H.J. Res. 49, Proposing*
     Equal-Rights Amendment to the Constitution. 79th Cong., 1st sess., July 12,
     1945. H. Rep. No. 907. Washington DC: Government Printing Office.

———. *Extending the Right of Suffrage to Women.* 48th Cong., 1st sess., April 24,
     1884. H. Rep. No. 1330. Washington DC: Government Printing Office.

U.S. Congress. House Judiciary Subcommittee. *Amend the Constitution Relative*
     to Equal Rights for Men and Women: Statements Presented on H.J. Res. 1. (and
     other Resolutions), Proposing an Amendment to the Constitution of the United
     States Relative to Equal Rights for Men and Women. 79th Cong., 1st sess.,
     February 21–March 1945. Washington DC: Government Printing Office.

———. *A Bill to Provide for Equal Rights.* 75th Cong., 1st sess., May 26, 1937.
     Washington DC: Government Printing Office.

———. *Equal Rights Amendment to the Constitution and Commission on Legal Sta-*
     tus of Women: Hearings on H.J. Res. 49, 62, 85, 86, 89, 104, 110, and H.R.
     1972, 1996, 2003, 2007, 2035, and 3028. 80th Cong., 2nd sess., March 10
     and 12, 1948. Washington DC: Government Printing Office.

———. *Report to Accompany H. J. Res. 397, Proposing an Amendment to the Consti-*
     tution of the United States Relative to Equal Rights for Men and Women. 80th
     Cong., 2nd sess., June 4, 1948. H. Rep. No. 2196. Washington DC: Gov-
     ernment Printing Office.

U.S. Congress. House Committee on Labor. *Thirty-Hour Week Bill: Hearing before the Committee on Labor, S. 158 and H.R. 4557, and Proposals offered by the Secretary of Labor.* 73rd Cong., 1st sess., April and May 1933. Washington DC: Government Printing Office.

U.S. Congress. House Committee on Rules. *To Amend the Law Relative to Citizenship and Naturalization and for Other Purposes: Hearings before the Committee on Rules on H.R. 3674.* 73rd Cong., 2nd sess., March 24, 1934. Washington DC: Government Printing Office.

U.S. Congress. Senate Committee on Appropriations Subcommittee. *Legislative Establishment Appropriation Act for 1933, Part II—To Effect Economies in the National Government: Hearings before a Subcommittee on Appropriations of the United States Senate on Senate Resolution Numbered 279.* 72nd Cong., 2nd sess., 1933. Washington DC: Government Printing Office.

U.S. Congress. Senate Committee on Education and Labor. *Joint Hearings on the Fair Labor Standards Act.* 75th Cong., 1st sess., June 2–15, 1937. Washington DC: Government Printing Office.

U.S. Congress. Senate Committee on Immigration. *American Citizenship Rights of Women: Hearing before a Subcommittee of the Committee on Immigration.* 72nd Cong., 2nd sess., March 2, 1933. Washington DC: Government Printing Office, 1933.

———. *To Provide Equality in Matter of Citizenship between American Men and American Women and to Clarify Status of Their Children.* 73rd Cong., 2nd sess., April 26, 1934. S. Rep. No. 865. Washington DC: Government Printing Office.

U.S. Congress. Senate Committee on the Judiciary. *Arguments of the Woman-Suffrage Delegates before the Senate Committee on the Judiciary.* 46th Cong., 2nd sess., January 23, 1880. Washington DC: Government Printing Office.

———. *Equal Rights Amendment to Accompany S.J. Res. 61.* 79th Cong., 2nd sess., March 5, 1946. S. Rep. No. 1013. Washington DC: Government Printing Office.

———. *Equal Rights Amendment: Report to Accompany S.J. Res. 65.* 75th Cong., 3rd sess., April 20, 1938. S. Rep. No. 1641. Washington DC: Government Printing Office.

———. *"Equal Rights": Report to Accompany S.J. Res. 25.* 81st Cong., 1st sess., March 22, 1949. S. Rep. No. 137. Washington DC: Government Printing Office.

———. *A Memorandum prepared by Stephen Rice, Assistant Legislative Council of the United States Senate, and an Answer written by George Gordon Battle, Attorney at Law.* 77th Cong., 1st sess., August 15, 1941. Senate Committee Print. Washington DC: Government Printing Office.

———. *Report to Accompany S.J. Res. 8, Proposing an Amendment to the Constitution of the United States Granting Equal Rights to Women.* 77th Cong., 2nd sess., May 11, 1942. S. Rep. No. 1321. Washington DC: Government Printing Office.

———. *Report to Accompany S.J. Res. 25, Proposing an Amendment to the Constitution of the United States Granting Equal Rights to Men and Women.* 78th Cong., 1st sess., May 24, 1943. S. Rept. No. 267. Washington DC: Government Printing Office.

U.S. Congress. Senate Judiciary Subcommittee. *The Equal Rights Amendment: Hearings before the Subcommittee on Constitutional Amendments of the Committee on the Judiciary.* 91st Cong., 2nd sess., May 6, 1970. Washington DC: Government Printing Office.

———. *Equal Rights Amendment Hearings on S.J. Res. 61, Proposing an Amendment to the Constitution of the United States Relative to Equal Rights for Men and Women.* 79th Cong., 1st sess., September 28, 1945. Washington DC: Government Printing Office.

———. *Equal Rights Amendment: Hearing on S.J. Res. 64, Proposing an Amendment to the Constitution of the United States Relative to Equal Rights for Men and Women.* 70th Cong., 2nd sess., February 1, 1929. Washington DC: Government Printing Office.

———. *Equal Rights for Men and Women: Hearing on S.J. Res. 1, Proposing an Amendment to the Constitution of the United States Relative to Equal Rights for Men and Women.* 73rd Cong., 1st sess., May 27, 1933. Washington DC: Government Printing Office.

———. *Equal Rights for Men and Women: Hearings on S.J. Res. 65, Proposing an Amendment to the Constitution of the United States Relative to Equal Rights for Men and Women.* 75th Cong., 3rd sess., February 7–10, 1938, and supplemental statements, March 7, 1938. Washington DC: Government Printing Office.

———. *Equal Rights Hearing on S.J. Res. 52, Proposing an Amendment to the Constitution of the United States Relative to Equal Rights for Men and Women.* 71st Cong., 3rd sess., January 6, 1931. Washington DC: Government Printing Office.

———. *Proposing an Amendment to the Constitution of the United States Relative to Equal Rights for Men and Women: Report to Accompany S.J. Res. 76.* 80th Cong., 2nd sess., April 30, 1948. S. Rep. No. 1208. Washington DC: Government Printing Office.

U.S. Congress. Senate Committee on Privileges and Elections. *A Sixteenth Amendment to the Constitution of the United States, Prohibiting the Several States from Disfranchising U.S. Citizens on Account of Sex: Hearing before the Senate Comm. on Privileges & Elections.* 45th Cong., 2nd sess., January 11–12, 1878. Washington DC: Government Printing Office.

U.S. President's Commission on the Status of Women (PCSW). *American Women: Report of the President's Commission on the Status of Women.* Washington DC: Government Printing Office, 1963.

———. *Report of the Committee on Civil and Political Rights.* Washington DC: Government Printing Office, 1963.

———. *Report of the Committee on Education*. Washington DC: Government Printing Office, 1963.

———. *Report of the Committee on Home and Community*. Washington DC: Government Printing Office, 1963.

Unrau, William E. "Charles Curtis." In *The New Warriors: Native American Leaders since 1900*, edited by David Edmunds, 17–34. Lincoln: University of Nebraska Press, 2001.

Urofsky, Melvin. "State Courts and Protective Legislation during the Progressive Era: A Reevaluation." *Journal of American History* 72, no. 1 (1985): 63–91.

VanBurkleo, Sandra. *"Belonging to the World": Women's Rights and American Constitutional Culture*. New York: Oxford University Press, 2001.

Van Voris, Jacqueline. *Carrie Chapman Catt: A Public Life*. New York: Feminist Press at the City University of New York, 1986.

Voss, Kimberly Wilmot. *Women Politicking Politely: Advancing Feminism in the 1960s and 1970s*. New York: Lexington Books, 2017.

Waller, Willard. *The Veteran Comes Back*. New York: Dryden Press, 1944.

Waltz, Emerson. *The Nationality of Married Women: A Study of Domestic Policies and International Legislation*. Urbana: University of Illinois Press, 1937.

Wandersee, Winifred. *Women's Work and Family Values, 1920–1940*. Cambridge MA: Harvard University Press, 1981.

Warbasse, Elizabeth. *The Changing Legal Rights of Married Women, 1800–1861*. New York: Garland, 1987.

Ware, Susan. *Beyond Suffrage: Women in the New Deal*. Cambridge MA: Harvard University Press, 1981.

Weiner, Lynn. "Maternalism as a Paradigm: Defining the Issues." *Journal of Women's History* 5, no. 2 (1993): 96–98.

Welter, Barbara. "The Cult of True Womanhood, 1820–1860." *American Quarterly* 18 (Summer 1966): 151–72.

Westbrook, Robert B. "Fighting for the American Family: Private Interests and Political Obligations in World War II." In *The Power of Culture: Critical Essays in American History*, edited by Richard W. Fox and T. J. Jackson Lears, 195–221. Chicago: University of Chicago Press, 1993.

Wheeler, Marjorie Spruill, ed. *One Woman, One Vote: Rediscovering the Woman Suffrage Movement*. Troutdale OR: New Sage Press, 1995.

Wilson, Jan Doolittle. *The Women's Joint Congressional Committee and the Politics of Maternalism, 1920–1930*. Urbana: University of Illinois Press, 2007.

Young, Louise. *In the Public Interest: The League of Women Voters, 1920–1970*. New York: Greenwood, 1989.

Zimmerman, Joan. "The Jurisprudence of Equality: The Woman's Minimum Wage, the First Equal Rights Amendment and *Adkins v. Children's Hospital*, 1905–1923." *Journal of American History* 78, no. 1 (1991): 188–225.

INDEX

abortion, 224, 228

Acheson, Dean, 58, 66, 75, 132, 136

activism: anti–gender-discrimination movements, 240; of conservatives, 119; feminism within, 223–24; social and political, 218–24; success of, 238–39; of women, 13, 23–30

Adkins v. Children's Hospital, 36, 63

American legal tradition, protectionist viewpoint of, 83–84

American Woman Suffrage Association (AWSA), 26

American Women (PCSW), 207–8

Anderson, Mary: Alice Paul and, 60; Emanuel Celler and, 198; ERA and, 60; leadership of, 168; New Deal and, 119–20; as protectionist, 10; quote of, 79, 123, 124, 125, 169, 188, 190, 210, 266n60; viewpoint of, 120–21; work of, 167–68, 187

Anthony, Susan B., 26, 27

anti–gender-discrimination movements, 240

Austin, Warren, 118, 133

autonomous domicile, rights to, 43–44

Avery, Edwina Austin, 97, 104

Baldwin, Mrs. Harris, 105

Barkley, Alben, 163–64

Barney, Nora Stanton, 145

Bates, Henry, 75

Battle, George Gordon, 61, 152, 156

Bethune, Mary McLeod, 174

Bill of Rights for Women (NOW), 225

Bingham, Hiram, 97–98

biological determinism, 285n75

Black Americans, 28, 39, 201–2, 249n96, 250n110

Black-Connery Bill, 100, 264n35

Blackstone, William, 17, 38

Borchardt, Selma, 83

Bradley, Joseph P., 21

Bradwell, Myra, 20–21

Bradwell v. Illinois, 20–21

Brandeis, Louis, 24–25, 35

Brandeis Brief, 24

Breedlove v. Suttles (1937), 285–86n81

Brennan, William, Jr., 233

Bresette, Linna, 80

Brewer, David J., 24

Brief for Action: The Status of Women (LWV), 193

Broomall, John Martin, 22

Brown, Clarence J., 170

Brown, Helen Elizabeth, 144

Brown v. Board of Education (1954), 213

Burke, Edward, 6, 10, 118, 130, 134

Burn, Harry, 31

Butler, Sally, 166–67

Cable, John, 32

Cable Act (Married Women's Independent Citizenship Act of 1922), 32–34, 106–12, 267n64

Cadwalader, Thomas, 83, 84

California, 95, 237